ANCIENT AND MEDIEVAL
CONCEPTS
OF FRIENDSHIP

SUNY series in Ancient Greek Philosophy
—————
Anthony Preus, editor

ANCIENT AND MEDIEVAL
CONCEPTS
OF FRIENDSHIP

Edited by

Suzanne Stern-Gillet

and

Gary M. Gurtler, SJ

SUNY PRESS

Published by State University of New York Press, Albany

For information, contact State University of New York Press, Albany, NY
www.sunypress.edu

Production by Eileen Nizer
Marketing by Michael Campochiaro

Library of Congress Cataloging-in-Publication Data

Ancient and medieval concepts of friendship / edited by Suzanne Stern-Gillet and
    Gary M. Gurtler, SJ
        pages cm. — (SUNY series in ancient Greek philosophy)
    Includes bibliographical references and index.
    ISBN 978-1-4384-5365-1 (hardcover : alk. paper)
    ISBN 978-1-4384-5366-8 (e book)
    1. Friendship.   2. Philosophy, Ancient.   3. Philosophy, Medieval.   I. Stern-Gillet,
Suzanne, 1943– editor of compilation.   II. Gurtler, Gary M., 1947– editor of
compilation.

    B187.F75A53 2014
    177'.6209—dc23   2013049696

                          10 9 8 7 6 5 4 3 2 1

To Ranjan, with love
—Suzanne

In Memoriam John Cleary
—Gary

CONTENTS

PART 3
PATRISTIC AND MEDIEVAL PHILOSOPHERS

PART 4
ENLIGHTENMENT THINKERS

PREFACE

The concept of friendship (*philia*) looms large in the philosophical reflections of the ancients and their medieval successors. For all their differences, the definitions of friendship put forward by Plato, Aristotle, the Stoics, Augustine, and Aquinas are the background against which subsequent Western treatments of friendship are to be understood. Our aim in the present volume is twofold: to give an account of friendship as it emerged as a topic in those philosophies which proved to be the most significant of all time, and to sketch the evolution that the concept itself underwent after Plato first gave it ethical currency. Philosophical exegesis and history, although our main concerns in this volume, are not, however, the only ones; while highlighting discrepancies between ancient, medieval, and modern intuitions, the contributors also draw attention to what we, moderns, stand to learn from the study of ancient and medieval texts.

This anthology has no ambition to provide a comprehensive history of the concept of friendship in the Western tradition; our more modest aim is to direct a spotlight on the most salient points in what proved to be an enduring theme in philosophical literature. The volume falls into three parts. The first part treats of the moral and political values with which the philosophers of pagan antiquity invested the bond of friendship; the second part deals with the profound changes brought about by Christianity in the conception of the nature and moral value of interpersonal relationships; the third part indicates how more recent philosophers have retrieved and synthesized this rich and complex heritage. While ancient pagan thinkers regarded friendship as secular and selective by definition, the Christian philosophers of late antiquity and the Middle Ages, having stripped the concept of virtue (*aretē*) of its aristocratic connotations, grounded friendship and its associated excellences in the creaturely status of human beings. Teaching that the love of God ought to precede and supersede individual choice and inclination, these authors understood friendship and its obligations in relation to the virtue of charity (*caritas*). Since the soul's relation to Christ was the only friendship worthy to be called perfect, human friendship took on a more complex character. While Christian philosophers such as Augustine regarded friendship as a possible obstacle to the development of moral reasoning, others such as Aquinas sought to integrate the love of individual friends into the ideal of neighborly love.

The reception of ancient and medieval texts on friendship by later authors brought further assumptions to the fore. After an eclipse of a few centuries, Enlightenment figures such as Kant and Hölderlin turned for inspiration to the ancients and sought to combine their insights with their own, different, assumptions concerning the value and autonomy of the individual. Again, some two centuries after the Enlightenment, the revival of virtue ethics and the rise of ethical particularism, defined as the theory that moral reasons, far from being universalizable by definition, are to be responsive to the particularities of agents and circumstances, combined to make interpersonal relations, once again, a topic of lively philosophical debate. Recently published studies on the subject, by philosophers working in both the Anglo-American analytic tradition and various Continental European schools, testify to the vitality and continuing relevance of the classical and medieval heritage.

It is generally assumed that Aristotle's treatment of friendship in the three versions of the *Ethics* that have come down to us represents the peak of ancient thinking on the subject. This is the assumption that Dimitri El Murr undertakes to challenge. Without seeking in any way to diminish the importance of Aristotle's views on the matter, El Murr argues that Plato's contribution to the philosophy of friendship is greater than has so far been recognized. Through a close analysis of a short passage in book eight of the *Laws*, El Murr argues that in his last pronouncement on friendship Plato introduced a distinction between three forms of *philia*. In friendship from opposites, which aims at sensual repletion, each party is but a means to the satisfaction of the needs of the other. In friendship from resemblance, by contrast, which bonds those who are similarly driven by a desire for virtue, each party seeks the good of the other, and the resulting relationship, therefore, constitutes the paradigm of friendship. In a third form of friendship, composed of elements of the other two, the parties seek sensual gratification while also having a genuine desire for the good of the other. Such a threefold distinction, so El Murr contends, sheds retrospective light, not only on the aporetic argument on friendship and resemblance in the *Lysis*, but also on the distinction between kinds of love drawn in the *Pha-*

edrus. Returning to the *Laws*, El Murr goes on to show how the legislator of Magnesia is to rely on shared activities of a social and political nature to encourage the formation of virtuous interpersonal relations among all the citizens. As conceived in the *Laws*, therefore, civic friendship, El Murr concludes, represents a welcome enlargement of the corresponding notion in the *Republic*, where the majority of the population is excluded from political life.

Aristotle formalized the distinction, largely left implicit by Plato until the *Laws*, between various kinds of friendship—pleasure, utility, and virtue—alongside which he also listed civic virtue. How the three kinds of friendship are related to each other has been an object of debate since the time of the earliest Aristotelian commentators. Although it is generally agreed that the friendship of virtue, being friendship in its most complete form, provides the standard of reference for the other two, there is no consensus as to the precise nature of its classificatory preeminence. In his contribution to the present volume, Gary M. Gurtler offers a new model, derived from Aristotle's own explanation of the four kinds of cause (*aitia*), for describing the interrelation between the friendships of pleasure and utility and the friendship of virtue. In all three kinds of friendship, Gurtler argues, the formal cause is the wishing of the good of the other, the material cause is the character of the two friends, the moving cause is good will, while the final cause is the good, whether real or apparent. Thus pleasure, utility, and virtue, rather than being the motives for entering into a friendship, describe how character qualifies the kind of friendship possible for the individuals concerned.

Although Aristotle held civic friendship to be a powerfully cohesive force in the state, he wrote surprisingly little about it, never explaining in detail what it entailed, who is capable of it, or how it might most efficiently be cultivated. Suzanne Stern-Gillet brings elements of answer to these questions. A close reading of the passages devoted to *megalopsychia* (literally, greatness of soul) in the corpus leads her to argue that Aristotle's great-souled man is paradigmatically capable of engaging in civic friendship. His overall excellence or virtue, which Aristotle regards as compatible with his self-sufficiency, aloofness, and (justifiable) pride, fits him to play a key political role, not only in states where the principle of distributive justice dictates that the best and most able should rule, but also in states with a democratic constitution, where the citizens take it in turn to rule and be ruled. Focusing on chapter 8 of book IX of the *Nicomachean Ethics*, she goes on to show how an Aristotelian *megalopsychos* can benefit his city and friends; not only is he in a position to make handsome financial contributions to the city, but, in exceptional circumstances, he is even prepared to lay down his life for it. Turning then to the mysterious and so far ill-understood vice that Aristotle calls smallness of soul (*mikropsychia*), Stern-Gillet shows that it involves an intellectual as well as a practical failure. Unduly preoccupied with his own safety and comfort, the small-souled man (*ho mikropsychos*) of Aristotle's description fails to take a just measure of the contribution he would otherwise be capable of making to his city and fellow citizens.

With the Hellenistic period came a progressive waning of interest in civic friendship. This, however, did not mean a loss of philosophical interest in friendship *tout court* since Stoics and Epicureans both brought to bear on the subject their characteristic concepts and preoccupations. Drawing inspiration from seminal Platonic texts, the Stoics sought to resolve what they perceived to be a tension in Plato's conception of love as stemming from lack and need. They further developed the view, first mooted by Pausanias in Plato's *Symposium*, that love finds its fulfillment in friendship and concord. This is the conceptual territory covered in Bernard Collette-Dučić's contribution. Focusing on the Stoic sage, whose virtue is by definition perfect and his self-sufficiency complete, Collette-Dučić argues that the sage's love is necessarily of a pedagogical nature in so far as he aims at setting those he loves onto the path of knowledge and virtue. But then, Collette-Dučić wonders, what benefit can the sage himself possibly draw from friendship with those who, while having natural predispositions to virtue, are too young to actualize them? The answer, it turns out, is that the sage's love for and friendship with such happily predisposed young people provide him with welcome opportunities to practice his own virtues.

Cicero's eclectic brand of Stoicism and his familiarity with Aristotle's teleological ethics and conception of virtuous friendship as "other selfhood" gave him added resources to resolve the paradox of love and friendship that he found articulated in Plato's *Symposium*. In her contribution to the volume, Robin Weiss disentangles the descriptive and normative elements in the key concept of Stoicism, *oikeiōsis* (generally rendered as the drive for self-preservation), to show how deftly Cicero sidesteps the Platonic view that love is born of need. Weiss explains that, from Cicero's point of view, human beings do not so much yearn for what they lack as reach out for what, being *oikeios* to them, enables them to preserve their being, actualize their rational capacities, and more generally, attain their end. Assuming, like all Stoics, that there can be no love greater than self-love, Cicero contends that in true friendship the self of each partner is so closely integrated in the self of the other as to contribute uniquely to its self-realization. True friendship, therefore, cannot but be virtuous friendship. For Cicero, Weiss concludes, "love is born of an internal abundance of the very things we seek outside ourselves in another—virtue."

It is well known that the Epicureans' desire for a trouble-free existence led them to seek release "from the prison of public affairs and politics." It is less well known that it also led them to discourage their followers from erotic love. Why did it do so? To account for the Epicurean distrust of *erōs*, Harry Lesser turns to Lucretius' *De rerum natura*, in which the issue is dealt with at telling length. Erotic love, so Lucretius claims, breeds violent emotions, generates desires which cannot all be fulfilled, is prone to turn into hate, and is indifferent to the virtue or its possible lack in the beloved. It is nothing short of a mental illness (*furor, rabies*). Rationally based friendship with like-minded individuals, by contrast, favors the achievement of the Epicurean ethical goal, namely, freedom from pain and anxiety (*ataraxia*). Since they conceived of love and friendship as being poles apart, the Epicureans, Lesser shows, did not follow Plato and the Stoics in believing that love could transform itself into friendship.

Tamer Nawar's contribution highlights the shift from the Greco-Roman to the Christian conception of friendship. Chronicling the stages of Augustine's various autobiographical accounts of friendship, from the early writings, which are much indebted to Cicero, to the *Confessions* and the *City of God*, in which Augustine speaks in his own voice, Nawar shows how Augustine remained suspicious of friendship and its attendant seductions throughout most of his writing life. In books I to IV of the *Confessions*, Augustine presents friendship as an occasion for sin, which is liable to bring out in our unredeemed nature evil motives and emotions such as pride and shame. Although less severely critical of friendship in books VI and VII, Augustine still argues that delight in the creature can detract from delight in the Creator and that it is an illusion to assume that human friendship, as opposed to the love of God, can make good perceived deficiencies in our character and dispositions. As for the good that we can do to others by befriending them, it, too, is likely to be an illusion, stemming from our failure to realize that we cannot ever be more than occasions for God to work His beneficent interventions in our lives. The well-known limitations that Augustine set to human agency, Nawar suggests, dominate Augustine's account of friendship.

John Panteleimon Manoussakis, too, refers to those aspects of friendship that many a Christian author of late antiquity considered to be pernicious. The letters between Gregory Nazianzen and Basil the Great provide him with an opportunity for identifying and developing themes specific to Christian friendship. Like Augustine, Gregory analyzed friendship in direct relation to his own experience, yet without exposing himself to the same critical, not to say suspicious, gaze as did Augustine. Manoussakis organizes Gregory's accounts of his friendship with Basil in terms of three episodes of denials and reconciliations, moving each time from *agapan* to *philein*. The distinction enables him to show how the epistemological and ethical grounds of Christian friendship differ from those of ancient pagan friendship. He shows that, in common with Augustine, Gregory discusses his own experience, recording in minute detail the differences, discords, and seeming betrayals that transformed, but did not entirely destroy, his friendship with Basil.

Many centuries later, Aelred of Rievaulx and Thomas Aquinas were each reacting to a classical text on friendship, Cicero's *De Amicitia* and Aristotle's *Ethics*, respectively. Both returned to a more systematic and less autobiographical mode of philosophical discourse. John Sommerfeldt highlights the importance of friendship for Aelred, who added *affectus* to Augustine's triad of memory, intellect, and will. Although the concept of *affectus* enabled Aelred to account for the intimacy that is characteristic of authentic friendship, it did not, even so, eliminate the difficulties highlighted by Augustine and Gregory in their respective autobiographical narratives. In Aelred, however, the goodness of creation so dominates his conception of friendship that the potentially negative aspects of this interpersonal relation are absorbed within the positive aspects. Becoming a friend, for Aelred, entails a rigorous process in the course of which the loyalty, integrity, and patience of the parties are tested in a manner reminiscent of the role that Cicero assigned to virtue in the *De Amicitia*, but with a new emphasis on self-revelation, a notion that Kant would later place at the center of his conception of friendship.

Fergus Kerr brings the writings of Thomas Aquinas to bear on the nature of *caritas* and friendship. In his early *Scriptum* on the *Sentences* of Peter Lombard, Aquinas states that charity supplements friendship in so far as the friend is God, so that it is God whom we love in charity, while human beings are loved only to the extent that they belong to God. Aquinas, Kerr shows, abandoned this thesis in the *Summa*, in which he argued that charity makes us friends with God. By taking over Aristotle's view that friends are equals and that each friend delights in the other's existence, Aquinas showed that friendship with God enables us to be truly friends to others. Friends do not disappear in our love for God, but their possession of intrinsic value entails that they are loved for their own sake. In so capturing the value that the human experience of friendship has for all Christian authors, Aquinas, as interpreted by Kerr, provides an Aristotelian antidote to what many scholars have perceived to be the Platonic conception of love, according to which the particular is discarded in the ascent to the purest form of love, love of the Forms. In a remarkable way, therefore, our two medieval thinkers, Aelred and Thomas Aquinas, are able to articulate a positive evaluation of friendship within their understanding of charity and thus make human friendship compatible with the love of God.

The interplay of self-disclosure and self-knowledge in friendship, as theorized by Aristotle and Kant respectively, is the theme of Andrea Veltman's chapter. To highlight the different assumptions about human nature that the two philosophers brought to the discussion of self-disclosure, she undertakes a close reading of a number of relevant passages in all three versions of Aristotle's ethics before highlighting Kant's vacillations on the issue, from the *Lectures on Ethics* to the *Metaphysical Principles of Virtue*. She articulates the premises of the argument that led Aristotle to conclude that the good of self-knowledge can be secured only through the mutual self-disclosure that is characteristic of virtue friendship. Rather than investing self-disclosure with intrinsic value, Aristotle, she infers, regards it as a means through which the virtuous agent gains the intrinsic good of self-discovery and self-knowledge. What matters for Aristotle is to know oneself rather than being known by another. The reverse, so Veltman proceeds to show, is true of Kant, who prized friendship mainly for the opportunity that it gives us to rise above the reticence and anxiety that cloud most forms of social interaction and thus to satisfy our deep-seated impulse to share thoughts and sentiments with another human being. While for Aristotle, who was more sanguine than Kant on the inherent sociality of human beings, trust is presupposed in the shared activities of virtuous friendship, for Kant, trust is a good that is achieved through communion with another and the refuge from our fellow human beings that true friendship alone can provide.

Sandra Dučić-Collette's intertextual reading of Hölderlin and Plato enables her to show how *Hyperion*, the epistolary novel that Hölderlin wrote in 1797, is permeated by Platonic notions, filtered through the prism of Christian beliefs. Love, as highlighted in Hölderlin's interpretation of the myths of Plato's *Symposium* and *Politicus,* represents a state of nature and is asymmetrical, as opposed to friendship, a symmetrical relation that points to the advent of a new age, rejuvenated and governed by spirit. The love of Plato's myths is repeatedly expressed as an opposition between life and death, "having" and "lacking," while friendship expresses a new and different relationship, namely, a relationship between equals. Being a state of plenitude, friendship transcends the love that Hölderlin found in Plato.

It is agreeable in an anthology on friendship to record a debt of gratitude to the friends and colleagues who have made the editorial task lighter and contributed to the quality of the finished product. Together with the two referees appointed by the State University of New York Press, Daniel La Corte, Denis O'Brien, Gerard O'Daly, Richard Parry, and Svetla Slaveva-Griffin have commented insightfully on some of the contributions submitted for inclusion in this volume. Four editorial assistants have provided valuable help at different stages of the preparation of the manuscript: while David Ellis and Stephanie Rumpza (Boston College) did much useful preliminary work on a number of submissions, the final formatting, standardization of notes and bibliographies, and preparation of the index were done by Ryan Wesley and Albert Yates (University of Bolton), whose eye for detail and readiness to work long hours ensured that the preproduction manuscript was as flawless as these things can be. Last, Menahem Luz (University of Haifa) provided the material for the cover illustration, from a photograph of a second century AD mosaic on the ancient site of Sepphoris, described by Josephus as the "jewel of Galilee." Warmest thanks to them all.

Although the chapters in this volume have been adapted to a uniform format of referencing, no attempt has been made to change individual style or mode of argument. Each contributor speaks in his or her own voice.

Manchester (UK), 24th October 2013

PART 1

PLATO AND ARISTOTLE

PHILIA IN PLATO*

Dimitri El Murr

Introduction

The Platonic conception of love (*erōs*) is one of most the debated issues in the canon. By comparison, the Platonic conception of friendship (*philia*) suffers from underexposure. This exegetical imbalance is rooted in the widespread belief that, when compared to Aristotle's grander and supposedly more stimulating account of friendship, significantly placed at the heart of his ethical theory, Plato does not seem to have much to say, philosophically, about friendship.

One of the main reasons for what is hardly more than a prejudice is that Plato seems to ignore deliberately the distinction Greek culture and Greek terminology made between *philia* and *erōs*, between friendship and erotic love.[1] Indeed, in several passages where Plato considers *philia* a form of interpersonal relationship (see *Symp.* 179c, 182c, 184b, 185a, 192b, 209c), he seems more interested in explaining the power of *erōs* than in defining a specific relationship of *philia*.

The *Lysis*, Plato's dialogue devoted to *philia*, is paradigmatic of this ambiguity. The relationship between lover (*erastēs*) and beloved (*erōmenos*) provides the general setting for the investigation of *philia* (see *Lys.* 206a–e), so much so that most commentators would agree with David Konstan in claiming that "the dialogue commonly read as Plato's treatment of friendship [. . .] has as much to do with *erōs* and other kinds of affection as with friendship. Plato was chiefly concerned with the nature of desire or attraction in general, of which friendship is one type."[2] Whereas Aristotle considered in depth the specific nature of *philia*, as distinct from erotic love, and the essential role it is given in the good life, Plato's account of friendship seems to narrow *philia* to *erōs*, leaving friendship itself untreated.

Admittedly, the topic of friendship is massively in evidence in the political dialogues.[3] It might therefore seem natural to suppose that the core of Plato's conception of friendship is political, which would fit neatly with the traditional association, in ancient Greek political thought, between friendship and concord (*homonoia*), as well as with the classic trope of the indispensability of friendship to the inner harmony of any city.[4] No matter what interest Plato had in interpersonal friendship, there can be no doubt that he considered friendship a primarily political phenomenon, perhaps even to the exclusion of any other.

From a purely philosophical point of view, this would be a deeply unsatisfactory outcome. How could a serious philosopher like Plato consider that interpersonal *philia* is not sufficiently interesting to give rise to independent philosophical treatment while at the same time making it an essential ingredient of the cement of society? A quick comparison with Aristotle will help bring out the problem.

As Aristotle makes clear in the *Politics*, friendship is an indispensable means to the good life which any city endeavors to achieve.[5] As is repeatedly claimed in the *Nichomachean Ethics*, friendship is the choice to "live together" (*suzēn*). The three forms of friendship that Aristotle famously distinguishes in the *Nichomachean Ethics*—friendship based on pleasure, utility, and virtue—require a common life.[6] The shared activities that inevitably result suggest that any citizen involved in any form of friendship will feel embedded, so Aristotle thinks, in the smaller-scale institutions he is a part of, based, for example, on kinship or religion. Civic life as a whole, according to Aristotle, depends on, and is a development of, such associations.[7] Hence the political importance of friendship and Aristotle's crucial remark in the opening chapter of book VIII of the *Nichomachean Ethics*: "Friendship also seems to keep cities together, and lawgivers seem to pay more attention to it than justice."[8] Not only does Aristotle succeed in developing a theory of friendship comprehensive enough to account for the importance of *philia* in both the ethical and the political spheres; even more significantly, his analysis of the political importance of friendship stems from, and depends on, his ethical views on *philia*.

Plato's theory of friendship, so I shall show in this chapter, is quite as coherent as Aristotle's. Plato not only makes a distinction between erotic love and friendship, but he, no less than Aristotle, has a distinct conception of virtuous friendship. Such a conception of virtuous friendship requires that there be between the friends a form of resemblance which obeys a specific law of attraction, namely, the principle that "like loves like." Virtuous friendship so conceived may well throw light on the contrast between Plato's treatment of civic friendship in the Kallipolis of the *Republic* and his treatment of the same subject in the city of Magnesia as described in the *Laws*.

Studies of friendship in Plato inevitably, and rightly so, start from the complex arguments of the *Lysis*.[9] My sole aim here will be to scrutinize a short passage from book eight of the *Laws* (*Leg.* 836e–37d) which, until now, has received little attention[10] but which, so I shall argue, will open the way to a fresh understanding of Plato's conception of friendship. In what will prove to be his last pronouncement on *philia*, Plato, looking back to earlier treatments of friendship in the dialogues, provides, for the first time, a clear-cut definition of three forms of *philia*: friendship from opposites, friendship from resemblance, and a mixed form of friendship. We shall first (part 1) examine each of these three forms taken singly. We shall discover that Plato holds a distinct conception of virtuous friendship, a conception which will offer a solution to the aporetic argument of the *Lysis* on friendship and resemblance (*Lys.* 213c–15c). We shall then need (part 2) to take a close look at the three speeches on love in the *Phaedrus* where kinds of friendship similar to those to be found in the *Laws* are distinguished. The philosophical form of *philia* described by Socrates in the *Phaedrus*, so we shall see, illustrates virtuous friendship as it will be defined in the *Laws*. Only then (part 3) shall we be able to consider what bearing, if any, the definition of virtuous friendship provided by the *Laws* has on the dialogue's conception of civic friendship, and how far, if at all (part 4), such a conception conflicts with the approach to the same topic in the *Republic*.

1. Friendship and the Laws of Attraction: Leg. 8, 836e–837d

One of the issues raised by the Athenian Stranger in book eight of the *Laws* concerns sexual behavior. The young men and women of Magnesia will devote their time to the activities of music, dancing, and sacrificing, all activities which require a life of leisure with little or no time spent on hard physical labor. Even so, the Athenian notes, physical labor has the obvious advantage of "starving" the appetites for pleasure by distracting the body (*Leg.* 841a). Since they will experience no such labor, what shall we make of the bodily needs of the young people of Magnesia "as they associate with each other on friendly terms" (835d5)? How can the law control their sexual desires? In order to adopt an appropriate legislation, one that will be able to counterbalance the irrational power of sexual attraction, the Athenian suggests we should be clear about what is at stake. Hence the urge to define with all due precision the laws of erotic attraction.

> ATHENIAN. [. . .] If you want to get these things straight, you have to analyse the nature of friendship and desire and "love," as people call it (*tēn tēs philias te kai epithumias hama kai tōn legomenōn erōtōn*). There are two separate species, plus a third which is a combination of both (*ex amphoin triton allo eidos*). But one term (*hen onoma*) covers all three, and that causes no end of muddle and confusion.

> CLEINIAS. How's that?

> ATHENIAN. I suppose that we call "friend" (*philon*) (1) what is similar (*homoion*) to what is similar regarding virtue and what is equal to what is equal (*kai ison isōi*); but we also call friend (2) what is needy (*to deomenon*) to what has grown rich (*tou peploutēkotos*), even though it is opposite in kind (*enantion on tōi genei*). In either case, when the friendship becomes particularly ardent, we call it love (*erōta*).

> CLEINIAS. Yes, we do.

> ATHENIAN. And (2) a violent and savage form of friendship it is which comes from opposites, and only seldom do we see it reciprocated (*kai to koinon ou pollakis echousa en hēmin*), whereas (1) the form of friendship which comes from resemblance is a calm and mutual affection that lasts a lifetime. But (3) there is third category compounded of the other two (*meiktē de ek toutōn*). The first problem here is to discover what this third kind of lover is really after. There is the further difficulty that he himself is confused and torn between two opposing instincts: one tells him to enjoy his beloved, the other forbids him to. On the one hand, the lover of the body, hung for his partner who is ripe to be enjoyed, like a luscious fruit, tells himself to have his fill, without showing any consideration for his beloved's character and disposition. But, on the other hand, physical desire will count for very little and the lover will be content to gaze

upon his beloved without lusting for him—a mature and genuine desire of soul for soul. That body should sate itself with body he'll think outrageous; his reverence and respect for self-control, courage, high principles and intelligence will make him want to live a life of purity, chaste lover with chaste beloved. This combination of the first two is the "third" love we enumerated a moment ago.

So there's your list of the various forms love can take: should the law forbid them all and keep them out of our community? Or isn't it obvious that in our state we'd want there to spring up the kind that is virtuous and that desires the youth to become as excellent as possible? It's the other two we'll forbid if we can. (*Leg.* 8, 836e5–37d8, trans. Saunders, with modifications)[11]

The importance of this passage for Plato's conception of *philia* should not be overlooked. There is first an account with a definition of *philia* where three different forms are distinguished, each one obeying a specific law of attraction. In that respect, the structure of the passage is particularly significant. The second paragraph (i.e., 837a6–9) provides an analysis of what it is we call *philon*, "friend," in general terms,[12] whereas the remainder of the passage, in accordance with the immediate context, concerned as it is with the regulation of sexual behavior, applies the threefold distinction by illustrating what kind of lover corresponds to each form of *philia* and what kind of behavior is distinctive of each of them.

In providing such an account—this is another reason why the importance of this passage should be duly acknowledged—the Athenian not only elucidates the relations between *philia*, *erōs*, and desire, but also solves a problem raised by the *Lysis* as to whether friends (*philoi*) are like (*homoioi*) one another. This appeal to categories (similar and opposite) and psychic dispositions (desire and *erōs*) which, obviously enough, are already present in the *Lysis* in connection with *philia*, should not come as a surprise. In the *Laws*, Plato, more often than not, summarizes earlier treatments of a subject and looks back to them.[13] As far as *philia* is concerned, I suggest that this is exactly what he does in this passage.

A. THREE KINDS OF *PHILIA*

The Athenian starts by emphasizing the need to analyze the "nature" (*physin*) of friendship, desire, and what people call love. He then notes that there are two distinct species, and a third one composed of the other two. We are not yet told what these species are. But the Athenian points out from the start that there is a single name covering all three, thus causing the confusion a good legislator needs to dissipate. There are, it is true, three different species, the last one being a combination of the other two, but people do not usually recognize these species, so he tells us, because a single name is used to cover all three. What is that single name? In the next paragraph, the Athenian points out that we "call friend" (837a6) what is similar in relation to what is similar and also what is needy to what has grown rich, and he adds that when either of the two relationships flares up, we "call it love" (837a9). The Athenian thus draws attention to the names commonly used in our affective vocabulary: we make use of the term *philon* to refer to two very different kinds of relationship, and we call *erōs* the form of relationship either kind of *philia* takes when it becomes intense. As a result, it should be clear that the single name covering all three forms not as yet specified cannot but be *philia*. If one's legislation is to succeed in regulating the passions of the young, one should therefore define each species of *philia* with all due precision.

Neither desire nor love will turn out to be that species. The Athenian is not providing a threefold division where one species corresponds to *philia*, a second one to *epithumia*, and a last one to *erōs*. So much is clear from the rest of the passage where the Athenian shows that desire is involved in all three forms of *philia*. When considering the first type of friendship, the Athenian indicates that it is "a genuine *desire* of soul for soul" (837c5: *tēi psychēi de ontōs tēs psychēs epitethumēkōs*; see also 837d5: *ton neon epithumounta hōs ariston gignesthai*); similarly for the second type of *philia* where the lover, described as "a lover of the body" (837b8–c1), has physical desire for his beloved (837 c 4). Since the third type of *philia* is a combination of the other two, it will include desire as one of its components.

As far as *erōs* is concerned, the Athenian twice mentions a "third love" (837b6 and 837d1–2). Are we then to suppose that the third form of *philia* that the Athenian wishes to isolate is none other than *erōs*? This seems unlikely insofar as the Athenian explicitly says that *erōs* is not a specific form of *philia*, but the name we give to the first two types of *philia* whenever they reach a certain degree of intensity (837a8–9: *gignētai sphodron*). *Erōs* is thereby a variation of *philia*, not a distinct species of it. For that very reason, we should refrain altogether from identifying the third type of *philia*, the mixed type, with *erōs*. The three species which are about to be analyzed are three species of *philia* which involve desire and which can, under certain conditions, turn into an erotic form of relationship. The Athenian thus distinguishes (1) the form of *philia* which comes from similars

(837b3–4), (2) the form of *philia* which arises from opposites (837b3) and (3) the form of *philia* which is a mixture of the previous two (837b5). Let us label them (1) *friendship from resemblance*, (2) *friendship from opposites*, and (3) *mixed friendship*.

B. FRIENDSHIP FROM OPPOSITES

Consider, first, friendship arising from opposites, a form of friendship which stands in contrast to friendship arising from resemblance. Friendship from opposites involves "what is needy" (837a6) and "what has grown rich even though it is opposite in kind" (837a6–7). What exactly does the Athenian mean when he specifies that what is needy is, in relation to what is rich, opposite in kind? When, further on, he illustrates mixed friendship, he depicts the third kind of lover as "confused and torn between two opposing instincts" (837b7: *eis tounantion hup' amphoin helkomenos aporei*), one of which corresponds to friendship from opposites and proves to be no more than a search for bodily pleasures.

The question therefore arises: what is one who seeks physical love and sensual pleasures really after? Such a lover desires the body of his beloved, but in so doing, he aims at sensual repletion (cf. 837c2) by, as it were, filling the lack he suffers from. Thus, what one is really after in such a circumstance is not an opposite object, but an opposite state of the soul (note the use of the perfect participle, "one who has been enriched," *tou peploutēkotos*, which expresses not simply the end point of the process but its completion).[14] Hence, in this type of friendship, the other is used as a means, not as an end: the beloved is only an instrument used to convert the lover's sense of inner deficiency into a sense of plenitude. In this way, the lover ultimately loves only himself. This is why this particular type of friendship is necessarily "violent and savage" (837b2: *deinē kai agria*) and cannot last. The friendship can no longer continue once the object of desire has been achieved.

C. FRIENDSHIP FROM RESEMBLANCE AND MIXED FRIENDSHIP

Fortunately, there is a form of friendship where reciprocity is possible and where the friend is loved as an end and not as a means. This is friendship from resemblance. It arises between two terms, each of which is similar (*homoion*) and equal (*ison*) to the other.[15]

The appeal to resemblance, or so I suggest, is a direct echo of what we read in the *Lysis*. In the *Lysis* (214a–b), Socrates proposed to identify *philon* (friend) and *homoion* (like), in order to define the latter. But this option immediately turned out to be misleading. One should therefore ask why resemblance in the *Laws* should adequately capture what friendship is, whereas, in the *Lysis*, it seems to lead to a dead end. To answer this question, we first need to get a clear picture of the *Lysis*' argument against the identification of *philon* and *homoion*.

Socrates calls in aid "the prose-writings of the wisest people" who hold, he says, that "like is necessarily always friend to like" (214b3–4).[16] Note the absence of any qualification and the very strong modality of the thesis. Unsurprisingly, Socrates feels at once obliged to qualify the claim: it cannot concern bad people inasmuch as a bad person will inevitably try to harm others and thus will prove incapable of friendship. Moreover, the bad cannot be like the bad since a bad person is at odds with himself. So the bad will never become a friend to anyone else or like to anyone else. If the principle of "like loves like" is true, it is therefore true of the good. What the wise men meant by this principle then is that "the good person alone is friend to the good person alone" (214d5–6: *ho agathos tōi agathōi monos monōi philos*). But another difficulty soon faces us: "Is the like person friend to the like to the extent that he is like him, and is such a person useful to another such?" (214e3–5). Answering this question leads Socrates to consider the two options at his disposal and raise two questions accordingly: when two persons are friends, is the person who is like loved because he is like (214e4), or is it because he is good (215a5)? Both options turn out to be unsatisfactory as they lead to the same aporia: the like person does not need anybody like him, and the good one, being good and self-sufficient, has already all he needs.[17] This passage makes clear that Socrates is after the cause of the love felt by one friend for the other. But at the end of the passage, what remains obscure is why a friend should love his friend if both are alike or both are good.

Even so, it should be noted that, right at the beginning of the passage, Socrates alluded to the possibility of an alternative understanding of the "like loves like" principle. Before raising serious doubts about the validity of the principle as far as the bad is concerned, Socrates had asked Lysis if he thought the wise men were right about friendship and resemblance. Lysis thought they might be right. And Socrates added: "Perhaps half of [what they say], and perhaps the whole of it, but we're just not understanding" (*Lys.* 214a7–8). Although one might imagine Socrates being ironical here, I think that he is hinting at an understanding of the principle of "like loves like" that will truly account for *philia* and will allow us to move beyond the aporetic argument of the *Lysis* (213c–15c). This refinement is what will come from our passage of the *Laws*.

In the *Lysis*, as I have pointed out, both identifications of the friend to the similar, and to the good, made it impossible to understand what attracted a friend to his friend. However, we do know that one of the main outcomes of the *Lysis* is to show that "desire is cause of friendship, and that what desires is friend to that thing it desires and at such time that it desires it" (*Lys.* 221d2–4). Given the treatment of *philia* in the *Laws* and given the insistence on the need to regulate the sexual behavior of young people, the Athenian starts where Socrates left off: in the *Laws*, desire is, as it were, a given.

Now, why should desire make any difference? And why should Socrates' arguments against the principle of "like loves like" in the *Lysis* be considered unsound when the Athenian appeals to resemblance in his definition of the first type of friendship? The point, it seems to me, is that, when it is considered exclusively from the point of view of logical or physical properties, as in the *Lysis*, the *homoion* cannot explain any attraction whatsoever since it is not an object of desire. Indeed, why would the like person desire another like person, *to the extent that he is like*? Why would a good person desire another good person, *insofar as he is good*? In order to account for *philia* as a force of attraction, we need to consider the terms envisaged in the *Lysis* (like, contrary, neuter) not as logical properties, and not so much as physical properties, but more as qualities that can be objects of desire. It is not the use of *homoion* as such which is problematic, but its conception in the manner of Presocratic philosophers.[18] Once the role of desire has been recognized, such categories as *like* or *contrary* can be seen as pertinent to a general theory of *philia*.

It is true that the Athenian does not content himself with endorsing the principle of "like loves like" without any qualification, when he claims that "what is similar is friend to what is similar regarding virtue" (837a6). Although such a formulation inevitably recalls Socrates' successive attempts at definition in the *Lysis* (214b–15b) it also marks a significant difference.[19] Here, the question is not so much whether two friends are alike, but whether they are alike "regarding virtue." As far as interpersonal relationships are concerned, our passage claims therefore that the good can be a friend to the good inasmuch as their similarity concerns the identical desire for virtue which drives them.[20] This distinction is not to be found in the *Lysis*: in the passage from the Laws, goodness is understood as constitutive of the relation of resemblance, not as an accidental feature added to it.[21] The identity of two friends matters less than their similar desire for a common objective, virtue.

Plato's point here is not that the personal identity of the two friends has nothing to do with this kind of friendship. Obviously enough, desiring the same thing, in this case desiring virtue, is not a sufficient condition for friendship insofar as two people with the same desire are not, for this reason, automatically as it were, friends to one another.[22] This kind of friendship, meant to last a lifetime (837b4), necessarily involves personal acquaintance and affection.[23] It is, even so, the shared desire for virtue that accounts for the principle of "like loves like" and allows the Athenian to move beyond the aporetic argument of *Lysis* (213c–15e). True and everlasting *philia* can accommodate personal difference, but only so long as an identical desire for virtue drives the two friends' lives.

With this type of friendship, two souls, however different they may be, resemble one another inasmuch as both desire, for itself and for the sake of the other soul, to become as virtuous as possible. The contrast with the previous form of friendship is striking. What both friends now desire is a *tertium quid* which they desire to acquire as the result of common search. Moreover, perfect and everlasting reciprocity is embedded in this kind of friendship. Indeed, since the desire to be virtuous never ceases, but is constantly nurtured by the joint effort of the two friends, this kind of friendship will last forever. Resemblance according to virtue also explains why this type of friendship is intrinsically chaste: if the two friends are to remain in a perfectly reciprocal form of relationship, bodily desires, which are asymmetrical by nature, cannot be part of their relation.[24]

The third and final form of friendship addressed by the Athenian is mixed friendship. It is a combination of the two opposed types, and the lover is here "confused and torn between two opposing instincts" (837b7). The Athenian points out that one of these instincts is sexual appetite, and the other a genuine concern for the beloved's own good. One instinct drives the lover to make the beloved an instrument for the satisfaction of his bodily appetite; the other sees him as a soul whose good should be pursued. Mixed friendship thus shares some of the characteristics of friendship from resemblance, for all that it shows some concern for the other's soul. However, because it also includes a bodily desire for repletion, it can be neither perfectly harmonious nor perfectly coherent.

The Athenian has argued that we use the single name *philia* to refer to three kinds of relationships which differ widely, even though desire is involved in all three of them. When *philia* stems from a desire to fulfill one's own bodily appetite, it is a violent and savage relationship where the beloved is treated as a means to satisfy one's needs. Such a relationship is asymmetrical and leaves no room for consideration of the beloved's own good. *Philia* can also stem from resemblance regarding virtue: it is then a "genuine desire of soul for soul" (837c5: *tēi psychēi de ontōs tēs psychēs epitethumēkōs*) where each friend will seek his friend's own good. As the final lines of our passage make clear, the Athenian's understanding of this form of friendship, "the kind that is virtuous and that desires the youth to become as excellent as possible" (837d4–5), seems to be modeled on the pedagogical relationship displayed by two souls engaged in the common search for moral excellence.[25] Although there is a third type of *philia* which is a combination of the first two and which can be seen as reciprocal, only the form of friendship which comes from resemblance is perfectly and everlastingly reciprocal, since it does not include any bodily desire which could jeopardize the reciprocal relation of the two friends in making one of them the means to the other's satisfaction.

Before considering the political and legislative consequences the Athenian draws from his account of friendship and addressing the issue as to whether this account has any bearing on the social cohesiveness of the political community of Magnesia, I shall argue in the next section that the analysis of friendship provided at *Leg.* 8, 836e–837d takes stock of earlier assessments of the subject.

2. Forms of Friendship in the *Phaedrus*

Commenting on friendship and resemblance, I have argued already that in the passage of the *Laws* scrutinized so far Plato provides a solution to some of the puzzles raised by his earlier account of *philia* in the *Lysis*. As a consequence, should one consider that "the present disquisition [i.e., *Leg.* 836e5–837d8] amounts to a distinct recantation of many of the views expressed in the earlier erotic discourses (*Lysis, Symposium, Phaedrus*)"?[26] Quite the opposite. "Plato's last pronouncement on the subject of friendship"[27] in book 8 of the *Laws*, so I would claim, is in perfect harmony with earlier accounts of friendship in the dialogues.

Such an idea is not new. It has been argued, long since, that there is a "triad of *philia*, manifest in the *Laws* and present also in the *Symposium* and *Phaedrus*."[28] Consider only the *Phaedrus*. The reason for limiting our choice is that in this dialogue, as has been shown recently, "friendship is at the heart of the speeches [of the *Phaedrus*]. Each of the speeches argues for a particular characterization of friendship, shaped by different conceptions of desire."[29] Drawing on recent studies of the dialogue, I will claim that the three forms of friendship distinguished in the *Phaedrus* correspond to the forms spelled out at *Leg.* 8, 836e–837d.[30]

The kind of *philia* Socrates depicts in the *Phaedrus* at the end of his first speech is a good illustration of what the Athenian describes as friendship from opposites: "So these, my boy, are the things you must bear in mind, and you must understand that the friendship of a lover (*tēn erastou philian*) does not come with goodwill (*met' eunoias*): it's like an appetite for food, for the purpose of having one's fill (*charin plēsmonēs*) (*Phaedrus*, 241c6–d1, trans. Rowe, slightly modified)."[31] Note how *Phdr.* 241d1 (*charin plēsmonēs*) is echoed by *Leg.* 837c6 (*tēn peri to sōma tou sōmatos plēsmonēn*).[32] This, admittedly, is not how Socrates pictures true friendship. Worked out as a response to Lysias' paradoxical praise of the lover's lack of love, Socrates' first speech aims at demonstrating that there is nothing valuable in the way Lysias understands love.[33] One reason for this is that love, as Lysias sees it, makes the beloved a mere instrument for the satisfaction of the lover's needs. Therefore, the fulfilling of the lover's appetitive desires is the only thing sought in such a relationship where goodwill (*eunoia*), a form of consideration of the good of others, has no part to play.

Socrates' conception of true friendship is pursued in his palinode. We know that, in explaining the psychological genesis of the true lovers' mutual attachment, Socrates' second speech intends to prove, *contra* Lysias, that the friendship of a lover is a good thing. We have no need not consider in detail the whole psychological process leading to establishing that final claim. Suffice it to say here that, although Socrates depicts the relationship of the true lovers as including at first a sexual aspect, the erotic nature of the relationship is progressively transformed[34], by joint philosophical activity, into a relation of mutual benefit, where the lover promotes the good of his beloved.[35] Just as the life of the true friends of the passage from the *Laws* is to remain chaste, the philosophical lovers of the *Phaedrus* come to resist the desire for physical pleasure. Here is how Socrates describes their life of bliss.

> And then, well, if the better elements of their minds get the upper hand by drawing them to a well-ordered life, and to philosophy, they pass their life here in blessedness and harmony, masters of themselves and orderly in their behaviour, having enslaved that part through which badness attempted to enter the soul and having freed that part through which goodness enters; and when they die they become winged and light, and have won one of their three submissions in these, the true Olympic games—and

neither human sanity nor divine madness has any greater good
to offer a man than this. (*Phaedrus*, 256a6–b7)

Note the common characteristics between the kind of friendship bonding the philosophical pair of the *Phaedrus* and what the Athenian says of
virtuous friendship in the *Laws*: in either case, the affection lasts a lifetime
(*Phdr.* 256b1: *ton enthade bion diagousin*; *Leg.* 837b4: *dia biou*), it is reciprocal (*Phdr.* 255a3–4: *kai autos ōn physei philos tōi therapeuonti*; *Leg.* 837b4:
koinē), it never indulges in sexual pleasure, but is characterized by reverence for the other (*Phdr.* 254e9: *aidoumenēn te kai dediuian*; *Leg.* 837c8:
aidoumenos hama kai sebomenos) and self-control (*Phdr.* 256b1–2: *egkrateis
hautōn kai kosmioi ontes*; *Leg.* 837c6–7: *to sōphron*). Here too the life of the
true lovers depicted by Socrates' second speech is a perfect illustration of
what the Athenian describes as a mutual and everlasting affection grounded
on friendship from resemblance.

This being said, on what grounds can we claim that the principle
of "like loves like" holds for the kind of *philia* bonding the philosophical
pair of the *Phaedrus*? Even though there is no direct formulation of that
principle to be found in the specific context of Socrates' second speech in
the *Phaedrus*, we should not overlook his observation that the two lovers are
"of one mind" (*Phdr.* 256b1).[36] Because the love they feel is for the Form
of beauty and because their life is devoted to understanding the experience
they share, their desires are fully consistent and their lives dominated by
reason. To that extent, the two *philoi* resemble one another and can be said
to experience true friendship.[37] I claimed previously that friendship from
resemblance in the *Laws* was not grounded on the perfect similarity of the
friends (such a conception would lead back to the aporetic argument of
the *Lysis* on friendship and resemblance), but on the similarity of desire for
virtue that drives them and of the life led according to that desire. Socrates'
view of the friendship of the philosophical pair in the *Phaedrus* provides,
so it seems to me, a direct confirmation of that claim and vindicates the
Athenian's view that friendship from resemblance is the only truly virtuous
type of friendship (cf. *Leg.* 8, 837d4–5).

In the lines immediately following the lines quoted above, Socrates
suggests there is a third kind of friendship which, as it happens, illustrates
what the Athenian describes in the *Laws* as mixed friendship:

But if they live a coarser way of life, devoted not to wisdom but
to honour (*aphilosophōi, philotimōi de*), then perhaps, I suppose,
when they are drinking or in some other moment of careless-
ness, the licentious horses in the two of them catch them off

guard, bring them together and make that choice which is called
blessed by the many, and carry it through; and, once having
done so, they continue with that choice, but sparingly, because
what they are doing has not been approved by their whole mind
(*ou pasē tēi dedogmena dianoiai*). So these too spend their lives
as mutual friends, though not to the same degree as the other
pair, both during the course of their love and when they have
passed beyond it, believing that they have given and received the
most binding pledges, which it would be against piety to break
by ever becoming enemies. (*Phaedrus*, 256b7–d3)

This type of *philia* is based, not on the joint search for knowledge, but on
the love of honor (*philotimia*). As the end of the passage makes clear, such
a form of friendship is reciprocal, but it does not exhibit the same degree
of reciprocity as the first one. The reason why this is so should be clear:
from time to time, the two friends are subject to the pulls of appetitive
desire, which will lead one of them to treat his partner as an object of sexual
pleasure, so that they engage in what is now an asymmetrical relationship.
As Socrates points out, such friends will never come to hate one another,
but their inability to engage enduringly in the search for knowledge prevents
them from entering into a relation of perfect reciprocity and equality.

However succinct may be the account Socrates has given of this form
of friendship, he seems to see it as a combination of the *philia* of the
pleasure-seekers and the *philia* of the philosophical pair. The honor-loving
pair love one another since each one seeks the other one's good for the
sake of honor for himself, but because they occasionally yield to the pulls
of appetitive desire while disapproving of it, they cannot be of one mind
(cf. *Phdr.* 256c6–7).[38]

Schematic though the previous analysis may have been, I hope to
have shown that the three forms of friendship distinguished in the *Laws*
can be recognized in the speeches of the *Phaedrus*.[39] Returning now to our
starting point in this section, we may safely assume, as a result, that Plato
is not recanting his earlier views on *philia* in his last work. Additionally,
it seems that the previous examination of Socrates' approach to friendship
in the *Phaedrus* supports the interpretation held so far: the passage of the
Laws given over to *philia* is of great importance for the Platonic theory of
friendship because it provides, for the first time in the dialogues, a sharp
definitional account of friendship where Plato summarizes and assesses his
earlier treatment of the subject.

3. Civic Friendship in the *Laws*

Returning to our passage from the *Laws*, we need to examine what political and legislative consequences the Athenian draws from his analysis of *philia*. At the end of the passage, the Athenian observes that, although only virtuous friendship should be promoted, getting rid of the other two forms of *philia* seems barely possible (837d7). What can the legislator do with the nonvirtuous forms of friendship, given that he cannot eradicate them altogether?

A. LEGISLATIVE CONSEQUENCES

Consider the legislative measures put forward by the Athenian in the pages immediately following our passage (837e–42a).[40] Since any form of heterosexual relationship is a type of *philia* involving opposites, it is by definition a "violent and savage" form of friendship. The Athenian insists that the legislator of Magnesia will be compelled to prescribe conjugal loyalty (838e–39c), or, if this is too much to aim for, to have the laws bring shame on adulterers, force them to hide and feel bad about themselves (841a–b). It seems clear that, at this point, the main objective of the Athenian's prescription of conjugal fidelity is to transform this violent and savage form of friendship into a calm and mutual friendship which makes "men friends to their own wife" (my translation of 839b1: *gunaixi te hautōn oikeious einai philous*). As far as homosexuality is concerned, the Athenian's solution is far more radical, and he insists that homosexual relationships should simply be forbidden (841d): not only are homosexual relationships typical of *philia* from opposites, but it is impossible to appeal to the natural desire for procreation to justify them.[41]

Stemming directly from the Athenian's analysis of the forms of friendship and from the sharp contrast he draws between friendship from resemblance and friendship from opposites, these realistic measures show that the virtuous type of friendship serves as a paradigm for the legislator. The mutual affection brought about by the obligation of conjugal loyalty can be the closest some people seem to get to the virtuous form of friendship. From the point of view of policy making, this will nonetheless help the legislator strengthen civic unity by getting rid of the "raging fury of the sexual instinct" (839a7), which inevitably disturb the social order.

The Athenian also makes a much stronger claim: "[I]sn't it obvious that in our state we'd want there to spring up the kind that is virtuous and that desires the youth to become as excellent as possible?" (837d4–6).

Whenever and wherever possible, the legislator will facilitate the development of pedagogical relationships based on the joint search for virtue, and
he will do his best to impede other forms of *philia* as much as he can. I
think, however, that even though the Athenian has in mind a particular
type of friendship between individuals engaged in a specific form of activity, we may assume that he thinks the virtuous form of friendship is not
restricted to such exceptional cases and accounts for a more general form
of friendship, binding together each citizen to all others—civic friendship.

B. Friendship and Legislation

In several key passages of the *Laws*, the Athenian emphasizes that one of the
goals of legislation is the promotion of friendship among citizens.[42] In book
1, he proposes a critical survey of the constitutions of Sparta and Crete,
which, he argues, aim at courage and the preparation of war. Let us suppose, he says, a family with a majority of unjust sons and only a minority
of just sons: who will be the best judge of the conflict within this family?
The best judge is someone who "will take this single quarreling family in
hand and reconcile its members without killing any of them; by laying down
regulations to guide them in the future, he will be able to ensure that they
remain on friendly terms with each other" (*Leg.* 1, 627e4–28a3).[43] From this
analogy, the Athenian concludes that the best legislator is one who prevents
civil war, not by destroying one of the parties in conflict, but by bringing
about reconciliation which will eventually lead to "peace and friendship"
(628b8). The greatest good for a city is indeed "neither war nor civil war"
(628c9) but "peace and goodwill among men" (628c10–11: *eirēnē de pros
allēlous hama hai philophrosunē*).

   That friendship among citizens is the main goal of the Athenian's
legislation is also made obvious by his reflections on the history of both
Persian monarchy and Athenian democracy in book 3. As a prelude to this
historical survey, the Athenian suggests that even though there are different names used to indicate the goal a good legislator should pursue, these
names amount to the same thing: "When we say that the legislator should
keep self-control (*to sōphronein*) or good judgement (*phronēsin*) or friendship
(*philian*) in view, we must bear in mind that all these aims are the same not
different" (*Leg.* 3, 693c1–4). The Athenian then contrasts Persian monarchy
and Athenian democracy, two opposite types of constitution which, he says,
are both "mother-constitutions which [. . .] have given birth to all the others" (693d2–3). A good legislation should combine both regimes "if it is
to enjoy freedom and friendship allied with good judgment" (693d8–e1).

His point is that a well-ordered state is a happy medium between extreme repression and extreme freedom. For that reason, it will foster liberty and friendship in direct proportion.

Moreover, the history of both Persian monarchy and Athenian democracy provides a negative proof of this claim. The reason for the corruption of the Persian empire is "that [the Persians] were too strict in depriving the people of liberty and too energetic in introducing authoritarian government, so that they destroyed all friendship (*to philon*) and community of spirit in the state (*kai to koinon en tēi polei*)" (697c9–d1). The same is true of Athenian democracy, but for opposite reasons: it is not authoritarianism in government that destroyed all bonds of civic friendship, but excessive liberty which, as time went on, turned into license to do whatever one pleases and which transformed democracy into "theatrocracy" (701a3: *theatrokratia*).

So it is that, when at the beginning of book 4 of the *Laws*, the Athenian launches his exposition of the legislation proper to Magnesia, he is building on previous results. His observation in book 5 that "the whole point of our legislation was to allow the citizens to live supremely happy lives in the greatest possible mutual friendship" (*Leg.* 5, 743c5–6) is no more than a reminder.[44]

C. VIRTUOUS FRIENDSHIP AND CIVIC FRIENDSHIP

Returning now to the issue raised at the beginning of this section, we should ask: is the form of friendship encouraged by the laws of Magnesia the virtuous form of friendship which, the Athenian claims, ought to be promoted in the city, or is it some other kind of friendship, perhaps a form of general benevolence? As I argued previously, the Athenian's description of the virtuous form of friendship suggests that he has an intimate form of relationship in mind, not the kind of relationship that would be likely to extend to all citizens. Does this entail that the virtuous form of friendship will fail to be a genuinely civic friendship? How could the form of friendship which aims at virtue and binds together individuals seeking virtue in common be active among large groups of people?

Compelling as it may seem, this objection is unsound: in the *Laws*, as Christopher Bobonich has convincingly argued, "Plato does not think that friendship involving a non-instrumental concern for the friend's well-being must be restricted to intimate relations between two or a few people."[45] Bobonich shows that the several shared activities in which the citizens of Magnesia are involved, whether of a social or a political nature, will foster within the city many forms of cooperation.[46] These, in turn, will foster

virtue in all the citizens.[47] Even though the citizens of Magnesia, in contrast
with the intermediate class of citizens in the ideal city of the *Republic*, will
be allowed to own households and have private families and so will come
to find a specific and differential kind of *philia* addressed to their family
and intimate friends, the possibility of civic friendship is guaranteed by the
several social and political activities they share with their fellow citizens. It
is true, even so, that civic friendship cannot share in all the features of a
more intimate form of friendship as depicted by the Athenian in book 8,
but it will nonetheless arise from these shared activities aiming at virtue
and the well-being of all citizens. To that extent, the definition of virtuous
friendship provided by the Athenian in book 8 succeeds in accounting for
civic friendship: it aims at virtue, it includes mutual goodwill, and it is
based upon a form of activity which the friends have in common.

D. CIVIC FRIENDSHIP AND EQUALITY

A last piece of evidence can be provided in favor of the interpretation
proposed above.

I have already commented on the close connection between friendship and resemblance in the definition of virtuous friendship given in *Leg.*
8, 836e–37d. There is a second feature of the definition that I have not so
far commented upon, a feature that it no less significant for a full understanding of the theory.

Absent from the corresponding passage of the *Lysis*, the notion of
equality is introduced at *Leg.* 837a7 in the same breath as the principle of
"like loves like" but with no explicit justification. What is more, it appears
to be no sooner spoken of than forgotten in the continuation of the passage where no mention of equality occurs in the depiction of the behavior
characteristic of each type of friendship. Note that when the Athenian says
that we call *philon* "what is equal to what is equal," we still have to understand the qualification "regarding virtue"[48]

When the Athenian mentions "like to like" and "equal to equal," is he,
as he has been thought to be, merely using the two words synonymously?[49]
Perhaps so. From a philosophical point of view, this would be unsatisfactory.
Resemblance and equality, obviously enough, are different in kind. Admittedly, the association of friendship and equality is a leitmotif of the *Laws* and
a distinct feature of its political theory. Even so, this is not a good enough
reason for supposing that equality regarding virtue is to be understood as
a mere synonym of resemblance. Equality introduces a distinctly political
type of relation matching the conception of civic friendship sketched above.

Promoting friendship among the citizens, as I claimed previously, is one of the main goals of the legislation of Magnesia. This goal can be achieved, as we have seen, through the fostering of shared activities in which the citizens take part, and especially through their participation in the political institutions of the city. Therefore, it is no accident that the constitution of Magnesia, as the Athenian has already insisted in book 3, occupies a middle position between the two extremes of monarchy and democracy. The reason is that in neither of these two systems can friendship be secured.

As a passage of book 6 shows, any form of despotism prevents friendship from occurring because in such a constitution, there are no citizens but only slaves and masters who have radically unequal statuses and so cannot be friends. Hence the observation that slaves and masters can never become friends (*Leg.* 6, 757a1). So too, it is claimed, in a pure monarchical state, where "citizens" are not merely, as we might want to say "subjects." but for all intents and purposes "slaves." As for democracy, this form of constitution grants equal honors to the good and the bad, insofar as it gives equal access to public office to people who deserve it and to people who do not. For this very reason friendship cannot occur either. Instead of promoting friendship and social harmony, pure monarchy and pure democracy lead to *stasis* and discord (cf. 757a4–5). Pure monarchy does so because it destroys all forms of equality between the ruled (who are therefore comparable to slaves), pure democracy, because it is absurdly egalitarian.

Clearly, the Athenian's assumption is that one cannot secure friendship without promoting equality. As the old Pythagorean saying has it, "equality brings about friendship" (757a5–6: *isotēs philotēta apergazetai*).[50] The solution he puts forward, in order to secure friendship in the city, consists in distinguishing two forms of equality. The first form of equality is proportionate equality, or equality "according to nature" (757d4–5), which will provide better opportunities to better people and lesser opportunities to the less able. This is what the legislator should always aim at. But, as the Athenian notes, this form of equality is not sufficient, on its own, to guarantee friendship among the citizens, since resentment among the many and sedition can still arise. Hence the need to resort to another form of equality, "equality by lot" (757e3) to prevent such conflicts from occurring.[51] The legislator will hope, however, that the most important charges turn out to be apportioned to the best people. If so, friendship secured by equality will be achieved among the citizens.

The *Laws* thus show that civic friendship is the type of friendship produced in a just city operating as widely as possible on the principle of proportionate equality, "the most genuine and the best" form of equality

(757b5–6), but resorting only with parsimony to equality by lot. Proportionate equality is achieved when equals are granted what is equal, when therefore those with greater virtue occupy greater positions. Proportionate equality, the Athenian notes, "always [confers] greater honours on those who are greater regarding virtue" (757c3–4: *timas meizosi men pros aretēn aei meizous*).

The Athenian's mention of equality as a relation of equal to equal regarding virtue at *Leg.* 8, 837a7 confirms the point that we should not refrain from considering that the virtuous form of friendship so defined also accounts for civic friendship which binds citizens together. In the specific context of book 8 of the *Laws*, the Athenian is right to point out that friends of the first kind, friends united by the virtuous form of friendship, are also equals inasmuch as the overall political settlement devised by the legislator aims at promoting friendship chiefly through a form of equality concerned specifically with virtue.

4. Civic Friendship in the *Republic*

In the last section of this chapter, I turn to the conception of civic friendship presented in the *Republic*. That friendship in general and civic friendship in particular are topics addressed at any philosophical depth in the *Republic* may not be self-evident. As I have argued elsewhere, we should not overlook the importance of friendship in the social organization of Kallipolis because the part that it plays within the city is far more important and more elaborate than it may seem at first sight.[52]

First, because the traditional conception of *philia* built around a polarity of friend and enemy cannot be accounted for, Socrates' political project in the *Republic* partly amounts to removing any feeling of enmity within the city and, more generally, between Greek peoples.[53] Second, Socrates makes clear that one of the explicit aims of the primary education of future guards is to strengthen the bonds of friendship within their class.[54] Such bonds will of course be buttressed by their communal life, whose main thrust Socrates captures by citing twice the Pythagorean motto "everything is common between friends" (*panta . . . koina ta philōn*).[55] According to Socrates, friendship has therefore a decisive role to play in the solidarity of the intermediate class of citizens. Third, with respect to friendship between the social classes, Socrates emphasizes that bonds of friendship extend to the whole city insofar as philosopher-rulers will consider the members of the two lower classes as friends while guards, in turn, will consider the producers as friends.[56]

A. IS CIVIC FRIENDSHIP POSSIBLE IN THE IDEAL CITY?

As far as friendship between guards is concerned, it is a well-worn theme that it relies on an extension of family affection to the whole class of citizens and, simultaneously, on the abolition of private property, including wives and children. Because of this communal life, guards will be engaged in mutually beneficial relationships with one another. Discussing whether Socrates' extended argument on the education of guards and their communal life is cogent enough to justify his view that guards are bound by mutual friendship is not my concern in this chapter.[57] I shall concentrate on how Socrates accounts for the existence of civic friendship between auxiliary guards and producers.[58]

The possibility of civic friendship between the members of the two lower classes of Kallipolis is problematic. The reasons which, in my view, may ground the possibility of friendship between guards, namely, that they undergo a long process of education in common, share a life experience, and lead a life devoted to the common goal of protecting the whole city, are exactly the ones that make civic friendship with the producers difficult to vindicate. How could guards and producers be friends when the latter do not experience the same educational process as the former and when the latter live a private life and own private property while the former do not?

The political theory of the *Republic* lays great emphasis on the virtue of moderation in which each class of citizens participates. In the individual soul, moderation is identified as a form of concord and mutual friendship between the psychic parts, a form of concord which the soul achieves under the rule of reason.[59] Given the analogy of city and soul in the *Republic*, we are thus bound to ask if civic friendship amounts to moderation. Socrates defines moderation within the city as an agreement of all citizens on the general order of the city.[60] It seems clear then that for Socrates moderation is a condition of civic friendship, not civic friendship as such. Indeed, civic friendship implies more than agreement on who should rule and who should be ruled; it implies some form of active cooperation and mutual interest between the citizens. Admittedly guards and producers do have a relation of mutual interest because the freedom of the lower class depends on the power of the upper one, whose subsistence, in turn, wholly relies on the work of the producers. Thus Socrates is keen to emphasize that guards and producers will cooperate and enjoy mutual benefits.[61]

So much is confirmed by the Noble Lie, the foundational myth of the ideal city. Despite the differences in intelligence and capacity within the citizen body, and despite the hierarchical structure of the city which is intended to mirror these differences, the Noble Lie will implant in the soul of each citizen the belief that all citizens are akin to each other, brothers sharing the same earth mother.[62] This story shows that no citizen should think of himself as an isolated individual, following his own particular interests, as if he were disconnected from his fellow citizens. On the contrary, each member of the ideal city must consider himself to be part of a greater whole, a member of a larger family.

In spite of the belief fostered by the Noble Lie, Socrates' approach to civic friendship in the *Republic* falls short of the precise account provided by the *Laws* and in this respect remains unconvincing. As we have seen, civic friendship in Magnesia arises from the actual participation of citizens in the social and political groups they belong to and where they share activities and cooperate. Such active cooperation is a means to reaching the overall goal of legislation, which is to foster virtue in each citizen. Not so in the *Republic*, where the majority of citizens do not participate in the political life of the city and where guards and producers do not seem to share in joint activities of the kind described in the *Laws*.

Although Socrates provides us with very little information about the affective and mental life of the producers in the *Republic*, what we know of the kind of friendship experienced by the guards and based upon *homopatheia*, that is, the sharing of joys and sorrows rooted in their education and communal life, is sufficient evidence to claim that this very kind of friendship cannot extend across classes.[63] If it could, we would get yet another ideal city, where the community of property and of women and children extend throughout the entire city. As we are told in the *Laws*, we would get an ideal city "where the old saying [i.e., 'friend's property is genuinely shared'] is put into practice as widely as possible *through the entire state*" (*Leg.* 5, 739c1–2).[64] In this city, which the *Laws* call the "first city" (739b8), civic friendship as such would be none other than the friendship experienced by the intermediate class in the *Republic*.

B. FRIENDSHIP AND RESEMBLANCE

It is nonetheless a striking feature of the political theory of the *Republic* that Socrates considers that the social hierarchy of the city does not preclude the possibility of civic friendship. Why does he think this?

With respect to friendship between the citizens of Kallipolis, a crucial passage of the *Republic* should not be overlooked.[65] At the end of book 9, Socrates asks his interlocutors why manual occupations usually attract reproach (590c2). The answer, he argues, is that "they indicate that the best element in a person is too weak for him to be able to rule over the animal nature in him" (590c3–5). But, Socrates adds, "we suppose it better for everyone to be under divine and wise rule" (590d3–4), before concluding: "It will be best if he has that divinity and wisdom within him, but failing that, it will need to be set over him from outside, so that all may so far as possible resemble each other and enjoy mutual friendship, insofar as they are all ruled by the same thing" (*Resp.* 9, 590d4–6).[66] This passage makes clear that the just order of the soul can be achieved either by rational understanding (this is achieved by philosophers only) or by imposition "from outside." As the context indicates, the difference between these modalities amounts to a justification of the general hierarchy of the ideal city. As far as producers are concerned, it is clear that they are what they are and that they do what they do because a rational and complete understanding of how their soul should be ordered is out of their reach. Notice how Socrates concludes the passage: because they are governed by the one and same principle, each will resemble the other, and all will enjoy mutual friendship. With respect to civic friendship, this point is crucial. It shows that the possibility of civic friendship depends on a form of resemblance between the citizens fostered by the imposition of the philosopher's rule over the city as a whole. The rule of reason, imposed from outside on most of the citizens of Kallipolis, seems sufficient to ground a form of friendship pervading the city and likening every citizen to any other in spite of the general hierarchy of the ideal city.

Insofar as this hierarchy is imposed by the philosophers who are the only perfectly rational citizens, what the philosopher-kings do to make the city cohere is comparable to what the demiurge does with the elements of the body of the universe. This comparison may seem far fetched, but we should keep in mind that in book 6 Socrates sees no problem in likening the philosopher to a craftsman (500d6) of all forms of demotic virtue (500d7–8), the civic virtue which contrasts with his own excellence deriving from reason.[67]

Consider how the body of the universe is brought into being in the *Timaeus*. "For these reasons and from such constituents, four in number, the body of the universe was brought into being, coming into concord by means of proportion, and from these it acquired friendship, so that coming into unity with itself it became indissoluble by any other save him who bound it together" (*Tim.* 32b8–c4, trans. Cornford, slightly modified).[68] The body of the universe has a specific organization that is bestowed upon it by the demiurge. This order stems from geometric proportion binding the four primary elements together. In this context, friendship is the sort of harmony that the body of the universe acquires from such organization of its elements.[69] The reason why the demiurge harmonizes these elements geometrically is to make them cohere with one another into a single *kosmos*: "[I]n that way," Timaeus says, "all will necessarily come to play the same part towards one another, and by so doing they will all make a unity" (Cornford's translation of *Tim.* 32a5–7: *panth' houtōs ex anagkēs ta auta einai sumbēsetai, ta auta de genomena allēlois hen panta estai*). Although each of the four basic elements which the universe is made of has its own specific properties and its own part to play according to these properties, the highest degree of unity which the whole can attain to depends on their being rendered similar to one another with respect to the role they play in relation to the whole.

In the ideal city of the *Republic*, the three classes of citizens have a distinct role to play in relation to the good of the whole to which they belong, but because the rule of reason is imposed upon each class and each citizen within each class, whether from rational understanding or "from outside," they resemble one another and are thus able to cohere as parts of a single whole. Just as the body of the universe acquires friendship from the binding of its elements, the city becomes one and friendly with itself insofar as each citizen becomes part of a structured whole.

So also in the *Republic*, civic friendship is a form of assimilation dependent upon resemblance. Whereas in the *Laws* civic friendship is seen as stemming from a similar desire for virtue fostered by the constitutional settlement of the city and as a means to achieve social cohesiveness, the *Republic*'s holistic approach seems to make civic friendship the mere consequence of the social order.

Although there are hints in the *Republic* that some form of mutual interest or benevolence extends through social classes, the life experience and virtues of the citizens belonging to the two lower classes seem too remote to allow for a form of civic friendship to arise that would be based upon a similar desire for virtue. The philosopher kings will indeed love and care for all the citizens of Kallipolis, and the guards will care for their fellow guards, but it is difficult to see how guards and producers will enjoy mutual friendship.

Aristotle was right, I believe, to express doubts about the very possibility that the constitution of Kallipolis could foster "a marvelous friendship of all for all" (*Politics*, 2, 5, 1263b17–18). Even though I am convinced that the political theory of the *Republic* is deeply concerned with the happiness of all citizens, the way Plato approaches civic friendship in this dialogue, as a consequence rather than a condition of civic unity, shows that this kind of friendship is merely concerned with the happiness of the whole, not with the happiness of its parts.[70]

Conclusion

Defined as a form of attraction grounded on resemblance according to virtue, Plato's conception of virtuous friendship is comprehensive enough to embrace the intimate and philosophical relationship of two souls engaged in the search of excellence as well as the wider form of friendship which pervades the city of the *Laws*. Not unlike Aristotle, Plato has a coherent account of interpersonal friendship on which his conception of civic friendship heavily depends.

Without wishing to impose an artificial unity on dialogues where Plato speaks of *philia* in ways that the modern reader may be tempted to find inconsistent, I do hope to have shown that there is a thematic unity underlying apparently disparate discussions. Two different and what may appear at first sight as conflicting notions of *philia* seem to run through the *Republic*: when Plato considers the intermediate class of citizens, his preoccupation is to work out a conception of friendship based on mutual affection and the sharing of common goals, but when he examines the unity of the whole city and considers civic friendship as such, he seems nonetheless to be appealing implicitly to a wider and more traditional notion of *philia* which can be given an explanatory role in his conception of the city and which will come into its own in the account he will give of the *kosmos* in the *Timaeus*. Such a conception, sharply criticized by Aristotle, has perhaps for that reason eluded the grasp of many of those who of recent years have sought to isolate this aspect of Plato's thought.

To capture the drift of Plato's thinking, as he passes from one dialogue to another, we must avoid being tied to a narrow conception of likeness, of friendliness, and of "excellence" that would, as in most modern discussions to the subject, be restricted to a discussion of human conduct. Plato, at the time he was writing, had a far more flexible use of these concepts, a use which enabled him to pass easily from discussion of individuals and states in the *Laws* to topics that we, unlike Plato, would find out of place, notably his presentation, in the *Timaeus*, of the *kosmos* itself as a unity held together by bonds of friendship. Such a wider view would have been wholly familiar to Plato's predecessors and explains much of the background of Plato's thinking.[71] It will reappear in some later views of the *kosmos* and man's place in it, but is not be found in Aristotle's writings, which have too often dominated the approach adopted by modern scholars intent on studying the notion of friendship in the ancient world.

In the preceding pages, I have hoped to recover the perspective that would enable us to approximate to Plato's conception of friendship. A critical review of Plato's handling of such a conception must be left for another day.

Notes

*My warmest thanks go to David Konstan, Christopher Rowe, and Suzanne Stern-Gillet for very helpful comments on earlier drafts and to Denis O'Brien, whose scrupulous criticisms led me to rethink many points of detail. I am also most grateful to the anonymous readers whose searching criticisms gave me much food for anxious thought.

1. On this distinction see Konstan 1996, 1–23, and Konstan 1997.

2. Konstan 2012,175. Konstan adds (176): "the frame of the dialogue concerns *erōs*, not friendship."

3. See, e.g., *Resp.* 351d, 386a, 442c, 576a, *Polit.* 311b, *Leg.* 627d–28a, 693c–e, 738d–e, 743c, 757a, 759b, 862c.

4. On *homonoia* in general, see the classic study of de Romilly 1972a; on *homonoia* in Plato, see de Romilly 1972b and Slings 1999, 187–93.

5. See, e.g., *Politics*, 3, 9, 1280b36–81a2.

6. On Aristotle's three forms of friendship (*NE* 8, 3) see the classic study by Cooper 1977. On Aristotle's theory of friendship in general, see Stern-Gillet 1995, and the papers by Gurtler and Stern-Gillet in this volume.

7. Cooper 1990, argues for the existence and the political importance of a special form of friendship in Aristotle, "civic friendship," consisting of "a concern of each citizen for each other citizen's character" (233). I find Julia Annas' critical discussion of Cooper's view convincing: see Annas 1990. For another very convincing analysis of political friendship in Aristotle's *NE* and *EE*, see Schofield 1998.

8. *NE* 8, 1, 1155a22–24: ἔοικε δὲ καὶ τὰς πόλεις συνέχειν ἡ φιλία, καὶ οἱ νομοθέται μᾶλλον περὶ αὐτὴν σπουδάζειν ἢ τὴν δικαιοσύνην. Translation is borrowed from Rowe in Broadie and Rowe 2002.

9. Such a study is to be found in Penner and Rowe 2005. Three hundred pages of tight philosophical commentary and thorough textual examination are needed to account for the philosophical argument of the *Lysis*. The final pages (352–58) are given over to a bibliographical record of recent studies of the *Lysis*.

10. To the best of my knowledge, there are only two studies devoted to *Leg*, 8, 836e–37d: a brief note by Follon 2002, and the detailed and useful study of Dixsaut 2005,, to which the first section of this chapter is indebted.

11. All translations of the *Laws* throughout this paper are borrowed from Saunders 1970.

12. So much is clear, I think, from the Athenian's choice of the neuter gender (φίλον at 837a6) which seems to be implied by the comparison with the second form of *philia*, the friendship of τὸ δεόμενον (neuter) for τοῦ πεπλουτηκότος. Regarding the translation of the adjective φίλον, I have followed what has become a common usage in scholarly publications on ancient friendship [see, e.g., Penner and Rowe 2005], and so favored "friend," rather than "friendly" or "dear" which are more natural in English but do not exactly capture the meaning of the Greek.

13. This characteristic of the dialogue has been rightly emphasized by Brisson and Pradeau 2007, 15: "les *Lois* paraissent à plusieurs reprises tirer profit des arguments et des leçons des autres dialogues platoniciens, en proposant des développements qui ont l'aspect de synthèse, de rappels ou de résumés."

14. As noted by Dixsaut 2005, 112.

15. On the mention of equality in this passage, see part 3, section D *infra*.

16. All translations of the *Lysis* throughout this paper are borrowed from Penner and Rowe 2005.

17. See *Lys.* 214e5–7: "what benefit would anything whatever that's like anything else whatever be capable of having for that other thing?"; 215a7–b3: "The one who's sufficient wouldn't be needing anything, with respect to his sufficiency. [. . .] The sort of person who doesn't need a thing wouldn't prize a thing either [. . .]. And what he didn't prize, he wouldn't love either."

18. See El Murr 2001, 77–80.

19. Compare *Leg.* 837a6 (φίλον μέν που καλοῦμεν ὅμοιον ὁμοίῳ <u>κατ'ἀρετήν</u>) with *Lys.* 214e3–4 (ὁ ὅμοιος τῷ ὁμοίῳ <u>καθ'ὅσον ὅμοιος</u> φίλος) and 215a4–5 (ὁ δὲ ἀγαθὸς τῷ ἀγαθῷ <u>καθ'ὅσον ἀγαθός</u>).

20. A few lines before the end of the passage, the Athenian makes this point clear, when, looking back to this form of friendship, he says: "[I]sn't it obvious that in our state we'd want there to spring up the kind that is virtuous *and* that desires the youth to become as excellent as possible?" England 1921, 346 is right to point out that the conjunction "and" here "connects two *aspects* of the same passion: to desire what is excellent 'is the same thing as desiring excellence to be as great as possible.'"

21. See Dixsaut 2005, 115. Inasmuch as virtue belongs to everyone (see *Gorg.* 506d–e), resemblance according to virtue throws light on the distinction put forward provisionally by Socrates at the end of the *Lysis* (222b) between the *oikeion* (what belongs to us) and the *homoion* (like). On the relation between *oikeion* in the *Lysis* and *oikeiōsis* in Cicero, see Weiss in this volume.

22. The Stoics seem to have held that personal acquaintance was not a necessary component of true friendship. All Stoic sages are indeed said to be friends without even knowing one another: see Clement of Alexandria, *Stromata*, V, xiv, 95, 2 (= SVF I, 223) and Cicero, *De Natura deorum*, I, 121 (= SVF III, 635). On the Platonic background of Stoic friendship, see the papers by Collette-Dučić and Weiss in this volume.

23. Fraisse 1974, 155–56 has rightly observed that this aspect of friendship is absent from the *Lysis* but crucial to Plato's later accounts of *philia*: "il apparaît, en maint autre dialogue, que la *philia* du sage, malgré ses fins rationnelles, est liée dans son apparition à des conditions empiriques qui tiennent à l'affectivité." As we shall see, this is true of the account of friendship to be found in the *Phaedrus*.

24. Michel Foucault has rightly insisted on the importance of reciprocity in Platonic love: see Foucault 1984, 309–10.

25. This has been rightly observed by Bobonich 2002, 429.

26. England 1921, 344–45.

27. Hoerber 1959, 27.

28. Hoerber 1959, 27. Interestingly, Hoerber also detects this triad in the depiction of character within the *Lysis*: see 24–25.

29. Sheffield 2011, 255. See also Hoerber 1959, 26, and most recently Belfiore 2012, who writes (239): "His [Socrates] myth about erotic madness ends not with *erōs*, but with friendship, thus emphasizing, as have all three speeches in the *Phaedrus*, the importance of friendship within an erotic relationship."

30. As pointed out by Hoerber 1959, 27 and Sheffield 2011, 258, n. 12.

31. All translations of the *Phaedrus* throughout this paper are borrowed from Rowe 2005.

32. On the same note, compare *Phdr.* 241c7–8 (οὐ μετ' εὐνοίας) and *Leg.* 837c2–3 (τιμὴν οὐδεμίαν ἀπονέμων τῷ τῆς ψυχῆς ἤθει τοῦ ἐρωμένου).

33. As Léon Robin rigthly claimed long ago: see Robin's Introduction to the *Phaedrus* in Robin (1995, lxxxix–xc.

34. For details, see Sheffield 2011, 255–58 and Belfiore 2012, 228–39.

35. The *Phaedrus* provides evidence against Vlastos' famous view that Plato is guilty of the charge of "cold-hearted egoism" and that the Platonic analysis of love and friendship shows no concern for the friend's own well-being and happiness. See Vlastos 1973. For a criticism of Vlastos' position, see Sheffield 2011, 262–70.

36. Notice too how Socrates explains the true lovers' absence of jealousy (*phthonos*) towards their beloved: "rather, they act as they do because they are trying as much as they can, in every way, to draw him into complete resemblance to themselves and to whichever god they honor" (*Phdr.* 253b8–c2).

37. See Foucault 1984, 310: "à la différence de ce qui se passe dans l'art de courtiser, la 'dialectique d'amour' appelle ici chez les deux amants deux mouvements exactement *semblables*; l'amour est *le même*, puisqu'il est, pour l'un et pour l'autre, le mouvement qui les porte vers le vrai" (my italics).

38. See Belfiore 2012, 238–39.

39. According to Hoerber 1959, 26, this is also true of the *Symposium*.

40. On this section of the *Laws*, see Brisson and Pradeau 2006, 320–22, Schöpsdau 2001, and Schöpsdau 2011, 195–213.

41. It seems to me, however, that the way the Athenian depicts virtuous friendship is an indication that the pedagogical relationship between men and adolescent boys should not be subjected to this interdiction, provided they are driven by the joint search for knowledge and so progressively turn into virtuous friendship. On this see Foucault 1984, 260–62.

42. On the relevant passages, see Morrow 1960, 561–62, Bobonich 2002, 427–28, and Schofield 2013.

43. On this passage, see Schofield 2013, 286–88.

44. Compare, e.g., *Leg.* 3, 701d with *Leg.* 5, 743c.

45. Bobonich 2002, 427. My analysis of civic friendship is much indebted to Bobonich's treatment of other-regarding concerns in the *Laws*: see Bobonich 2002, 418–36.

46. "Social": for example common meals or, one might add, *symposia*. On common meals in the *Laws*, see Morrow 1960, 389–98. On the relation between *symposia* and friendship, see *Leg.* 1, 640c–d and Morrow 1960, 316–18. "Political": on the Assembly in Magnesia, see *Leg.* 6, 753b and Bobonich 2002, 432: "The political structure of Magnesia makes possible an essentially political form of shared activity, that is, sharing in the business of running the city, supporting its constitution, and furthering its political goals."

47. As the Athenian repeatedly claims, the promotion of all the virtues in the citizens is the main objective of the law in Magnesia: see *Leg.* 1, 630c; 4, 705d–06a.

48. England 1921, 345 rightly, so it seems to me, takes the qualifying expression κατ' ἀρετήν with both ὅμοιον and ἴσον.

49. See England 1921, 345 who writes: "Here we have ἴσον added as a synonym, and the qualifying κατ' ἀρετήν [. . .] is to be taken both with ὅμοιον and ἴσον. The likeness or equality must be a likeness or equality in excellence. This is assumed below at c6." I can see no trace of such an assumption "below at c6." Furthermore, the fact that "the qualifying κατ' ἀρετήν [. . .] is to be taken both with ὅμοιον and ἴσον" has no bearing on the question whether likeness and equality should be identified.

50. See Diogenes Laertius, *Vita* 8, 10 and Aristotle, *NE* 1157b36 and *EE* 1240b2.

51. See, for example, *Leg.* 6, 759b–c on the elections of priests, for which the two forms of equality are used to produce friendship between the citizens.

52. See El Murr 2012.

53. See El Murr 2012, 588–93.

54. Throughout the last section of this paper, I shall refer to the members of the ideal city's intermediate class as "guards," not "guardians," as is usually preferred. It seems to me that "guards" captures more neatly what they are, i.e. soldiers and protectors of the city. Rowe 2012, also favors "guards." On friendship and the education of guards, see *Resp.* 3, 386a1–4.

55. See *Resp.* 4, 424a2 and 5, 449c5.

56. On the love of the rulers for their fellow-citizen, see *Resp.* 3, 414b1–5 with El Murr 2012, 594–95. On friendship between guards and producers, see *Resp.* 8, 547b7–c4 with El Murr 2012, 599–602.

57. In the *Politics* 1262b4–24,, Aristotle famously expressed doubts about the very possibility of a bond of *philia* between guards, arguing that their friendship is necessarily "watery" (cf. 1262b15–16) since they have no reason to care for one another. I think a response to Aristotle's criticisms is not out of reach, provided we take into account the long process of affective and social maturation to which guards are subjected during their education, and provided we see how this process aims at fostering other-regarding concern in each guard. My attempt at such a response will be developed in an as yet unpublished paper. Proclus responded to Aristotle's objections against the possibility of the ideal city, but did not concentrate on the issue of friendship within the intermediate class: see *In Remp.* 2, 360, 5–368, 16 Kroll.

58. On friendship between the guards, see the recent and insightful study of Caluori 2013.

59. See *Resp.* 4, 442c10–d1: σώφρονα οὐ τῇ φιλίᾳ καὶ συμφωνίᾳ τῇ αὐτῶν τούτων, ὅταν τό τε ἄρχον καὶ τὼ ἀρχομένω τὸ λογιστικὸν ὁμοδοξῶσι δεῖν ἄρχειν καὶ μὴ στασιάζωσιν αὐτῷ.

60. See *Resp.* 4, 432a. On this passage and more generally on the importance of agreement in the political theory of the *Republic*, see Kamtekar 2004.

61. See, e.g. *Resp.* 5, 463a–e with El Murr 2012, 599–600.

62. See *Resp.* 3, 415a2–3: πάντες οἱ ἐν τῇ πόλει ἀδελφοί and a7–8: ἄτε οὖν συγγενεῖς ὄντες πάντες. On this aspect of the Noble Lie, see Schofield 2007, 149–63.

63. On *homopatheia*, see El Murr 2012, 597–99.

64. That the ideal city of *Leg.* 5 is not the city of the *Republic* has been convincingly argued by Laks 2001, 108–10.

65. My thanks to Franco Ferrari for pointing out the importance of this passage to me.

66. All translations of the *Republic* are borrowed from Rowe 2012.

67. See *Resp.* 6, 500d4–8. For a parallel between the Demiurge of the *Timaeus* and the legislator of the *Laws*, see the classic study by Morrow 1954.

68. Translation borrowed from Cornford 1937.

69. Plato, obviously enough, has Empedocles in mind here. On the Empedoclean background of this passage, see Cornford 1937, 40 and O'Brien 1969, 144–45.

70. On the distinction between the happiness of the city as a whole and the happiness of its individual members, see the insightful study of Morrison 2001.

71. See Aristotle, *NE*, 8, 2, 1155a33–55b13, trans. Rowe in Broadie and Rowe 2002: "But there are not a few disputes about the subject. Some people suppose that it [friendship] is a kind of likeness, and that those that are alike are friends, which is the source of sayings such 'Like tends to like,' and 'Jackdaw to jackdaw,' and so on; whereas others take the contrary position and say that like to like is always a matter of the proverbial potters. And in relation to these same things they pursue the question further, taking it to a more general and scientific level—Euripides claiming that 'Ever lusts the earth for rain' when it has become dry, 'Lusts too the mighty heaver, filling full with rain, / To fall on earth,' Heraclitus talking of hostility bringing together, the divergent making finest harmony, and of all things coming to be through strife; but taking a view contrary to these there is Empedocles, for one, who says that like seeks like. Now those problems that come from natural science we may set to one side, since they are not germane to the present inquiry; let us look further into those that belong to the human sphere and relate to characters and affective states."

Bibliography

Annas, J. 1990. "Comments of J. Cooper." In Patzig, 1990: 242–248.

Belfiore, E. 2012. *Socrates' Daimonic Art: Love for Wisdom in Four Platonic Dialogues.* Cambridge: Cambridge University Press.

Bobonich 2002. *Plato's Utopia Recast: His Later Ethics and Politics*. Oxford: Oxford University Press.

Brisson, L., and Pradeau, J.-F. 2006, *Platon: Les Lois*. Traduction, introduction et notes. Paris: GF-Flammarion.

———. 2007. *Les Lois de Platon*. Paris: Presses Universitaires de France.

Broadie, S., and Rowe, C. 2002.Aristotle, *Nicomachean Ethics*. Translation, introduction and commentary. Oxford: Oxford University Press.

Caluori, D. 2013. "Friendship in Kallipolis." In D. Caluori, ed., *Thinking about Friendship: Historical and Contemporary Philosophical Perspectives*. Basingstoke: Palgrave Macmillan, 47–64.

Cooper, J. M. 1977. "Aristotle on the Forms of Friendship." *Review of Metaphysics* 30, no. 4, 619–648.

———. 1990. "Political Animals and Civic Friendship." In Patzig 1990: 220–241.

———. ed. 1997. *Plato. Complete Works*. Edited with Introduction and Notes. Indianapolis, Cambridge: Hackett Publishing Company.

Cornford, F. M. 1937. *Plato's Cosmology: The* Timaeus *of Plato*. Translated with a running commentary. London: Kegan Paul.

Dixsaut, M. 2005. "La *philia* et ses lois." In Végléris, E. ed., *Cosmos et psyché. Mélanges offerts à Jean Frère*. Hildesheim—Zürich—New York: G. Olms, 101–122.

El Murr, D. 2001. *L'Amitié*, choix de textes avec introduction, commentaires et glossaire. Paris: GF-Flammarion.

———. 2012. "L'amitié *(philia)* dans le système social de la *République*." *Revue philosophique de Louvain*, 110, n°4, 587–604.

England, E. B. 1921. *The Laws of Plato*. The Text Edited with Introduction and Notes. Manchester: Manchester University Press.

Follon, J. 2002. "Note sur l'idée d'amitié dans les *Lois*." In L. Brisson and S. Scolnicov, eds, *Plato's Laws: From theory into practice*. Sankt Augustin: Academia Verlag, 186–190.

Foucault, M. 1984. *Histoire de la sexualité*, II: *L'Usage des plaisirs*. Paris: Gallimard.

Fraisse, J.-C. 1974. *Philia. La notion de l'amitié dans la philosophie antique*. Paris: Vrin.

Hoerber. 1959. "Plato's *Lysis*," *Phronesis*, 4, n°1, 15–28.

Kamtekar, R. 2004. "What's the Good of Agreeing?: *Homonoia* in Platonic Politics." *Oxford Studies in Ancient Philosophy*, 26, 131–70

Konstan, D. 1996. "Greek Friendship." *American Journal of Philology*, 117, 1, 71–94.

———. 1997. *Friendship in the Classical World*. Cambridge: Cambridge University Press.

———. 2012. "Friendship." In Gerald Press ed., *A Companion to Plato*. London: Continuum Books, 175–177.

Laks, A. 2001. "In What Sense Is the City of the *Laws* a Second-Best One?" In Lisi 2001: 107–114.

Lisi, F., ed. 2001. *Plato's Laws and Its Historical Significance*. Sankt Augustin: Academia Verlag.

Morrison, D. 2001. "The Happiness of the City and the Happiness of the Individual in Plato's *Republic*." *Ancient Philosophy* 21, 1–24.

Morrow, G. 1954. "The Demiurge in Politics: the *Timaeus* and the *Laws*." *Proceedings and Addresses of the American Philosophical Association* 27, 5–23.

———. 1960, *Plato's Cretan City: A Historical Interpretation of the "Laws."* Princeton: Princeton University Press.

O'Brien, D. 1969. *Empedocles' Cosmic Cycle. A Reconstruction from the Fragments and Secondary Sources.* Cambridge: Cambridge University Press.

Patzig, G., ed. 1990 *Aristoteles' 'Politik,'* Göttingen: Vandenhoeck und Ruprecht.

Penner, T., and Rowe, C. 2005. *Plato's Lysis.* Cambridge: Cambridge University Press.

Romilly, J. de 1972a. "Vocabulaire et propagande ou les premiers emplois du mot *homonoia*." In *Mélanges de linguistique et de philologie grecques offerts à Pierre Chantraine.* Paris: Klincksieck, 199–210.

———. 1972b. "Les différents aspects de la concorde dans l'œuvre de Platon." *Revue de philologie, de littérature et d'histoire anciennes* 46, no. 1, 7–20.

Rowe, C. 2005. Plato. *Phaedrus.* Translated with introduction and notes. London: Penguin.

———. 2012. Plato. *Republic.* Translated with introduction and notes. London: Penguin.

Schofield, M. 1998. "Political friendship and the ideology of reciprocity." In P. Cartledge, P. Millet, and S. Von Reden, eds, *Kosmos: Essays in Order, Conflict and Community in Classical Athens.* Cambridge: Cambridge University Press, 37–51.

Schofield, M. 2007. "The Noble Lie." In G. R. F. Ferrari ed., *The Cambridge Companion to Plato's Republic.* Cambridge: Cambridge University Press, 138–164.

———. 2013. "Friendship and Justice in the *Laws*." In G. Boys-Stones, D. El Murr, and C. Gill, *The Platonic Art of Philosophy.* Cambridge: Cambridge University Press, 283–297.

Schöpsdau, K. 2001. "Die Regelung des Sexualverhaltens (VIII, 835c1–842a10) als ein Exempel platonischer Nomothetik." In Lisi 2001: 179–199.

———. 2011. *Platon. Nomoi (Gesetze). Buch VIII–XII*, übersetzung und kommentar. Göttingen: Vandenhoeck und Ruprecht.

Sheffield, F. C. C. 2011, "Beyond *eros*: Friendship in the *Phaedrus*." *Proceedings of the Aristotelian Society* 111, no. 2, 251–273.

Slings, S. 1999. *Plato. Clitophon.* Edited with introduction, translation and commentary. Cambridge: Cambridge University Press.

Stern-Gillet, S. 1995. *Aristotle's Philosophy of Friendship.* Albany: SUNY Press.

2

ARISTOTLE ON FRIENDSHIP

INSIGHT FROM THE FOUR CAUSES

Gary M. Gurtler, SJ

1. Introduction

In teaching Aristotle's *Ethics* it is almost impossible to keep the students from taking partial friendships as merely friendly relations and perfect friendship as the only one that really counts as friendship. It is easy to sympathize with them, since a host of scholars seem to share the same view, with various arguments that attempt to explain how this makes sense of what Aristotle says in the text. The difficulty is that it does not take seriously the emphasis Aristotle gives to friendship as necessary for human beings, even in cases such as the virtuous or the vicious where it does not seem necessary or possible. In resorting to analogies or examples to explain what Aristotle might mean, I chanced on analyzing his argument in terms of the four causes. My initial analogy was that a house built of wood is just as much a house as one built of stone, even if it is more prone to destruction by fire or water or the ordinary wear and tear of time and use. Similarly, partial friendships share the same essence as perfect friendships, even though they too are prone to break up. By looking more carefully at Aristotle's definition of friendship as wishing the good of the other, especially as he expands this definition when he begins to speak of proper self-love, and also at his careful discussion of good will as the condition needed for beginning a friendship, I attempt to discern how the different aspects of friendship can be understood in terms of the four causes. In brief, good will is the moving cause, the activities associated with wishing the good of the other constitute the formal cause or essence, the character of the individual is the material cause, and the other as good is the final cause. The character of the individual determines both the capacity to know the good and the degree of maturity needed to engage in the activities that constitute friendship. A virtuous character is the right material for forming a friendship; a vicious one falls short and is in fact counterproductive; and a character between these extremes serves as the material for friendships of different kinds, as the individual is more or less successful in following the model of the virtuous.[1] One other assumption I make is that justice is related to friendship in the same way that the practical virtues are to contemplation in *NE* X, 6–8.[2] This gives a context for understanding the good of friendship in terms of shared contemplative activities that seems missing in many accounts that look on friendship as if it were solely a moral virtue.

2. Wishing the Good (*boulesthai tagatha*)

Aristotle begins his discussion of friendship by claiming that it is both a necessary good and a virtue in some sense. In *NE* VIII, 1, he mentions the rich and powerful as well as the poor and unfortunate, as a way of indicating that friendship is necessary for everyone. The more crucial test, however, concerns the wicked, for whom friendship seems impossible (*NE* VIII, 1, 1155b11–12), and the virtuous, for whom it seems unnecessary (*NE* IX, 9, 1169b4–5). Aristotle's discussion thus rests on the tension between the necessity of friendship for everyone and its relation to virtue. Most commentators take virtue as more fundamental and thus contrast perfect friendship with the two partial varieties.[3] Aristotle's argument, however, is more complicated and nuanced. Discussing friendship in terms of the extremes makes his distinctions precise, but sometimes makes the general application of his principles harder to discern. Aristotle reminds us throughout, however, that he has not jettisoned the idea that friendship is necessary for all human beings, even if some will fail in their efforts.

A careful reading of *NE* VIII, 2 indicates key factors in the definition of friendship and distinctions that are central for keeping friendship open to everyone. He deals with friends in the dual sense of objects that can be liked and of subjects capable of liking. Examining the object first, he separates the likeable from other kinds of objects. "It seems, however, that not everything is liked but only the likeable; and this is either good, or pleasant, or useful. One would think that the useful is that by which something good or pleasant comes to be, so that the good and the pleasant would be likeable objects as ends" (*NE* VIII, 2, 1155b18–21.)[4] The good, the pleasant, and the useful have generally been taken as the motives of the subject, but they are introduced here in terms of objects that can be liked, and Aristotle immediately does something rather odd but not atypical. He reduces them first to the good and pleasant and in the next few lines to the good alone. What drives this reduction to the good is a shift in his focus from the object as likeable to the subject that can like them. Since he regards the object as a final cause, this is natural, for the subject always chooses the good. Thus, in dealing with the subject the issue he must face is not the good, the pleasant or the useful, but the real or the apparent good. In other words, the difference between the virtuous and the rest of us, including the wicked, is precisely the choice of the apparent over the real good, and this choice rests on our character and not on choosing the useful or the pleasant instead of the good. In Aristotle's view everyone chooses the good, and "it makes no difference," for the real good or the apparent good "will both appear likeable" (*NE* VIII, 2, 1155b26–27). This shift from looking at the object as good, useful, or pleasant to looking at the subject as always choosing the good is an initial indication of the complexity of the definition, which concerns not one individual but two and the specific activities these individuals share as friends. Failing to take this complexity into account is one of the sources for the tendency to reduce friendship to virtuous friendship alone. This distinction between subject and object will arise again in the later analysis of good will as the moving cause, but at this point Aristotle clarifies a few more details about friendship itself.

In the next few lines, this general distinction between likeable objects and the subject's choice of the good alone is applied to friendship. Aristotle separates the proper objects of friendship, other human beings, from other likeable objects, such as inanimate things and, at least implicitly, other animals. Inanimate things are ruled out because they cannot like us back, and we do not wish for their good, at least not for their sake but for our own, which perhaps includes animals, to judge from his next statement that "they say it is necessary to wish good things for a friend for the friend's sake" (*NE* VIII, 2, 1155b31). Wishing good things for the other thus emerges as the essence of friendship, but only if it is reciprocated. The complexity of friendship as involving two people means that the proper likeable objects are at the same time the subjects who are choosing the other as good. Here we come to the heart of friendship, not merely liking or having good will toward someone, but that specific situation where two individuals have this good will for one another, are aware of it, and actually start becoming friends. We can thus have good will (*eunous*) toward the whole range of likeable objects, but good will is related to friendship only when it can be reciprocated. Aristotle ends this section by putting these elements together and relating them once more to the three ends that make things likeable, the useful, the pleasant, and the good. Thus he concludes with the following definition of friendship: "It is necessary then to have good will and to wish good things for one another, with both [individuals] not unaware [of the good will] because of some one of the [ends] spoken about above" (*NE* VIII, 2, 1156a3–5).

Having defined friendship in general, Aristotle next speaks of its species. It is in this context that we need to pay careful attention to Aristotle's causes in order to understand what he means."These [ends] differ from one another in kind, and so also the affections and friendships. Thus, there are three kinds of friendship, corresponding in number to likeable objects. In each case they are not unaware of reciprocal affection, but having affection for one another they wish one another good things on the basis of that [likeable object] for which they have affection" (*NE* VIII, 3, 1156a6–10).[5] This text is generally taken as describing the motive or intention of the subjects for initiating a friendship, indicating the particular end the individuals have in mind from the very beginning.[6] This does not seem to describe what actually happens between people, since all of us would make a mad dash away if we suspected someone of being interested in us solely for the pleasant or useful. It also undermines Aristotle's sense of the necessity of friendship in his initial description where the range of people who seek friendship is deliberately inclusive. I will argue that this text and subsequent sections of *NE* VIII 3 are examining friendship formally. That is, the three kinds of friendship are not what we intend but define formally what the possible kinds of friendship are, given that likeable objects can be useful, pleasant, or good. Support will come from an examination of three topics, Aristotle's development of the notion of good will in *NE* IX 5, of proper self-love in *NE* IX 4, and of happiness and self-knowledge in *NE* IX 9.

3. Good Will (*eunoia*)

The context of *NE* IX is different from *NE* VIII, since Aristotle is concerned with issues other than the definition of friendship and its division into species. In *NE* IX, 5, good will is thus discussed as the beginning of friendship, its precondition. Aristotle compares the role of good will in friendship with that of beauty when falling in love.

It seems then that [good will] is the beginning of friendship, just as what is pleasing to the eye is the [beginning] of love, for no one falls in love who has not already been overcome by the vision [of the beloved]. Enjoying the look, however, is not yet being in love, but only when one misses the absent [beloved] and desires his presence. So also it is not possible to be friends without sharing good will, but having good will is not yet being friends, for they only wish good things for those for whom they have good will, but they do nothing to help them get it nor do they trouble themselves about them. (*NE* IX, 5, 1167a3–10)

The comparison shows that good will is a necessary condition for friendship, but it is not sufficient. Good will thus capture one aspect of wishing the good of the other. In terms of Aristotle's principle of potency and act, it is merely a first potentiality, indicating that these two individuals can in fact become friends. As the condition of possibility and starting point of friendship, good will thus is the moving cause that changes two individuals from being potential to actual friends. "Therefore one might say in an extended sense that [good will] is inactive friendship, but that if it continues over time and reaches a habitual state it becomes friendship, not one on account of utility or pleasure, for good will does not arise for these ends" (*NE* IX, 5, 1167a10–14). In its extended or metaphorical sense, therefore, good will can be understand as friendship, but only potentially, needing time and habit to become actual friendship. Friendship itself, therefore, needs to do more than just wish good things for the other. One has to be committed to helping one's friend acquire these goods and this commitment, Aristotle avers, is both a matter of concern and of effort. Thus, wishing the other good as it operates in friendship oscillates between second potentiality (first actuality), friendship as a characteristic or habit the two friends possess, and second actuality, when they engage in the activities of friendship.

Some take the final lines of the above text, as well as the rest of the chapter, as overwhelming evidence against my thesis.[7] Let me begin to show how they actually support it. Aristotle examines utility and pleasure under two different formalities. In *NE* VIII, 1–3, they are considered relative to the object as an end, whereas in *NE* IX, 5 they are considered as possible causes of good will in the subject. In *NE* VIII, 1–3, utility and pleasure are characteristics of the object and, relative to the definition of friendship, formally divide it into three species, perfect friendship and its two partial kinds. In *NE* IX, 5, by contrast, the subject may take the other as good erroneously, as an apparent good, but Aristotle is clear that the other cannot be taken as merely useful or pleasant for the purposes of developing a friendship. In this context, therefore, utility and pleasure are related not to the definition of friendship but to good will as its moving cause. Aristotle argues in this context that utility and pleasure cannot be causes of the kind of good will that is necessary to move individuals to actual friendship.[8] With this in mind, Aristotle's comments in *NE* VIII, 3 and 13, on friendships of utility and pleasure take on a different function. First, Aristotle describes the elderly and ambitious young people as prone to friendships of utility, while the young in general, as especially subject to passions, are prone to friendships of pleasure. He is not talking about their intentions but about aspects of their character that carry certain tendencies with them. It is, in other words, an extrinsic analysis, and not about how anyone in these groups goes about forming a friendship. Second, Aristotle observes that friendships of utility often break up in terms of conflict and complaint and those of pleasure do so more from change of circumstance or situation. These distinctions between the two types of friendship are more retrospective than intentional. They thus illuminate our actual experience. Only when our friendships are over are we in a position to evaluate what kind they may have been; while we are in them we regard them as friendships pure and simple.

His further comments on utility in *NE* IX, 5 describe an individual who has received a good deed and whose good will is seen as the just return for the deed done. In this case, good will, in wishing the benefactor well, expresses one's hope for further favors and does not look to the good of the benefactor as such. One wants the relationship to be friendly, but there is no interest in becoming friends. This situation describes a vast number of our interactions with others, where we are quite content with creating this friendly atmosphere in which to carry out the various pursuits that the routines of life entail. Aristotle's concluding words, moreover, give us a clear indication of what he thinks does serve as a motive for friendship. He states that "generally, good will comes to be on account of some virtue and decency, when someone appears to another good or brave or some such thing, as we said of competitors" (*NE* IX, 5, 1167a18–21).[9] The individual whom one wants to befriend stands out in some way as good and not merely as useful or pleasant. Thus our motive for friendship is that we like someone in such a way that we see in him some good that we want to get to know in the intimate way that friendship offers. While we may be mistaken, the motive conforms to his earlier reduction of the useful and the pleasant to the good and also serves to confirm the discussion of proper self-love in *NE* IX, 4. To conclude so far, while good will can lead to friendship, under certain conditions where the other is seen as good and where each party has good will for the other for the other's sake, there are other situations, where utility or pleasure are the moving causes, that do not lead to friendship, but other relationships beneficial to both parties, but each for one's own sake. The confusion of many commentators can be traced to not recognizing this distinction.

4. Self-Love and Another Self (*philein heauton kai allos autos*)

Aristotle claims at the beginning of *NE* IX, 4 that we are to our friends as we are to ourselves. This involves two complementary assumptions, that our self is somehow double (*NE* IX, 4, 1166a34–b2) and that our friend is another self (*NE* IX, 4, 1166a31–32; 9, 1170b6–7). A contemporary articulation of this assumption can be found in the writings of John Macmurray, where he explores how the self is constituted in relation to the other.[10] While Aristotle does not use Macmurray's precise language, he is getting at the same kind of thing. In part, this expresses the fact that we cannot have direct self knowledge and therefore that we need to achieve self knowledge in relation to others, especially a friend, examined in the next section concerning *NE* IX, 9. Initially, however, these assumptions allow Aristotle to articulate more fully the definition of friendship that he gave rather succinctly at *NE* VIII, 2, 1156a3–5.

> Some hold that a friend wishes and works for good things or things appearing so for his friend; or who wishes the friend to be and to be alive for the friend's benefit, as mothers feel for their children and even as in the case of friends who have quarreled. But others [hold] that a friend goes through things with and desires the same things as [his friend]; or that one shares the sorrows and joys of his friend, and this also happens especially among mothers. Thus they define friendship by one or another of these [characteristics]. A mature individual, moreover, has each of these [characteristics] toward himself (but for the rest, insofar as they undertake to be [mature], since virtue or the excellent man seems to be the measure in every case, as has been said). (*NE* IX, 4, 1166a2–13)[11]

Wishing good things for one's friend is fundamental to the definition that Aristotle proposed in *NE* VIII, 2, 1156a3–5, adding here a list that articulates what some of those goods are and how friends express the wish for them both in their concern for one another and in the effort they exert in acquiring these goods for one another, the two elements of friendship noted at *NE* IX, 5, 1167a9–10. This concern is expressed strikingly in the example of the concern of mothers for the welfare of their children and in their ability to identify with their children's sorrows and joys.

The introduction of character in the next passage allows for the examination of the material cause of friendship, since the character of an individual signals the kind of friendship one is capable of establishing, whether with oneself or another. There are two aspects that emerge in this context, the role of the moral virtues in developing friendship and then the role of friendship itself in contributing to the self knowledge and happiness of the friends. Both aspects prefigure and complement the discussion of happiness in *NE* X, where moral virtue also functions as a necessary precondition for happiness, which is constituted by contemplation. Aristotle begins by describing the self-love of someone of good character.

> He also wishes and works for real and apparent goods (for it belongs to the good man to cultivate the good) and he does this for his own sake (for it is for the benefit of the thinking part, which is what each one seems to be). He also wishes for himself to live and to stay alive, especially for the part by which he is wise. For to be is good for the virtuous, since everyone wishes good things for himself and no one would choose to have everything but become someone else. (*NE* IX, 4, 1166a14–21)

It is worth noting that Aristotle mentions both real and apparent goods in the case of the virtuous, not claiming for them a knowledge that goes beyond the limits of human nature. He thus leaves open the possibility that someone of good character may have not only friendships based on virtue, but also those based on pleasure and utility. In addition, these efforts of the virtuous have their finality in the thinking part, the center of the self and the focus for the integration of all one's activities.[12] While one would not choose to become someone else, Aristotle notes at the end of this section that the virtuous man has these characteristics not only toward himself but towards his friend as well, "for a friend is another self." (*NE* IX, 4, 1166a31–32)

The dual or multiple nature of human beings is at the root both of friendship to one's self as well as of the importance of the friend as another self, but Aristotle first turns his attention to the many and to the vicious before exploring some of the implications of this insight.

It seems the things mentioned belong to the many, even to those who are immature. Now then, do they share in these things in this way, insofar as they accept themselves and undertake to be mature? [Yes], since not one of those utterly immature and engaged in evil possesses these things, nor even appears to. For they don't even have [their act together]: they are at odds with themselves, desiring some things but wishing for others, just like the morally weak, even choosing pleasant but harmful things instead of what actually seems to them to be good. (*NE* IX, 4, 1166b2–10)[13]

The differences among the good, the many and the vicious are not described in terms of their intentions, but rather of how their character facilitates or hinders their choices and thus the possibility of proper self-love as well as friendship with others. The many are not excluded from self love and friendship, but share in these characteristics insofar as they take the virtuous and mature as their models. Those who are bent on evil, however, are described in terms reminiscent of Socrates' description of the tyrant in *Republic* IX. They still want friends but all their efforts are counterproductive, since they are basically at war with themselves and Aristotle concludes that they are "not likeable at all" (*to mēden echein phileton*: *NE* XI, 4, 1166b26).

5. Virtue and Activity

While *NE* IX, 8 gives a full defense of self-love, establishing its foundation in the moral virtues and the dominant part of the soul, *NE* IX, 9 shifts to the role of friendship in happiness as an activity and the particular benefits of friendship for self knowledge, grounding the earlier comments on the multiple self and the friend as another self. The context of happiness alerts us that friendship cannot be reduced to the moral virtues, which have been more central in his analysis of the kind of character needed for friendship to develop. Aristotle is anticipating *NE* X 7,1178a2, where happiness is the activity of contemplation that integrates all the activities in the life of the sage. Since this aspect of friendship goes beyond the moral virtues, Aristotle can also explain why friends have no need of justice. Justice is concerned with those relations that precede friendship, as pointed out in *NE* IX, 5, as well as those conflicts that arise in friendships that turn out to be based on utility, discussed in *NE* VIII, 9. Nonetheless, the particular role of friendship in happiness, like contemplation and the virtue of wisdom in *NE* X,

7–8, presumes the moral virtues that establish the kind of character that is capable of developing friendship as well as contemplation.

Two small sections of this chapter will suffice for examining self-knowledge and the life friends share together. The first passage occurs when Aristotle reflects that happiness is an activity and not some kind of thing that one can possess. The assumption, mentioned earlier, that human beings are double or complex is very much in play, since Aristotle holds that knowledge of someone else is more direct and immediate than self-knowledge.

> But if happiness is in living and being active, and the activity of the good man is excellent and pleasant in itself, as we said at the beginning, and what is one's own is also among these pleasures, [and given that] we are able to contemplate our neighbors better than ourselves and their actions better than our own, and the actions of those who are excellent friends are pleasant for good men (for both are pleasant by nature), then one supremely happy will need friends of this sort, since he chooses to contemplate actions both noble and proper to him, and such actions are those of a good man who is a friend. (*NE* IX, 9, 1169b30–1170a4)[14]

There is as sense in which we come to know ourselves and see the depths of our own nature in that peculiar mirroring that the other provides for us, especially in friendship. In the present context, moreover, Aristotle reminds us that the sage's happiness includes and makes possible the best kind of friendship, where the contemplation of each other's activities manifests and enhances the activity of happiness in each friend.[15]

The second passage meditates on life itself as pleasant and desirable. Aristotle points out the intricate relation between awareness or, as we would say, self consciousness and the pleasure one takes in being alive. In this case, too, the friend is essential, precisely as another self who facilitates this awareness and with whom we share our lives and our thoughts.

> As the virtuous man has [the same feeling] toward himself and toward his friend (for the friend is another self), then just as one's own being is desirable for each one, so also is that of his friend, or nearly so. But one's being was [shown to be] desirable through his perception of being good, and such perception is pleasant in itself, so it is necessary to be conscious also of the friend that he is, and this can come about in living together and sharing in discourse and thoughts. (*NE* IX, 9, 1170b5–12)

Self awareness is the way in which we exist and take pleasure in our existence. Such existence, however, is not restricted or reduced to our perceptions and thoughts as if they are private; as human, our perceptions and thoughts are intrinsically the substance of what we share with one another, especially with our friends. Aristotle is claiming in both these passages that the knowledge and awareness excellent friends make possible is not an accidental extra but a deeply constitutive part of the self knowledge and self awareness of each; it thus helps to place the description of contemplation in *NE* X, 7–9 in context. While contemplation is the kind of thing that is most self-sufficient in its formal structure, the role of others in contemplation and happiness is clearly essential in terms of the social character of human nature and the indirect character of human self knowledge. Finally, his earlier comments on the many, I would also venture to argue, do not exclude this kind of self knowledge and awareness, although it may be less complete and less frequent, as subject more to the vicissitudes of human imperfection.

6. Conclusion

I have used two strategies in this account of friendship in Aristotle, attention to how the various factors in his analysis function in terms of his theory of causes and care in translating certain terms more neutrally. The role of the causes bares the weight of the argument, while the translation gives supporting corroboration. Central is Aristotle's definition of friendship in terms of wishing the good of the other, with the precise conditions under which this constitutes friendship. In this way friendship is defined as a virtue, a habitual state which has certain activities associated with it, in the concerns and efforts exerted for the friend. Among these concerns Aristotle includes wishing and working for the friend to be and be alive, undergoing and desiring the same things, sharing sorrows and joys. The range of people capable of these attitudes and actions is interestingly extensive, starting with mothers (mentioned twice within a few lines), specified most fully in terms of the mature (who have these toward themselves as well as others), and finally including the rest of us (who take the mature as our model).

The assumption behind this definition is that we all choose the good, but the problem is that the good can be real or apparent. Real goods are known and sought most especially by those who are good, with both moral and intellectual virtues, from Aristotle's point of view, but all of us, including the virtuous, also wish and work for apparent goods of all kinds. In terms of friendship, this distinction between real and apparent goods is the key for differentiating the kinds of friendship and the kinds of character capable of having them. Friendship thus has three kinds, complete or virtuous, with two partial kinds, pleasant or useful. As friendships, the partial kinds, moreover, include wishing all these goods and exerting effort and concern in helping a friend achieve them, but are qualified since the friend (or both friends) may not have the character and self-knowledge necessary to sustain the friendship when difficulties or quarrels arise and even when there are changes in the friends or their circumstances. There are similarly three kinds of character, the virtuous, the many and the vicious. The differences here relate to the different degrees in which people possess virtues, and a more restrained translation of Aristotle's terms allows for a less rigid identification of friendship with the virtuous alone. Aristotle is actually careful to indicate that the many, especially as they have a more adequate self appraisal and seek to follow the example of the virtuous, are capable of friendships of various kinds, while only the vicious are excluded from achieving friendship, despite their efforts.

When Aristotle examines good will as the origin of friendship, he emphasizes that one sees the good in the other, under some aspect, and states explicitly that good will leading to friendship cannot arise from utility or pleasure. He is distinguishing here the difference between the point of view of the subject, who always chooses what appears good, and the objective nature of things, where the likeable may only be pleasant or useful, an apparent good, or where the subject has limitations that prevent knowing whether a good is real or apparent. Thus, one always, as it were, intends the good in becoming a friend, but one cannot always deliver on that intention. This is much more cogent than an interpretation that eviscerates the partial kinds of friendship by making pleasure or utility the intention for entering the friendship. Aristotle makes clear that such intentions cannot and do not lead to friendship at all, but to other relationships that may be called friendly but are different from friendship since they do not wish the good of the other precisely for the other's sake. His earlier comments on wishing the good of the other, when more discretely translated, indicate that, as the essence of friendship, this is not restricted to the virtuous, even if they are the ones most capable of friendship, but includes the many as well, especially insofar as they are morally strong and seek to be virtuous. The wicked, while incapable of friendship, still testify to its necessity for all human beings. They continue to seek friendship, even if their efforts can only be counterproductive.

Friendship has also its own end or good, which Aristotle is able to articulate most clearly in the case of the virtuous. The comments on self-knowledge and happiness make abundantly clear that friendship goes beyond justice in the same way that the life of contemplation goes beyond the life of the moral virtues, by integrating them into a more complete and active human life. The primary good one has toward oneself or one's friend is, as he says, toward one's thinking part, that which each of us is. But this part functions within a living human being, who does not have direct self knowledge and for whom the friend is another self, whose actions both noble and proper can be seen or contemplated and with whom one can live and share one's conversation and thoughts. These comments on friendship, further, give the context in which the analysis of happiness and contemplation of the sage in *NE* X, 7–8 have their first articulation and proper context, showing a much richer understanding of the human condition as rooted in our relation to one another.

Notes

1. Stern-Gillet 2013 (in this anthology), focuses on certain character types, the great-souled and the small-souled, and their relation to friendship. This helps expand a restrictive reading of *NE* VIII–IX, where the virtuous and the wicked become the only alternatives.

2. Gurtler 2003, 801–834, argues that the practical virtues and contemplation are not so much in competition as exclusive choices, but rather that practical virtues have their end in contemplation as that end that is complete and final. Similarly, justice only sets up the conditions in which friendship can develop and flourish.

3. Cooper 1980, discusses the "forms of friendship" in the first part of his essay (301–17). He describes moral character, pleasure and advantage as causes of friendship and what binds or cements the friends together. "Cause" seems taken in the modern sense of prior condition, here the intention or motive for entering and maintaining a friendship. This has two deficiencies: it does not exploit Aristotle's diverse senses of cause, and as a result takes pleasure, advantage, or virtue as the motive or intention of the one befriending rather than as descriptions of the friendship. Aristotle examines the intention, however, in terms of good will as the origin and moving cause. Using Aristotle's more complex notion of cause brings consistency to his presentation, is based on his own philosophy, and does not relegate the partial friendships to merely friendly relations.

4. All translations are my own, using the Greek text of Bywater, 1920.

5. Translating *tauta* as motives, causes, or reasons seems to be the source for seeing the virtuous, pleasant, or useful as moving causes, the reason why one as subject starts a friendship, rather than as ends related to the friend as likeable object, whether a real or apparent good.

6. Cooper 1980, 310–11, discusses the three ends in analyzing *dia*, which I have translated as "on the basis of," specifying the end as the likeable object. For

the partial friendships, *dia* has been interpreted prospectively, so that one wishes good to the friend in order to secure one's own pleasure or advantage. For perfect friendship, however, Cooper argues that *dia* more likely means in recognition of the friend's good character. In this sense it is a consequence of the friend's character rather than some purpose in the one befriending him. He argues that all three cases should be the same, so that *eunoia* applies to all three types of friendship. His further discussion turns on the distinction between the *haplōs* character of perfect friendship and the *kata symbebēkos* of partial friendships. Here, however, by making the three ends the motive or intention of the one befriending, Cooper continues to take the partial friendships as not friendships at all (using the example of the businessman with certain of his clients). His distinction about *dia* confirms the presence of *eunoia* in all three types, but I make the further distinction that Aristotle is talking here about the definition of friendship formally considered, with the character of the friends as the material cause that qualifies the friendship. Thus partial friendships are fragile not because the two friends intend to use or find pleasure in one another, but because their character limitations or immaturity interfere with their intention to be friends.

7. Cooper 1980, 310, says that *NE* IX 5 seems to deny "that εὔνοια exists in pleasure- and advantage-friendships at all," and is followed by Susanne Foster, 2003, 82. This reading misses the context of this passage and the nature of good will in the development of any kind of friendship. Despite Cooper's nuanced counter-argument (see n. 9), both he and Foster seem in fact to understand partial friendships as only friendly relations, as in the case of a businessman. Aristotle here, however, distinguishes the three types of friendship from such friendly relations in that friends wish good for the sake of the friend, whereas these friendly relations are for one's own sake. See n. 13 for Smith Pangle's, 2003, rejoinder to Foster's view.

8. Smith Pangle 2003, 92, discusses the three types of friendship based on virtue, utility and pleasure, but adds that good will does not arise from utility and pleasure. She notes that the essence of friendship is the shared activities, which applies to all three types. The only things missing in her account is the different contexts of VIII 1–3 and IX 5, and that good will is not only the root of friendship but is so precisely as the moving cause.

9. At this point, my translation does not inflate the case; where I have "some virtue and decency," for example, Ostwald 1962, 256, translates it as "some sort of excellence and moral goodness." The context of competitors for whom a spectator might spontaneously develop good will indicates not the perfect case of the virtuous, but the common experience of finding something good in another, when someone appears good, as Aristotle says here with precision.

10. Macmurray 1961 are the two volumes of his Gifford Lectures on *The Form of the Personal*. Macmurray argues that the person, as opposed to the subject, is constituted in relation to the other. Thus the person is never merely self-constituted, but the other is necessarily involved. Attention to his argument gives a context in which Aristotle's position need not be reduced to the abstract "subject" of modern

thought. Cooper 1980, 317–34, examines the relation of friendship to the good. For Cooper, it is necessary to establish why the virtuous individual needs or wants friends in the first place. This continues his restriction of friendship only to the virtuous, but includes the assumption that such an individual is self-constituted, so Aristotle's position that friends are indeed necessary for virtuous individuals needs to be supported by several convoluted arguments, that are neither convincing nor illuminative of Aristotle's different assumption about human nature.

11. Here again my translation attempts to be more neutral, so that *tō epieikei* is rendered as mature (earlier at 1167a18–21, as decent) rather than good or virtuous. Moreover, I have rendered *hupolambanousin* as "undertake" rather than regard, think, or suppose, highlighting Aristotle's emphasis on friendship as an activity. Aristotle, in addition, does not seem to be taking the many as self deluded, but as having a self appraisal that leads them to follow the example of the mature; see 1166b2–10 below.

12. *Hoper hekastos einai dokei* seems to prefigure *NE* X, 7, 1178a2, *einai hekastos touto*. See Gurtler, 2003, 826–830, which examines the thinking part in terms of contemplation and its integrative function in *NE* X 7–8 and also, 2008, which examines Aristotle's teleology based on the need of the body, the need of the soul, and their integration for us in the thinking part. See also Stern-Gillet, 2013, 8, who also sees the centrality of the thinking part for the virtue of the *megalopsychos*. This integrative role of the thinking part reveals how Aristotle actually connects the different parts of his ethical synthesis.

13. The many as immature (*phauloi*) are clearly distinct from those utterly immature (*komide phaulon*), for the many have some self-knowledge and desire to follow the good. I deliberately translate the term in a more neutral fashion.

14. Macmurray 1962, vol. 1, emphasizes the self as doer, with thinking as secondary. Cooper, 1980, 323–24, translates *theōrein* as "study," to emphasize its active character rather than a mere sense of awareness. I prefer "contemplation" because it emphasizes the activity of seeing the other as whole or complete. This is not mere awareness, but the product of sharing a life together and is related to the sense of contemplation in *NE* X 7–8, which is active not in the sense of studying someone or something, but in regarding it as a whole.

15. Stern-Gillet 2013, 9–14, places friendship in the context of Aristotle's understanding of human nature as social and that one's self sufficiency has its locus in community with others, to whom and with whom one can exercise those activities that are peculiarly human. Her paper also brings out the relationship of theses virtues to self-knowledge, central to Aristotle's concern in the present context.

Bibliography

Burger, Ronna. 2003. "Hunting Together or Philosophizing Together: Friendship and *Eros* in Aristotle's *Nicomachean Ethics*. Edited by Eduardo Velásquez. Lanham, MD: Lexington Books, 37–60.

Bywater, Ingram. 1920. *Aristotelis Ethica Nicomachea*. Oxford, Clarendon Press (reprint).

Cooper, J. M. 1980. "Aristotle on Friendship." In *Essays on Aristotle's Ethic.*, Edited by A. O. Rorty. Berkeley: University of California Press, 301–340.

Foster, Susanne. 2003. "Aristotle on Moral Considerability." In *Proceedings of the Boston Area Colloquium in Ancient Philosophy* ed. J. Cleary and G. Gurtler. Leiden: Brill, 75–88.

Gurtler, S. J., Gary M. 2003. "The Activity of Happiness in Aristotle's Ethics." *The Review of Metaphysics* 56: 801–834.

———. 2008. "Happiness and Teleology in Aristotle." In *Yearbook of the Irish Philosophical Society Fealsúnacht*, ed. Fiachra Long (Maynooth), 17–31.

Konstan, David. 1997. *Friendship in the Classical World*. Cambridge University Press.

Macmurray, John. 1961. *The Self as Agent* and *Persons in Relation*. New York: Faber and Faber.

Ostwald, Martin. 1962. *Aristotle, Nicomachean Ethics*. New York: Prentice Hall.

Sherman, Nancy. 1993, "Aristotle on the Shared Life." In *Friendship: A Philosophical Reader*. Ithaca: Cornell University Press, 91–107.

Smith Pangle, Lorraine. 2003. "Comment on Foster." In *Proceedings of the Boston Area Colloquium in Ancient Philosophy*, ed. J. Cleary and G. Gurtler, 89–93.

Stern-Gillet, Suzanne. 1995. *Aristotle's Philosophy of Friendship*. Albany: SUNY Press.

———. 2013. "Souls Great and Small" In *Ancient and Medieval Concepts of Friendship*. Albany, SUNY Press.

3

SOULS GREAT AND SMALL

ARISTOTLE ON SELF-KNOWLEDGE, FRIENDSHIP, AND CIVIC ENGAGEMENT*

Suzanne Stern-Gillet

Friendship we believe to be the greatest good of states and what best preserves them against revolutions.

—*Politics* II, 4, 1262b7–9[1]

Introduction

Aristotle's philosophy of friendship has recently benefited from a good deal of scholarly attention. While such renewal of interest, which comes after centuries of neglect, has shed new light on some of the puzzles already identified by the ancient commentators, it has also thrown up fresh cruces and complexities. At one end of the spectrum are the many scholars who, in the second half of last century, sought to identify the nature of the relationship between the three forms of friendship distinguished in the *Ethics*. In so doing, these scholars have taken up and developed a question that had already been formulated in the second century AD when Aspasius the Peripatetic asked whether the friendship of virtue, the friendship of utility, and the friendship of pleasure are related analogously or by virtue of the focal meaning that Aristotle ascribed to the friendship of virtue.[2] At the other end of the spectrum are the scholars who, more recently, have probed the meaning of Aristotle's definition of virtue friendship as "other selfhood" or who have taken position on the vexed question as to whether Aristotelian *eudaimonism* can be described as a form of ethical egoism.[3] At the heart of these questions are concepts such as self, egoism, and altruism, which had no currency in antiquity or had a very different meaning from the one they came to acquire later. To avoid projecting modern meanings on ancient concepts, therefore, scholars interested in questions of this latter kind must be clear as to how and why the key notions in which Aristotle expressed his views differed from their own. Only so can they hope to mine his ethical insights for all their considerable worth.

The present chapter is concerned with questions of this second kind. Taking friendship as my focus, I shall address two clusters of questions. Turning first to Aristotle's paragon of virtue, the great-souled man (*ho megalopsychos*),[4] I shall ask whether, or to what extent, his many excellences prepare him for engaging in friendship at both the personal and the civic levels. Is his virtuous self-sufficiency so great as to make the formation of personal ties redundant? Can he be counted upon to engage readily in the association that Aristotle calls "civic friendship" (*politikē philia*)? Turning then to the mysterious character whom Aristotle describes as the small-souled man (*ho mikropsychos*), I shall ask why he is presented as vicious and, more specifically, why he is held to be a potential source of harm to the state. Both sets of questions have mostly been ignored by ancient and modern commentators alike, eager to turn to what they perceived to be weightier matters in the master's *Ethics*. In this, as I hope to show, they were mistaken. Aristotle famously tells us on more than one occasion that "friendship . . . seems to hold states together, and lawgivers apparently devote more attention to it than to justice."[5] This being so, we need to understand why he considered that the great-souled man, for all his aloofness, is nonetheless an asset to the state. Correspondingly, we need to understand why he held that the vice of the small-souled man, whose civic dimension is far from being immediately apparent, involves a failure of friendship and responsible citizenship.

These are not easy questions to deal with. Not only is Aristotle's description of *mikropsychia* (literally, "smallness of soul") terse in the extreme, but it also comes as a corollary of his analysis of the most elusive and most misunderstood of all the virtues listed in the *Ethics*, namely, *megalopsychia* (literally, "greatness of soul"). The absence of any ready equivalent in our modern vernaculars for either the virtue of *megalopsychia* or the vice of *mikropsychia* suggests that, as far as modern readers are concerned, Aristotle's characterization of *mikropsychia* as a vicious deficiency of *megalopsychia* is truly a case of explaining the obscure by the more obscure.

In an attempt to overcome the exegetical and philosophical difficulties involved in coming to terms with these twin dispositions of character, I shall proceed as follows. In section 1, I shall offer some introductory remarks on the difficulties that Aristotle's translators encounter in rendering the two concepts into modern vernaculars. If nothing else, a survey of their largely unsuccessful efforts will begin to give us a sense of the conceptual territory covered by the Aristotelian notions. In section 2, I shall briefly sketch what I take to be those features of *megalopsychia* that make it most likely to con-tribute to the realization of the end of the city-state, as Aristotle conceived it. In section 3, I shall turn to the political dimensions of *megalopsychia* and show how, in Aristotle's viewpoint, a *megalopsychos* is likely to be the source of considerable benefits to both his friends and his city. Section 4 will be devoted to an analysis of Aristotle's definition of *mikropsychia* and of his claim that, in contrast with *megalopsychia*, it is incompatible with both the best kind of friendship and an optimal level of civic engagement. In section 5 I shall offer some brief remarks on the normative gap that separates Aristotle's concept of pride from ours.

1. A Translator's Headache: *Megalopsychia* and *Mikropsychia*

In the fourth book of the *Nicomachean Ethics* Aristotle defines "*megalopsy-chia*" as the virtue of the "man who thinks he deserves great things and actually does deserve them."[6] A page later he writes that *megalopsychia* is the "crown of the virtues" insofar as "it magnifies them and cannot exist without them."[7] Taken together, the two statements have long been a source of perplexity for Aristotle's later readers, most of whom were brought up in one or the other of the Abrahamic religions. As is well-known, these reli-gions teach that pride is a sin and the proud man "an abomination to the Lord." Unlike Aristotle, who viewed the *megalopsychos*' keen awareness of his merit as an integral part of his virtue, these religions discourage the faithful from dwelling on their own deserts and attainments.[8] It should therefore come as no surprise that, from the Middle Ages onwards, translators found *megalopsychia*, with the commendatory connotations that it has in Aristotle's usage, well nigh impossible to render into Latin or their own vernacular.

Of the most common renderings of *megalopsychia*—"pride," "magna-nimity," "high-mindedness," "great-soulness," and "great-heartedness"—none is semantically close enough to the Aristotelian concept while also carrying its highly commendatory connotations. Least acceptable of all is "pride."[9] Not only has it become too negatively connotated to enable modern readers to understand how Aristotle could hold it to be the crown of the virtues, it is also the traditional rendering of *superbia*, the Latin word by which medieval commentators rendered Aristotle's name for the vicious excess of *megalopsychia*, namely, *chaunotēs*. "Magnanimity,"[10] which is an exact rendering of the Greek *via* the Latin *magnanimitas*, tends nowadays to denote the virtue of those who are disposed to overlook the slights and offenses of which they may have been the object. As such, "magnanimity" lacks the cognitive import that lies at the very core of Aristotelian *megalopsychia*. "High-mindedness"[11] sounds an archaic note. Furthermore, insofar as it has long denoted the state of one who is generally "high-principled" or "moral" (in the modern sense of the word), it is too vague to convey the very specific virtuous disposition that Aristotle classifies under the name of *megalopsychia* in both versions of the *Ethics*. Attempts at literal renderings of the Greek, such as "greatness of spirit"[12] and "greatness of soul"[13] have no resonance for modern readers, and do not, therefore, serve their needs any better than would a mere transliteration of Aristotle's own word. As for "great-heartedness"[14], it is too close to "big-heartedness" to be a possible contender since it tends nowadays to characterize the generosity of those whose response to appeals on behalf of victims of natural disasters is immediate and pre-reflective. As will presently be seen, the generosity of Aristotle's *megalopsychos* is of a different kind.

Aristotelian *mikropsychia* is almost as alien to modern mentalities as *megalopsychia*. Insofar as Aristotle holds it to be a culpable (*psektos*) disposition of character which leads people to underassess their capabilities and merits,[15] it, too, runs counter to the moral intuitions of readers of the *Ethics* brought up in any one of the Abrahamic religions. What could be morally worthier, their religiously based intuitions intimate, than to refrain from proclaiming one's own merit and from actively seeking to reap one's due rewards? Admittedly, there is some resemblance between Aristotelian *mikropsychia* and the modern psychological concept of "low self-esteem."[16] But the resemblance is no more than skin deep: while the Aristotelian concept denotes a moral vice for which one is to be blamed, the modern day concept denotes a psychological dysfunction for which one is to be pitied or even, in some extreme cases, offered treatment. Furthermore, while Aristotelian *mikropsychia* affects only men of substance who shy away from the kind of civic engagement that is part and parcel of a life well lived, as objectively conceived, low self-esteem is a condition that can affect anyone and stands in the way of self-fulfillment and happiness, as subjectively conceived.

Such discrepancy between Aristotle's viewpoint and later intuitions has caused *mikropsychia*, like *megalopsychia*, to fare badly at the hands of his translators. Of all the renderings to be found in currently available translations of the *Ethics*—from pusillanimity to humility—none successfully conveys the meaning and the connotations of the Greek concept. "Pusillanimity,"[17] the Latinized equivalent of *mikropsychia* (*pusillus animus*), once the standard rendering of *mikropsychia* in English, is now almost obsolete. Although, like the Greek word, it does denote excessive timidity, it fails to convey what, in Aristotle's outlook, stands at the vicious core of *mikropsychia*, namely, lack of self-knowledge. "Small-mindedness"[18] denotes a preoccupation with petty, narrow-minded concerns rather than the cognitive failing that Aristotle identifies as the root of *mikropsychia*. As for "small-soulness,"[19] "little-soulness,"[20] and weak-heartedness,[21] they have no ready meaning at all for modern readers and set no barrier, therefore, to the construal of *mikropsychia* as "modesty" or even "humility." As will presently be shown, such construal is the most misleading of all since it actively invites the anachronistic projection of religiously grounded notions onto a philosophy to which they are profoundly alien.[22]

To guard against all such assumptions and misapprehensions I shall here leave untranslated both *megalopsychia* and *mikropsychia*. Although this may well be taken to be a counsel of despair, it has the advantage of setting no semantic barrier between Aristotle and ourselves.

2. *Megalopsychia* and Self-knowledge

Aristotle's definition of *megalopsychia* as "the crown of the virtues"[23] together with his characterization of the *megalopsychos* as "a man who thinks he deserves great things and actually does deserve them" (*NE* 1123b1–2) entail that there is in his view an objective ratio of public recognition (or honor) to individual desert and that the *megalopsychos* correctly surmises that, in his own case, the ratio is particularly high. His specific virtue, which is also the highest point of virtue, is therefore made up of two elements, exceptional merit and accurate self-assessment. These will now be taken in turn.

"Crown of the virtues" is, on the face of it, a curious expression to use on the part of a philosopher who holds a unitary theory of the virtues. Since, according to this theory, one person cannot have some virtues while lacking others, and anyone possessing one virtue also possesses all the others, the question arises as to why there should be a "crown" of the virtues and, if there be occasion for one, why it should go to *megalopsychia*. The answer, as inferred from the text of both *Ethics*, is that the crown-like status of *megalopsychia* is grounded in its necessary association with greatness (*megethos*, *NE* 1223b8) and nobility (*kalokagathia*, *EE* 1249a16). The link between *megalopsychia* and *kalokagathia*, which is but tenuous in the *Nicomachean* version, is the object of a helpful, though compressed, argument in the *Eudemian* version. *Kalokagathia*, Aristotle there explains, is "perfect virtue" (*aretē teleios*); it is the virtue of a man for whom the things that are good by nature are "fine" and valuable in and for themselves (*ta kala di' hauta*), rather than solely for their consequences. Since wealth, birth, and power enable such a man to perform actions that are both advantageous and fine (*sympheronta kai kala*),[24] it is just that these goods of nature should be his. As Aristotle will have further occasions to argue in the *Politics*, "what is just (*dikaion*) is fine, and what is according to worth (*kat' axian*) is just."[25] In performing fine and advantageous actions, therefore, the Aristotelian *kalokagathos* or *megalopsychos* shows himself worthy of the incidental advantages that nature and circumstances have bestowed upon him. He is therefore in a position to lead the best human life possible, namely, a "life of excellence, when excellence has external goods enough for the performance of good actions."[26] Modern readers of Aristotle, of course, will point out that, given the nature of the incidental conditions that he takes to be necessary for the possession of *megalopsychia*, it is unlikely that it could ever be practiced by more than a handful of individuals at any one time. Women,[27] slaves,[28] resident aliens,[29] the unintelligent, the less than wealthy, and those whose achievements fell short of the highest could not realistically aspire to it in fourth-century Athens, however great their merits and determined their efforts. The unpalatable conclusion, therefore, appears unavoidable that Aristotle restricted the achievement of the crown of the virtues to the aristocratic rich.

A careful reading of the text of the *Nicomachean* version, however, reveals that the conclusion is not quite as unpalatable as it might appear at first glance since Aristotle presents the possession of such incidental advantages as wealth and high birth as necessary, as opposed to sufficient, conditions of *megalopsychia*. To these necessary conditions, he added another one, namely that, in order to be worthy of wearing the crown of the virtues, a wealthy nobleman needs also to be consistently disposed to perform the fine actions that circumstances call for and to confer upon the state and his fellow citizens the high benefits that his position enables him to confer. No one, Aristotle takes care to add, can lay claim to the virtue of *megalopsychia* who does not fulfill both conditions: "[W]hoever possesses the goods of fortune without possessing excellence or virtue is not justified in claiming great deserts for himself, nor is it correct to call him a *megalopsychos*, for neither is possible without perfect virtue."[30] Insofar as the *megalopsychos'* entitlement to civic recognition and honors is conditional upon the fulfillment of this latter, moral, condition, he is within striking distance—surprisingly so—of the faithful servant of the synoptic gospels: "[T]o whom much is given, of him much will be required."[31]

Other aspects of Aristotle's account of *megalopsychia* have proved more difficult to reconcile with our moral intuitions. One such is the claim that it is characteristic of the *megalopsychos* to be fully aware of the extent of his merit and achievements. While no commentator has disputed that the ability to take the measure of one's own worth is to be esteemed in proportion to its rarity, many have resisted Aristotle's claim that it is a moral virtue. Far more virtuous it is to be aware of one's limitations than of one's merits, goes a long-standing and widespread view. Holding such a view, modern commentators have mostly been united in expressing their dismay at Aristotle's commendation of the *megalopsychos* for his keen awareness of the extent of his deserts. So put out, for example, were Burnet and Joachim by the portrait of the *megalopsychos* drawn in the *Ethics* that they could not believe that Aristotle had meant it in earnest; it was, they conjectured, quietly "humorous," "half-ironical,"[32] or obviously exaggerated.[33] Rather than seeking to provide a detailed account of this particular difference between Aristotle and ourselves—a task that would far exceed the space available in this volume—I shall here, more modestly, try to make Aristotle's position appear less distasteful to those who regard pride as a vice (or a sin) and modesty (or humility) as a virtue. Accordingly, I shall now proceed to outline the cognitive excellences that enable the *megalopsychos* to take a just measure of his merit and, on that basis, to accept, graciously if not enthusiastically, whatever high civic honors come his way.

The self-knowledge that an Aristotelian *megalopsychos* needs to have in order to be worthy of the name goes far beyond the particularities of his own person and situation. To begin with, he must have a secure grasp of the standards and criteria by which merit happens to be assessed in his city; only so will he be able to measure his attainments against his capabilities and to compare both with those of his peers. More crucially, however, he must have an understanding of the standards and criteria by which it is right and proper that merit should be measured; only so will he be able, not only to keep his own standards of excellence independent of local contingencies, but also to value in himself and his friends what is most truly valuable. In Aristotelian terms this means that the *megalopsychos* must identify himself with his thinking element (*nous*), on the understanding, whether explicit or not, that "the thinking element is what each of us mostly is" (*NE* 1168b34–5), and that it behoves us, therefore, to cultivate and promote it over all others. Truly to have identified himself with his *nous* and become a *megalopsychos*, such a character will therefore have had to nurture the thinking element in himself and trained his appetitive and emotional drives into habits of easy compliance with it. If such self-training has been successful, the *megalopsychos* will, in all relevant circumstances, consistently choose the good of his soul in preference to all external goods. This will make him a self-lover (*philautos*) in Aristotle's commendatory sense of the word, someone who "loves and gratifies the most sovereign element in him" (*NE* 1168b33–34) and "obeys it in everything" (*NE* 1168b31). The *megalopsychos*' self-knowledge, it can now be concluded, is of a virtuous nature since it gives him, beyond the certainty of his own worth, the assurance that his life is consistently governed by the element in him that is best suited to rule.[34]

Whether the *megalopsychos*' correct understanding of the end of human life be theoretical[35] or practical,[36] one thing is certain: it consistently informs his deliberations in matters related to his personal and civic life. Amongst these, honor and public recognition figure more prominently than we would expect, and the question will presently have to be asked as to why Aristotle should have assigned honor such a significant role in the life of the *megalopsychos*. For the moment let us simply note that, having classified honor as "the greatest external good" (*NE* 1123b20–21),[37] he proceeds to claim that it is entirely proper for the *megalopsychos*, not only to strive after such honors as his merit warrants (*NE* 1123b19), but also to be chagrined at being denied them (*EE* 1232b12–3). This, however, does not mean that the *megalopsychos*' attitude to honor is one of anxious concern. Far from it. Aware that honor depends as much upon luck and the opinion of those who have it in their gift as it does upon the merits of the recipient, the *megalopsychos* regards it as an external good unfit to play more than a minor role in the best life for a human being to lead. Thus he disdains the small and ill-judged honors bestowed upon him by the unthinking many[38] and, although he is moderately pleased at being the object of the highest honors, he yet knows better than to attach undue importance to them: "From great honors and those that good people confer upon him he will derive a *moderate* (cf. *metriōs*) amount of pleasure, convinced that he is only getting what is properly his or even less. For no honor can be worthy of perfect virtue. Yet he will accept such honors, because they have no greater tribute to pay to him" (*NE* 1124a5–9, tr. Ostwald, modified). As can be seen, therefore, virtue has distanced the Aristotelian *megalopsychos* from worldly success, wealth, and power, all of which are for most men objects of anxious concern. Not being at the mercy of fortune and the opinion of others, the *megalopsychos* has made himself as self-sufficient as a human being can be.

Does this mean that his self-sufficiency is so complete that he has no reason or need to engage in friendship? Indeed not. Besides holding that human self-sufficiency cannot ever be such as to preclude the need for friendship,[39] Aristotle gives us clear grounds in both versions of the *Ethics* and in the *Politics* for thinking that his paragon of virtue, far from remaining aloof from the affairs of men, has an important political role to play in the city and that he readily engages in friendship at both the civic and the personal levels. Let us see how.

3. *Megalopsychia* and Civic Friendship

A. THE END OF THE CITY-STATE

In book I of the *Politics* Aristotle summarily restates his teleological conception of human nature. Human beings, he teaches, cannot achieve self-sufficiency on their own or in isolation; they need a social context in which to grow to maturity and develop their power of reason. This is why nature, which does nothing without a purpose or in vain,[40] has implanted in human beings a social instinct.[41] This instinct prompts them, in the first place, to form communities (*koinōniai*), such as households and villages, with the immediate purpose of securing for themselves the "bare necessities of life." Once a community, or group of communities, has grown materially self-sufficient or very nearly so, it evolves into a *polis* or sovereign city-state in which "the limit of self-sufficiency" is attained (*Pol.* I, 2, 1252b29). In Aristotle's outlook the city-state is the optimal political unit, being inclusive enough to be self-sufficient, but not so large as to make it impossible for the citizens to know each other by reputation, if not personally. Mutual acquaintance, he held, breeds mutual confidence (*pistis pros allēlous*) and instills in the citizens a desirable sense of community. So much is evident, he pointed out, from the fact that tyrants, who must divide in order to rule, "take every means to prevent people from knowing one another"[42] and, for that reason, forbid the practice of meals in common (*sussitiai*) and the formation of clubs and fellowships (*hetairiai*). Precisely because Aristotle wanted the citizens to know each other and to interact in leisure as in work, he favored the custom of taking meals in common for the opportunities it provided for the discussion of topics of mutual interest.[43] Although, surprisingly enough, the issue of civic friendship is hardly ever broached in the *Politics*, Aristotle's insistence on the desirability of social and educational interaction between the citizens would seem to justify Richard Kraut's conclusion that Aristotle "sees common meals as a way of fostering civic friendship."[44]

From the a priori anthropological considerations offered in the opening remarks of the *Politics*, Aristotle concluded that the state is obviously (cf. *phaneron*) a creation of nature and that human beings are political animals by nature.[45] He did not, however, stop there and proceeded to draw from his conception of the state and human sociality as "natural" the norm which lies at the very foundation of his ethics and political philosophy. The city-state (*polis*), he taught, being the completion or end (*telos*) of associations formed for the sake of survival and self-sufficiency, is the best form of political association; it alone provides humans beings with the conditions in which they can flourish and lead the best possible human life. To the realization of this end, friendship, as created by associations of various kinds between the citizens, plays an important part. As we read in a characteristically dense passage:

> It is clear then that a state is not a mere society, having a common place, established for the prevention of mutual crime and for the sake of exchange. These are the conditions without which a state cannot exist; but all of them together do not constitute a state, which is a community of families in well-being, for the sake of a perfect and self-sufficing life. Such a community can only be established among those who live in the same place and intermarry. Hence there arise in cities connexions, brotherhoods, common sacrifices, amusements which draw men together. But these are created by *friendship, for to choose to live together is friendship.* The end of a state is the good life, and these are the means towards it. And the state is the union of families and villages in a perfect and self-sufficing life, by which we mean a happy and honorable life. Our conclusion, then, is that *political society exists for the sake of noble actions, and not of living together.* Hence they who contribute most to such a society have a larger share in it (*tēs poleōs metesti pleion*) than those who have the same or a greater freedom or nobility of birth but are inferior to them in *political excellence* (cf. *tēn politikēn aretēn*); or than those who exceed them in wealth but are surpassed by them in excellence. (*Pol.* III, 9, 1280b33–40)

Aristotle here highlights two factors that contribute to the realization of the end of the *polis*: friendship between the citizens and compliance with the principle of distributive justice that dictates that those best qualified to hold political office should be given a share in the government of the city commensurate with their ability.

B. EGALITARIAN AND ARISTOCRATIC CONSTITUTIONS

While the promotion of civic friendship is entirely consonant with Aristotle's conception of the state as a relatively compact community aiming at a self-sufficing and good life, the application of the principle of distributive justice, as alluded to in the above lines, runs counter to the egalitarian conception of the state that Aristotle defends elsewhere in the *Politics*, when he claims that "it is obviously necessary on many grounds that all the citizens alike should take their turn of governing and being governed. Equality consists in the same treatment of similar persons, and no government can stand which is not founded on justice" (*Pol.* VII, 14, b25–30).[46] So outlined here, the principle of citizenly equality grounds Aristotle's argument in book IV of the *Politics*, that the best constitution for most states is one in which the middle classes (*hoi mesoi*) are in charge. Citizens of the middle class, he there optimistically avers, being "equals and similars (cf. *isōn kai homoiōn*)"[47] and possessing the goods of fortune (beauty, strength, and wealth) in moderation, are more likely than the very rich or the very poor to follow the rule of reason (*logos*) and to lead a life lying in the mean, as defined in the *Nicomachean Ethics* II, 6–9.

"Equal and similar" to his fellow citizens is precisely what the *megalopsychos* is not. Being preeminent in virtue, nobility, and wealth, he is capable of making a greater contribution to the community than most other citizens. For that reason, the principle of distributive justice alluded to in *Politics* III 9 and 13 dictates that he should be given a proportionately larger share in the government of the city-state. Rather than simply taking it in turn to rule and be ruled, the *megalopsychos* is qualified, on the ground of his overall excellence, to play a consistently dominant role in the realization of the function of the city-state. When, later in book III, Aristotle returns to the question of the civic role best suited to the man—or men—of "pre-eminent excellence" (*diapherōn kat' aretēn*), he answers as follows:

> If . . . there be one person, or more than one, although not enough to make up the full complement of a state, whose excellence is so pre-eminent that the excellence or the political

> capacity of all the rest admit of no comparison with his or theirs, he or they can no longer be regarded as part of a state; for justice will not be done to the superior, if he is reckoned only as the equal of those who are so far inferior to him in excellence and in political capacity. . . . For men of pre-eminent excellence there is no law—they are themselves a law. (III, 13, 1284a4–14)[48]

Rather than prevent such exceptional men from being continuously active in government, Aristotle here claims that, in accordance with the principle of distributive justice, "the only alternative is that . . . all should happily obey such a ruler, according to what seems to be the order of nature, and that men like him should be kings in their state for life." (1284b12–14) While acknowledging the somewhat utopian character of such aristocratic, or monarchic, conception of the state, Aristotle, even so, presented it as preferable to all others, whenever circumstances were such as to permit its implementation.[49] The famous formula "excellence furnished with external means"[50] neatly encapsulates the requirements for holding high office in the kind of aristocratic regime he favored. That the *megalopsychos* described in *NE* IV 3 meets these requirements is beyond doubt. As Robinson aptly notes in an *ad loc.* comment to the above-quoted lines: "Aristotle did worship, or at least look up to with awed respect, some ideally highminded or 'megalopsychic' person who 'demands great honors and deserves them.' "[51]

To be sure, such aristocratic model of the constitution, according to which those who are preeminent in virtue and contribute most to the city deserve a proportionately large share in government, is not easily reconciled with the egalitarian model, according to which citizens of the middle class (*hoi mesoi*) should take it in turn to rule and be ruled.[52] Fortunately, however, since the present context does not require that an attempt be made at reconciling the two models, we can turn without further ado to Aristotle's conception of civic friendship. Which role, we shall now ask, can citizenly cooperation and concord, be it in an aristocratic or a democratic state, play in the life of a man who combines great wealth and supreme moral excellence?

c. CIVIC FRIENDSHIP

In *Politics* III, 9, 1280b33–40, as quoted above, Aristotle assigns to friendship, pithily defined as voluntary living together, a central role at every stage in the formation of the city-state. At the level of restricted associations within the *polis*, as he explains in the *Nicomachean Ethics*, friendship bonds individuals in the pursuit of common aims: "Men address as friends their fellow travelers on a voyage, their fellow soldiers, and similarly also those who are associated with them in other kinds of communities. Friendship is present to the extent that men share something in common, for that is also the extent to which they share a view of what is just" (*NE* VIII, 9, 1159b27–31). Insofar as such restricted associations are aimed at advantage, they readily fall under the category of friendship of utility. As such, one presumes, they do not outlive the realization of the particular common aim for which they were set up. Yet, in spite of their limited scope and life-span, they do contribute, albeit modestly, to the fulfillment of the end of the city-state, namely to ensure citizenly cooperation in the pursuit of specific aims.

In the formation of the *polis* itself, considerations of need and mutual advantage also play a crucial role. Civic friendship, Aristotle tells us in the *Eudemian Ethics*, is based on utility and can even be compared to a "cash-in-hand transaction"[53] since those who first set up the city had entered into a "definite agreement" (cf. *kath' homologian*)[54] to assist each other and to further their common interests. In book VIII of the *Nicomachean* version, too, Aristotle includes the *polis* itself among the associations entered in for the sake of advantage: "All communities are like part of the political community. Men combine with an eye to some advantage or to provide some of the necessities of life, and we think of the political community as having *initially* (*ex archēs*) come together and as enduring to secure the advantage [of its members]" (*NE*, VIII, 9, 1160a8–12). If, in the manner of Aristotle in these two passages, one concentrates on the motives behind the formation of the city-state, civic friendship cannot but be classified as a variety of the friendship of utility, a friendship which can vary in scope and duration depending on the character of the persons who come together.[55] To the extent that those who associate for reasons of advantage expect to receive benefits proportional to their outlay,[56] the basis of their friendship is equality of advantage gained or hoped for.

However, as Aristotle takes care to stress in book IX of the *Nicomachean* version, a state cannot become, or remain, a flourishing community, as opposed to a mere association of men and women banded together for survival, unless the friendship which binds the citizens evolves in depth as well as in scope.[57] Not only should it come to encompass the present as well as the long-term interest of the state, but it should also aim at the moral and intellectual fulfillment of the citizens. To this nobler bond, Aristotle gave the name of "concord" (*homonoia*): "We do attribute concord to states, when the citizens have the same judgment about their common interest, when they choose the same things, and when they execute what they have decided in common. In other words, concord is found in the realm of action, and in the realm of action in matters of importance and in those matters in which it is possible for both partners or all partners to attain their goals" (*NE* IX 6, 1167a26–30). So conceived, civic friendship transcends mere utility and can flourish only in states with a sound constitution.[58] It flourishes, paradigmatically, in states run along the aristocratic model, when "both the common people (*ho dēmos*) and the better classes (*hoi epieikeis*) wish that the best men (*hoi aristoi*) should rule."[59] In such a case citizenly concord consists in the recognition, on the part of the majority, of the moral and political superiority of a small minority among them. Unequal and hierarchical, such civic friendship involves gratitude and deference on the part of the inferior and good government on the part of the superior. The benefits conferred on to the citizen body as a whole by the *aristoi* in the city, who include the *megalopsychoi*, considerably outweigh the return they get from their fellow citizens. While the majority get the internal good of living in a city-state that is well run and dedicated to the pursuit of "a happy and honorable life," the *aristoi* in charge of public affairs gain nothing better in return than the external good of public recognition. Such external good, as Aristotle wryly notes in IV 3, 1124a5–9, gives them only a moderate amount of pleasure since honor is no match for moral excellence and political ability.

Modern readers will be reassured to learn that Aristotle did not restrict the disinterested kind of civic friendship to aristocratic constitutions. Having stated that it can prevail among good men of sound judgment, who are "of the same mind each with himself and all with one another" and who, in addition, wish "for what is just," he concluded that it could bond also those who are equal in both virtue and citizenly status.[60] As such, it can fit the democratic model of the constitution, in which the citizens take it in turn to rule and be ruled.[61] In such a democratic constitution, committed as it is to the principle that "political society exists for the sake of noble actions,"[62] the *megalopsychos*, although not consistently occupying the high political offices of the state, would nonetheless have considerable opportunities to make a disinterested contribution to the end (*telos*) of the state. Not only would he entertain relations of civic concord with other good men and citizens and, in association with them, promote justice, but his wealth would also enable him to bestow munificent gifts on the city. Lastly, in extreme circumstances, his "all-complete" (*pantelēs*) virtue[63] would prompt him to perform noble actions, not indeed for the sake of his own advantage, but to benefit both his personal friends and his fellow citizens. Let us now turn to the crucial lines in which Aristotle outlines how far his paragon of virtue would go in benefiting city and friends, be it in an aristocratic or a democratic constitution.

D. THE *MEGALOPSYCHOS* AS FRIEND

Take, to begin with, benefits of a financial nature. A *megalopsychos* could be relied upon to perform high-profile public services or "liturgies" (*leitourgiai*), all of which entail heavy financial liabilities, such as equipping a trireme or financing the cost of a chorus for one of the dramatic festivals. The importance of such contributions to the life of the city-state is not to be underestimated. Since there was no overall regulated system of direct taxation in classical Athens, the liturgies provided a large part of the public revenue needed by the city to maintain its fleet and public buildings as well as to provide for the regular scheduling of religious and dramatic festivals. So very considerable was the financial burden entailed by liturgies that many rich citizens sought exemptions from them or looked for loopholes in the regulations governing the institution.[64] Some even resorted to various expedients of doubtful legality to hide their wealth. Not so the *megalopsychos*. From the repeated references in both versions of the *Ethics* to the public honors bestowed upon him by the city on account of services rendered, it can safely be inferred that a *megalopsychos* would be highly unlikely to shirk his responsibilities as a potential liturgist.

Financial contributions are not, however, the only sacrifice that an Aristotelian *megalopsychos* would consent to make for his city. Far from it. I shall now argue, on the basis of chapter 8 of book IX of the *Nicomachean* version, that the *megalopsychos*, although no "lover of danger" (*oude philokindunos*: *NE* IV 3, 1124b7), would nevertheless be prepared, if the need arose, to lay down his life "for his friends and for his native land."

In *NE* IX 8 Aristotle mounts an intricate and highly compact argument to show that virtuous friendship is best understood by reference to self-love (*philautia*) properly so-called, which is the love of the highest and most sovereign element in oneself, namely reason. This kind of self-love, Aristotle contrasts with self-love the misnomer, which seeks the gratification of the lower appetites and impulses. While self-lovers of the first kind promote their reason by following its counsel in all things, self-lovers of the second kind seek mostly pleasure, comfort, and personal safety. The difference between the two kinds of self-love is highly relevant to the present issue. Self-love directed at the promotion of one's own reason tends not to produce interpersonal conflicts insofar as the demands of one person's reason are unlikely to conflict with the demands of another person's reason.

By contrast, self-love conceived as the gratification of appetitive wants and
needs is very likely to result in interpersonal conflicts whenever, as often
happens, the desired good is in such limited supply that one person's having more of it entails another person's having less. While rationality cannot
be an object of competition, money and honors tend to be eagerly sought
and fiercely fought over.

In Aristotle's viewpoint, therefore, a self-lover of the first kind will not
let considerations of personal safety or comfort stand in the way of what
he understands to be the demands of the situation he finds himself in. Far
from considering personal risk to be of any great moment, he will readily
sacrifice his comfort or safety to assist his friends or his native land, whenever either would benefit from his assistance. In some admittedly exceptional
circumstances, he will even be prepared to lay down his life for them.

At this point Aristotle's argument begins to take the appearance of
paradox. Even when the virtuous self-lover consents to the ultimate sacrifice, so Aristotle avers, he still stands to benefit. The argument, which
is consequentialist in nature, begins as follows: "Those . . . whose active
devotion to noble actions is outstanding win the recognition and praise of
all; and if all men were to compete for what is noble (*hamillōmenōn pros to
kalon*) and put all their efforts into the performance of the noblest actions,
all the needs of the community (cf. *koinēi*) will have been met, and each
individual (cf. *idiai*) will have the greatest of goods, since that is what virtue
is" (IX 9, 1169a 6–11).The paradox comes through a few lines later, when
Aristotle contends that the beneficiaries of noble actions are not restricted
to the agent's *philoi* and city, but that the self-sacrificial agent, too, stands
to benefit. Even if he were to lose his life, he would gain the (internal)
good of virtue and the (external) good of honor: "It is also true that many
actions of the man of high moral standards [*ho epieikēs*] are performed in
the interest of his friends and of his country, and if need be, he will give
his life for them. He will freely give his money, honors, and, in short,
all good things that men compete for, while he gains nobility (*to kalon*)
for himself" (*NE*, IX 9 1169a18–22., tr., Oswald, modified).[65] Aristotle is
not unaware of the paradox involved in holding that self-sacrifice can be
self-serving. As he knew well, the conventional view holds that heroes can
benefit others only by sacrificing themselves. But the conventional view,
Aristotle here argues, takes account of only one side of the issue. It fails to
understand that the agent who offers himself in sacrifice secures for himself,
albeit posthumously, the greatest of all goods, namely *to kalon*. Appearances
to the contrary notwithstanding, he concludes, the self-sacrificial agent is,

in this case, a gainer as well as a loser, and what he gains is greater than what he loses.

Who is the rare person whom Aristotle has here in mind? Who is the "man of high moral standards" (*ho epieikēs*), whose devotion to noble actions is such that he faces death with equanimity? From the context, we know that he is a man capable of the highest kind of friendship, namely, the friendship of virtue. My claim is that the *megalopsychos* is such a man. Not only is Aristotle's *megalopsychos* worthy of wearing "the crown of the virtues" but, from Aristotle's description of his character, we can safely assume that he is capable of the highest of the three kinds of friendship distinguished in both *Ethics*.[66] Indeed, far from presenting him as too self-absorbed to engage in friendship at all, Aristotle writes of him that "he cannot adjust his life to another, except to a friend" (*NE*, 1124b31–32). Clearly, such a paragon of virtue, who is forever disinclined to accept benefits from others (*NE*,, 1124b9–11), would not want to cultivate the friendship of utility. As for the friendship of pleasure, his general loftiness of purpose and demeanor would most likely make him despise it. Since we had already been told earlier in the *Nicomachean* version that the *megalopsychos* "will face great risks, and in the midst of them he will not spare his life, aware that life at any cost is not worth having" (*NE*, 1124b8–9),[67] we are entitled to infer that he is the paradigmatic *philautos* who, as described in chapter 8 of book IX, is prepared to die for his friends or country.

This may well seem to us an impossibly heroic ideal of friendship and civic engagement. Not so in ancient Greece, where a short and heroic life was traditionally held to be nobler than a long and undistinguished existence. This ideal, which we find already expressed in the *Iliad*,[68] was still current at the classical age, as testified by Isocrates' panegyric of Evagoras, the deposed ruler of Salamis. In that oration, likely to have been composed for political motives, the famous orator found it judicious to say that "men of ambition and greatness of soul (cf. *philotimous kai megalopsychous*) not only are desirous of praise for such things, but prefer a glorious death to life, zealously seeking glory rather than existence, and doing all that lies in their power to leave behind a memory of themselves that shall never die."[69] Since the oration was composed in the mid–360s, it is likely that Aristotle, who had arrived at Plato's Academy in 367, either heard or read it. What at any rate is certain is that the verbal parallels between the orator's lines and the above-quoted passage from *NE* IX 8 show that the conception of the *megalopsychos* as a man capable of heroic acts for the sake of his friends or country was far from unfamiliar to Aristotle's contemporaries. The honors they would readily bestow on the *megalopsychoi* amongst them are a reflection of that conception.[70]

4. *MIKROPSYCHIA*

Aristotle's eulogy of *megalopsychia* has cast a shadow over his disparagement of *mikropsychia*. So exercised have medieval and modern commentators been about his presentation of *megalopsychia* as a virtuous mean that they have mostly left out of account, or misunderstood altogether, his description of *mikropsychia* as the corresponding vice of deficiency. This is unfortunate insofar as a close reading of these passages would have given these commentators a further opportunity to appreciate the gap that separates the values of the ancients from those of later ages. A more immediately relevant reason for paying attention to Aristotelian *mikropsychia*, however, is that it stands to confirm—or to invalidate—a conclusion drawn earlier in this chapter, namely, that self-knowledge plays a crucial role in Aristotle's conception of friendship at both the personal and the civic levels.

From the number of times that *mikropsychia* is mentioned in the *Ethics*, it is clear that Aristotle attaches significance to it. However, since his various descriptions of it, besides being terse, do not appear to be entirely consonant with each other, at least at first sight, our first task must be to consider the passages in some detail. I shall begin with the *Nicomachean* account, which sets out the issue more fully and more discursively than the corresponding *Eudemian* passage.

In the *Nicomachean Ethics*, *mikropsychia* is first mentioned in the context of the broad taxonomical considerations offered in book II:

> As regard honor and dishonor the mean is *megalopsychia*, the excess what we might call vanity and the deficiency *mikropsychia* (*NE* II, 7, 1107b21–23, tr. Ostwald, modified).

In book IV, embedded in the chapter devoted to the *megalopsychos*, we find a highly compressed argument designed to show that the faults of the *mikropsychos*, like those of the vain man, are of a cognitive nature:

> Such then is the *megalopsychos*. A man who falls short is a *mikropsychos*, and one who exceeds is vain. Now here, too, these people are not considered to be evil—for they are not evil-doers—but only *mistaken* (*hêmartêmenoi*). For a *mikropsychos* deprives himself of the goods he deserves. What *seems* to be bad (*kakon*) about him is due to the fact that he does not think he deserves good

things and that *he does not know himself* (cf. *agnoein heanton*); if
he did, he would desire them, especially since they are good. Such
people are not regarded as stupid so much as timorous (*oknēroi*).
However, a reputation of this sort seems to make them even worse
(*cheirous*). For while everyone (cf. *hekastoi*) strives to get what they
deserve, these people keep aloof from noble actions and pursuits
(*aphistantai tōn praxeōn tōn kalōn kai tōn epitēdeumatōn*) and from
external goods as well, because they consider themselves unworthy
(*anaxioi*) . . . *Mikropsychia* is more opposed to *megalopsychia* than
vanity is, for it occurs more frequently and is worse. (*NE* IV 3,
1125a16–34, tr. Ostwald, modified)

As characterized in these lines, the *mikropsychos* is someone whose desires
and ambitions are more modest than they should be and whose achievements, as a result, fall short of the highest. Failing to know the extent of
his capabilities, he stands back from the internal good of performing noble
deeds and engaging in fine pursuits. Such diffidence, in turn, makes it
impossible for him to serve the city in ways that would make him worthy
of receiving from the city the external good of honor (*timē*). Although he
cannot be said to be "evil," there is nonetheless something bad about him,
since, in Aristotle's estimation, there is nothing meritorious in seeking to
obtain less than one's capabilities would warrant.[71]

In the more succinct *Eudemian* account there is no mention of fine
actions or noble pursuits. The focus is firmly placed on the external good of
timē, *micropsychia* being there described as a culpable (cf. *psektos*)[72] failure to
lay claim to goods which lie within one's reach and to which one is entitled:

The vice that pertains to one who is worthy of great things
without deeming himself to be is weak-heartedness (*mikropsychia*), since it seems to be the mark of the weak-hearted person
to fail to deem oneself worthy of anything great despite the
availability of that which would render the claim just. (*EE*, III,
5, 1233a12–15, tr. Inwood and Woolf)

What are the qualities that the *mikropsychos* fail to recognize in himself? As
we learn by implication later in the same chapter, they are mostly contingent
qualities relating to legal status and social rank: "[I]t would not be called
weak-hearted (*mikropsychos*) if a resident alien did not deem himself worthy
of high office but held back, whereas it would be in the case of a well-born
citizen who considered high office a great thing (*EE* III, 5, 1233a28–30,
tr. Inwood and Woolf).

This is the point at which we must take care not to project our own values onto Aristotle's text. Two mistakes in particular are to be avoided. Firstly, before deploring Aristotle's "elitism" or superficiality in his choice of criteria of civic worthiness, we should bear in mind that the conception of civic culture in classical Athens differed from our own in a number of respects. Although it was not impossible for resident aliens, slaves, and low-born citizens to achieve wealth and renown, civic obligations and privileges were mostly in the hands of those who, descended from citizens, were of high rank and possessed large estates. These were the citizens who were expected to contribute the most, financially as well as personally, to the city's renown and prosperity. As shown in section 3 above, in the absence of any comprehensive system of direct taxation, the civic obligations that went with wealth and rank were as onerous as the rewards for fulfilling them were considerable. Properly understood *timē*, therefore, was considered to be part and parcel of the performance of fine actions and noble deeds. Accordingly, to be the object of the highest civic honors was, for most citizens, a matter of legitimate pride. Correspondingly, citizens who, though high born and wealthy, avoided getting involved in costly or risky civic endeavors would be rebuked and shamed for their lack of public spiritedness. Their reluctance to seek such public esteem as normally rewarded the holding of high office or the bestowal of munificent gifts on to the city would be regarded, not indeed as commendable reticence, but as culpable reticence. In describing the vice of *mikropsychia* as he does in the *Eudemian Ethics*, Aristotle, therefore, expresses commonly held opinions (*endoxa*) as well as his own view.

Secondly and more importantly, *mikropsychia* is not to be thought of as the classical Greek counterpart of humility. To conflate, in the manner of many a later commentator, Aristotelian *mikropsychia,* defined as reticence, to lay claim to goods of which one is worthy, and humility, defined as a propensity to value others above oneself,[73] is to make Aristotle's position well nigh unintelligible. Aristotle's position, I shall now argue, becomes clear once it is appreciated that his reasons for castigating the *mikropsychos* are the converse of his reasons for praising the *megalopsychos* and that both sets of reasons flow directly from his conception of civic worthiness and friendship. Once this is understood, the gap between his values and ours, although considerable, will no longer seem unbridgeable.

The blameworthy *mikropsychos* of Aristotle's description is a person who combines external assets such as status, wealth, and leisure with other, less contingent, qualities such as physical strength, natural authority, and political intelligence. Although such a person cannot be assumed to be unaware of his lineage and the extent of his wealth, he yet fails to take the full measure of his capabilities and advantages, so reluctant is he to take on the civic onus that they place upon him. Such failure, together with the resulting discrepancy between what he could do and what he actually does for the city is precisely what Aristotle blames the *mikropsychos* for. So much is confirmed by his description in both versions of the *Ethics* of another character, the man of limited abilities and small achievements, who, keenly aware of his limitations, refrains from attempting to do great things and seeking high honors. Although Aristotle is not greatly interested in this lackluster character, who is in no position to contribute significantly to the life of his city, he yet expresses esteem for him, and if the praise he gives him is faint, as one would expect, it is praise nonetheless. To the extent that this man knows himself, so Aristotle contends, he resembles the *megalopsychos*, and his character is "as reason bids" (*EE*, 1233a23); in spite of his small worth, he deserves to be called "*sophrōn*" (*NE*, 1123b5).

This is more than can be said of the *mikropsychos* who, content to remain unaware of his capabilities,[74] harms the city by default. Just how much harm Aristotle considers him to inflict upon the city emerges from his claim, as put forward in the *Nicomachean* version, that *mikropsychia* is "more opposed to *megalopsychia* than vanity (*chaunotēs*) is, for it occurs more frequently and is worse (*cheiron*)."[75] To modern readers, this appears to be one more bemusing statement in a chapter that abounds in them. How, these readers wonder, could Aristotle believe that the tendency to underassess one's merits is worse than the tendency to overassess them? How, for that matter, could he flout the experience of everyday life by presenting the first tendency as more widespread than the second?

The fact that Aristotle made no attempt to justify either claim shows that he did not expect his contemporaries to find them contentious. In an attempt to understand how Aristotle's contemporaries would have received them, let me first elaborate somewhat on Aristotle's terse presentation of the *mikropsychos* as deficient in the very respects in which the *megalopsychos* excels. The *mikropsychos*, like the *megalopsychos*, has been blessed with the "goods of fortune," but, unlike him, he does not appreciate the moral onus that such goods place upon him. While the *megalopsychos*, who judges great and small goods at their true value, does not hesitate to shoulder the expenses of liturgies, for example, the *mikropsychos* takes advantage of legal loopholes to avoid incurring the financial responsibilities involved, in the mistaken belief that private wealth is a greater good than civic engagement. While the *megalopsychos*, who cares little for the opinions of the many and is open in love as in hate, speaks up in the Assembly and the law courts, even when it is dangerous to do so, the *mikropsychos*, who would do anything for a quiet life, is ever reluctant to stand and be counted. While the *megalopsychos*, who does not think life worth preserving at all costs, is prepared to lay down his life for his friends and country, the *mikropsychos* consistently chooses the good of personal safety over that of performing "noble actions" likely to put life and limb at risk. While the *kalon* is the ultimate good for the *megalopsychos*, it holds no motivating force for the *mikropsychos*. While the *megalopsychos* accepts graciously whatever honors the city bestows upon him for services rendered, the *mikropsychos* purposefully eschews honors in the mistaken belief that most of them cost too much. All in all, the differences between the two men stem from the fact that while the one effortlessly follows the guidance of his thinking element, which advises him that a life of safety is not the ultimate good, the other, who lacks an understanding of what befits a man of substance, aims at an easeful existence in the course of which his needs and wants will be met. To put the same point differently: both men aim at the good, but while the good of the *megalopsychos* is the real good, the good of the *mikropsychos* is only what appears to him to be the good.[76]

Can we find confirmation in the text that this comparison is in line with Aristotle's thinking on *mikropsychia*? A first encouraging piece of evidence comes from his use of *oknēros* to describe the man who, through self-ignorance, turns away (*aposterei*) from the great goods that he can, and should, aspire to and who becomes worse as a result (*NE* IV 3, 1125a24). In classical and postclassical Greek, *oknēros* and its cognate *oknein* most often connote timidity, reluctance, and weakness.[77] As for Aristotle's own use of *oknēros* and *oknein*, it is unfailingly deprecatory.[78] Thus in the *Historia Animalium*, he expresses the view that "in virtually all animals," including human beings, the female of the species is "more afraid of action" (*oknēroteron* VIII.1 613b13, tr. D. M. Balme) than the male, while the male is "more courageous" (*andreioteron* 613b16) than the female. In the *Politics*, he writes that "in time of war the poor are apt to hang back (*oknein*) unless they are fed; when fed, they are willing enough to fight" (IV.10, 1297b10–11, tr. Jowett/Barnes, modified). This is consonant with Aristotle's use of *mikropsychos*, again in the *Politics*, to refer to those who are too timorous to consider conspiring, even against a tyrant.[79] Taken together, these passages show that Aristotle labels *oknēroi* those who show reluctance to perform the courageous or noble actions of which they are capable, but which are incompatible with their comfort or safety. Such usage, which highlights the pejorative connotations of *mikropsychia*, brings into vivid relief the disanalogies between *mikropsychia* and the commendable disposition of character that we call modesty or humility (in the secular sense), words that denote the disposition to refrain, mostly out of consideration for others, from putting oneself forward or boasting about one's own capabilities and achievements. This latter disposition, Aristotle thought just as commendable as we do since, as we saw, he ascribes it to the *megalopsychos*. What, by contrast, he called *mikropsychia* is best understood, therefore, as culpable timidity or, in Grant's felicitous gloss, "want of spirit."[80]

Further confirmation that it is on grounds of civic disutility that Aristotle takes *mikropsychia* to be a vice comes from his contention that it is a worse vice than vanity. To find a justification of what is, to our minds, a counter-intuitive claim, we must turn, in succession, to books II and IX of the *Nicomachean* version. In II 8 (1108b35–1109a20), Aristotle expresses the view that some virtues present a greater similarity to one of their two extremes than to the other. Whenever human nature has a greater propensity to one extreme than to the other, he there explains, we take this extreme to be more opposed to the mean of virtue, and therefore worse than the other extreme. For example, because human nature is more prone to cowardice than to recklessness, he argues, we take cowardice to be more opposed to the mean of courage, and therefore worse than recklessness. The contention, as put forward in book IV, that *mikropsychia* is worse than vanity stems from a similar assumption. Since human nature, in Aristotle's viewpoint, is more prone to the kind of diffidence, or lack of spirit, that goes under the name of *mikropsychia* than to vanity, it must be regarded as a worse failing. Admittedly, it is not entirely clear at this point whether Aristotle himself agrees with the view he is reporting. The concluding sentence of the chapter, in which he switches from what "we describe" to "what is," however, makes it plain that he shares the view that he is reporting: "We describe (*legomen*) as more opposed to the mean those things toward which our tendency is stronger; and for that reason excess, manifested as self-indulgence (*ousa hyperbolē*), is more opposed (*enantiōtera*) to self-control than is its corresponding deficiency" (II, 8, 1109a16–19, tr. Ostwald, modified).[81] By analogy, we may infer, *mikropsychia* is worse than vanity since human beings have a greater propensity to shy away from noble undertakings than to boast of having undertaken them. Is Aristotle's argument as convincing as it is cogent? Not as it stands. For, after all, both the vain man and the "diffident" man are guilty of taking their worth to be other than what it actually is. And if the mistake is the same, why should Aristotle, who praises the *megalopsychos* above all for his self-knowledge, consider one kind of failure of self-knowledge to be morally worse than another? To understand Aristotle's position on the matter, we need to remind ourselves of the *megalopsychos* of his description, whose consciousness of his own worth, as shown in section 3(d) above, goes hand in hand with his willingness to benefit his friends, personal and/or civic. Compared with this noble character, the *mikropsychos* is likely to fail his friends and country both through his erroneous assessment of what he can do and his craven desire to lead a quiet life. His unwarranted diffidence leads him to shy away from all sorts of challenge, ranging from taking a leading part in a hazardous military expedition to holding the high offices to which his status and ability would suit him. In the process, his diffidence grows, and he becomes ever more reluctant to intervene in circumstances that call for decisive action or generous intervention. He becomes a man who generally prefers to play safe.[82] This downward spiral is the converse of the process of acquiring moral virtue. Just as it is by performing courageous actions that one becomes courageous,[83] it is by repeatedly refusing to run risks of all kinds on the ground of (assumed) personal inadequacy that one acquires, or re-enforces, the internal disposition of *mikropsychia*. To that extent, *mikropsychia* is an invidious and cumulative condition from which the state as a whole stands to suffer. To "shrink from rule," as Aristotle puts the matter in the *Politics*, "is an injury to the state."[84] By contrast, the vain man of Aristotle's description is less potentially harmful. Aping the manners and behavior of the *megalopsychos*, his exaggerated view of his own ability leads him to undertake "honorable enterprises" (cf. *tois entimois, NE* IV 3, 1125a29) which he is incapable of carrying through. Fortunately, however, his ineptitude is soon discovered (cf. *exelegchontai, NE* IV 3, 1125a29), and he becomes a figure of fun. To the extent that he is revealed to be more show than substance, he is rendered largely harmless and is therefore unlikely to inflict serious harm onto others by undertaking more than he is capable of carrying off.

5. Conclusion

Aristotle's *megalopsychos*, I have argued here, is a much maligned character, having fallen victim to the anachronistic projections of later commentators who approached the *Ethics* through the prism of their own, often religiously based, assumptions. A modicum of historical distance and attention to the larger cultural context of fifth- and fourth-century BC Athens, should have alerted us to the radical shift in values that began to take place not long after Aristotle wrote the texts that have come down to us under the titles of *Eudemian Ethics, Nicomachean Ethics* and *Politics*. Viewed from the perspective of these treatises, the *megalopsychos* is best understood as an asset to any city-state with a sound constitution, although an aristocratic regime in which government is in the hands of the best among the citizens would give him the greatest opportunity for putting his overall excellence at the service of the *polis*. To the *polis* he gives much, both of his wealth and his person, by consistently acting in such a way as to promote the end of political society, which, in Aristotle's viewpoint, is the performance of noble actions and the realization of the good life for all the citizens. To this end, the city must seek to achieve a high level of political and economic self-sufficiency as well as to instill into all its citizens the values which will enable them to fulfill their potentialities as rational beings. In the realization of these two aims, as we saw, the *megalopsychos* has a large part to play: not only is he in a position to contribute much to the material well-being of the city, but his political excellence makes him a suitable candidate for the highest offices. In return for services rendered, the city bestows great honors upon him. These honors he graciously accepts, in the knowledge that they are deserved and that the city has nothing greater than honor to give him. No doubt, this makes him a proud man, but his pride, which is grounded in an accurate assessment of his worth and merit, is not inordinate, nor is it vested in inappropriate objects, nor is it accompanied by any kind of unseemly rebelliousness. The pride of the *megalopsychos*, being focused on his consistent success in meeting standards that are both high and true, cannot without paradox be stigmatized as vicious. This being so, it offers modern readers of Aristotle an opportunity to question, or enlarge, the concept of pride they are familiar with.

Unlike the *megalopsychos*, the *mikropsychos* has mostly been neglected by commentators, some of whom have been content to describe him as "modest" or "humble." In leaving matters at that, they have failed to heed Aristotle's classification of *mikropsychia* as vicious. Neither modest nor humble, the Aristotelian *mikropsychos* is someone who, although blessed with the goods of fortune and natural ability, consistently shies away from public involvement. Rather than putting his talents and assets at the service of the state, he chooses to lead a retiring life in the course of which he remains unconcerned with public affairs. In his craven desire for safety and comfort, he fails to heed the counsel of reason; he lets lesser men come forward and take positions of high responsibility for which they have little or no talent, and who later claim civic rewards to which they would not otherwise be entitled. So doing, the *mikropsychos* undermines the capacity of the state to ensure that its citizens can lead the best possible human life. The harm he inflicts on the community by refusing political office is all the greater since the optimal Aristotelian *polis*, being relatively compact, can ill afford to lose the services of those who are recognized as having potentialities for statesmanship: "if the citizens of a state are to judge and distribute offices according to merit, then they must know each other's characters."[85]

Aristotle's censure of the *mikropsychos* for his lack of responsible citizenship would, within a few years, be seemingly forgotten, having fallen on the deaf ears of Epicurus and his followers who sought to release themselves "from the prison of affairs and politics."[86] But Aristotle's strictures would never be completely forgotten. In the intervening centuries distant echoes of them would be heard, particularly in times of war or international crisis. One such occasion occurred in 1961, when the citizens of one of the largest states on the planet were urged to "ask not "what your country can do for you," but "what you can do for your country.""[87]

Notes

*I am grateful to Denis O'Brien for helpful comments on an earlier draft of this chapter and to Malcolm Schofield for bringing home to me that Aristotle's *Politics* is an even more complex text than I had realized.

1. Except when otherwise indicated, all quotations from the *Politics* are in Jowett's translation, as revised by Barnes on the basis of Dreizehnter's 1970 edition.

2. See G. Heylbut 160, 29–162, 15, and Aspasius, tr. Konstan 2006, 1–4, 7–8. Recent commentators who have addressed the issue of focal meaning include Owen 1960, Gauthier et Jolif 1970, Fortenbaugh 1975, Walker 1979, and Berti in Alberti and Sharples ed. 1999.

3. See, e.g., Allan 1952, Madigan 1971, Kahn 1981, Millgram 1987, Schollmeier 1994, and Stern-Gillet 1995.

4. The *megalopsychia* with which I am here concerned is the ethical virtue analyzed in *EE* III.5 and *NE* IV.3. I shall therefore leave out of account both the terminological distinction that Aristotle draws in *A.Post* II, 97b15–25 and his description of the ordinary use of the concept in *Rhet.* 1362b12 and 1388b3.

5. *NE* VIII, 1; see also *Pol.* II, 4, 1262b7–9, as quoted earlier, and IV 11, 1295b23–25. Unless otherwise flagged, all translations of the *Nicomachean Ethics* are in Ostwald's translation (1962, with occasional modifications, flagged as such.

6. *NE* IV 3, 1123b1–2; see also *EE* III, 5, 1233a2–3.

7. *NE* IV 3, 1124a1–3.

8. For the Old Testament, see, e.g., Proverbs 21:4 and 16:5; for the Qur'an, see, e.g., 7.146 and 16.23.

9. Ross' historical sense seems to have been temporarily deserted him when he so translates *megalopsychia* and writes in an *ad loc.* comment to *NE* IV 3, 1123a34: "'Pride' of course has not the etymological associations of *megalopsychia*, but seems in other respects the best translation." One wonders which "other respects" the great commentator had in mind.

10. In his translation of the *Rhetoric* Freese renders *megalopsychia* alternately as "magnanimity" or "high-mindedness."

11. So Grant 1858 and Ostwald 1962.

12. So Rackham 1935.

13. So Crisp 2000, Sachs 2002, and Taylor 2006.

14. So Inwood and Woolf 2013.

15. *EE* III, 5, 1232b39–1233a1.

16. Thanks are due to John Dillon for drawing my attention to possible parallels between Aristotelian *mikropsychia* and low self-esteem in the modern sense of the word.

17. So Irwin 1985.

18. So Ostwald 1962, and Taylor 2006.

19. So Rackham 1952, Crisp 2000, and Sachs 2002.

20. So Rowe and Broadie 2002.

21. So Inwood and Woolf 2013.

22. For an example of such projection, see, e.g., Curzer 1990 and E. Lavielle 1999.

23. *NE* IV 3, 1124a1–2. See also *EE* III, 5, 1232a31–2.

24. *EE* VIII, 3, 1249a5–16.

25. *EE*, VIII, 3, 1249a7–8.

26. *Pol.* VII, 1, 1323b41–1324a2.

27. See, e.g., Thucydides 2.45.2 (Pericles' funeral oration), according to whom "the greatest glory of woman is not to slip beneath the level at which nature has pitched her" (my tr.). This cannot but exclude noble deeds for which a debt of public recognition might be appropriate.

28. *Politics* I, 13.

29. This particular category of individuals is explicitly excluded in *EE* IV 3, 1233a29–30.

30. *NE* IV 3, 1124a26, tr. Ostwald, slightly modified. See also *Pol.*, III, 9, 1280b33–40.

31. See, e.g., Luke 12:35–48.

32. So J. Burnet 1900, 179, in an *ad loc.* comment on 1123b1 sqq.

33. So H. H. Joachim, 1951, 125. Let it be noted, however, that Joachim makes a point of expressly endorsing Aristotle's view that claims should match deserts.

34. Please note that I am not here arguing that *all* the characteristics that Aristotle ascribes to the *megalopsychos* are morally admirable. His disdain for the many, for example, as expressed in *NE* IV 3, 1124b5–6, hardly seems morally justifiable, even within an Aristotelian perspective. I cannot therefore fully agree with Michael Pakaluk's, (2004) otherwise convincing attempt at rehabilitating this much maligned character. The issue is discussed at some length in Stern-Gillet 2012. For an enlightening comparison between Aristotle's views on self-knowledge and Kant's, see Andrea Veltman's article in the present volume.

35. As Gauthier 1970, 290–91, claims.

36. As Hardie 1978, 68, more justifiably in my view, contends.

37. Aristotle is not entirely consistent in the matter since at 1169b1–10, in the course of a dialectical argument leading to the conclusion that "a happy man needs friends," Aristotle writes that friends "*are thought* to be the greatest of external goods," 1169b9–10. However, the fact that Aristotle needs to rely on this particular *endoxon* (received opinion) as a premise to ground his own conclusion suggests that he shares it.

38. *EE* III, 5, 1232a39.

39. *EE* VII, 12 and *NE* VIII, 1, 1155a5–9 and IX 9.

40. *Pol.* I, 1, 1253a9 and I, 2, 1256b21.

41. *Pol.* I, 1, 1253a29–30; see also *NE* I, 7, 1097b11.

42. *Pol.* V 11, 1313b5–6, and 1313a41. The same point is made in Plato's *Symposium* (Pausanias' speech), 182c1–7.

43. Pol. VII, 10, 13b5–25, where Aristotle justifies the practice mainly on grounds of its antiquity.

44. Kraut 1997, 110.

45. *Pol.* I, 2, 1253a2–3.

46. See also I, 12, 1259b4–6, I, 7, 1255b20, II, 2, 1261a34–b5, and III, 13, 1283b. Of the three Aristotelian models of the *polis* and citizenship discussed by Schofield 1999, this is the rational model (103–106).

47. *Pol.* IV 11, 1295b25–26.

48. See also *EE* VII, 10, 1241b36–37.

49. As aptly noted by Paul Cartledge 2000, 162, "when forced to choose between equality and hierarchy, Aristotle regularly went for hierarchy."

50. *Pol.* IV 2, 1289a33,and VII, 1, 1323b41–1324a2.

51. Robinson 1995,58; first ed. 1962.

52. In Pericles' funeral oration, Thucydides effected an equipoise between the two models: "Our constitution is called a democracy because power is in the hands not of a minority but of the whole people. When it is a question of settling private disputes, everyone is equal before the law; when it is a question of putting one person before another in positions of public responsibility, what counts is not membership of a particular class, but the actual ability which the man possesses." *History of the Peloponnesian War*, II.37, tr. Warner.

53. *EE* VII, 9, 1242a22–27.

54. Ibid., VII, 10, 1242b35.

55. As usefully pointed out in Cooper 1977.

56. *EE* VII, 10, 1242b32–33.

57. As can be seen, there are considerable differences between the two versions of the *Ethics* on the categorization of civic friendship: while the *Eudemian* account is of a fundamentally self-regarding relationship, the account given in book IX of the *Nicomachean* version is of a relationship that is indicative of the citizens' virtue and can therefore be engaged in at varying degrees of depth. For a detailed account of the differences between the two versions of the *Ethics*, see Stern-Gillet 1995, 149–55, and, in a more developed form, Schofield 1999, 87–91. See also Leigh 2012.

58. This puts me at odds with Schofield 213, 287–88, who claims that Aristotle "regards civic friendship as the social glue of mutual advantage between individuals who are personally acquainted, seeing it as exhibited above all in exchange and commerce." As the above-quoted lines make clear, citizens of states with a sound constitution do not have to be personally acquainted in order to cooperate in political and social matters of importance. The matter is further dealt with in section 3(d) *infra* in which it is argued that an Aristotelian *megalopsychos* is prepared to go to great lengths in order to benefit his country or assist his fellow citizens, whether or not he is personally acquainted with them.

59. *NE* IX 6, 1167a35–1137b1.

60. In *NE* IX 6, 1167b5–6 and 9–10, Aristotle describes civic friendship as beyond the capability of bad men (*hoi phauloi*).

61. See note 45 above.

62. As quoted above.

63. *NE* IV 3, 1124a7–8.

64. For the rules and regulations governing the institution of liturgies, see Aristotle, *Athenian Constitution*, LXVI and LSVII. For a detailed account of the institution and how it was implemented, see Gernet 1955. For the cultural background of all these issues in the fifth and early fourth centuries, see Davies 1978, ch. 6.

65. For a reconstruction and attempted justification of the argument, see Madigan 1992, Stern-Gillet 1995: chapter 5, *passim* and Pangle 1999: 191–96. In *NE*, V 9, 1136b20–22, Aristotle makes a similar point when he explains that the good man (*ho epieikēs*), in taking less than his fair share, secures for himself a higher good, namely glory or *to kalon*.

66. *NE* VIII, 2 and 3; *EE* VII, 2.

67. See also *NE*, X 7, 1177b16–17 and *EE* III, 5, 1232b10–12. According to Collins 1999, 140–41, the *megalopsychos'* disdain of external goods, which extends to life itself, accounts for his "willingness to forgo [his] own good in favor of the noble which is not [his] good." While this is certainly a factor in his readiness to die for his country and *philoi*, it is not the sole one since, as Aristotle takes care to note, the *megalopsychos'* willingness "to adjust his life . . . to a friend" provides an additional and powerful motivation for the ultimate sacrifice.

68. See, e.g., *Iliad* XVIII, 97–104, in which Achilles, after the death of Patroclus, counters his mother's counsel of prudence by saying that he would rather die forthwith than abide "a useless burden to the earth."

69. Isocrates *Evagoras*, 3, tr. Larue Van Hook. See also Thucydides, *History of the Peloponnesian War* II 42.

70. See also *Rhetoric* I, 9, 1666b3–4. As Hardie 1978, 73, well said: [T]he great man earns honors by his active services to his friends and country in great matters."

71. *NE* IV 3, 1232b38–39.

72. *EE* III, 5, 1232b39–1233a1. See also *NE* IV 3, 1125a18–27.

73. The distinction between two kinds of humility, religious and secular, however interesting in itself, is not directly germane to the present issue. Humility, as consistently praised by biblical authors (see, e.g., Matthew 19:30, Luke 1:52, and

Paul, *Philippians* 2:3,) is awareness of our creaturely status; secular humility, on the other hand, is the disposition to place others above oneself. Aristotle would hardly have been able to make sense of the religious kind of humility.

74. Contemporary philosophers of an existentialist persuasion might be tempted to describe *mikropsychia* as a form of self-deception, but Aristotle, who was the author of the distinction that these philosophers question, would not, of course, have done so.

75. *NE* IV 3, 1125a32–34.

76. The relevance of character to the choice of one's good is brought out clearly in section 1 of Gary Gurtler's contribution to this volume.

77. See L.S.J, s.v. *oknaleos* and *oknēros*, I.2; Chantraine 1974. Such evaluative divergences make translation a hazardous undertaking, and readers of ancient texts must avoid relying exclusively on the choice of words of even the best of translators. Ostwald's rendering of *oknēros* as "retiring" and Irwin's as "hesitant" both concede too much to modern assumptions insofar as the two adjectives lack the negative undertones that the words had in ancient Greek.

78. Bonitz 1831, s.v.

79. *Pol.* V 11, 1314a16.

80. Grant 1858: ad. loc. comment on 1125a17.

81. For particularly clear comments on those lines, see Broadie in Broadie and Rowe, 2002, 309–10.

82. As also noted by Gauthier, 1970, 297–98.

83. As Aristotle claims in *NE* II, 1, 1103b2.

84. *Pol.* IV 3, 1295b12.

85. *Pol.* VII, 4, 1326b15–16.

86. *Sententiae Vaticanae*, fr. 58, tr. Bailey. This particular aspect of Epicureanism is explored in Harry Lesser's contribution to the present volume. J. F. Kennedy's inaugural address, January 20, 1961.

87. J. F. Kennedy's inaugural address, January 20, 1961.

Bibliography

I PRIMARY LITERATURE

Aristotelis Ethica Nicomachea. 1894. Edited by I. Bywater. Oxford: Clarendon Press.
———. *Ethica Eudemia.* 1991. Edited by R. R. Walzer and J. M. Mingay. Oxford: Clarendon Press.
———. *Aristotelis Politica.* 1957. Edited by W. D. Ross. Oxford: Clarendon Press.
Aristoteles' Politik. 1970. Eingeleitet, kritisch herausgegeben und mit Indices versehen bei A. Dreizehnter. Munich: Fink.
Aristotle. 1944. *Politics.* Translated by H. Rackham. Cambridge MA: Harvard University Press, Loeb Classical Library.

The Politics of Aristotle. 1948.Translated with notes by E. Barker. Oxford: Clarendon Press.

Aristote. *Les Politiques.* 1993. Traduction et présentation par Pierre Pellegrin. Paris: GF Flammarion.

Aristotle. 1995. *Politics. Books III and IV.* Translated with Introduction and Comments by R. Robinson. Oxford: Clarendon Press.

———. 1997. *Politics. Books VII and VIII.* Translated with a Commentary by R. Kraut. Oxford: Clarendon Press.

The Ethics of Aristotle. 1900. Edited with an Introduction and Notes by J. Burnet. London: Methuen.

Aristotle. *Nicomachean Ethics.* 1999. Translated with an Introduction and Notes by M. Ostwald. Upper Saddle River NJ: Prentice-Hall.

———. *Nicomachean Ethics.* 2000. Translated and edited by R. Crisp. Cambridge: Cambridge University Press.

———. *Nicomachean Ethics.* 2002. Translation, Introduction and Commentary by S. Broadie and C. Rowe. Oxford: Oxford University Press.

———. 1952. *The Athenian Constitution, The Eudemian Ethics, On Virtues and Vices.* With an English Translation by H. Rackham. Cambridge MA: Harvard University Press, Loeb Classical Library.

Aristote. 1999. *Ethique à Eudème* Suivi de *Des Vertus et des Vices.* Traduction, préface et notes d'E. Lavielle. Paris: Pocket.

Aristotle. 2013. *Eudemian Ethics.* Translated and Edited by B. Inwood and R. Woolf. Cambridge: Cambridge University Press.

———. 1926. The *"Art" of Rhetoric.* With an English Translation by J. H. Freese. Cambridge MA: Harvard University Press, Loeb Classical Library.

———. 1991. *History of Animals.* Books VII–X. Edited and Translated by D. M. Balme. Cambridge MA: Harvard University Press, Loeb Classical Library.

Isocrates. 1945. *Evagoras. Helen. Busiris. Plataicus. Concerning the Team of Horses. Trapeziticus. Against Callimachus. Aegineticus. Against Lochites. Against Euthynus.* Translated by Larue Van Hook. Cambridge MA: Harvard University Press, Loeb Classical Library, 1945.

II Secondary Literature

Alberti, A., and R. W. Sharples, (eds.). 1999. *Aspasius: the Earliest Extant Commentary on Aristotle's Ethics.* Berlin: De Gruyter.

Allan, D. J. 1952. "Aristotle's Account of the Origin of Moral Principles." *Actes du XIIème congrès de philosophie* (Brussels). Reprinted in Barnes, J., M. Schofield, and R. Sorabji (ed.), 1977.

Anagnostopoulos, G. (ed.). 2009. *A Companion to Aristotle.* Chichester: Wiley-Blackwell.

Anton, J. P., and A. Preus (eds.). 1992. *Essays in Ancient Philosophy* IV. Albany: State University of New York Press.

Baltzly, D., and N. Eliopoulos. 2009. "The Classical Ideals of Friendship." In B. Caine (ed.). 2009. *Friendship: A History.* Sheffield: Equinox.

Bailey, C. 1926. *Epicurus: the Extant Remains.* With Short Critical Apparatus, Translation and Notes. Oxford: Clarendon Press.

Barnes, J., M. Schofield, and R. Sorabji (ed.). 1977. *Articles on Aristotle: 2. Ethics and Politics.* London: Duckworth.

Bartlett, R. C., and S. D. Collins (eds.). 1999. *Action and Contemplation. Studies in the Moral and Political Thought of Aristotle.* Albany NY: State University of New York Press.

Boys-Stones, G., D. El Murr and C. Gill, C. 2013. *The Platonic Art of Philosophy.* Cambridge: Cambridge University Press.

Bostock D. 2000. *Aristotle's Ethics.* Oxford: Oxford University Press.

Caine, B. (ed.). 2009. *Friendship: A History.* London: Equinox.

Cartledge, P. 2000. Review of *Saving the City: Philosopher-Kings and Other Paradigms* by M. Schofield. *The Classical Review* 50, no. 1.

Chantraine, P. 1974. *Dictionnaire Etymologique de la Langue Grecque.* Tome III. Paris: Editions Klincksieck.

Clarke, T. 2004. *Ask Not: The Inauguration of John F. Kennedy and the Speech That Changed America.* New York: Henry Holt and Co.

Collins, S. D. 1999. "The Moral Virtues in Aristotle's *Nicomachean Ethics.*" In R. C. Bartlett and S. D. Collins (ed.).

Cooper, J. 1977. "Aristotle on the Forms of Friendship." *The Review of Metaphysics* 30, no. 4.

Corrigan, K., J. D. Turner, and P. Wakefield (eds.). 2012. *Religion and Philosophy in the Platonic and Neoplatonic Traditions: from Antiquity to the Early Medieval Period.* Sankt Augustin: Academia Verlag.

Curzer, H. J. 1990. "A Great Philosopher's Not so Great Account of Great Virtue: Aristotle's Treatment of 'Greatness of Soul,'" *Canadian Journal of Philosophy.* Vol. 20 no. 4.

Davies, J. K. 1978. *Democracy and Classical Athens.* Hassocks, Sussex: Harvester Press/Glasgow: Collins-Fontana.

Düring, I., and G. E. L. Owen (eds.). 1960. *Aristotle and Plato in the Mid-Fourth Century.* Göteborg: Elanders Boktryckeri Aktibolag.

Fortenbaugh, W. W. 1975. "Aristotle's Analysis of Friendship: Function and Analogy, Resemblance, and Focal Meaning." *Phronesis* 20, no. 1.

Gauthier, R. A. et J. Y. Jolif. 1970. *L'Ethique à Nicomaque: Introduction, Traduction et Commentaire.* Tome 2. Louvain: Publications Universitaires et Paris: Béatrice-Nauwelaerts.

Gernet, L. 1968. *Droit et Institutions en Grèce Antique.* Paris: Flammarion.

Grant, A. 1858. *The Ethics of Aristotle Illustrated with Essays and Notes* in three volumes. London: John W. Parker and Son, West Strand.

Hardie W. F. R. 1978. "Magnanimity in Aristotle's Ethics." *Phronesis* 23, no. 1.

Heylbut, G. (ed.). 1889. Aspasii in Ethica Nicomachea quae supersunt commentaria, Commentaria in Aristotelem Graeca XIX 1. Berlin.

Jones, H. S., and J. E. Powell (eds.). 1942. *Thucydides' Historiae*. Vol. II. Oxford: Clarendon Press.

Joachim, H. H. 1951. *Aristotle:* The Nicomachean Ethics. A commentary edited by D. A. Rees. Oxford: Clarendon Press.

Kahn, C. H. 1981. "Aristotle and Altruism." *Mind* 90, no. 357.

Keyt, D. 1995. Supplementary Essay to *Aristotle:* Politics *Books III and IV.* Tr. with introduction and commentary by R. Robinson.

Konstan, D. 1997. *Friendship in the Classical World.* Cambridge: Cambridge University Press.

Leigh, F. (ed.). 2012. *The Eudemian Ethics on the Voluntary, Friendship, and Luck: the Sixth S.V. Keeling Colloquium in Ancient Philosophy.* Leiden and Boston: Brill.

Madigan, A. S.J. 1992. "*Eth. Nic.* 9.8: Beyond Egoism and Altruism?" In J. P. Anton and A. Preus (eds.).

Marchant, E. C. (ed.). 1901. *Xenophontis Opera Omnia.* Tomus II. Oxford: Clarendon Press.

Miller, F. D. 2009. "Aristotle on the Ideal Constitution." In G. Anagnostopoulos (ed.).

Millgram, E. 1987. "Aristotle's Account of Friendship in the 'Nicomachean Ethics.'" *The Canadian Journal of Philosophy* 17, no. 2.

Ober, J. 1989. *Mass and Elite in Democratic Athens: Rhetoric, Ideology, and the Power of the People.* Princeton NJ: Princeton University Press.

Owen, G. E. L. 1960, "Logic and Metaphysics in some Earlier Works of Aristotle." In I. Düring and G. E. L. Owen (eds.).

Pakaluk, M. 2004. "The Meaning of Aristotelian Magnanimity." *Oxford Studies in Ancient Philosophy.* Vol. 26. Oxford: Clarendon Press.

Pangle, L. S. 1999. "Friendship and Self-Love in Aristotle's *Nicomachean Ethics.*" In R. C. Barlett and S. D. Collins (eds.).

Schofield, M. 1996. "Sharing in the Constitution." *The Review of Metaphysics* 49, no. 4.

———. 1999. *Saving the City: Philosopher-Kings and Other Paradigms.* London: Routledge.

———. 2013. "Friendship and Justice in the *Laws.*" In G. Boys-Stones, D. El Murr, and C. Gill (eds.).

Schollmeier, P. 1994. *Other Selves: Aristotle on Personal and Political Friendship.* Albany: State University of New York Press.

Stern-Gillet, S. 1995. *Aristotle's Philosophy of Friendship.* Albany: State University of New York Press.

———. 2012. "Virtues of Self-Knowledge: Aristotle, Augustine, and Siger of Brabant." In K. Corrigan, J. D. Turner. and P. Wakefield.

Walker, A. D. M. 1979. "Aristotle's Account of Friendship in the *Nicomachean Ethics.*" *Phronesis* 24, no. 2.

PART 2

HELLENISTIC PHILOSOPHERS

4

MAKING FRIENDS

THE STOIC CONCEPTION OF LOVE
AND ITS PLATONIC BACKGROUND*

Bernard Collette-Dučić

Introduction

Right from its foundation, the Stoa asserted particularly bold claims about friendship. Zeno, especially, in his *Republic*, says that "only the *spoudaioi* are citizen, *friend*, kin and free."[1] Given the rarity of the Stoic sage, Zeno's claim was condemned by his detractors[2] as outrageous because of its extreme negative consequence: to hold the sage as the only true friend (who, as a matter of fact, is as elusive as the Egyptian phoenix)[3] is to put the rest of humanity "at enmity" (virtually everybody, including parents and children).[4] Zeno's claim and the reaction it triggered show therefore how important friendship was from the beginning for the Stoics.[5]

The Stoa recognized friendship as a kind of knowledge of a most general type[6] that does not really instruct us about the particulars of *how to be* a friend. They did, however, acknowledge a virtue[7] and an art[8] of *how to make* friends. This art of how the sage can transform someone else into a friend was called erotics or the science of love. The Stoic conception of friendship appears therefore inseparable from that of *erōs*.[9]

In this chapter, I intend to clarify the relationship the Stoics drew between love and friendship, where friendship is presented as the aim and effect of love. We shall see that the Stoic idea of love as the cause or maker of friendship, first asserted by Zeno, likely stems from a reading of Plato's

Symposium. However, a comparison of Zeno's account of love with Plato's reveals a major discrepancy between the two, in particular on the pedagogical nature of love as Zeno understood it. Contrary to Plato, where it is the lover who appears to benefit the most from the love relationship (love being love of wisdom), Zeno's pedagogical view of love, where the lover is a sage (not properly a philosopher) and the beloved necessarily a non sage, makes it difficult to understand what kind of good love is for the sage. If, as Zeno reportedly said, "continuous association with young boys does not benefit the intelligence of the teachers" (cf. *infra* text 11), then what good if any does it do for the sage to fall in love and make friends? We shall address this final difficulty in the last part of this chapter, through a study of Seneca's *Letter 9*, a key Stoic text on friendship.

1. Friendship as the Aim of Love

A. THE PEDAGOGICAL DIMENSION OF STOIC LOVE[10]

In order to understand Stoic friendship we need first to study how it is produced, and hence its cause: love. I start with the analysis of an important testimony in Stobaeus, in which we find an obvious difference between love and friendship. Indeed, whereas friendship only occurs among sages and is therefore to be taken as a good, love occurs among both sages and non sages and is thus what the Stoics call an "indifferent": love, in itself, is neither good nor bad. Now love is never to be found just by itself, but always either in the sage or in the non sage. And since friendship only takes place among sages, we shall therefore focus our attention on how the Stoic sage loves:

> **1.** [The Stoics] hold that the sage has good sense, acts appropriately in matters of discussion, banquet and love (*dialektikōs, . . . kai sumpotikōs kai erōtikōs*); but the erotic man (*ton . . . erōtikon*) is so called in two senses, one who gets his quality from virtue (*kata tēn aretēn*), being spoudaios, and one who gets his quality from vice, and is blamed, being some sort of erotomaniac (*erōtomanē tina*). [. . .] And being worthy of love is similar to being worthy of friendship and not to being worthy of enjoyment (*ton t' axieraston homoiōs legesthai tō(i) axiophilētō(i), kai ou tō(i) axiapolaustō(i)*; for he who is worthy of the sage's love is worthy of love. They understand virtue exercised at a symposium as similar to virtue in erotic matters, the one being knowledge

(*epistēmē*) which is concerned with what is appropriate at a symposium, viz. of how one should run symposia and how one should drink at them; and the other [sc. erotics] is knowledge of how to hunt for young boys that are naturally predisposed [to virtue] (*epistēmēn neôn thêras euphuôn*), which encourages them to virtuous knowledge; and in general, knowledge of nobly loving (*kalōs eran*). That is why they say that the man with good sense will be in love (*erasthēsesthai*). To love (*to de eran*) by itself is an indifferent, since at times it also occurs among base men. But love (*ton de erōta*) is not desire nor is it directed at any worthless thing, but is an effort to make friend from the appearance of beauty (*epibolēn philopoiias dia kallous emphasin*). (Stobaeus, *Eclogae* II. 7, p. 65, 15-66, 13 Wachsmuth [W] = *Stoicorum Veterum Fragmenta* [*SVF*] 3.717,translation by Inwood and Gerson, adapted)

According to the Stoa, the sage possesses all the virtues and acts according to all of them, although not all the time.[11] The Stoics admit not only the four cardinal virtues (courage, moderation, justice, and *phronesis*), but also a large variety of less well-known virtues among which one finds erotic virtue. Being a virtue,[12] *erōs* is therefore also "knowledge" (*epistēmē*), the knowledge of "how to hunt for young people that are naturally predisposed <to virtue>."

By exercising his erotic virtue, the sage then encourages the young to become virtuous. Stoic love is, therefore, essentially pedagogical:[13] it aims at transforming a young person who lacks virtue, but displays a natural inclination to it, into a sage. The pedagogical dimension of love is made particularly clear, in our text, when it is said that the one who is "worthy of love" is in no way similar to the one who is "worthy of enjoyment." In other words, if the sage engages in a relationship with a young person, it will not be for the sake of enjoying sexual favors, but for that of teaching him the virtues so that he also may become virtuous.

According to the Stoics, there is no intermediate between foolishness and wisdom: because the sage possesses all the virtues (rather than a limited number of them), to become a sage does not consist in progressively emancipating oneself from vice; rather, it is a genuine *transformation* from being a fool to being wise. The definition of love that is given in our passage suggests that this transformation consists in nothing but "friend making," *philopoiia*. In other words, the erotic virtue of the sage aims at actually transforming the *axieraston* into an *axiophilēton*.

B. LOVE, FRIENDSHIP, AND THE BEAUTIFUL

To understand properly the relation between love and friendship, we need to introduce a new text, drawn from Plutarch's *On Common Conceptions*:

> **2.** All members of the school, however, are involved in the ab-
> surdity of the philosophical tenets of the Stoa that are at odds
> with the common conceptions on the subject of love. [a] For
> their position is that, while the young are ugly, since they are
> base and stupid (*phaulous . . . kai anoētous*), and the sages are
> fair (*kalous*), none of these who are fair is loved or worth being
> loved (*axieraston*). [b] And this is not yet the awful part. They
> say further that when the ugly have become fair, those who have
> been in love with them stop. Now who recognizes love like this,
> which at the sight of <depravity> of soul together with deprav-
> ity of body is kindled and sustained, and at the birth in them
> of beauty together with prudence accompanied by justice and
> moderation wastes away and extinguished? Lovers like that, I
> think, do not differ at all from gnats, for they delight in scum
> and vinegar but palatable and fine wine they fly from and avoid.
> (Plutarch, *On Common Conceptions* 28, 1072F–1073A, transla-
> tion by Cherniss, slightly amended)

What Plutarch, with obvious delight, presents as a most absurd paradox—to love what is ugly and, when it has become beautiful, to stop loving it—is actually of great help for retrieving the original Stoic doctrine.

I. LOVE AND THE APPEARANCE OF BEAUTY

I shall study the two parts of the passage separately, starting with the claim that the sage is beautiful and the young ugly (part [a]). Plutarch's account is here *almost* completely right. He is right when he says that only sages are beautiful. Indeed, virtue and wisdom are the only things genuinely beautiful according to the Stoa, and since only the sage possesses them, he is the only one (other than god and the cosmos) who can be said to be beautiful. Similarly, Plutarch is right when he says that the young are ugly because they are base and stupid. By definition, since they lack wisdom, young people lack what would make them beautiful, hence they should be considered (morally) ugly. He is not right when he says that *all* young people, because they lack wisdom, are necessarily ugly. Indeed, the Stoics recognize that some adolescents, because they have *euphuia*,[14] have *at least* the "appearance of beauty" or *emphasis kallous*.[15] Plutarch does not ignore this fact, nor try to conceal it from the reader, but thinks that "there is no plausibility in their assertion that love is incited by what in their terminology they call an appearance of beauty."[16]

This last remark shows that the Stoics have given the word *emphasis* a technical meaning in order to solve a difficulty occasioned by their own ethical doctrine, in which only the beautiful is good,[17] and there is no good other than virtue. Indeed, when the Stoics speak of *emphasis kallous*, they do so presumably because they want to avoid two pitfalls: to attribute to young people with *euphuia* either genuine beauty or ugliness. It is not possible to attribute true moral beauty to the young since, as already stated, only the sage (or virtue) is beautiful. But it is also not possible for the young to be morally ugly, since it is then extremely difficult to see what could drive the sage to fall in love and try to make the young into a friend.

In order to see how they managed to get out of this difficulty, we need to grasp the Stoic meaning of the word *emphasis*. We do not know much about it, and some cryptic lines in Diogenes Laertius provide our only real insight:

> **3.** An impression (*phantasia*) is different from a figment (*phantasma*). A figment is the kind of fanciful thought, which occurs in dreams, whereas an impression is a printing in the soul: i.e. an alteration, as Chrysippus suggests in his *On soul* . . . One thinks here of the impression as what is engraved, stricken and imprinted, arising from what exists in accordance with what exists, in such a way that it would not occur if its object did not exist. Some sensory impressions arise from what exists, and are accompanied by yielding and assent. But impressions also include appearances (*emphaseis*), which occur as if they were coming from what exists (*hōsanei apo huparkhontōn ginomenai*). (Diogenes Laertius 7, 50–51 = *SVF* 2.55 and 61; Long and Sedley [LS] 39A), translation by Long and Sedley)

What makes this account particularly difficult to interpret is that it presents *emphaseis* as a special sort of *phantasia*, but nevertheless describes them in terms that seem to suit better what the Stoics call "figments" of *phantasmata*. Even the wording used to describe them (*hōsanei apo huparkhontōn ginomenai*) seems to recall the way Stoics define *ennoēmata*, which are themselves sorts of figments: an *ennoēma* is "a figment of thought (*phantasma dianoias*), which is neither something nor qualified, but a quasi-something and a quasi-qualified (*hōsanei de ti on kai hōsanei poion*), as when the mental image (*anatupōma*) of a horse occurs when no horse is actually present (*mē parontos*)."[18]

It is pivotal to understand properly the distinction between *phantasia* and *phantasma*[19] in order to comprehend what an *emphasis* is. Figments are pure mental products and do not refer to anything that is actually present. Figments are thus fictions. Examples of *phantasmata* given by the Stoics are Platonic Ideas and things appearing in dreams and delusions provoked by a mad mind.[20] What is distinctive of figments, then, is that they are unreal objects of thought producing *empty* affections in the soul,[21] that is, affections with no real corresponding "impressor."[22] *Phantasiai*, on the contrary, are affections of the soul triggered by an impressor, that is, some actually present *thing* that impresses itself on the soul of the perceiver.

If we take Diogenes Laertius' report seriously and look upon *emphaseis* as cases of *phantasiai* rather than *phantasmata*, then we must assume that *emphaseis* are not just mental fictions but real affections in the soul produced by some present external impressor. Now the description of *emphaseis* as occurring "as if" (*hôsanei*) they were coming from what exists is troubling as it suggests that these appearances do *not really* come from what exists, hence that no impressor is responsible for their occurring. There is however another way to read this sentence, which will appear more clearly if we consider a different example. Leaving aside the case of the appearance of beauty in a young person worthy of love and friendship, the only example of *emphasis* available in our sources is the face of the man in the moon. According to Plutarch, the Stoics claimed that the actual shape of the moon, when the air running on its surface is getting darker, generates the *emphasis* of a man's face.[23] What this example shows is that *some thing* that *is not* human (the moon) can, in some circumstances, *look like* a human being, by taking on *the actual appearance* of the face of a man. Clearly, here, we are not dealing with a fiction made up by our mind, but with a genuine physical appearance. For, what is here potentially delusional is not the appearance itself, but only the temptation to infer from it the actual existence of a man while there is none.

While the emptiness attached to *phantasmata* tends to make them some sort of non-beings, *emphaseis*, on the contrary, refer instead to some sort of *superficial* being: they are, quite literally, what appears at the surface of some perceived thing. The idea that *emphaseis* are of a fickle nature is found in Epictetus, who compares them to opinions and shows how the changeability of their nature makes them unsuitable to serve as genuine criteria for knowledge:

> **4.** Is [right only] *what seems* so to us (*ta hēmin dokounta*)? Why to us, rather than to Syrians; or, rather than to Egyptians; or rather than to me or to anybody?—There is no reason why.—Therefore, the opinion (*to dokoun*) which each man holds is not sufficient for determining the truth; for also in the case of weights and measures we are not satisfied with mere appearance (*psilē(i) tē(i) emphasei*), but we have invented a certain standard (*kanona tina*) to test each. (Epictetus, *Discourses*, II, 11, 15)

The superficial nature of *emphaseis* in the Stoic doctrine on love is again well confirmed by another testimony where the word *emphasis* seems to be replaced by that of *eidos*:

> **5.** The sage will be in love with youths that exhibit by their appearance (*dia tou eidous*) a natural predisposition to virtue (*tēn pros aretēn euphuia*), as Zeno said in his *Republic*, Chrysippus in his *On Kinds of Lives* Book I, and Apollodorus in his *Ethics*. (Diogenes Laertius, 7, 129)

The "appearance" or *eidos* in this passage refers to the external manifestation of *euphuia* and we have seen in other testimonies that it is the possession of *euphuia* that is responsible for the young person to have at least an *emphasis kallous* (rather than being simply ugly). "*Eidos*" is therefore likely used here in place of *emphasis*, a point that strongly suggests that an *emphasis* is the *external* aspect of a given thing.[24]

It is now possible to see better how and why the Stoics chose to speak of an *emphasis kallous* in their doctrine of love. An appearance of beauty is obviously not genuine beauty, but it is not fake beauty either. It cannot be genuine beauty since *emphasis*, as we have seen, refers to the superficial and external semblance of a given thing or being. But it cannot be simply fake beauty, since *emphasis* is not the empty affection of a *phantasma*, but a *phantasia*. As a matter of fact, our accounts explain the very cause of this appearance: if the young person whom the sage falls in love with manifests the appearance of beauty, it is because he possesses *euphuia*, that is, a natural predisposition to virtue. *Euphuia* is not virtue, and hence cannot generate true beauty; rather, it is a natural ability to become virtuous that some of us possess and which, when present, generates a sign or mark[25] of (future, possible) beauty in the form of an appearance. Here it may be useful to recall that the Stoics acknowledged physiognomics as a science, and affirmed it is possible to perceive the inner moral character of a given person from the external appearance.[26] All these elements combined explain therefore how they were able to claim, as they did, that love is an effort at friend making through the appearance of beauty.

II. FRIENDSHIP AND TRUE BEAUTY

Let us now turn to the second part of Plutarch's passage (part [b] of text 2): "They say further that when the ugly have become fair, those who have been in love with them stop." The reason for this is easily explained if we bear in mind the fact that love only occurs relative to the *appearance* of beauty, not genuine beauty. So, if the young person, thanks to the sage's love, turns into a friend, then the appearance of beauty vanishes and becomes true beauty. This is a further confirmation that Stoic love is essentially pedagogical, hence also *asymmetrical*: only the sage *loves*, and only the naturally well-disposed young *is loved*. Now, we have seen (from text 1) that the transformation of the *axieraston* (one worthy of being loved) into a friend and a sage is the true aim of love and, since love is defined as an *epibolē philopoiias* (effort of friend making), we must then conclude that, once the young has been changed into a sage, he ceases to be *axieraston* and becomes *axiophilēton*. So Stobaeus was certainly not incorrect to say that the two expressions are held to be "similar" by the Stoics: one who is worthy of being loved is also worthy of being a friend, although not at the same time.

   Love is then eventually replaced by friendship. The major difference between the two, apart from the one already mentioned, that friendship is a good whereas love is an indifferent, is that friendship is a *symmetrical* relationship, due to the fact that it takes place between morally equal beings (as sages indeed are).[27]

2. The Platonic Background

The Stoic doctrine on love and friendship just presented goes back as far as Zeno of Citium himself and was initially developed in his *Republic* (cf. text 5 *supra*), a book that most scholars accept as an early work. In this treatise, where he developed the principles on which his ideal city shall be built, Zeno made *Erōs* the tutelary god of his state:[28]

6. Pontianus said that Zeno of Citium took *Erōs* to be the god of friendship and freedom (*theon einai philias kai eleutherias*), and even the provider of concord (*homonoias paraskeuastikon*), but nothing else. This is why he said in his *Republic* that *Erōs* was the god who contributed to the preservation of the city (*tēn poleōs sōtērian*). (Athenaeus XIII 561 C = *SVF* 1.263)

Why Zeno chose to pick *Erōs*, rather than another divinity, as the protecting god of the Stoic city is easily explained if we connect this to the central idea of Zeno, that *erōs* is an effort or attempt "at friend making." Indeed, in the epitome of Stoic ethics preserved in Stobaeus, friendship is defined as "concord (*homonoia*) about things concerning the way of living," and concord is itself the science of common goods.[29] So, to assert that *Erōs* is "provider of concord" is virtually the same as to say that it is an *epibolē philopoiias*.

A. PLATO'S SYMPOSIUM ON FRIENDSHIP AS THE AIM OF LOVE

Now, an interesting question to answer is why Zeno believed that *erōs* is the cause of friendship and concord in the first place. My suggestion is that it is a doctrine he first encountered while reading Plato's *Symposium*,[30] probably in his early years when he was attending lectures at Polemon's Academy. Indeed, there are several aspects of Zeno's conception of love and friendship that appear reminiscent of the *Symposium*. Two of them, as we are going to see, are already asserted in Pausanias' speech:

7. I don't think it is convenient for those in power that there should be big ideas about if these belong to their subjects, or for that matter strong friendships and partnerships (*philias iskhuras kai koinōnias*), and that is just what all the other things, but especially love, most tend to bring about in us (*ho dē malista philei ta te alla panta kai ho erōs empoiein*). The tyrants here in Athens themselves learned this from experience, because it was Aristogeiton's love (*ho . . . Aristogeitonos erōs*) for Harmodius, and Harmodius' friendship (*hē Harmodiou philia*) for him, when both became firm and constant (*bebaios*), that brought their regime to an end. (Plato, *Symposium*, 182 c1–6, trans. Rowe, adapted)

Pausanias' account of love is certainly not to be confused with Plato's own, but we should not look upon it as utterly incompatible with Plato's philosophical views on *erōs* as expressed by Diotima to Socrates. David Sedley has shown that the many discourses in Plato's *Symposium* are all approximations, with variable success, of the truths Diotima is disclosing to Socrates.[31] There are at least two elements in this passage that will actually be taken over in Diotima's account and that we have already identified as pivotal in Zeno. First, the idea that what love tends to bring about (*empoiein*) is "strong friendships and partnerships," thus, that friendship is what love effects. Second, the idea that while friendship refers to an equal and symmetrical relationship (as shown through its connection with the notion of *koinōnia*), love does *not* and implies on the contrary a sort of asymmetry between a lover and a beloved where *only* the lover is said to exercise love. This is suggested here when Pausanias contrasts Aristogeiton's *love* for Harmodius with Harmodius' *friendship* for Aristogeiton:[32] Pausanias is careful not to speak of the young Harmodius as a lover, but rather speaks of his friendship for Aristogeiton as the natural outcome of Aristogeiton's love for him.

In his Introduction to the *Symposium*, Christopher Rowe reminds us that love, as an essentially asymmetric relationship, was "a regular feature of Athenian society":

> **8.** The standard case of *erōs*, from which most of the speakers begin, is the *erōs* felt by an older, male, lover for a younger, also male, beloved, and at least includes the desire for sexual gratification—on the part of the lover—as a central component. Such essentially asymmetric relationships, in which the benefit to the younger partner would no doubt have varied in proportion of the quality of the older, were evidently a regular feature of Athenian society. (Rowe 1998, 5)

It is this feature that we find again in Diotima's speech, in a passage that appears also to have been influential on Zeno:

> **9.** When someone is pregnant with these things [sc. the civic virtues of moderation and justice] in his soul, from youth on, and by divine gift, and with the coming of the right age, desires to give birth and procreate, then I imagine he too goes round looking for the beautiful object (*to kalon*) in which he might procreate; for he will never do so in what is ugly. So he warms to beautiful bodies rather than ugly ones, because he is pregnant, and if he encounters a soul that is beautiful and noble and *naturally predisposed [to virtue]* (*kale(i) kai gennaia(i) kai euphuei*), his welcome for the combination—beautiful body

and soul—is warm indeed; to this person, he is immediately
full of resource when it comes to things to say about virtue,
what sort of thing the good man must be concerned with, and
the activities such a man should involve himself in, and tries
to educate him (*epikheirei paideuein*). (Plato, *Symposium*, 209
b1–c2, trans. Rowe, adapted)

Like Zeno and the Stoics later (cf. the previous section of this chapter), Plato
thought of love as a non-reciprocal relationship where the lover (*to erōn*)
and the beloved (*to eraston*) refer to two distinct functions (*Symp.* 204c)
incarnated in two distinct persons. In this passage, drawn from the section
on the Lesser Mysteries in Diotima's account, the lover is described as a
man who, "from youth on, and by divine gift, is pregnant (with virtues) in
his soul, and, with the coming of the right age, desires to give birth and
procreate." It is by looking for "a beautiful object" in which to procreate
that he falls in love with a beloved, namely a young person with a "soul
that is beautiful and noble and naturally predisposed [to virtue]." So not
only do we find here already asserted the idea (endorsed by the Stoics)
that what sparks love must be, somehow, related to beauty and youth, but
also that one of the essential qualities the beloved must bear is *euphuia*: a
natural predisposition to virtue.

As noted above, the asymmetrical nature of the erotic relationship is
not peculiar to Plato since it is shared by all the interlocutors in the *Symposium*. What is genuinely Platonic (or nearly so), is making love the cause
of friendship and concord. It is first asserted by Pausanias, as we have seen
(cf. text 7), but only to prepare the reader for the revelations of Diotima's
own account, in a passage that appears right after the one quoted above:

10. For, I imagine, it's by contact with what is beautiful (*tou
kalou*), and associating with it, that he [sc. the lover] brings to
birth and procreates the things with which he was for so long
pregnant, both when he is present with him [sc. the beloved] and
when he is away from him; and he joins with the other person in
nurturing what has been born, with the result that such people
enjoy a much greater partnership with each other (*polu meidzō
koinōnian . . . pros allēlous*) than the one people have in their
children, and a firmer friendship (*philian bebaioteran*) between
them, insofar as their sharing is in children of a more beautiful
and more immortal kind. (Plato, *Symposium*, 209 c1–7, trans.
Rowe, slightly adapted)

The passage here recalls undoubtedly the words used by Pausanias himself.
Like him, Diotima associates friendship with *koinōnia* and reciprocity, and
underlines the firmness of the friendship caused by love.

b. Plato on Love as Philosophical

It seems reasonable enough to think that it is these principles about love
and friendship that the Stoics, and first of all Zeno in his *Republic*, took
from Plato's *Symposium*. However, we should be careful not to consider
Zeno's conception of love as crypto-Platonic, for, as we are going to see
now, besides the obvious similarities between the two doctrines, one finds
also great and even possibly irreconcilable differences. To see that, we must
first note that the similarities between the two doctrines are limited to one
section of Diotima's account: the Lesser Mysteries (cf. 207 c–209 e). Any
student of Plato knows well however that it is *not* in this part that we can
expect to find Plato's last word on *erōs*. For that, we must be initiated, like
Socrates, to the "final revelation" or Greater Mysteries (starting at 210 a).

This is not the place to engage in a full interpretation of these Greater Mysteries, but one can at least underline two major differences that
Diotima introduces there. First and foremost, Diotima presents us with a
third character: next to the lover and the beloved, she mentions a "guide"
(*ho hēgoumenos*, 210 a6) or "teacher" (*paidagōgēthē(i)*, 210 e3) who shows
the lover "the correct kind of boy-loving" (*to orthōs paiderastein*, 211 b6).
Contrary to the case in the Lesser Mysteries (cf. text 9), where the respective natures of the lover and of the beloved are spelled out, the nature and
identity of the guide are here left unstated. I believe the reason for this is
that Diotima is willing to make a very straightforward point: contrary to
the case in the Lesser Mysteries, where the lover is pregnant in virtues only
"by divine gift" (cf. again text 9), in the Greater Mysteries he is truly and
correctly taught and instructed by a guide.

This point is directly related to a second difference that Diotima is
introducing: whereas the Lesser Mysteries are concerned only with love as
a productive force at work in poetry, craftsmanship and politics (209a4–6),
the Greater, on the other hand, are a place where one is initiated to genuine
philosophical love: the desire for knowledge and contemplation of Forms.
Now, in the *Dialogues*, the difference between the two groups (poets, craftsmen, statesmen, on the one hand, and philosophers, on the other)[33] is
precisely that while the former pretend to possess wisdom but are in fact
ignorant (they are, at best, divinely inspired,[34] and cannot give an account
of what they claim to know), the latter (the philosopher) is the one who
recognizes his own ignorance and therefore seeks after a *teacher*. The rec-

ognition of ignorance is essential in Platonic *erōs*, a desire for wisdom that has its very essence "in creative *lack*, rather than in actual possession of the good it seeks."[35]

c. PEDAGOGICAL v. PHILOSOPHICAL LOVE

If Zeno limited his references to the Lesser Mysteries in Diotima's account, it may well be because he felt the genuine Platonic doctrine expressed in the Greater Mysteries was incompatible with his own understanding of what love and wisdom are. Since the Stoics dismissed Platonic Forms as *phantasmata*, it is no wonder that Zeno wanted to distance himself from a section where Diotima is explaining how to get to the contemplation of the Form of beauty. But I believe the real bone of contention lies elsewhere, in the doctrine of love itself.

For the Stoics, love (the good one) is genuinely *pedagogical* in the sense that, in terms of acquisition of knowledge, *it benefits the beloved only*. It is by instructing his beloved that the sage makes him a friend, that is, transform him into another sage. Thus the sage can only play the role of the lover/instructor since he already possesses knowledge and is therefore in a position to guide and teach the beloved young. On that subject, one apophthegm recalls an interesting anecdote about Zeno conversing with a "boy lover":

> **11.** To a lover of boys (*pros de ton philopaida*), he said that continuous association with young boys does not benefit the intelligence of the teachers, nor of those of his kind [i.e. boy lovers]. (Diogenes Laertius, 7, 18 = *SVF* 1.295)

If there is one potentially philosophical point that can be salvaged from this passage, it is that continuous association with a young boy cannot in any way benefit the intelligence of the mature man who is associating with him. This is true in any kind of association involving a young boy, but most obviously so in a pedagogical one. Indeed, how could a mindless boy improve in any way the intelligence of the one who is supposed to instruct him? This fits perfectly Zeno's conception of love, in which the lover and instructor is at the same time a sage: one can hardly see how the intelligence of the sage, who does possess full wisdom, could benefit from that of his young beloved, even if the latter possesses *euphuia*.

Now, if we apply this Stoic principle to Plato's own doctrine, in particular the one expressed in the Greater Mysteries, then we see something unexpected, namely that Platonic (i.e. philosophical) love does not seem to be truly pedagogical. Indeed, if there is any pedagogical dimension to be found, it is not so much between the lover and the beloved, but between the guide or *Hēgoumenos* and the one who is being led by him (the lover). And, although this is not positively stated in the text, the relationship between the guide and the one he leads does *not* appear to be an erotic one[36]. As I wrote earlier, Diotima is rather secretive when it comes to determining who exactly the guide is. The only point she recurrently emphasizes is not that the one being led is himself being loved by his teacher, but rather that he is being *correctly led* by him.[37] Thus, one can see that, in the Greater Mysteries, the pedagogical dimension is somehow separated from the erotic relationship itself (occurring only between the lover and his beloved).

Furthermore, and in contradiction with the Stoic principle mentioned above, in Diotima's account the intelligence of the *lover* does indeed benefit from the lover's association with his young beloved. This holds, actually, for the doctrines expressed in the Lesser *and* the Greater Mysteries. Already in the Lesser Mysteries we observe that it is *once* engaged in a relationship with his beloved that the lover finds himself "immediately full of resource" when "it comes to things to say about virtue, what sort of thing the good man must be concerned with, and the activities such a man should involve himself in." *Only then* will he "try to educate" the beloved (cf. text 9). In the Greater Mysteries, this is even more obvious: having been instructed how to love boys correctly,[38] it is through the love for his beloved that the lover is progressively freeing *himself*[39] from false opinions about beauty and then starts ascending the *scala amoris* up to the top until he is finally able to contemplate the Form of Beauty.

Even if the pedagogical dimension of love in Diotima's account is not totally absent, one cannot but have the overwhelming impression that the one who really benefits from the erotic relationship, in terms of gaining intellectual insight on what beauty really is, is the lover, not the beloved. And this has to do, as I noted earlier, with Plato's conviction that the true essence of love is *philosophical*. If love is first and foremost love for wisdom and if love can only be exercised by the lover, then it is clear enough that only a lover can truly seek after wisdom and benefit from it. The downside of such a philosophical understanding of love is that it then becomes difficult, if not impossible, to ascribe to love a genuine pedagogical dimension, and this is precisely reflected in the Greater Mysteries by the introduction of a guide that is leading, pedagogically but lovelessly, the apprentice lover of wisdom. The model of such a relationship is provided by Diotima and Socrates themselves, Diotima playing the role of a teacher who, while not being in love with Socrates, nevertheless teaches him the very science of love.

Knowing how influential the *Symposium* was on Zeno's doctrine of love and friendship, we can also now see more clearly how his own conception may implicitly at least reflect a criticism directed against Plato's *erōs*. Indeed, since Zeno, as any other Stoic after him, would only praise a love that is truly pedagogical (where the young beloved is transformed and made a friend and a sage), he could but only disagree with Plato's final account of *erōs*, and he may even have considered it as being falsely and deceivingly pedagogical.[40]

3. The Good of Friend Making

A. WHY DOES THE SAGE MAKE FRIENDS?

The comparison of the Stoic doctrine with Plato's account of *erōs* in the *Symposium* has eventually shown a major discrepancy: while in Plato it is first of all the lover himself who is being transformed and becomes wiser thanks to love, in Zeno, on the contrary, the lover, already a sage, remains apparently unaffected. Such a difference raises an interesting question: if the sage cannot, by definition, become wiser, and if, at any rate, a continuous association with young boys is the last thing one should want to do if one wishes to improve one's intellect (see text 11), then what good (if any) does it do for the sage to engage in a relationship with the non wise? It may sound silly enough to ask for the motive for falling in love. Margaret Graver may well be right to warn us about that: "[W]e should be careful not to conclude that the educative dimension of the love relationship is what justifies wise *erōs* in the eyes of the Stoics. *Erōs* does not require justification; it is a good thing in its own right, as are all *eupatheiai*.[41] The wise fall in love for no other reason than that it is their nature to want to be intimate with those whom they see as beautiful."[42] Certainly, she is quite right to say that *erōs* is "a good thing in its own right" if by *erōs* we mean the sage's. But the question is: Why is it a good? On what ground? While the answer to this question is rather straightforward in Plato, it is not in the Stoa. Even if we take Stoic love to be a natural impulse, common as it is to any human being, it remains for us to ask ourselves exactly how the sage can benefit from such an intimate relationship with a non sage.

B. THE STOICS ON COINCIDENTAL GOODS

We cannot simply rely here on a well-known Stoic doctrine concerning the reciprocity of goodness, recalled by Stobaeus:

12. All goods are common to the virtuous, and all that is bad
to the inferior; therefore, one who benefits another also benefits
himself, and one who does harm also harms himself. All virtuous
men benefit one another. [Even when they are not aware of each
other and do not live at the same place], they nonetheless are
in attitude well-disposed and friendly to each other, and prized
and accepted by one another. The foolish are in the opposite
situation. (Stobaeus, *Eclogae* II. 7, p. 101, 21-102, 3 W = *SVF*
3.626, trans. Long and Sedley)

We cannot rely on such a doctrine because the reciprocity of goodness only
applies between sages, and this is precisely the reason why Zeno affirmed
that only the sages are friends, having the science of common goods.[43] Now,
what we are interested in here is not how two Stoic friends benefit one
another, but how a sage can benefit from loving a non sage.

The question is especially important in a Stoic context since for the
Stoics there is no true good but virtue, and virtue is itself nothing else but
wisdom. Should we then suppose that to love does not actually benefit the
sage at all, only his unwise beloved, and that the sage's natural impulse to
fall in love is a matter of genuine altruism? Unfortunately, as we are going
to see, altruism does not seem to be a kind of good available to a Stoic.

Evidence shows that the *oikeiōsis* doctrine (i.e., the natural affection
one has for oneself and the tendency to preserve one's life), which is at the
basis of their entire ethics, led the Stoics to assert that men as well as gods
"do everything primarily *for themselves*"[44] (cf. *infra* text 13). In particular,
we find them resorting to this claim in order to explain the possibility of
divine providence, that is, how god, master of men, can benefit men without however becoming their servant and slave. The relationship in question
is actually structurally close to the one occurring between the sage in love
with a non sage trying to make the latter a friend: in the two cases, we are
presented with one master (god or the sage) and one inferior (the human
kind or the unwise beloved) who benefits from the action of the master
either though providence or through love. In an asymmetrical relationship
between unequal as that between god and men, the Stoics say, there is no
reciprocity of goodness, for the goods of each one are not shared but are
only *in coincidence* (*sundromos*):

13. How can gods be our masters, if what a master considers is
not the good of the slave but his own good? . . . And what good
could come to god because of man? [The answer is that] their

respective goods do coincide with one another. Thus, the Stoics say, the master cares for the slave, but only for his own sake [i.e. the master's sake] (*phrontidzei de kai ho tē(i)de despotes tou doulou, alla di' heauton*), and so too the gods: they do everything chiefly for themselves (*di' heautous proēgoumenōs*). (Damascius, *Commentary on the* Phaedo, 32 = *SVF* 2.1118.3)

We have evidence that, for some Stoics at least, the doctrine according to which one does everything for oneself was not confined to theology but used quite generally as a matching piece of the *oikeiōsis* doctrine. Epictetus, in particular, explains how it must not be confused with egoism:

> **14.** This is not selfishness (*touto ouk estin philauton*), this is the nature of the animal: he does everything for his own sake (*hautou heneka panta poiei*). For even the sun does everything for its own sake, and so, for that matter, does Zeus. But when Zeus wishes to be 'Rain-giver,' and 'Fruit-giver,' and 'Father of gods and men,' you see that he cannot accomplish these acts or earn these epithets without also contributing to the common good. And, in general, Zeus has so constituted the nature of rational animal that he can attain none of his proper goods without contributing to the common good. And so, it is no longer anti-social (*akoinōnēton*) to do everything for one's own sake. Well, what did you expect? That a man would stand aloof from himself and his own interest? And how can there any longer be one and the same principle for all beings: namely, appropriation to themselves (*hē pros auta oikeiōsis*)? (Epictetus, *Discourses*, I, 19, 11–15, trans. Dobbin, adapted)

It is a law of nature that an act cannot benefit its author without also contributing to the common good, that is, to the good of everyone else. This holds true for god who, for instance, cannot be the god of rain without at the same time having human beings (and animals in general) also benefiting from it by having their lands saved from drought (to take a simple example). And this holds true for any living animal since such a law stems directly from the universal principle of *oikeiōsis*.[45]

If we apply this Stoic principle (that one does everything primarily for one's own sake) to the sage in love, we have to assume that the sage does indeed benefit from his relationship with his beloved: he would not do it if it were not (also) for his own sake. Somehow, his good must *coincide* with the good of the young person with whom he is in love and whom he tries to change into another sage.[46] But how? I believe the answer is preserved in Seneca's *Letter 9*, a very important account of Stoic friendship.

C. SENECA ON THE ARTISTRY OF FRIEND-MAKING

The topic of Seneca's *Letter 9* is about friendship and wisdom: does the sage need friends? If the sage is self-sufficient, then it seems obvious that he does not need friends. And indeed, Seneca recognizes that having friends is not necessary for the happy life of the sage. But then, one should ask, for what purpose should the sage make friends?[47] Seneca is thus addressing a question similar to the one just raised by the comparison of Zeno's doctrine on love with Plato's own account in the *Symposium*: what good does it accomplish for the sage to fall in love and try to change his young beloved into a friend? Here, however, the reader must be warned that Seneca is not, in this letter, resorting to the Stoic doctrine of love we have been studying so far. He is concerned only with friendship and, when he brings love into the discussion, it is not the kind that causes friendship, rather a love he calls "insane friendship" (*insana amicitia*).[48] But this does not in any way detract from its relevance, for Seneca's letter is not so much concerned with friendship as it is with friend *making*, something that, after all, Zeno's love is precisely about.

I. THE SAGE AS AN ARTIST

After having recalled the orthodox Stoic doctrine that the sage seeks to have friends, but that, at the same time, he would remain perfectly happy if he had to be friendless, Seneca adds that, actually, it does not make sense even to think of the sage as being deprived of friends since the sage is an "artist at friend making." Seneca uses here a striking analogy, comparing the sage to Phidias:

> **15.** But in truth he [sc. the sage] will never be without a friend, for it rests with him how quickly he gets a replacement. Just as Phidias, if he should lose one of his statues, would immediately make another, so this artist at friend making (*faciendarum amicitiarum artifex*) will substitute another in place of the one who is lost. (Seneca, *Ep.* 9, 5)

Some commentators are not really happy with Seneca's analogy. Margaret Graver, in particular, thinks that the image of the sage as a sculptor capable of replacing any lost statue with a new one tends to present the figure of the friend as a passive recipient of the sage's artistry and, as a consequence, to present the sage and his friend as unequal partners.[49] I am not sure this is a totally fair criticism for what the Phidias analogy is about is not having friends but rather *making* friends. So, in fact, at this stage, there is not yet any friendship going on (involving the sage and his friend), only a friend in the making. Thus, the inequality and asymmetry conveyed by the Phidias metaphor is only reflecting the inequality and asymmetry that are at work between a sage and his beloved non sage.

II. THE USE OF VIRTUES

Seneca's image reminds us that, for the Stoa, virtues are not only sciences, but also *arts* (*tekhnai*),[50] and this makes him who possesses them not only supremely happy, not only perfectly wise, but also a true artist or *artifex*. So, to compare the sage to Phidias is not to present the sage as some kind of omnipotent demiurge, capable of transforming anything into whatever he wants, but only to reveal what being a sage is about, namely, *making use* of virtues as productive arts. This point is made clear two paragraphs later, when Seneca recalls what the Stoic Attalus (who was Seneca's master)[51] said about making friends:

> **16.** The philosopher Attalus used to say: "It is more pleasant to make than to have a friend (*iucundius esse amicum facere quam habere*) as it is more pleasant to the artist to paint than to have finished painting." When one is busy and absorbed in one's work, the very absorption affords great delight (*ingens oblectamentum*); but when one has withdrawn one's hand from the completed masterpiece, the enjoyment is not so keen. Henceforth it is the fruits of his art (*fructu artis*) that he enjoys; but it was the art itself (*ipsa arte*) that he enjoyed while he was painting. (Seneca, *Ep.* 9.7)

Making friends, says Attalus, is more pleasant than having friends. In fact, making friends affords "great delight" (*ingens oblectamentum*) for the artist himself.[52] It seems we finally start to grasp what good friend making can do to the sage. While the fruits of art can be enjoyed both by the artist and the admirers of his work, art itself cannot be enjoyed by anyone but the artist, that is, the sage. An art or a science becomes useful not by its mere possession, but by its *use* and exercise. So, to define, as in Zeno, the erotic art as an art of friend making actually means that all the good that the sage gets from love lies in the *making* of the friend. And if we take friendship to be a virtue, as in Seneca,[53] then the desire of the sage for making friends can also be explained by the wish not so much to have a friend, but to *exercise* friendship with a friend:

> **17.** The wise man, I say, self-sufficient though he be, nevertheless desires friends if only for the purpose of practising friendship (*ut exerceat amicitiam*), in order that such a great virtue may not be dormant (*ne tam magna virtus iaceat*). (Seneca, *Ep.*, 9.8)

What is here said of friendship holds true for any virtue, including love. It would not make sense to possess some good and not make use of it.[54] But the gain is not so much the external fruit of the art (the friend that has been made), as the actual *exercise* of the art. When the sage makes use of love (an art and virtue) to make a friend, he is enjoying the greatest of all possible goods: the exercise of virtue.

The emphasis on the *usus* or exercise of virtues in Seneca's letter helps us to make sense of a passage apparently desperately altruistic and thus at odds with the Stoic principle according to which it is the nature of an animal (including men and gods) to do everything for its own sake (cf. *supra* text 13 and 14). Here is what Seneca says:

> **18.** For what purpose then, do I make a man my friend? (*In quid amicum paro?*) In order to have someone for whom I may die, whom I may follow into exile, against whose death I may stake my own life, and pay the pledge, too. The friendship which you portray [i.e. one for the purpose of *utilitas*] is a bargain and not friendship; it regards convenience only, and looks to the results. (Seneca, *Ep.*, 9.10)

The passage must be understood against the backdrop of a criticism of the Epicurean conception that links friendship with utility and interest.[55] If we seek to make a friend, says Seneca, it is not because we foresee the utility a future friend will provide us, such as going to our rescue whenever we are in some danger (cf. *Ep.*, 9.9). On the contrary, if we consider making a friend, it must be for the sake of following him or her in case he or she is condemned to exile, putting our life at stake for the sake of saving his or hers, etc. Seneca seems here to depict an attitude genuinely altruistic in the sense that the purpose of making a friend is presented as prompted out of sheer selflessness. There is no doubt that a Stoic sage will do exactly what Seneca contemplates. But this does not necessarily make him altruistic. For, as Seneca has continuously emphasized in his letter, the sage shall enjoy *ingens oblectamentum*, resulting not from the product of his virtues, but from their actual exercise. It is not the case that the Stoic virtue of friendship is in itself altruistic.[56] But even if it were, it would remain that if a sage seeks to make a friend, it is first of all because he is eager to exercise his virtues and benefit from them.[57] After all, is that not what being a sage is all about?

III. THE NEED OF FRIENDS

We finally have reached an essential tenet of Stoicism, namely the coincidence between virtue and use, *khreia*, a word that can mean either "use" or "need." The Stoics played on this ambiguity in the meaning of the word *khreia* to formulate one of their famous paradoxes about the sage: the sage, though self-sufficient, will *need* plenty of things.[58] It is precisely this paradox that Seneca exposes at the end of his letter on friendship:

> **19.** Chrysippus says that "the wise man is in want of nothing (*nulla re egere*), and yet needs many things (*multis illi rebus opus esse*). On the other hand, nothing is needed by the fool (*nulla re opus est*), for he does not understand how to use anything (*nulla enim re uti scit*), but he is in want of everything (*sed omnibus eget*)." The wise man needs hands, eyes, and many things that are necessary for his daily use (*cotidianum usum*); but he is in want of nothing. For want implies a necessity, and nothing is necessary for the wise man. Therefore, although he is self-sufficient, yet he has need of friends. (Seneca, *Ep.*, 9.14–15)

The sage, being an artist, is here characterized by his ability to make use of everything and it is for this reason that he is said to *need* many things. Indeed, if you know how to play the piano, you will need a piano; if you know how to paint, you will need canvas and brush, etc. Now, the sage possesses not a particular art, nor even a plurality of particular arts, but one single universal art: the art of making use of everything. The fool, on the other hand, because he is lacking such a universal art, finds himself, paradoxically, in need of nothing. But of course, to say that the sage is in need of everything is not the same as saying that he is in want of everything. Actually, the sage is in want of nothing, since he is self-sufficient. In that respect, the sage is not in want of friends, in the sense that friends are not necessary for his happiness. But he needs them anyway, and, more importantly perhaps, he needs to *make* them anyway, so that he can *exercise* his virtues.

Conclusion

The Stoic doctrine on *erōs* was, from the outset, one in which love is presented as a formidable pedagogical power that drives a sage in love to change his beloved into a friend, that is, into another sage. The pedagogical dimension of Stoic love has been well acknowledged in modern scholarship. But what is not found there and what I hope this chapter has now shown, is how distinctive the Stoic idea of a pedagogical love is. Indeed, it is only when we place the doctrine of Zeno, founder of the Stoa, in its historical and Platonic background that we can really appreciate how it sought to improve on Plato's own conception of *erōs* in the *Symposium*. For there, while somehow assuming in the Lesser Mysteries section of Diotima's account that the lover shall indeed "try to educate" his beloved (*Symposium*, 209c2), Plato nevertheless ends up in the Greater Mysteries separating education and love as two distinct relationships, one between a guide and the one whom he (or she) is guiding, and one between a lover (who happens to be the same as the one guided) and his beloved. This separation was the natural outcome of Plato's understanding of *erōs* as philosophical in nature, that is, a love of wisdom that has its very essence in creative lack, and is therefore in need of a guide and a teacher. Zeno was probably disappointed to see how Plato's final account eventually parted from what Zeno thought was Plato's initial program. He then undertook to unite the two relationships distinguished by Plato, affirming that love, the knowledge of how to hunt for young boys naturally predisposed to virtue, is that by which the sage "encourages them to virtuous knowledge."

Having thus changed the Platonic parameters about love, Zeno and the rest of the Stoics after him found themselves in a rather unprecedented predicament. One new issue in particular needed to be addressed: while, to a potential lover, the appeal of Platonic love was rather straightforward, since Plato's lover is one that seeks after and eventually benefits from wisdom, the appeal of a pedagogical love like the Stoic one was apparently much less obvious. Indeed, the question became: what good, if any, is accomplished when the Stoic sage falls in love? Zeno made it clear that continuous association with young boys was certainly not a way to improve one's own intellect and, in any case, since the Stoic lover is a sage, one understands well that he cannot benefit from the kind of love Socrates is initiated into by Diotima in her Greater Mysteries. Seneca's *Letter 9* helps us to reconstruct how the Stoics responded to this difficulty. It shows, in particular, that what is distinctive of the Stoic sage is his (her) capacity to make wise use of everything. He (or she) has this talent of making use of any given situation as a way to *exercise* his (her) virtues. So, if an unwise young boy cannot in himself be a good for a sage (since he is not, or not yet, a friend), he is nonetheless valuable in the sense that he provides the Stoic sage with a unique opportunity:[59] that of exercising one of the greatest virtues, namely love. To modern ears, this may sound like sheer egoism or utilitarianism. But the Stoics emphatically rejected Epicurean utilitarianism. And, as to the accusation of egoism, Epictetus responded that if it is a natural law that any animal will do everything chiefly for itself, nature will also provide that something done for one's own sake will also benefit someone else. Love as "an effort at friend making from the appearance of beauty" is probably one of the best illustration of this Stoic principle.

Notes

*My thanks go to Gary M. Gurtler, S.J., and Suzanne Stern-Gillet for kindly polishing and correcting my English. I also thank David Sedley for comments and suggestions on an earlier version of this chapter.

1. Diogenes Laertius, 7, 33: *politas kai philous kai oikeious kai eleutherous*.

2. We know one of them: Cassius the skeptic (as reported in Diogenes Laertius, 7, 32–33), on which see Schofield 1999, 3–21, and Goulet-Cazé 2003, 41 et seq.

3. Cf. Banateanu 2002, 155–81.

4. Diogenes Laertius, 7, 33. See Schofield 1999, 3 et seq.

5. Even though the Stoics list friendship among the goods, either external or of the soul (cf. Stobaeus, *Eclogae* II. 7, p. 70, 8-20 W = *SVF* 3.97 and II. 7, p. 94, 21-95, 2 W = *SVF* 3.98), and claim that "one's friend is worth choosing for his own sake" (cf. Diogenes Laertius, 7, 124), being another "I" (cf. Diogenes Laertius, 7, 23), they nevertheless do not seem to have regarded friendship as a virtue. Neither in Diogenes Laertius nor in the epitome of Stoic ethics in Stobaeus (sometimes attributed to one Arius Didymus) is friendship formally identified as a virtue. Seneca, however, claims *amicitia* to be a virtue (see *Epistulae* [*Ep.*] 9, 8; the passage is quoted in the last section of this chapter).

6. In *SVF* 3.630, friendship is defined as "being of one mind" (*homonoia*) about "things concerning the way of living" (*peri tôn kata ton bion*) and *homonoia* is said to be the science (*epistēmē*) of common goods.

7. I do not share the interpretation according to which Stoic *erōs* is a kind of "good emotion" or *eupatheia*. This interpretation is actually based only on a reconstruction by some Modern commentators (see in particular Graver 2007, 188–189) and is not found in the extant evidence: it is not in Diogenes Laertius' list of "good emotions" (7.116 = *SVF* 3.431) nor in the pseudo Andronicos' (= *SVF* 3.432). (On this, see Graver 2007, 232, n. 45 and 48.) On the other hand we have evidence from Stobaeus that the Stoics took one kind of *erōs* (the one that is found in the *spoudaios* only) as a virtue. Stobaeus reports that when the Stoic sage is in love, he is thus qualified (an "*erōtikos*") because of a virtue ("*kata tēn aretēn*"), presumably the erotic virtue or *erōs* (cf. Stobaeus, *Eclogae* II. 7, p. 65, 17–18 W = *SVF* 3.717= text 1 in this chapter). In this chapter, I shall assume that *erōs* is a virtue for the Stoics.

8. *Erōs* is a kind of hunting: the knowledge of "how to hunt for naturally well-endowed young people" (see text 1 in this chapter). See also Seneca's *Ep.* 9 (cf. text 15) where the sage is presented as an "artist at friend-making (*faciendarum amicitiarum artifex*)."

9. It is striking to observe how studies on Stoic friendship tend to ignore its connection with *erōs*. See, for instance, Lesses 1993 and Banateanu 2002, neither of whom comments at any length on *erōs* as the origin of friendship according to the Stoa. There are, however, exceptions: see Price 2002.

10. The most thorough study on the topic is to be found in the classicstudy by Malcolm Schofield, *The Stoic Idea of the City* (Schofield 1999, 22–56). Among other important studies, see Inwood 1997, Price 2002, Laurand 2007, and Graver 2007, 173–90.

11. I have addressed this topic in Collette-Dučić 2009.

12. Cf. note 7.

13. The point has been convincingly made in Schofield 1999.

14. On the importance of this notion in the Stoa, see Stobaeus, *Eclogae* II. 7, p. 107, 14–108, 4 W = *SVF* 3.366.

15. Cf. Plutarch, *On Common Conceptions* 28, 1073B.

16. Cf. Plutarch, *On Common Conceptions* 28, 1073B.

17. Cf. Diogenes Laertius, 7, 101: "They say that only the beautiful is good, according to Hecaton in book three of his *On Goods* and Chrysippus in his book *On the Beautiful*; and this is virtue and that which participates in virtue; this is the same as [saying] that everything good in beautiful and that the good is equivalent to the beautiful—which is equal to it. For 'since it is good it is beautiful; but it is beautiful; therefore it is good.'" (Translation by Inwood and Gerson, slightly changed).

18. Diogenes Laertius, 7, 61.

19. Technically speaking, while *phantasiai* are affections of the soul, *phantasmata* are rather objects of affection (unreal objects though). In what follows, however, I shall assume that by "appearance of beauty" or *emphasis kallous* the Stoics refer not simply to the affection left in the soul of the sage following the view of the beautiful appearance of his young beloved, but also to the actual objective appearance itself, that is the external physical manifestation of *euphuia* in the beloved.

20. On this, see Long and Sedley 1987, section 39.

21. Cf. pseudo-Plutarch (= Aetius), *Placita philosophorum*, 900F (= LS 39B and *SVF* 2.54): "A figment is that to which we are attracted in the empty attraction of imagination; it occurs in people who are melancholic or mad." (Translation by D. Sedley and A. Long.)

22. Cf. pseudo-Plutarch (= Aetius), *Placita philosophorum*, 900E (= LS 39B and *SVF* 2.54): "The cause of an impression is an impressor: e.g., something white or cold or everything capable of activating the soul." (Translation by D. Sedley and A. Long.)

23. Cf. *SVF* 2.673.

24. It is not implausible that the original formulation of the Stoic doctrine, expressed by Zeno in his *Republic*, used *eidos* rather than *emphasis*. Zeno, who was trained at the Academy under Polemon, may have borrowed this expression from a reading of *Symposium* 210 b2, where Diotima speaks of to *ep' eidei kalon* (the context is that of the beauty of bodies). I will later show that there are other parts of the Stoic definition of *erōs* that can be traced back to the *Symposium*.

25. Cf. Cicero, *De Officiis* 1.46: "Since life is passed not in the company of men who are perfect and truly wise, but those who do very well if they show likenesses of virtue (*simulacra virtutis*), I think it must be understood that no one should be entirely neglected in whom any mark of virtue (*significatio virtutis*) is evident," translation Long and Sedley. Cf. Price 2002, 186.

26. On this see Schofield 1999, 31–32, Price 2002, 182–183, and Boys-Stones 2007.

27. This has well been seen by Price: "A pederastic relationship that makes a person virtuous and wise cannot be equally reciprocal, but the benefit that it bestows [sc. friendship] is greater and equally shared" (Price 2002, 188).

28. On this fragment, see Boys-Stones 1998.

29. Cf. *SVF* 3.630. On the idea of defining friendship in terms of concord, see Schofield 1999: Annexe E, in which the author shows convincingly how the Stoic doctrine on the question was probably inspired by a reading of *Cleitophon* 409 e.

30. The suggestion that Zeno's concept of *erōs* stems from a reading of Plato's *Symposium* is not new. One finds it in Inwood 1997, Schofield 1999, 32, and Laurand 2007. But these commentators disagree on deciding what part of the *Symposum* has been the most influential on Zeno. While Brad Inwood shows interesting similarities with Pausanias' speech, Valéry Laurand provides elements in favor of Diotima's dialogue with Socrates. I tend to side with Laurand's interpretation, although, as will further be shown, I think that Zeno's reminiscence of Diotima's account is *deliberately* limited to the Lesser Mysteries part.

31. Cf. Sedley 2006.

32. Cf. Rowe's commentary *ad loc.* p. 143: "That Aristogeiton is said to feel *erōs* for Harmodius, and Harmodius *philia* ('friendly affection') for Aristogeiton, is the clearest indication yet of the expected asymmetry of the relationship between lover and beloved (cf. 180a7–b4n.)."

33. This distinction is already at work in the *Apology of Socrates* (21 b–23 b) where Socrates recalls how he used to cross-examine and prove ignorant poets, craftsmen and statesmen.

34. Cf. what is said of the poets in *Apology of Socrates*, 22 b–c.

35. Sedley 2006, 50.

36. This is a debated issue; see Price 2002, 48, n. 56.

37. Cf. *Symposium*, 210 a4–5, a6, c8, e2–3 and 211 c1–2.

38. Cf. *Symposium*, 211 b6.

39. Cf. *Symposium*, 210 d3.

40. The idea that Zeno's conception of love may implicitly include a criticism directed against Plato is here more of a conjecture on my part. One could imagine that Zeno did not intend to have his own account read in this light and that he only sought to show the right (Stoic) way to read some of Plato's doctrines in the *Symposium*. There is no doubt that Zeno did use this strategy in the cases of doctrines displayed in Plato's early dialogues (the so-called Socratic dialogues), doctrines that he probably viewed as more Socratic than Platonic. But I doubt very much that Zeno could have ever thought of the *Symposium* as a Socratic dialogue and this is why I think we should read his doctrine on *erōs* not simply as a Stoic interpretation of Plato's *Symposium* but also as reflecting a criticism against Plato.

41. As explained earlier (cf. *supra* note 7), I disagree with M. Graver on this particular point.

42. Graver 2007, 188–89.

43. Cf. *SVF* 3.630.

44. Cf. Damascius, *Commentary upon the* Phaedo, 32 = *SVF* 2.1118.3.

45. According to Valéry Laurand (who develops an idea initially expressed in Pembroke 1971, 130), love understood as an *epibolē* may have a peculiar link with Stoic *oikeiōsis* or appropriation. See Laurand 2007, 74–75.

46. Malcolm Schofield, although through a different approach, reaches a similar conclusion: "Which is more fundamental? The disinterested concern that my beloved achieve virtue (. . .)? Or the pursuit of him, in the attempt to get him to be my friend? The authors of definitions [A = love is a chase] and [B = love is about making friends] in effect take the second option. Rightly so. My concern is not the impartial desire that those with the right make-up for virtue should realize their promise, still less the impersonal wish that virtue should be achieved where there is the potentiality for it. It is *my* beloved I want to achieve virtue, because he is or could be in a particular relationship with *me*: which is not incompatible with wanting it for *his* sake, not mine" (Schofield 1999, 35). However, I think we would be wrong to suppose that the good of the sage lies only with the prospect of *having* a friend eventually, for, in that case, love would not be a virtue in its own right and would only serve as means to friendship. If we take *erōs* as a virtue, then we have to assume also that it is a good the sage can actually benefit from when he is in love.

47. Cf. Seneca, *Ep.* 9, 10: *In quid amicum paro?*

48. Cf. Seneca, *Ep.* 9, 11. Compare this with the *erôtomanê tina* in text 1.

49. Cf. Graver 2007, 184: "[T]he comparison [with Phidias] is still troubling in that it seems to imply that friends are merely the passive recipients of one's own artistry as friend maker. Asymmetry need not be incompatible with friendship: it can be argued, for instance, that Seneca's endeavor in the *Moral Epistles* as a whole is to engender a notional friendship between himself as author and Lucilius—or any potential reader—as aspirant to wisdom. Outside the literary context, though, one would like to have the assurance that a Stoic wise person also thinks of the friend as an equal whose existence is as important as his own."

50. Cf. Stobaeus, *Eclogae* II. 7, p. 63, 6-8 W (= *SVF* 3.280; LS 61D): "All the virtues which are sciences and expertises (*epistēmai kai tekhnai*) share their theorems and, as already mentioned, the same end. Hence they are also inseparable."

51. On Attalus, see Inwood 1995, 69.

52. Attalus may be here referring to Stoic *terpsis*, which is a kind of joy, hence a *eupatheia* (cf. Diogenes Laertius, 7.116).

53. Cf. note 8 in this chapter.

54. Contrary to Aristotle who claims that to possess virtues is one thing, but to make use of them is another (for the sleeping sage is not, according to him, using his virtues and therefore not also benefiting from them), the Stoics, and first of all Zeno, hold that it is not possible to possess virtue without at the same time making use of it. Cf. Cicero, *Academica posteriora*, I, 38 = *SVF* 1.199. On this, see Bénatouïl 2006, 152–59.

55. See, for instance, Cicero, *De finibus*, II, 84: *Utilitatis causa amicitia est quaesita; Praesidium amicorum.*

56. It is better described as disinterested, that is, not seeking *utilitas*. See Cicero, *De Finibus*, III, 70: "Stoics consider that friendship should be cultivated (*Amicitiam autem adhibendam esse censent*), since it falls under the category of what is helpful (*quia sit ex eo genere, quae prosunt*). Some say that in a friendship the interest of one's friend will be as precious to the wise as one's own, though others claim that one's own will be more precious. But even these latter declare that it is incompatible with justice, for which we seem to be born, to take something from another for the purpose of enriching oneself. Indeed the school that I am discussing rejects absolutely the adoption or approbation of justice or friendship for utility's sake (*propter utilitates*), since the same utility might ruin or corrupt these. There can be no justice or friendship at all except where sought for their own sake (*nisi ipsae per se expetuntur*)." (Translated by Woolf)

57. On this, see again the remarkable book by T. Bénatouïl, dedicated to the study of the concept of usage in Stoicism (Bénatouïl 2006).

58. Consequently, "the fool has need of nothing (*ho phaulos oudenos deitai*), has use for nothing (*oudenos ekhei khreian*); to him, nothing is serviceable

(*khrēsimon*), appropriate (*oikeion*) or harmonized (*harmotton*)," Plutarch, *On common conceptions*, 20, 1068A. See also *On Stoic self-contradictions*, 12, 1038A–B.

59. On the importance of opportunity (*opportunitas, eukairia*) in Stoic ethics, see Cicero, *De Finibus*, III, 47: *Non intellegunt valitudinis aestimationem spatio iudicari, virtutis opportunitate.*

Bibliography

I Primary Literature

Cicero. 1998. *De Finibus Bonorum et Malorum.* Edited by L. D. Reynolds. Oxford: Clarendon Press.
———. 2001. *On Moral Ends.* Edited by J. Annas and Translated by R. Woolf, Cambridge: Cambridge University Press.
Diogenes Laertius. 1999. *Vitae Philosophorum.* Edited by M. Marcovich. 2 vol. Stuttgart/Leipzig: Teubner.
Epicteti Dissertationes ad Arriani Digestae. 1965 [1916]. Edited by H. Schenkl. Stuttgart: Teubner.
Epictetus. *Discourses Book 1.* 1998. Translation and Notes by R. F. Dobbin, Oxford: Oxford University Press.
Hellenistic Philosophy. Introductory Readings. 1997. Translation by B. Inwood and L. P. Gerson. Indianapolis: Hackett.
Ioannis Stobaei Anthologium [Eclogae]. 1884–1923. Edited by C. Wachsmuth and O. Hense. 4 vols. Berlin: Weidmann.
L. Annaei Senecae ad Lucilium Epistulae Morales. 1966. Edited by L. D. Reynolds. 2 vol. Oxford: Clarendon Press.
Plato. 1998. *Symposium.* Edited with an Introduction, Translation and Notes by C. J. Rowe. Oxford: Oxbow books (Aris and Phillips Classical Texts).
Plutarch. 1976. *Moralia XIII Part II: On Stoic Self-Contradictions* and *On Common Conceptions.* Introduction and Translation by H. Cherniss. Cambridge: Harvard University Press, Loeb Classical Library.
Seneca. 1917–1925. *Ad Lucilium Epistulae Morales.* Edited and translated by R. M. Gummere. 3 vol. Cambridge: Harvard University Press, Loeb Classical Library.
Stoicorum Veterum Fragmenta. 1903–1905. Edited by H. von Arnim. Stuttgart: Teubner, Vol. I: *Zeno et Zenonis discipuli*; Vol. II: *Chrysippi Fragmenta logica et physica*; Vol. III: *Chrysippi Fragmenta moralia—Fragmenta successorum Chrysippi*; Vol. IV: *Indices conscripsit Maximilianus Adler* (1924).
The Hellenistic Philosophers. 1987. D. N. Sedley and A. A. Long, eds. Cambridge: Cambridge University Press. Vol. I: Translations of the Principal Sources, with Philosophical Commentary; Vol. II: Greek and Latin Texts with Notes and Bibliography.

II Secondary Literature

Banateanu, A. 2002. *La théorie stoïcienne de l'amitié. Essai de reconstruction.* Fribourg: Editions du Cerf.

Bénatouïl, T. 2006. *Faire usage: la pratique du stoïcisme.* Paris: Vrin.

Bonazzi, M., and C. Helmig (eds.). 2007. *Platonic Stoicism—Stoic Platonism. The Dialogue between Platonism and Stoicism in Antiquity.* Leuven: Leuven University Press.

Boys-Stones, G. 1998. "Eros in Government: Zeno and the Virtuous City." *The Classical Quarterly* 48, no. 4.

———. 2007. "Physiognomy in Ancient Philosophy" in S. Swain, (ed.).

Collette-Dučić, B. 2009. "On the Chrysippean Thesis That the Virtues are Poia." Proceedings of the Boston Area Colloquium in Ancient Philosophy 25.

Goulet-Cazé, M.-O. 2003. *Les Kynica du stoïcisme.* Stuttgart: Franz Steiner Verlag.

Graver, M. R. 2007. *Stoicism and Emotion.* Chicago/London: University of Chicago Press.

Inwood, B. 1995. "Seneca in His Philosophical Milieu." *Harvard Studies in Classical Philology* 97.

———. 1997. "Why Do Fools Fall in Love?" In R. Sorabji (ed.).

Laurand, V. 2007. "L'érôs pédagogique chez Platon et les stoïciens." In M. Bonazzi and C. Helmig (eds.).

Lesses, G. 1993. "Austere Friends. The Stoics on Friendship." *Apeiron* 26.

Long, A. A. (ed.). 1996 [1971]. *Problems in Stoicism.* London: The Athlone Press.

Nussbaum M. C., and J. Sihvola (eds.). 2002. *The Sleep of Reason: Erotic Experience and Sexual Ethics in Ancient Greece and Rome.* Chicago/London: The University of Chicago Press.

Pembroke, S. G. 1996 [1971]. "Oikeiôsis." In A. A. Long (ed.).

Price, A. W. 2002. "Plato, Zeno, and the Object of Love." In M. C. Nussbaum and J. Sihvola, eds.).

Reis, B. (ed.). 2006. *The Virtuous Life in Greek Ethics.* Cambridge: Cambridge University Press.

Schofield, M. 1999. *The Stoic Idea of the City.* Chicago/London: The University of Chicago Press.

Sedley, D. 2006. "The Speech of Agathon in Plato's Symposium." In B. Reis (ed.).

Sorabji, R. (ed.). 1997. *Aristotle and After.* London: Institute of Classical Studies.

Swain, S. (ed.). 2007. *Seeing the Face, Seeing the Soul Seeing the Face, Seeing the Soul. Polemon's Physiognomy from Classical Antiquity to Medieval Islam.* Oxford: Oxford University Press.

5

ERŌS AND *PHILIA* IN
EPICUREAN PHILOSOPHY

Harry Lesser

1. Epicurean Arguments against *Erōs*

As with some other parts of Epicurean philosophy, our main source for the
Epicurean view of *erōs*, or *amor*, is Lucretius' *De rerum natura*, an account
of Epicureanism that is much longer than any of the surviving works of
Epicurus himself. There are, though, two objections to taking Lucretius as
one's main source. The first is that he is talking about *amor*, which is not
the same as *erōs*, since, unlike *erōs*, *amor* is used in reference to different
kinds of love, and not only sexual passion. To this one may reply that the
context makes it absolutely certain that in book IV of Lucretius' poem
amor refers to sexual passion. Second, there is the question whether Lucretius' view of *erōs* is that of an orthodox Epicurean. It is certainly possible
that the attack on *amor* in book IV of the poem derives its impetus from
Lucretius' personal history or from his psychological makeup: but we know
virtually nothing about Lucretius except that he lived, probably from 99 to
55 BC, and was a fairly prosperous farmer. It is also true that the passages
on love and the suffering it causes sound as if they come from experience.
However, what Lucretius says is not in any way out of line with other
Epicurean comments, though it does in its intensity go beyond anything
extant attributed to Epicurus himself.

   Epicurus' treatise on *erōs* is lost, but several references to sex and
marriage survive. According to Diogenes Laertius (10.119), in his account

of Epicurus' philosophy, "the wise man will marry and father children, as Epicurus says in his *Problems* and the *On Nature*." Moreover, "the wise man will not have intercourse with a woman in a manner forbidden by the laws" (Diogenes 10.118). In the context of the ancient world, this would not, for men, exclude all sex outside marriage, but it would exclude intercourse with married women or with free unmarried virgins who were living with their parents, leaving permissible intercourse with prostitutes, slave women, or other women for whom the rules of respectable society were, for one reason or another, not operative. Even this should be kept to a minimum. In the *Letter to Menoeceus* Epicurus says explicitly (Diogenes 10.132) that by pleasure (the aim of life), he does not mean "the pleasures of the profligate or the pleasures of consumption," but "the lack of pain in the body and disturbance in the soul." The basis for this is expressed in the *Principal Doctrines* 8: "No pleasure is a bad thing in itself. But the things which produce certain pleasures bring pains many times greater than the pleasures." Diogenes sums this up (10.118) by reporting the Epicureans as saying "Sexual intercourse never helped anyone, and one must be satisfied if it has not harmed him": this presumably refers to sex outside marriage.

All this relates to sex without *erōs*, to lust or desire rather than love. The two "outlets" are (to simplify the point a little) marriage and prostitution, the latter to be kept to a minimum, if one is wise. Since in ancient society, whether Greek or Roman, marriage was arranged by the families, neither type of relationship was likely to involve *erōs*. And Diogenes tells us, in the same passage, that "they do not believe that the wise man will fall in love . . . nor that love is sent by the gods." So there is a place for sex, but none for erotic love. With this in mind, as an account of the general Epicurean attitude, we may now consider what Lucretius has to say about *amor*, that is, *erōs*.

Lucretius discusses love and sexuality (always from a male point of view, and mainly, though not only, male sexuality) at the end of book IV of *De rerum natura*, lines 1037–1286. At first, he does not seem to distinguish love from sex in general, but at 1273 he makes a clear distinction. Like the Epicureans in general and in line with what has been quoted above, he distinguishes pure sexual desire from the emotion of erotic love and objects only to the latter:

> Nec Veneris fructu caret is qui vitat amorem,
> sed potius quae sunt sine poena commoda sumit;
> nam certe purast sanis magis inde voluptas
> quam miseris.

(Nor does he who avoids love lack the fruit of Venus, but rather takes the advantages without the penalty; for certainly the pleasure from this is more unmixed for the healthy than for the unfortunate; IV 1073–76).

This perhaps, though not certainly, goes beyond Epicurus himself, in that it sees *erōs* not simply as undesirable, like all violent emotion, but as an actual mental illness: those in love are contrasted with the "healthy," who want nothing more than sexual pleasure, and if they are healthy, this implies that the lovers are unhealthy. More explicitly, at line 1069 love is called "furor," and later on, at 1117, it is called both "furor" and "rabies," "frenzy" and "madness." What is somewhat unclear is how, for Lucretius, erotic love differs from sexual desire without love and why love is not healthy.

On the first point, it looks as if sexuality becomes *erōs* when it is an obsessive desire (as the Epicureans would see it) for intercourse with a particular person, for whom no other can be a substitute, as opposed to a desire that is for the moment, or even over a long period, as in an arranged marriage, directed toward a particular person, but capable of being satisfied by many others. Lucretius indeed recommends, as part of the cure for love:

> et iacere umorem collectum in corpora quaeque,
> nec retinere, semel conversum unius amore,

> (and to cast the collected liquid into any bodies, and not to retain it, as being wrapped up once for all in the love of one; IV 1065–66).

But why is this intense desire for one person a mental illness? The answer appears to be, because it is a desire that cannot be satisfied. For an Epicurean, to nurture such a desire is peculiarly irrational: to be "wounded" by it may be something one cannot help, but one can take steps to get rid of it, rather than feeding it. It is irrational because happiness consists in having no unsatisfied desires, and the way to achieve this is by eliminating those desires whose satisfaction cannot be guaranteed. This is strongly advisable even with desires whose satisfaction is possible in principle but uncertain in practice, such as the desire for elaborate meals; if a desire certainly cannot be satisfied it becomes, for an Epicurean, essential to eliminate it.

Now, Lucretius makes it clear (1084–1120) that even if the lovers are successful, and able to be with each other all the time, and to make love whenever they wish, they still cannot be satisfied. *Amor*, for Lucretius, is the one desire that it is in principle impossible to satisfy:

> unaque res haec est, cuius quam plurima habemus,
> tam magis ardescit dira cuppedine pectus.

> (and this is the one thing for which, the more we have, the more the breast burns with terrible desire, IV, 1089–90).

The desires for food and drink, he continues, are easily satisfied by eating and drinking: and presumably the desire for sex without *amor* can be satisfied. But, he argues, nothing satisfies *amor*. In the absence of the beloved there are only thin images, and even when the lovers are together and consummating their love, they cling to each other but have something unappeasable—sometimes, he says, they seem to want the impossible, to be literally absorbed in each other's body. Even after the climax, there is no relief, but only a short pause and then the same frenzy and madness return: *inde redit rabies eadem et furor ille revisit* (1117).

So love of this kind is always painful as well as pleasant: indeed much more painful than pleasant, even if it is regularly consummated, and apparently not thwarted in any way. It is not that some lovers are fortunate, if there is no obstacle to the consummation of their love, and others are, as it happens, unlucky: certainly the lovers who are prevented from being with their beloved will suffer even more (see 1141ff), but even those who possess their beloved are suffering. To be in love, as opposed to merely feeling sexual desire, is necessarily to be in mental pain: consummation of the love brings a short temporary relief from the pain, but it will soon start again.

However, this kind of pain, that of unfulfilled desire, is, according to Epicurean doctrine, and as indicated above, exactly the kind of pain from which one can save oneself, if, instead of nursing and feeding the desire (*ulcus enim vivescit et inveterascit alendo*, "for the sore quickens and grows inveterate with feeding," 1068), one sets oneself to get rid of it, using the methods which Lucretius describes in lines 1063–64: *sed fugitare decet simulacra et pabula amoris/absterrere sibi atque alio convertere mentem* (but it is right to flee from images, to scare away what feeds love, and to turn the mind in other directions), in particular, as the following lines indicate, by finding other partners. *Vatican Collection* of Epicurean maxims (18) suggests that simply avoiding the object of one's passion can be enough: "If you take away the chance to see and talk and spend time, then the passion of sexual love is dissolved."

On the other hand, if, instead of working to get rid of the desire, one allows oneself to be dominated by it, one crucial effect of the pain this produces is hate for the person who is the cause of it. Lucretius says that the behavior of lovers typically shows hate as well as love, as seen in their desire to hurt each other physically even while giving and getting pleasure:

> Quod petiere, premunt arte faciuntque dolorem
> corporis, et dentis inlidunt saepe labellis
> osculaque adfligunt, quia non est pura voluptas
> et stimuli subsunt qui instigant laedere id ipsum,
> quodcumque est, rabies unde illaec germina surgunt.

(They press tightly what they desire, and hurt the body, and often set their teeth in the lips and kiss roughly, because the pleasure is not unmixed, and there are stings within them, which urge them to hurt that very thing, whatever it is, from which those seeds of madness arise, 1079–83).

Lucretius differs here from his younger contemporary Catullus, who found it incomprehensible but true that he could both hate and love:

> Odi et amo. quare id faciam, fortasse requiris?
> nescio, sed fieri sentio et excrucior.

(I hate and I love. Perhaps you ask how I might do this. I do not know, but I feel it happening and I hang on a cross, *Poem 85*, my tr.)

Lucretius in contrast regards this as entirely the normal state of lovers, while agreeing with Catullus that it is an extremely painful one. What one should especially note is that it is a very poor basis for a long-term commitment: the lovers want to be fastened to each other forever and at the same time to be free from the torment the other is causing them; and sooner or later the second desire will win, and the affair will end. If *erōs* is, as Lucretius and Epicurus agree, a state of violent emotion, occasionally ecstatic but mostly unhappy ("Plaisir d'amour ne dure qu'un moment; chagrin d'amour dure toute la vie," to quote the classic French song by J. P. E. Martini, 1784), and always involving hate as well as love, then, even if the lovers are able to marry, the only way the relationship can last is if *erōs* is replaced by *philia* before it is too late: this is not explicitly stated by Epicurus or Lucretius, but it is a necessary consequence of what they say.

But are Epicurus and Lucretius saying the same thing? Bailey in his commentary (3: 1303) concludes that "Lucretius was rather more lax than his master in permitting intercourse as a satisfaction of lust and far more vehement in his denunciation of the passion of love." However, R. D. Brown correctly points out, in his *Lucretius on Love and Sex* (121) that this is a difference in tone and emphasis, and not a difference in doctrine, Earlier (112), he says, again correctly, that the "extant opinions on love of Epicurus and his followers" (few as these are, as he also reminds us) combine with the evidence of Lucretius to "form a consistent picture." Brown also notes (121) that we do not need to suppose that the difference in tone is necessarily due to Lucretius' personal experience: it might be simply due to his taking the opportunity to write some powerful poetry about human emotion. However, we equally cannot say with any certainty that Lucretius' hatred of sexual passion was not due to experience.

What we can say is that for both Epicurus and Lucretius long-term relationships must be based on *philia/amicitia*. In this connection, we must remember that *philia/amicitia* includes domestic and family relationships. Robin Weiss' chapter in this volume demonstrates the close connection between *to philon* and *to oikeion*; and in Latin *familiaris* can be a synonym for *amicus* (see Lewis and Short, 1975, volume 1, *s.v. familiaris*). Family relationships are included, at some length, in Aristotle's two books on *philia* in the *Nicomachean Ethics,* VIII and IV; and Cicero makes the point explicitly in *De Amicitia* VIII. Epicurus and Lucretius do not make the point explicitly; but, since people did not leave their families in order to join an Epicurean community, Epicureans must have seen *philia* within the family as being as important as, if not more important than, *philia* among people unrelated. The family has always been the place where affection starts and develops: as pointed out by Xenophon (*Hiero* 3.7), "The firmest friendships, I suppose, appear to be from parents towards children and children towards parents and brothers towards brothers and wives towards husbands and comrades towards comrades" (my tr.).

It is instructive at this point to compare Lucretius with Plato, and in particular with Dimitri El Murr's exposition of Plato in this volume. Plato, like Lucretius, holds that physical *erōs* cannot be a basis for a long-term relationship. He does so for three reasons, two of which are emphasised by El Murr. The first is that *erōs* is not accompanied by any goodwill toward the person who is its object, but is only concerned with obtaining pleasure. This is similar to what Lucretius says, but different in two ways. Plato makes no distinction between *erōs*, when it is physical, and sexual desire in general, and he regards *erōs* as being accompanied by indifference to the welfare of the "beloved," whereas Lucretius thinks there is actual hatred.

Second, *erōs* involves only the other person, as an object of pleasure, whereas a long-term relationship requires a third thing in which both parties are involved, ideally a search for wisdom and virtue (this is very well shown and developed by El Murr). Lucretius does not say this, but he makes much of the point that the lovers cannot satisfy each other and that their desire for each other is an unfulfillable desire. And it is clear that in the Epicurean communities of friends there were many kinds of shared and communal activities.

Third, because everything physical is in a state of change, love directed toward the body, and not the soul, of the loved one is equally liable to change: I think we may take it that Pausanias speaks for Plato himself when at *Symposium* 183e he says of the "bad" lover, who loves only the body, that "he is inconstant, because what he loves is inconstant: as soon as the body's bloom, which is what he fell in love with, is fading, he takes wing and is off" (my tr.). Lucretius would agree, but he parts company with Plato over how one should deal with this. Plato's recommendation is to work at making oneself a lover of the higher sort, who is in love with the soul; Lucretius' recommendation, for men, is to accept the promiscuous quality of one's sexual feelings and concentrate on satisfying those feelings in ways that do the minimum harm to oneself and others, which in particular requires the avoidance of *erōs* and its suppression if it arises. Nevertheless, he would agree with Plato that physical attraction, whether or not involving *erōs*, is not a basis for long-term relationships.

We may thus say that both Plato and Lucretius think that one must get beyond purely physical relationships and move toward relationships involving the personality. The difference is that Plato thinks that one should, if possible, get away from the physical altogether, whereas Lucretius thinks one should simply minimize its emotional importance. There are also differences in how the relationships are thought of. Some of these may relate to the metaphysical differences in their theory of the soul, which Lucretius regards as physical and Plato as nonphysical, but these need not concern us here. More importantly, Plato, or at least the Plato of the *Symposium*, regards these relationships as still erotic, but with *erōs* directed toward the soul rather than the body; whereas Lucretius probably would deny that a nonsexual relationship could be a manifestation of *erōs*. Perhaps one can say that for Plato *philia* is not the less *philia* because it is also the higher form of *erōs*, whereas for Lucretius the two cannot exist together as attitudes toward the same person at the same time. Indeed, for Plato the best kind of *philia* requires that one abandon sexuality, but not *erōs*; for Lucretius *philia* requires that one abandon *erōs*, but might, as in a successful arranged marriage, retain sexuality, especially in order to have children. We should remember that Lucretius' poem is dedicated to Venus, (see I, ll.1–49), but it is to Venus as the source of procreation, not to Venus as the goddess of erotic love (ll.29–49, about the surrender of Mars to Venus, are in contrast to this; but the serious point behind the poetic beauty of this passage might be only that even love is preferable to war).

We can also compare the Epicurean view with the Stoic one, as set out in this volume by Bernard Collette-Dučić. The Stoics saw *erōs* as something that could operate between teacher and pupil and positively assist the development of knowledge and virtue, a view that is found also in the *Symposium* (183–85). The Epicureans do not consider this, in any of the extant literature, but it is clear that they would see any such emotion, even if it did not lead to sexual activity, as an obstacle to learning and not a help. They also, unlike Plato and the Stoics, do not discuss homosexual *erōs*. Thus, in Lucretius' account, homosexual desire gets a brief mention (IV, l.1053), and even then it is for a "boy with womanish limbs" (*puer membris muliebribus*), but *erōs* is presumed to be between a man and a woman.

But what is particularly important is that Plato and Lucretius differ in their assessment of the state of being unsatisfied or unfulfilled. For Lucretius, *erōs* is bad because it cannot be satisfied, and the state of unfulfillment is painful and therefore bad. For Plato, there is nothing wrong with dissatisfaction as such. What is wrong with the "inferior" lover is that he is dissatisfied for the wrong reason. To be dissatisfied because one cannot possess a particular body is unworthy; but to be dissatisfied because one, or one and one's friend, is or are insufficiently wise or virtuous is entirely healthy, and much better than being a satisfied fool or rogue.

2. Epicurean Friendship

How does this help us to understand the Epicurean view of friendship, in contrast to the Platonic? It brings out the fundamental point that essential to Epicurean ethics is the idea that our aim should be the long-term satisfaction of our wants and long-term peace of mind. *Erōs*, in any form, is incompatible with these and needs to be either avoided or got rid of as soon as possible. I have tried to show in detail why the Epicureans take this view. But this is only half the story. There remains the positive side:

Why do they think that *philia* can supply the kind of basis for contentment that *erōs* cannot?

In other words, what is it that friendship has to offer which *erōs* does not? It offers pleasure without pain, if one chooses one's friends carefully, but also a lot more. To see this, we need to go back to what should be, according to Epicurus, our basic aim, namely, pleasure. Pleasure requires above all freedom from care and anxiety, *ataraxia*, which, according to Epicurus, gives happiness, whereas intense pleasure is paid for with suffering that makes it never worthwhile. Now, one major cause of a troubled mind, as we have seen, is the suffering caused by unfulfilled wants; and the way to deal with this is to reduce one's desires to those that can easily be satisfied. The other main cause of care and anxiety is fear; and a major cause of fear, a major potential threat, is other people.

In theory, one might try to deal with this by simply avoiding other people and living alone. But in practice a person cannot live alone and be entirely self-sufficient: we are all dependent on other people. So the only way in which one can have an anxiety-free life is by living with people one can absolutely trust. But one can only receive absolute commitment if one is prepared to give it: if it is known that one will do anything for one's friends and will always stand by them, they will also stand by one. Lovers of course often promise to do this, but the promise is based on an emotion always likely to burn itself out or be transferred to another object and always accompanied by hatred, so it is always unreliable.

In contrast, friendship is rationally based, on a need that will never go away, a need to trust people absolutely, and on an acceptance of what is required if the need is to be met. As was said above, what is required for Epicurean friendship is total mutual commitment. Epicurean friendship is thus not a strong motivation, if "strong" means "violent." But if "strong" means that the motive is long lasting, and that it will win out over all other motivations, whether springing from desire or from fear, the commitment that Epicureans are required to make to their friends could not be stronger. It even means being genuinely prepared to endure death or torture for one's friends; but unless and until this happens (and, the Epicureans would say, if it does it will be soon over) one can live with an entirely peaceful mind, among people one can trust absolutely. Thus 56 and 57 in the *Vatican Collection* declare, "The wise man feels no more pain when he is tortured than when his friend is tortured, and will die on his behalf, for if he betrays his friend, his entire life will be confounded and utterly upset because of a lack of confidence." Similarly, Diogenes Laertius, in the account of Epicurus' ethical views in his *Life of Epicurus*, reports him as holding that the wise

man will betray none of his friends and that he will sometimes die for a
friend (10.120a; 121b).

The position is in fact entirely consistent, even though it seems odd
that the consequence of making pleasure one's aim is that one be prepared
for the ultimate self-sacrifice. Indeed Plutarch accused Epicurus of "brazen"
inconsistency (*Against Colotes* 1111b); but Cicero (*De finibus* 1) saw the
point clearly. To repeat, the argument is as follows. A pleasant life requires
freedom from anxiety. This requires friends one can trust absolutely and
unconditionally. This in its turn means that one has to be the kind of person one's friends can trust unconditionally, even to the point of enduring
death or torture. For, even if this is required, and it may be, the peace of
mind one enjoys up to this point, the way one can rely on help from one's
friends, and the pleasure one gets from their company easily outweigh the
pain endured at the end of one's life: hence the commitment is not a gamble,
according to Epicurean values, because even if the sacrifice is required, it
is a good price to pay for the previous gains. (A similar conclusion, that
the requirement of self-sacrifice, if necessary, is consistent with the claim
that freedom from pain is everyone's ultimate aim, is reached, via a different route, by Suzanne Stern-Gillet in her paper "Epicurus and friendship"
(*Dialogue* XXVIII, 275–88).

Epicureans thus have a rich notion of friendship, involving mutual
enjoyment of each other's company, mutual activities, mutual help, and
mutual cooperation, whatever the sacrifices involved. Also, unlike *erōs, philia*
can involve a group of people and not simply a pair, as we see in Cicero's
statements that Epicurus assembled large congregations of friends in a small
household and that the Epicureans of his day did the same (see above).
Above all, again very unlike *erōs, philia* is based not on a violent emotion
which may (the Epicureans would say, will) one day depart and leave only
hatred behind, but on the rational realisation that this is the only way to
be happy. "Rational" here does not mean calculation, since calculation will
destroy friendship, which has to be unconditional. Thus number 39 in the
Vatican Collection says "The constant friend is neither he who always searches
for utility, nor he who never links [friendship to utility]. For the former
makes gratitude a matter for commercial transaction, while the latter kills off
good hope for the future." The collection (34) says, "We do not need utility
from our friends so much as we need confidence concerning that utility."

So what is rational is to realize that the way the world and human
nature are structured has the consequence that a vital part of a happy life
is mutual help and trust among friends, and to realize that anything less
than unconditional commitment will destroy the friendship, or turn it into

an inferior kind of relationship. Cicero, in *De amicitia*, section 16, similarly pointed out that the maxim, advocated by some "Love with the consciousness that you may one day hate" (my tr.) would utterly destroy friendship; and in section 18 he says that the crucial quality needed in friendship is loyalty. And erotic lovers, the Epicureans would no doubt say, are notoriously disloyal. Under the influence of the emotion they will, at the time sincerely, promise eternal faithfulness and any sacrifice; once the emotion has subsided and left behind at best indifference, and most likely hatred, the promises will all be forgotten and no doubt prove to be written on "wind and fast-flowing water," to quote Catullus once again (poem 70, l.4).

Perhaps it is for analogous reasons that Epicurus and his followers discouraged entry into political life. Diogenes praises the patriotism of Epicurus, but says immediately afterward that he was "so gentlemanly that he did not even participate in political life" (10.10). In his account of Epicurus' philosophy, he says that Epicurus wrote that the wise man "will not participate in civic life" (10.119), though he will be public spirited, serving as a juror, erecting statues, opening a school (though not drawing a crowd to it), giving public readings (though only if pressed), and being prepared to "serve a monarch, when the occasion is appropriate" (10.119–21). A possible reason for this is suggested by two of the maxims in the *Principal Doctrines*: "The natural good of public office and kingship is for the sake of getting confidence from men, from those from whom one is able to provide this" (6) and, "The purest security is that which comes from a quiet life and withdrawal from the many, although a certain degree of security from other men does come by means of the power to repel and by means of prosperity" (14).

For, as compared with real friendship, political alliances have the same weakness as love affairs, though for different reasons: they tend not to last, and the reasons for this are inherent in the relationship, and not accidental. Political alliances, whether between individuals or groups, and whether formal or informal, are entered into for supposed mutual benefit, sometimes genuinely benefiting both parties, sometimes in fact benefiting only one, or even neither. Whatever the situation, once they are no longer seen as advantageous they will be ended: at best, the parties will first honor the commitments they have already made and then end the alliance, and at worst they may simply break it off. And the knowledge that this may happen means that the security of true friendship cannot be obtained in politics: as indicated in the maxims above, political power can give some security, but only up to a point. One might add that the behaviour of tyrants, who try to obtain security through the creation of a culture of fear, seems to be another case of a self-defeating strategy: the more violence is used to quell opposition, the more people are alienated, so that security is never obtained and the amount of violence required keeps increasing. To try to obtain peace of mind by gaining political power is analogous to trying to obtain it by seeking the consummation of erotic passion: there is a short period of calm, and then the fear, or the desire, returns in a more intense form. Only a commitment to other people, based on the benefits of the relationship itself and not on the pleasures or benefits for which it is a means, can provide long-term *ataraxia.*

So, to repeat, the Epicurean conception of friendship is of an unconditional commitment to enjoying each other's company, doing pleasant and worthwhile things together, mutual help and cooperation, and mutual support for as long as it is required and whatever the sacrifice, It is the most essential element in a happy life, and it contrasts with the temporary storm of emotion that is *erōs* and the temporary alliances for supposed mutual benefit found in political life. One question remains: Must *erōs* and politics be opposed to true friendship, or can they in fact coexist with it? Epicurus and Lucretius concentrate on dealing with *erōs* by working to get rid of it and presumably then leaving the beloved. But what about working to convert *erōs* into *philia*? Here, we should simply note that there are two views of love in general. There is the view that the various kinds of love and lust are radically different from one another and should not be confused; and there is the view that, although psychologically and morally they are very different, they are all connected, and the inferior kinds can be converted into superior kinds. Epicurus and Lucretius take the first view; Plato, especially in the *Symposium*, takes the second. They agree, indeed, that erotic lovers of what is physical are mad. But they disagree as to whether the madness is infernal or divine and as to whether one should try to get rid of it or to convert it into a more nobly directed passion, as the prophetess Diotima (who may or may not have been a real person) describes the process in the *Symposium* (201–12).

About politics, they also agree up to a point and then disagree. There is a reading of the *Republic* which sees Plato's ideal society as the one described in book II, of an economically very simple society, requiring no central or state authority, in which people are content to satisfy their basic physical needs, live healthy lives, treat each other justly, and use their spare time for such things as study, music, conversation, and religion. The state is seen as a response to human corruption, to people wanting more than they need and coming into conflict as a result. It would seem that the life of Plato's "prestate" people, though not identical with the life of the Epicurean communities, would be very similar, in its relative physical austerity, its mutual cooperation, and its intellectual activities. But Plato, though he may have regarded all political societies, imagined as well as actual, and even his own Kallipolis, as falling short of the ideal, and even though he himself kept out of active politics, still seems to have thought that there could be a place for good people in the running of society and that the effort to improve things was worth making, whereas Epicurus seems to have thought that the best option was to withdraw from civic life and look to individual nonpolitical communities to promote human happiness.

Moreover, Dimitri El Murr has shown very convincingly that, although there is no explicit discussion of *philia* in the *Republic*, what Plato envisages is a society largely operating through the fellow feeling among its citizens. Indeed, what Plato says in book V of the *Republic* seems to envisage a society in which the ruling class has become one big family, in which everyone is, emotionally, the child of all members of the previous generation, the parent of all members of the next, and the sibling of all those too young to be their parents and too old to be their children. And the rulers and ruled will be fellow citizens, still governed by *philia* toward each other.

But—a very large but—the society envisaged by Plato has a great deal of *philia*, but it has no politics. If we mean by politics what is so well described and defended, as being the only way to have a free society in which everyone's interests are given some weight, by Bernard Crick in *In Defence of Politics* (2000), namely, the arguing and making of deals between the various interest groups in a society, resulting in various compromises and settlements, this would not exist in Kallipolis, but would be replaced by administrative activity by the ruling class, fully supported by the rest of society, and in the public interest of the whole society. If one has a taste for epigram and is prepared to be only partly original, one might say that in the *Symposium* Plato argues for taking the sex out of sex, and in the *Republic* for taking the politics out of politics. He is committed to *erōs* and to the public good, but without the messiness of physical sexuality and political negotiation and horse trading.

The question is then whether this ideal, which does have a certain nobility, is either possible, given human nature as it is, or desirable. For the Epicureans, it would seem, it would be desirable but impossible. They therefore conclude that a person's involvement with both should be as limited as is practicable, their involvement with sex being only what is needed for physical relief and for procreation, and their involvement with politics being, rather similarly, only what is needed for self-protection or to discharge one's duties as a public-spirited person. The long-time and fully committed emotional and active center of one's life should be neither with one's partner in *erōs* nor with the public, but with one's family and friends, that is, in *philia/amicitia*.

To sum up, this chapter has had three aims. The first is to show that the Epicurean conception of friendship, involving nothing less than commitment until death, is a much richer and more morally powerful idea than it is often given credit for. The second is to show how understanding this enables us to understand the Epicurean view of *erōs* and of political life. The third is simply to raise a question: Granted that we should respect the Epicurean ideal, is it in the end more appropriate to follow this ideal, and to devote oneself to *philia*, whenever possible keeping clear of sex and politics, or to follow Plato, by engaging with sex and politics with the aim of turning them into *philia*; or to accept that one must always operate in the messy world of human sexuality and politics, and within that pursue *philia* as much as one can?

Bibliography

Aristotle. 1984. *Nicomachean Ethics.* Translated by Ross, W. D. and J. Urmson. *The Collected Works of Aristotle,* edited by J. Barnes. Princeton: Princeton University Press.

Bailey, C. 1947. *Titi Lucreti Cari: De rerum Natura. Libri Sex.* Vol. III, ed. with Prolegomena, Critical Apparatus, Translation and Commentary. Oxford: Clarendon Press.

Brown, R. D. 1987. *Lucretius on Love and Sex: A Commentary on* De Rerum Natura IV, 1030–1287, with Prolegomena, Text and Translation. Leiden and Boston: Brill.

C. Valerii Catulli. 1958. *Carmina.* Translated by R. A. B. Mynors. Oxford: Clarendon Press.

M. Tulli Ciceronis. 2006. *De Re Publica, De Legibus, Cato Maior De Senectute, Laelius De Amicitia.* Edited by J. G. F. Powell. Oxford: Clarendon Press.

———. 1998. *De Finibus Bonorum et Malorum.* Edited by L. D. Reynolds. Oxford: Clarendon Press.

Crick, B. 2000. *In Defence of Politics.* 5th ed. London: Continuum.

Diogenes Laertius. 1994. *Life of Epicurus* (extracts) in Inwood Gerson.

Epicurus. 1926. *Epicurus: The Extant Remains.* Translated with notes by C. Bailey. Oxford: Clarendon Press.

The Epicurus Reader. 1994. Edited and translated by B. Inwood and L. P. Gerson. Indianapolis: Hackett Publishing Company.

———. 1994. Letter to Menoeceus. Principal Doctrines. Vatican Collection of Epicurean Saying. Inwood and Gerson.

Lewis, C. T., and C. Short. 1975. *A Latin Dictionary.* Oxford: Oxford University Press.

Lucretius, Titus Carus. 1992. *De Rerum Natura.* Tr. W. H. D. Rouse. New version by Martin Ferguson Smith. 2nd ed. revised. Cambridge MA: Harvard University Press.

Martini, J. P. E. 1784. "Plaisir d'amour" (song). de Florian, J.-P. Celestine. Paris.

Plato. 2007. *Republic.* Translated by D. Lee. 2nd edition revised,. Harmondsworth: Penguin Books.

Platonis Opera. 1901. Tomus II. Edited by J. Burnet. Oxford: Clarendon Press.

Plutarch. *Against Colotes* (extracts). 1994. Inwood and Gerson.

Stern-Gillet, S. 1989. "Epicurus and Friendship." *Dialogue* 28.

Xenophon. 2007. *Hiero. On Government.* Edited by V. J. Gray. Cambridge: Cambridge University Press.

6

Cicero's Stoic Friend as Resolution to the Paradoxes of Platonic Love

De Amicitia alongside the Symposium

Robin Weiss

Ne amores quidem sanctos a
sapiente alienos arbitramur.
The passions of love, when pure,
we do not think alien to the sage.

—Cicero (*Fin.* III.xx.68)

Introduction

Odd as it might be for us to speak of a loved one as "belonging" to our-selves, lovers find it easy enough to speak of themselves as "belonging" to each other, and none of us would have any difficulty in describing what we feel among intimates as a sense of "belonging." No wonder then that the Greeks used the same word for their personal effects and for those loved ones they claimed as "their own."

The root of the word they used is *oikos*, or "household." The *oikeia* were originally the things of which the *oikos* was composed, and they com-prised everything from the furnishings to the equipment that was needed to run the household. But among these physical belongings were also slaves and family members who contributed to the running and upkeep of the household. When it took on expanded meaning, *oikeioi* became a term broadly applied to all those who formed an integral part of one's life and with whom one lived connected in close intimacy.

Any Greek who observed that feelings of attachment were felt most strongly for *oikeia,* or "our own belongings," and that feelings of fondness were felt most strongly for those who were *oikeioi,* or "our own," would have made the same assumption as Socrates. The assumption he begins by making in Plato's dialogue on friendship, the *Lysis,* is that the *philon* or the "beloved" is *to oikeion,* or "that which belongs to oneself" (*Lys.* 210d).[1] Whatever is "beloved" or "cherished," whatever seems "friendly to us," whatever is denoted by *to philon* initially remains shrouded in obscurity, and this obscurity is only partially dissipated when *to philon* is equated with *to oikeion.*[2]

The *Lysis* ends in *aporia* owing to a confusion as to the meaning of the word *oikeion* itself, which can be taken now in the sense of "that which is akin to," now in the sense of "that which is good for" oneself. What we love, whether we call it *to philon* or *to oikeion,* can thus be conceived in two different ways—*either* as something that is a source of benefit to us or as something in which we find a reflection of ourselves.

Interpreting *to oikeion* as though it signified *to agathon,* or "the good," is a strategy that fails Socrates. Supposing that one would consider nothing *oikeion* that one didn't consider beneficial for the management of one's household, Socrates first counsels Lysis to endear himself to his parents by becoming integral to the management of their affairs, saying that "everyone will be *philoi* to you and *oikeioi* when you are useful and good" (210d). But to assume that we love the good is to assume that our love is reserved for the goodness we lack, and this, because of our own badness (220d). Because the idea that the search for goodness has its origins in badness is one that Socrates finds abhorrent, he wavers between this interpretation and another that takes *to oikeion* to refer to that in which we find our own mirror image (222a). But it is equally abhorrent because it means that, governed by the law of "like seeks like," our affection for others stops at those in whom we find a semblance of ourselves (222b).

In previous chapter, Dimitri El Murr reminds us that the question the *Lysis* cannot answer is "What *causes* us to form friendships?" What is loved must be lovable either because it is *like us* or because it is *good for us.* But is it similarity or goodness that draws us to friends? In the *Symposium,* the same dilemma recurs. Aristophanes represents the view that we love what is already *similar to* or *a part of* us, and Socrates, speaking on behalf of the Diotima, represents the view that we desire the good. We leave it to

El Murr to determine whether Plato ever in fact reconciles these two positions. Here, we wish only to remark that the dialogue form allows Plato to
represent two mutually contradictory perspectives on love, each of which
he places in the mouth of a different character.[3]

Instead of adopting either one or the other of these views, Cicero
writes his own dialogue. In this dialogue of his, however, he places in
the mouth of one character, Laelius, two apparently contradictory assertions. Laelius speaks at some moments like Aristophanes, and at others like
Socrates. But if Laelius appears inconsistent, my claim is that it is because
Cicero is trying to do justice to *the contradictory nature of love itself* by
attempting to reconcile the two apparently contradictory sets of assertions
we often make about it. Cicero, in brief, says that love can be conceived
as a search for ourselves *and that at the same time*, it can be conceived as
a search for the good.

Cicero is uniquely equipped to reconcile to these disparate accounts
of love because he can rely upon a Stoic conception of desire. The Stoic
tradition had to offer him an account of desire that did not take for granted
the one assumption upon which these two Platonic visions of love, different
as they may be, are both premised. Both assume that *we desire what we
lack*, while the Stoic tradition upon which Cicero draws does not assume
that "the loved" will always be "the lacked."

Loving the *oikeion*

How do we know the views Laelius is about to espouse on friendship are
Stoic ones? We know, not just because friendship thrives among Stoics, nor
much less because the historical Laelius was a well-known Stoic,[4] though
it is a fact of which we are reminded every time Laelius is flattered for his
stoical nature.[5] We know that he voices ideas that are not just Peripatetic,
but specifically Stoic because the source to which Laelius traces friendship
lies in a *societas* or an "association" that increases with our proximity to one
another so that we unite ourselves in love with fellow citizens more than
foreigners, but with family members most of all. This *vis amicitiae concor-
diaeque*, this "force of friendship and concord," while so pervasive that "if
it were taken out of the universe, no household or city could stand," is a
propinquitas, a "nearness or closeness," but one still lacking that essential
kind of love that makes it *amicitia* proper (v.19).

This *propinquitas* must become *benevolentia* before it can draw two
people together so closely that the two are melded together, and a single

soul is made of two (v.19).[6] But while it can take on this extraordinary power among friends, it has its humble origins in a love that is originally for ourselves. Indeed, it has its origins in nothing but that *carum sibi esse*, or "being dear to oneself," to which Cicero refers in almost all his works; it is, for him, as much as for all Stoics, *the* force that makes the world go round and the force whose reality is always defended in passages like these:[7]

> From the beginning, nature has assigned to every type of creature the tendency to preserve itself, its life and body, and to reject anything that seems likely to harm them, seeking and procuring everything necessary for life, such as nourishment, shelter and so on. Common also to animals is the impulse to unite for the purpose of procreation, and a certain care for those that are born. The great difference between man and beast, however, is this: The latter adapts itself only in responding to the senses, and only to something that is present at hand, scarcely aware of the past or future. Man, however, is a sharer in reason, this enables him to perceive consequences, to comprehend the causes of things, their precursors and their antecedents, so to speak; to compare similarities and to link and combine future with present events; and by seeing with ease the whole course of life, to prepare whatever is necessary for living it. This same nature, by the power of reason, unites one man to another for the fellowship of common speech and of life, creating above all a particular love for his offspring. It drives him to desire that men should meet together and congregate, and that he should join them himself; and for the same reason to devote himself to providing whatever may contribute to the comfort and sustenance not only of himself, but also his wife, his children, and others whom he holds dear and ought to protect. (*De Officiis* I.iv.12)

Compare that passage from *De Officiis* with the following from *De Amicitia*:

> Now it is evident in animals, whether of the air, the water, or the land, and whether tame or wild, first, that they love themselves (*se ipsae diligant*)—for this feeling is born alike in every living creature—and, secondly, that they require and eagerly search for other animals of their own kind to which they may attach themselves—and this they do with a longing in some degree resembling human love (*cum quadam similitudine amoris*

humani)—then how much more, by the law of his nature, is this the case with man who both loves himself and uses his reason to seek out another whose soul he may so mingle with his own as to make one out of two (*quanto id magis in homine fit natura ! qui et se ipse diligit, et alterum anquirit, cuius animum ita cum suo misceat, ut efficiat paene unum ex duobu*s). (*Am*. xxi.81)

Though not referred to here or anywhere else by name, this is the Stoic doctrine of *oikeiōsis*. *Oikeiōsis* is what we might today call the drive toward self-preservation. But, for the Stoics, it impels us not *just* to seek out the means of our own self-preservation; it impels us to seek out the means by which the growth of the body and the development of its faculties—physical *and* mental—may be sustained. It directs us toward the things that, incorporated into the self, preserve and sustain its continued growth.

The Stoics might have availed themselves of the language of *orexis* employed by Aristotle in order to refer to the way human beings strain and exert themselves as they "stretch out" toward things outside themselves. The Stoics believe that we reach out for what allows us to attain our end in life. What we reach out for is thus what furthers us along the path we travel in life toward our final end, and just as this end is attained with the full actualization of all one's latent faculties for Aristotle, so it is for the Stoics attained with the full realization of one's human potential.[8]

It may at first appear that for the Stoics we desire what we lack. Indeed, they often speak this way. But the Stoics adopted another way of speaking about desire that lent the process of "laying claim to" and "making ours" a desired object—a phenomenon they called *oikeiōsis*—deeper significance. The word *oikeiōsis* is one for which we only have "making-one's-own-ization" as a possible English translation. But the word was important to the Stoics because it implied that the things one "appropriated" or "made one's own" were things that one took for oneself *because* they were *oikeia* to oneself *in advance*. That is to say, one established possession over the things that one could, in some sense, consider to "belong to" or "to be proper to" oneself. *But in what sense do the objects of our desire "belong" to us before we have taken them for ourselves?*

Although the things we desire allow us to realize our potential, we desire them not because we are in particular need of *them* if we are to realize our potential, but because they present themselves as potentially "belonging" or "proper to" the entity we are becoming. Since desired objects are the *means* by which self-actualization is attained, it would in some sense be correct to say that, without them, *one could not be what one is striving to become.* An integral part of one's self-actualization, they are an integral part of who one *is*. As much as water and sunshine are an elemental part of a plant, the things we desire are parts of the person we *are. Thus, they "belong" to us before we even try to possess them.* In another sense, however, we do not desire these things because we need and would otherwise lack them. Other objects can for the Stoic always be substituted as the means by which one achieves self-actualization.[9]

Let us now turn to the contradictory statements Laelius makes over the course of the dialogue:

1. he states that we love those who are similar to ourselves and then that we love those who help us to attain a good (xvii.50; xxii.82);

2. he states that we need those we love and then that we do not need them at all (viii.29; xviii.82);

3. he states that we must love our friends and never abandon them, even when it means compromising our virtue and then that we should break with friends when they prove a greater impediment than aid to virtue (xvii.61; xvii.42);

4. he states that we should not dissolve old friendships for the sake of new one and then that old friendships must not hold us back from forming new ones. (xx.74; xix.68)

Let us try to understand why someone like Laelius, taking his departure from the Stoic conception of desire just delineated, would be led to such apparently contradictory conclusions about the nature and practice of friendship.

To Love the Virtuous or Those like Ourselves?

The tradition to which Stoicism belongs is one that denies the reality of any love greater than self-love.[10] Other people and things are depicted as portions of the self lying *outside* it so that outwardly directed love aimed at *them* becomes an extension of the love directed at *the self*. Claiming that a loved object was already a component part of the self, the Stoics participated in a tradition that could be traced back at least as far as the Greek belief that one found pieces of oneself in loved ones. One's children were a part of oneself that would outlive one's earthly demise, and they were held dear for that reason. Even Diotima capitalizes upon the idea that everything that strives after its own self-preservation "naturally values its own offshoot (*apoblastēma*)" (*Sym.* 208b5). To say that one person was *oikeios* to another was usually to say *sungenēs*. This was to say the two came into being from out of the same source, that they shared a single origin.[11] Family members carried within themselves the same seeds from which other family members sprang. Kin relations had the same blood flowing through their veins and the same marrow in their bones, and it was expected that they would be loved because they were made of the very stuff as oneself. The *oikeion* therefore lay wherever one's roots could be seen to lie.[12]

In the *Symposium,* Aristophanes plays upon the assumption that there is something intrinsically lovable about those who are made from the same stuff as ourselves. But to what degree does Cicero agree with Aristophanes that we love those with whom we share a common nature? He does not depart from the commonplace that we love, first and foremost, people who share the same constituent nature as ourselves, and that the strongest love is initially felt for those who are literally flesh of our flesh, blood of our blood. But though family relations are *oikeioi*[13] in the sense that they partake of the things constitutive of our nature, other people can loosely be called *oikeioi* because they are "cut from the same cloth as ourselves," in a sense that is more figurative than literal. Thus, the strange character of the feeling of love when it is directed at those whose nature does not share any literal kinship with our own:[14]

> What this feeling is may be perceived even in the case of certain animals, which up to a certain time, so love their offspring and are so loved by them, that their impulses are easily seen. But this is much more evident in man; first, from the affection existing between children and parents, which cannot be destroyed except by execrable crime, and again from that kindred impulse of love, which arises when once we have met someone whose habits and character accord with our own, because in him we seem to behold a sort of light of uprightness and virtue (*si aliquem nacti sumus, cuius cum moribus et natura congruamus, quod in eo quasi lumen aliquod probitatis et virtutis perspicere videamur*). For there is nothing more lovable than virtue, nothing that allures us more to affection, since on account of their virtue and uprightness we feel a sort of affection even for those whom we have never seen. (viii.27, trans. mod.)

One way to interpret the relationship between two things with a basic affinity is to say that they are similar. Friendships often begin between those who have similar habits and dispositions. Laelius does not deny this. Laelius does not seem to mean, however, that those who love each other do so *merely* because they are similar and that this affinity can be reduced without remainder to the fact that each finds reflected in the other the mirror image of himself. According the Stoic theory of desire, the potential friend must attract because she presents herself as the means to the actualization of our own virtue. Insofar as they attract at all, these habits and inclinations must therefore hold promise of fostering the virtue inside us striving to express itself. Perhaps we sense that if we were to form a partnership with the friend-to-be, her virtuous qualities would bring out our own, or in some other way prompt us to perform virtuous deeds. But the fact that we are drawn to those of a nature that "accords" with our own does not mean that love is *merely* governed by the law of "like attracts like." This is manifest in Cicero's choice of the word *congruere*.

The way in which, in English, we describe two things as "akin" to one another also captures well the way in which the relationship between them extends beyond a relationship of mere family resemblance. When we say that things are "akin," we can mean to imply that they share a common progenitor, and thus, that they are inwardly similar, but we can also mean, in a much broader sense, that they are moved by the same inner force. Two things that are "akin" share what the Greeks called an *archē*. What this also means is that, moved by the same guiding impetus, they are likely to travel a similar trajectory and to live a parallel existence. This is exactly the kind of the affinity between two people connoted by the word *congruere*, which captures the way in which another person's life can "run parallel to" or "converge and coincide" with our own, such that he or she tends to further rather than impede our movement along the path we travel.

But Laelius not only counsels us to find a friend who is moved by the same forces as ourselves (*qui rebus isdem movetur*: xviii.65). He goes on, in the passage above, to say that we will love "once we have met someone whose habits and character accord with our own, *because in him* we seem to behold a sort of light of uprightness and virtue," and nothing is more lovable than virtue. Here, the claim that we love those who are like ourselves coexists alongside the claim that we love the virtuous. Similarity attracts. But virtue attracts, and attracts more powerfully and lastingly *because*, we may surmise, the more virtuous a person is, the more their character "accords" with our own. *This* shall be argued in what follows. But even here, Laelius seems to assume that we will only ever find a friend whose character fully

accords with our own when we find a virtuous friend. If what we are looking for is a friend traveling a path convergent with our own, we can only
hope to find a virtuous person. A virtuous person is uniquely valued us as
a furtherance along the path to our ultimate destination in life.

Laelius will eventually *arrive* at a Platonic conclusion—that, in the
end, we love those who are similar to ourselves only insofar as they strive,
like us, toward virtue. But because he does not begin from this assumption,
he does not exclude from the outset other forms of friendship as pretenders
to the name and exclude friendships that, only with time, become Platonic.
True, we are drawn instantly to virtue:

> let us believe that the sentiments of love and kindly affection
> (*sensum diligendi et benevolentiae caritatem*) spring from nature,
> when intimation has been given of moral worth; for when men
> have conceived a longing for this virtue they bend towards it
> and move closer towards it, so that, by familiar association with
> him whom they have begun to love (*diligere*), they may enjoy
> his character, equal him in affection (*amore*), become readier to
> deserve than to demand back his favors (*propensioresque ad bene
> merendum quam ad reposcendum*), and vie with him in a rivalry
> of virtue. (ix.32)

But how does this first inclination to befriend someone give rise to the
kind of friendship Plato would recognize as such? The humble origins of
friendship for Laelius lie in the giving and receiving of love through the
exchange of favors and then the attempt to outdo the other in virtue. (We
shall later see why these all amount to the same thing, since giving without
need or expectation of return is the very substance of virtue itself.) But
here, it is the exchange of favors that initiates friendship: "And yet love
(*amor*) is further strengthened by the receiving of kindly service (*beneficio
accepto*), by the evidence of another's care for us (*studio perspecto*), and by
closer familiarity (*consuetudine adiuncta*), and from all these when joined to
the soul's first impulse to love, there springs up, if I may say so, a marvelous glow and greatness of goodwill (*benivolentiae magnitudo*)" (ix.29). It is
evident that what is formed over time between two friends is nothing less
than a symbiotic relationship. It is important to note that the support the
other provides us may be of a very material kind and come in the form of
the exchange of personal favors. Friends supply the material preconditions
for our self-realization, but this, far from diminishing the importance of the
friend, makes it all the more possible to say that the friend is a "part" of us,

because he *literally* becomes that without which, we begin to feel, we cannot be what we are. And of course, the result is the feeling of *benevolentia* evidenced in one friend's treatment of the other as though he *were* himself. Cicero speaks often and highly of the feeling of love that knits (*contrahit*) two souls together and makes each treat the other as himself:

> But, since, as I said before, virtue knits (*contrahat*) friendship, if there should be exhibition of shining virtue to which a similar spirit (*similis animus*) may attach and adjust itself (*adplicet et adiungat*), when that happens, love must spring forth (*exoriator*). For is there anything more absurd than to delight (*delectari*) in many inanimate things like public office, fame, and stately buildings, or dress and personal adornment, and to take little or no delight in a being endowed with virtue (*virtute praedito*), who is capable of loving (*amare*), and as I will say, loving back (*redamare*)? For nothing is more pleasant (*iucundius*) than the return of goodwill (*remuneratione benevolentiae*) and the interchange of eager performance of duty (*vicissitudine studiorum officiorumque*). (xiv.49)

Cicero does not regard the *benevolentia* that he says manifests itself in the willingness to serve the other as though he were himself, as a means to some further end, as Epicurus would have it. For "it is the friend's love and his love alone that gives us delight" (xiv.50). But how is it possible in friendship that "its whole fruit is in love" (*omnis eius fructus in ipso amore inest*: ix.31)?

The activity of loving and being loved, for which Cicero coins the term *redamare*,[15] is one that actually allows us to become, for all intents and purposes, fused with another person. When we join with another person, the aggregate of virtue between us is much larger than would be amassed by any one of us on our own. We pool our virtue, so to speak, and in doing so we attach ourselves (*applicet*), as Cicero so beautifully puts it, to a larger font of virtue. It is therefore from an external source that we draw more of the virtue that wells up within us from internal sources. Eventually, these two springs of virtue are commingled and become a single raging river.

What that means, of course, is that friends are the people from whom we draw the strength and the power we need to become full human beings. Immediately, a parallel can be drawn between Cicero's friends and the lovers Aristophanes portrays as drawing their human strength and vigor from each other, each being *anthrōpou sumbolon*, or "half a man" without the other (*Sym.* 191d4). "Thus anciently is mutual love ingrained in mankind, reassembling our early estate and endeavoring to combine two in one and heal the wound of human nature" (*esti dē oun ek tosou ho erōs emphutos allēlōn tois anthrōpois kai tēs archaias phuseōs sunagōgeus kai epicheirōn poiēsai hen ek duoin kai iasasthai tēn phusin anthrōpinēn*: *Sym.* 191c8–d3, tr. mod.). So says Aristophanes, making the point that we desire to return to and reconnect with a lost point of origin. In departing from the source from which we drew our strength and energy like a stream from its wellspring, we were debilitated and enfeebled. For Cicero, this is not literally the case, but desire is nothing if not the urge to drink from that fountainhead from which our life force flows. Without drinking from this font, we cannot be who we are, or to put it another way, we have not the strength fully to become what we might. Yet, though we form a symbiotic relationship with the other that allows virtue to grow in the first place, we should nonetheless be able to retain that virtue if the other departs. Like two plants that have twined around each other in order to climb upward toward the sunlight, one should be able to hold itself upright if the other is cut down.[16]

Briefly, the attraction of one person to another may be described as a case of the law of "like attracts like," and yet the law cannot be so narrowly interpreted that it appears to conflict with the Socratic doctrine that we are really attracted to the good.[17] Cicero articulates both the law of "like attracts like" *and* the law that "moral goodness attracts," without seeing the two postulates to be in any way contradictory. In passages like the following it even appears that one is the logical corollary of the other: "And what if I also add, as I may fairly do, that nothing so allures (*inliciat*) and attracts (*trahat*) to itself as likeness does to friendship? Then it surely will be granted as a fact that good men love and join to themselves (*diligant adsciscantque sibi*) other good men, in a union that is almost that of relationship and nature. For there is nothing more eager (*adpetentius*) and more greedy (*rapacius*) than nature for what is like itself" (xiv.50). Aristophanes and Socrates appear to contradict each other when Socrates asserts that *virtue* is what we desire, and Aristophanes, the *self*. These two conceptions of love are thrown into sharp relief when Diotima questions the degree to which our love for others can be considered an extension of our love for ourselves:

> And certainly there runs a story," she continued, "that all who go out seeking their other half are in love; though by my account love is neither for the half nor for the whole, unless, of course, my dear sir, this happens to be something good. For men are prepared to have their own feet and hands cut off if they feel

these things of theirs of be harmful. The fact is, I suppose, that
each person does not cherish his own except where a man calls
the good *to oikeion*, and the bad another's; since what men love
is simply and solely the good. (*Sym.* 205d10–e7, trans. mod.)

According to Diotima, self-love is not enough to account for people's love
for others. The love they show others is not *merely* an extension of the love
they show themselves. What they love is *to agathon* (the good). We must
assert therefore that they don't love what is *already* theirs, or what *was once*
theirs, but that "they love the good to be theirs" (*einai to agathon hautois
erōsin*: *Sym.* 206a6–7).

But the one distinguishing feature of the symbiotic union between
friends in Cicero is that it is not pregiven, but *made*. It is made once one
man finds another with whom he can join (*coniuncti esse possunt*: iv.29). For
Diotima, love has its start in the longing for that which we have *yet* to make
our own, and therefore, Cicero presents love as the search for that which is
not *already* a part of ourselves. He depicts love not as a backward-looking
search for that which either *was*, or still *is* a part of us, but as a forward-
looking search for a not-yet-attained future self, a search that is part of a
larger journey we travel toward an unrealized state of virtue, along the path
to which the loved friend serves as a stepping stone to our final destination.
Since it is therefore as much for the sake of virtue as it is out of mutual
sympathy that we seek friends, we conclude that Cicero's account of love
incorporates the best elements of Socrates' and Aristophanes' speeches.

Desiring without Dependence

"The oftener, therefore, I reflect on friendship, the more it seems to me
that consideration should be given to the question, whether friendship is
desired on account of weakness and want" (*inbecillitatem atque inopiam*). Is
it by "giving and receiving gain" (*dandis recipiendisque meritis*), that "each
one accepts from the other and returns that which he is less able to get for
himself" (*quod quisque minus per se ipse posset, id acciperet ab alio vicissimque
redderet*)? Though each friend provides what the other is lacking, is not the
very cause of this mutual support, which is the mark of true friendship,
to be found in a source outside itself in something "more ancient, more
beautiful, and originating from nature itself" (*antiquior, et pulchrior, et magis
a natura ipsa profecta*: viii.26)?

This is the question with which Laelius begins because, although he may lend equal credence to aspects of Socrates' and Aristophanes' accounts of love, he is led into disagreement with both on the matter of its ultimate source. Different as their accounts may be, both take for granted that love's origins lie in an empty void at the center of our being, in a hole that the loved object promises to fill, the consequence being that the loved one plays the role of compensating for some internal deficiency. For Aristophanes, the deficiency for which the other compensates is the loss of some essential aspect of oneself. For Socrates, although love is the child of abundance, it is nevertheless also the child of want. After we have had a taste of the good, our appetites are whetted for more, and being deficient in it, we long for more of that in which we feel ourselves to be deficient. Laelius, meanwhile, refuses to assign love so ignoble a birth:

> If people think that friendship springs from weakness (*ab inbecil-litate*) and from a purpose to secure someone through whom we may obtain that which we lack (*ut sit, per quem adsequatur, quod quisque desideret*), they leave to friendship, if I may so say it, a birth far from noble, of lowly lineage, and they would make her born of poverty and want (*inopia atque indigentia*). If this were so, then whoever judged there to be least in himself (*quisque minimum esse in se arbitraretur*), would he be most fitted to friendship; whereas the truth is far otherwise. For to the extent that a man relies upon himself (*quisque sibi plurimum confidit*) and is so fortified by wisdom and virtue that he is dependent on no one and considers all his possessions to be within himself (*ut nullo egeat, suaque omnia in se ipso posita iudicet*), in that degree is he more conspicuous for seeking out and cherishing friendships. What need did Africanus have for me? By Hercules! None at all. And I certainly none for him. (ix.29–30)

This is the same Cicero who tells us in *De Finibus* that if friendships were founded on utility, then those same claims of utility "would be able to undermine or overthrow them" (*Fin.* III.xxi.70). Laelius is therefore of the Stoic view that this would reduce the friend to a mere tool to be used for the other's convenience. Then, it would be impossible to avoid the conclusion that the tool could be discarded as soon as it became an inconvenient hindrance to the meeting of those needs it once promised to fulfill. He presupposes that "on the assumption that advantage is the cement of friendships, if advantage were removed then friendship would fall apart" (ix.32). And yet, Laelius is often caught saying things of the following kind: "Indeed, I should be inclined to think that it is not well for friends never to need anything at all. Wherein, for example, would my zeal have displayed itself if Scipio had never been in need of my advice or assistance either at home or abroad?" (xiv.50). Laelius merely reiterates the Stoic claim, made in *De Finibus,* that there is a real sense in which friends can be said to need each other, and much more than anyone can be said to "need" any other external. For the Stoics readily acknowledge that the attainment of virtue is dependent upon friends. To be deprived of friends who can offer one moral counsel, even material assistance, is therefore, in some sense, to be deprived of something without which one remains incomplete. Laelius himself readily admits that "virtue *cannot* attain her highest aims unattended" (xxii.82). Indeed, for him, there is a sense in which, by bringing us into relationships of mutual assistance, nature intended us to come to rely upon each other for the fulfillment of our inner nature. For he says, "nature, loving nothing solitary, always strives for some sort of support, and man's best support is a very dear friend" (xxiii.82).

These two passages appear to leave Laelius in a state of flagrant self-contradiction, conceding, at one moment, that friendship arises from the mutual need of friends for each other and denying this fact the next. The contradiction is to be resolved as follows: although we depend upon friends materially and spiritually to attain virtue, we do not need them once virtue has been attained.[18] For virtue itself is the condition of not needing anything in order to be virtuous. One might well ask then, why the friendship endures when friends outgrow need of each other.[19] The answer is that it is too late. The bonds of friendship have already been formed. The friend is now another self.

Still, the picture we hold in our minds of the Stoic friend is confused: the Stoic friend appears to depend upon his companion for the provision of his needs, and he even faces hardship alongside him, fully expecting their friendship somehow to "lessen the burden of adversity by dividing and sharing it" (vi.22). Yet, their friendship is neither sought out for, nor contingent upon, either friend's ability to provide what the other lacks.

In the dialogue, the personage who embodies this Stoic friend is none other than Laelius, the closest companion of the recently departed Scipio, who is described as a man "dependent on no one." We are first introduced to him as a man whose *sapientia* consists in considering all his possessions to lie in himself (cf. *omnia tua in te posita esse ducas*: ii.7). But the question of how such independence coexists with the dependence of friends upon each other is raised almost immediately, at the same time as is raised the question of how Laelius has borne Scipio's passing. If he is a true friend, we expect him to admit to feeling that his friend's death has deprived him of something he needed and of which he now feels the painful loss. Laelius' response is instead, "I am indeed moved by the loss of a friend such as no man ever was to me, and whom I can confirm, no one ever will be." But he adds, "I am not without the remedy," this being his knowledge of the fact that anyone who is pained by his own inconveniences in this way "is a lover not of his friend, but of himself" (ii.10). This is to say, if one needed something from a friend, one never loved *him* to begin with—only what he could give.

Scaevola asks Laelius if he is right in concluding that not even the death of a close friend could keep such a man as himself from the discharge of his sacred duties. This is his way of asking if he needed Scipio to be virtuous. If he *needed* Scipio to be virtuous, two things follow: First, he was never really virtuous in the first place. To be virtuous he needed something outside himself to lean upon and prop up his virtue. If, however, he had achieved complete virtue, he should have been able to perform virtuously after Scipio's death. Second, he did not really love Scipio. He merely viewed him as a means to achieve a needed end—in this case, virtue. If he had achieved complete virtue, however, he could love Scipio solely as another self.

It remains unclear whether Laelius was, as he claimed to be, sick, or whether he was in fact too distraught to emerge from mourning on the one day he failed to discharge his duties. Scaevola assumes the best, observing of Laelius, "You bear with self-control the pain you accept with the death of a very great man and friend." Laelius graciously accepts the compliment, adding, "[N]o personal inconvenience ought to have kept me from the discharge duty," and further averring, "[N]or do I think it possible for any event of this nature to keep a man of strong character from his duty" (ii.8). Yet he does not deny the truth of what Scaevola says when he adds, "[N] either could you be unmoved" (*nec potuisse non commoveri:* ii.8).

The paradox with which we are confronted is that the greater one's self-sufficiency and the less one *needs* a friend, the better a friend one becomes. Here is how Cicero puts it: "And it is far from being true that friendship is cultivated because of need; rather, it is cultivated by those who are most abundantly blessed with wealth and power and especially with virtue, which is man's best defense; by those least in need of another's help; and by those most generous and given to acts of kindness" (xiv. 50). Paradoxically, he who "needs" his friend least is the man who can best care for his friend's needs. He is "most generous and given to acts of kindness" because he can give without need of return. The most self-reliant friend is the friend upon whom one can depend to care most, the toughest friend, the most tender. The greatest friends, then—those who become least dependent upon each other—end bonded in greatest interdependence.

The continuing love of two self-reliant friends for each other can only be explained by the Stoic conception of desire. It explains why each could love the other *without* lacking or needing him. For the Stoics, we desire what "belongs to us" as the means by which virtue *may*, but need not, be actualized. We desire the friend because he may help us to actualize our virtue, not because we necessarily need him to actualize it.

The actor need not be said to *lack* or to *need* any of the particulars after which she strives or to *depend* upon those particulars for the meeting of some internal need in order to strive after them. To pursue a desired object is to engage in an activity that is completely *self-sufficing*; it does not need to culminate in the attainment of the desired end in order to appear *finished* or *complete* (*Fin.* IV.xxi). Virtue itself, we might say, consists in nothing more than the undaunted pursuit of choice-worthy objects regardless of what befalls one. This, we might say, is why a woman who is virtuous in general also has the particular virtue of initiating friendships.[20] She pursues them undauntedly, conscious that she will not have retrospectively lost all reason for pursuing an object if she fails in the attempt. As we shall see all the more in what follows, the exercise our own virtue is not only the *result of* but also the *precondition for* a friendship of any longevity.

Friendship Made to Last

Laelius is reminded of the words of his departed friend, Scipio, who was often heard to remark that "no one thing was harder than for a friendship to continue until the very end of life" (x.34). For as he will later aver, "some cause of offence arises and we suddenly break the bonds of friendship asunder before it has run but half its course" (xxiii.86). These are, of course, the most frequent reasons Scipio saw for the dissolution of friendship:

> Now he, indeed, used to say that nothing was harder than for a friendship to continue until the end of life; for it often happened either that the friendship ceased to be mutually advantageous, or the parties to it did not entertain the same political views; and that, frequently too, the dispositions of men were changed, sometimes by adversity, and sometimes by the increas-

ing burdens of age. And then he would draw an illustration of this principle from the analogy of early life. "For," he said, "the most ardent attachments of boyhood are often laid aside with the boyish dress; but if continued to the time of manhood, they are broken off sometimes by rivalry in courtship, or sometimes by a contest for some advantage, in which both parties to the friendship cannot be successful at the same time. But should the friendship continue for a long time, it is often overthrown when a struggle for office happens to arise; for while, with the generality of men, the greatest bane of friendship is the lust for money, with the greatest men it is the strife for preferment and glory, and from this source have frequently sprung the deadliest enmities between the dearest friends. (x.34)

Lealius' answer to the question of how to make friendships last is not immediately forthcoming, but it is foreshadowed in passages like these. The problem is that many a friendship is based upon the Aristophanic assumption that the strongest ties bind similar people into a union of like and like. Scipio does not deny that two similar natures will be drawn together. In boyhood, our attachments will not extend beyond family members and those playmates who like the same games (xx.73). But he does say that a resemblance of character is not a sound basis for a love that will survive the changes that friends' dispositions undergo with time, and indeed must undergo as each friend's virtue is perfected. Much less can any present resemblance between two individuals serve as any guarantee of their future resemblance. Each friend's disposition is likely to fluctuate and vary, especially—and this is all important for the Stoics—as circumstances change, leading her to abandon a course of action for the sake of a perceived good, or for fear of a perceived evil. But let us return to this.

What then of a relationship based on the kind of love Socrates describes if it is based upon each friend's agonistic pursuit of virtue? If the friend is just as much needed to compensate for a deficiency, in this case, a deficiency of virtue, it shares the same fate.[21] For we cannot enlist the friend's assistance in our quest for virtue for long before the same friend who once sped us along the way to virtue's attainment becomes a stumbling block in our path. The friendship being a good merely subsidiary and instrumental to that higher good's attainment, it is readily cast aside in moments in which we must decide where our loyalties truly lie—with the ones we love or with our own virtue. Anyone who has read the *Symposium* will immediately recognize that this is one of the pitfalls of the Socratic approach to love.

Suffice it to say that a lasting relationship results neither from Aristophanic nor Socratic love. A sound basis for friendship resides neither in similarity of disposition nor entirely in the desire for virtue, but in the attainment thereof. First, Cicero finds a sound basis for a lasting relationship in the coincidence or harmony of opinions to which he alludes in the passage above. Placing much greater weight on quarrels than most philosophers would condescend to, Cicero claims that there can be no lasting friendship between two individuals prone to disagree with each other, and he presumes that friendship will be especially difficult among men whose opinions diverge on those questions of life and death raised in the political arena.[22]

However, the agreement between the two friends is impossible without the agreement of each friend with himself. For "since the effect of friendship is to make, as it were, one soul out of many, how will that be possible if not even in one man taken by himself shall there be a soul always one and the same, but fickle, changeable, and manifold?" (*sed varius, commutabilis, multiplex*: xxv.92).

Here, Cicero gives expression to the very old and venerable truth to which Plato gave voice when he wrote in his *Lysis* that "the bad, as is also said of them, are never like even their own selves, being so ill-balanced and unsteady (*emplēktous te kai astathmētous*) and when a thing is unlike itself and variable (*anomoion kai diaphoron*) it can hardly become like or friend (*homoion hē philon*) to anything else" (*Lys.* 214d1–3). This is the same point Aristotle made about the man who did not appear to be "amicably disposed even to himself." He observed of bad men that "their soul is rent by faction, and one element in it by reason of its wickedness grieves when it abstains from certain acts, while the other part is pleased, and one draws them this way and the other that, as if they were pulling them in pieces" (*NE* 1166b19–22). This being so, Aristotle concluded, we must "strain every nerve to avoid wickedness and should endeavor to be good; for so and only so can one be either friendly to one's self or friendly to another" (*NE* 1166b26–29).

Cicero adds to the observation that one cannot be in agreement with another if one is not in agreement with oneself, one additional insight. He adds that disagreements will only arise among the nonvirtuous (xx.77), since it is they who are in disagreement with themselves. As he puts it, "when the characters of friends are blameless, then there should be a complete harmony of opinions and inclinations between them without exception" (xvii.61), because they never disagree with themselves. This will be explained at greater length below. For the time being, we need only dwell on the one thing of which Laelius is utterly convinced: "But this I do feel first of all—that friendship cannot exist except among the virtuous" (iv.18). He then equates the ability to remain in accord with oneself with the classical Stoic virtues of *stabilitas* and *constantia*. Laelius says of virtue that "in her is harmony, in her stability, in her constancy" (xxvii.100). By the "good men" among whom he thinks friendship possible, he means men of *magna constantia*, "great constancy" (v.19). In short, when Laelius says that friendship can only exist among the virtuous, he must be interpreted to mean that friendship can only exist among those whose ability to remain in accord with themselves is guaranteed by their unwavering and unflinching Stoic virtue.

The Limits of Friendship

Some questions cannot be answered before others, and the question of how to make love last is one difficult to answer before one first has an answer to the question of when friendship has gone too far and ought to be curtailed before it outlasts its reason for being. The question to receive immediate attention is then the question of "how far love ought to go in friendship" (*quatenus amor in amicitia progredi debeat*: xi.36).

Here Laelius feels called to respond to those so-called sages who argue that each man has enough and more than enough things of his own and it is an aggravation to be involved in others (*statis superque esse sibi suarum cuique rerum: alienis nimis implicari molestum esse*)."These sages say "that it is best to hold the reigns of friendship as loosely as possible, so that we may draw them up or slacken them at will; for they say, an essential of a happy life is freedom from care." These men cut a crude caricature of the Stoic, remaining aloof and detached from others "lest it be necessary for one man to be disturbed for many" (*ne necesse sit unum sollicitum esse pro pluribus*), all to achieve a "freedom from care" (*securitatem*), which they believe is impossible "if one labors for many" (*parturiat unus pro pluribus*: xiii.45). But in the man who shields himself from upsets occasioned by emotional entanglement, he recognizes nothing of the Stoic friend he idealizes. He not only denies that a friend should approach a relationship with reluctance, lest he become too enmeshed in the lives of others, but that it is by an irresistible force of nature that we are drawn to do what we should, "to grant our friends whatever they wish, or to get from them whatever we wish," with the least possible hesitation and the greatest possible zeal (xiv.48; xi.38).

But can we really, along with the lovers who figure in Aristophanes' speech, allow ourselves to be fused with others for a lifetime, completely allowing our own identities to be submerged in their own, to remain at one in thought and action with the ones we love? If their thoughts were our thoughts, their desires our desires, then by those means and those means alone, would we fully realize the ideal of loving another as ourselves, since in that case alone could we say we loved them as ourselves, giving no preference to ourselves.

Marking out the *termini diligendi* or the "boundary lines of care" is necessary because we have to choose between the three traditional ways of doling out love. But Cicero refuses to agree with his predecessors that we must either (1) care for friends no more than ourselves, (2) care for them as much as they care for us, or (3) care for them to the same degree that they care for themselves (xvi.56). Complaining that all three ways of meting out care make something miserly and stingy of what appears "richer and more abundant" (*divitior . . . et adfluentior*), he protests that, in friendship, "there need be no fear that some bit of kindness will be lost, and that it will overflow the measure and spill upon the ground, or that more than is due will be poured into friendship's bin" (xvi.58).

If there is any reason to question the uninhibited outpouring of love, it is because it sometimes seems to deplete one's virtue. Many examples of this could be found in Rome. And in fact the most common problem Cicero observed firsthand was the following: A Roman statesman asks a friend to compromise his principles. The friend refuses, and his friend interprets the refusal as a betrayal (x.34). It all raises the question of what one should do when a friend appears to come between one and one's virtue, and whether one should allow virtue to be sacrificed to the demands of friendship, or whether one should, instead, put limits on friendship for the sake of virtue.[23]

Though he would rather seek his virtuous ends in company with Alcibiades, Socrates ultimately refuses to subordinate the attainment of virtue to the meeting of those of Alcibiades' needs he judges to be base in comparison with his own. Something is presciently revealed when Socrates explains why he rebuffs Alcibiades' advances. He will have to meet Alcibiades' needs at the cost of his wisdom and virtue and receive something of comparatively paltry value in return, a trade that he compares to that of gold for bronze (*Sym.* 218e–19a). This shows that however much he may be said to want the best for Alcibiades, Socrates, in refusing Alcibiades' advances, does keep his love for Alcibiades from extending so far as to acquiesce to his every desire; the conduciveness of affection to the attainment of virtue is ultimately the standard by which one decides, in individual instances, whether it is to be given or withheld.

Laelius says that friendship should not be abandoned too quickly at the first sign that a friend's wishes conflict with one's own virtuous aims. Even a friend who proves nonvirtuous is to be tolerated once chosen: "Indeed, Scipio thought that, even if we had been unfortunate in our choice of friends, we should endure it rather than plan an opportunity for a breach" (xvi.59). For, as he says, "if by some chance the wishes of a friend are not altogether honorable and require to be forwarded in matters which involve his life or reputation, we should turn aside from the straight path, provided however that utter disgrace does not follow" (xvii.61).[24] On the other hand, he says that friends "must not think themselves so bound that they cannot withdraw from friends who are sinning" lest they become complicit in their vice (xii.42).

Laelius' verdict is once again paradoxical because we can *neither* completely subordinate love to virtue, nor virtue to love. We cannot think, as Aristophanes does, that our individual aims can be subordinated to communion with the loved one. (It is noteworthy that, for Aristophanes, it is so as to be sure that we never endanger this union that we not seek to rival the gods.) However, we cannot simply think, as Socrates seems to, that virtue is that for the sake of which affection is given or withheld. Cicero is attempting some compromise between these two extremes.

Laelius' inability to give a straightforward, noncontradictory, response to the question of whether virtue always trumps love, or vice versa, is due to the fact that giving an answer, in the Platonic terms in which the debate is framed, is difficult for anyone subscribing to the theory of *oikeiōsis*. Given that theory of desire, any dichotomy that might be drawn between union with the beloved, on the one hand, and virtue, on the other, is a *false* dichotomy. That is because, as was previously remarked, the love that causes one to serve another is the same love that provides the conditions for the realization of the loved one's virtue. Your friend's love is the living substance of which your virtue is composed. Conversely, your friend's love for you literally becomes an essential part of the virtuous person you are becoming, and thus, the love which you feel for that person is exactly the same as the love you feel for your own virtue. In theory, it should be impossible to conceive drawing a distinction between serving one's own virtue and serving one's friend. The friend *is* our virtue, and our virtue *is* the friend.

Laelius can be found at one time asserting the necessity of putting virtue before love, and at another, the necessity of putting love before virtue, but it seems unlikely that a rhetorical mind like Cicero's could not have recognized such a contradiction. Much more likely is the possibility that he wanted to portray Laelius caught in a bind—affirming first that, as that for which friendship is sought, virtue is that to which friendship must be subordinated, and later, that you must occasionally sacrifice your own virtue to another person's much baser needs precisely in order to reach new heights of virtue.[25] What he is showing us through Laelius is that, since there is no virtue without love and vice versa, it is impossible to say that one should, in all circumstances, be subordinated to the other.

When this dichotomy drawn between virtue and friendship does become relevant is when our friends behave in such a way that we are confronted with the agonizing realization that our interests lie in different places: our love for a friend leads us in one direction; virtue calls us in another. Then, we have to make a choice between the two. This only occurs, of course, when our friends stray from the course of virtue. For were they to travel it unswervingly, our paths would perfectly coincide.

Thus, the more Laelius struggles to articulate the conditions that must be in place for lasting friendship to take hold, the more we see his discourse revolve back toward the original premise from which it took its departure: virtue is that which creates the bond of friendship and preserves it (xxvii.100). Yet, what we observe is that not just *any* kind of virtue will do. We need a virtue that will neither falter nor flag, one that will not waver or wane. That is because, as Laelius so often comments, the virtue which most men initially seem to us to possess is one that soon proves itself inconstant. It does so because men are too easily tempted from the path of virtue by the lure of external goods. They deviate from the course of action they should undertake because they are beckoned by the siren song of fame, fortune, pleasure, and comfort.

Thus, it is left for us to surmise that the only people who will be able to withstand these enticements without compromising their virtue will be those who pursue the good without allowing their activity to be interrupted by external attachments or the passions they arouse. In other words, those who possesses the particular kind of virtue requisite for a lasting friendship are model Stoics.

Of course, this is only to make, in a different way, the same point that Laelius makes when he says that the friend has to remain consistent with, and in agreement with, himself. For the very word that is used to describe that state of agreement with oneself, *constantia*, is also the same word that denotes an ability to remain imperturbable and unwavering in the face of externals. This is why the Stoics always found it usefully applied to the person who pursued the path of virtue without allowing himself to be deflected from it by passion-provoking externals. *Constantia* was, for them, the virtue *par excellence*, and by the end of the dialogue, we can see that despite Laelius' initial hesitancy to say more about it than that it was displayed by the great men of Rome past, it is undoubtedly *the* virtue he has in mind when he says that virtue "creates the bond of friendship and preserves it" (xxvii.100).

The consequences are several. First, the difficulty is to find friends who will not compromise their own virtue, and with it, the whole friendship, under pressure from externals:

> But the fair thing is, first of all, to be a good man yourself, and then to seek another like yourself. It is among good men that this stability of friendship, which I have been treating for some time, may be made secure; and when united by ties of goodwill, they will first of all subdue those passions to which other men are slaves; and, next, they will delight in what is equitable and accords with the law, and they will go to all lengths for each other; they will not demand anything of each other unless it is honorable and just, and they will not only cherish and love, but they will also revere, each other. (xxii.82)

We need to know that our friends can be relied upon not to swerve from the path of virtue and ask us to follow suit. But this requires that the initial impression we have that they are virtuous not be dispelled, and that they not give way to erratic and inconstant whims, conflicting with the longing for virtue. This is all the more important because the things to which we would sacrifice our friends' interests often have the look of virtue. But, in a society that places so much emphasis on the agonistic pursuit of honor—the shadow of virtue—Laelius asks, "[W]here shall we find those who do not put office, civil and military rank, high place and power, above friendship, so that when the former advantages are placed before them on the one side and the latter on the other they will not much prefer the former?" (xvii.63).

Returning then to the question of whether virtue or love holds precedence, the difficulty is not so much to choose which of the two is more important—virtue or love—since neither can exist without the other. The difficulty is to prevent from ever arising a situation in which we might have to choose between the two. If one of two friends "veers from the path of virtue," to use a common Stoic expression, then their paths will diverge, and one friend will have to decide what he loves more—his companion along the road of life, or the destination they originally had in mind in undertaking their shared journey. A truly enduring friendship is one in which the path that one friend travels perpetually coincides with the path his friend travels to the same end; neither friend ever needs to choose between pursuing his *telos* or furthering his friend along the route to less worthy ends.

However, a practical problem emerges when Laelius claims, "We ought, therefore, to choose men who are firm, stable, and constant, a class of which there is a great dearth; and at the same time it is very hard to come to a decision without a trial, while such trial can only be made in friendship" (xvii.62). For there is indeed one further sense in which only two Stoics will be capable of initiating a friendship, if it is indeed true that "you should love (*diligere*) your friend after you have appraised (*dilexeris*) him; you should not appraise him after you have begun to love him" (xxii.85). The impulse to sacrifice oneself without reserve is one that cannot be given way to *until* the virtue of the would-be friend is proven. The friend's character will, however, only reveal itself by degrees, as we give her more and more favors that she then returns. In this way, the bonds of friendship are slowly but surely strengthened, but the whole process must be brought to a halt once one party reveals her untrustworthiness, and her unworthiness for friendship. Too often, however, "friendship outruns the judgment and takes away the opportunity for a trial. . . . Hence it is the part of wisdom to check the headlong rush of goodwill as we would a chariot, and thereby so manage friendship that we would in some degree put the dispositions of friends, as we do those of horses, to a preliminary test" (xvii.63). Here we have a Platonic image, the image of the charioteer dragged by his horses. In Cicero's *œuvre*, the metaphor not only stands for the onrush of unchecked emotion, but the thing that causes it—reason's rushing ahead, hastily jumping to conclusions.[26] What this means is that friendship is only capable of being entered into by those who can restrain themselves from putting undue faith in the idea that their love will be returned and allowing themselves to be carried away by this belief.[27]

We may now venture an explanation of the relationship between friendship and erotic love. Erotic love is characterized by *erōs*, a particular form of love that usually involves the idealization of a person's character accompanied by the headlong impulse to possess them. For this reason, it is a feeling so intensely felt lovers give themselves over completely to each other long before they have any assurance that that relation can stand the test of time. Friendship seems to involve all the erotic components of romantic love, but without its pitfalls.[28]

Friends Old and New

For Aristophanes, love must be a lifelong attachment with an individual who cannot be replaced, else it is no love at all. But, for Socrates, the ties that bind seem never to be permanent, and the lover, faithless by nature, seems fated to find in an increasing variety of individuals what he first sought in his beloved. Accordingly, the question is raised of whether our attachments to one particular person are long lasting as Aristophanes suggests, or necessarily short lived and transitory, as Socrates would have it. For Cicero, it becomes necessary to answer the same question in a more practical way when it is put to him in the form of a question about when we should abandon old friends for new ones who show more promise. For him, the question is, "Are new friends who are worthy of friendship at any time to be preferred to old friends, as we are wont to prefer young horses to old?" (xix.67).

Again the two extremes between which Cicero's position negotiates evoke those of Socrates' and Aristophanes' speeches. For Socrates, the fact that relationships are born of a search for the *kalon*, for the "fine, beautiful, and virtuous," seems to entail that one is goaded onward in hot pursuit of ever greater degrees of it. There is even a tragic sense in which the virtue that a lover spies in another person and that is made "his own" can only ever have the effect of making the lover more virtuous, but therefore thirstier for a virtue that the beloved no longer suffices to supply. The virtue that one finds in one person is never enough in comparison with that which is eventually found elsewhere, so the same love that fixes on a particular person also carries us away from him, onward and upward, in pursuit of ever greater heights of virtue.

The future hope of attaining more of what one has—which is for Socrates a structural necessity, since one only wants that of which one could have a greater share—is foreign to Aristophanes because his claim seems to be that love is born, not of a desire for what one does *not yet* have, but of a need to recover what one *once* had but lost. For him desire is the feeling that we lack something, which can only be explained by the fact that we feel the absence of that which we once had. For this reason, desire is always a backward glance toward a moment in the past that has withdrawn from us; it always takes the form of a kind of nostalgia for the old and the familiar, whereas for Socrates, it is a forward-looking aspiration for a future good.

The choice between old and new friends is an important one because it is really a decision about whether the truest love is felt for the old and familiar or for that which promises a better future, but Cicero explains why neither account captures the whole truth about love. To believe that the old and familiar is where love lies is to believe that things grow lovable simply by virtue of our longtime association with them, or that having a shared past is enough to provide a stable basis for a relationship: "[N]or should men

who in boyhood were devoted to hunting and games of ball, keep as their
intimates those who they loved (*dilixerunt*) at that period simply because
they were fond of the same pursuits. For on that principle nurses and the
slaves who attended us to and from school, will, by right of priority of
acquaintance, claim the largest share of our goodwill" (xx.74). Meanwhile,
it would be heartless to assert that a shared past is of such little importance
that nothing keeps us from abandoning old friends for new ones when
their virtue captures our eye: "[Y]et the old friendships must preserve their
place, for the force of age and habit is very great. Nay, even in the case of
the horse just now referred to, everybody, nothing preventing, would rather
use one to which he is accustomed than one that is untrained and new.
And habit is strong not only in the case of animate but inanimate things,
since we delight even in places, though rugged and wild, in which we have
lived for a fairly long time" (xix.68). The example suggests a cooperation
between horse and rider that becomes possible when one learns the other's
habits and how to respond to them, and working in perfect harmony, both
are transformed into a single well-tuned machine. The way in which we are
habituated to others is an indication that they have indeed become a part
of us over time, since their own habits have become so bound up with our
own as to be inseparable from them. Thus, Cicero's answer to the question
of when to keep old friends and when to seek new ones is the following:

> The doubt is unworthy of a human being, for there should be
> no surfeit of friendships as there is of other things; and, as in
> the case of wines that improve with age, the oldest friendships
> ought to be the most delightful; moreover, the well-known ad-
> age is true: "Men must eat many a peck of salt together before
> the claims of friendship are fulfilled." But new friendships are
> not to be scorned if they offer hope of bearing fruit, like green
> shoots of corn that do not disappoint us at harvest time. (xvii.65)

Cicero's response is that we must try to heed both of these imperatives
simultaneously. On the one hand, the virtue of which we catch sight in new
acquaintances is something we can never get enough of, and we are therefore
called to let as many new friendships as possible blossom between us and
those we admire.[29] Socrates is right in this sense. On the other hand, this
imperative must be balanced with a deep respect for the kind of unity that
can only be built up over time, since this unity, after all, the product of a
long exchange of favors, and since one of the truest forms love takes is a
feeling of longing for that which has been, and continues to be, a part of us.

Even without using the word *oikeion*, Cicero seems well aware of the two senses it had for the Greeks. It could be understood to connote that which is "close to home" in the sense of "old and familiar," but it could also be understood to connote that which is bound up with our own well-being, and therefore "that in which our future good lies." The paradox with which the *Lysis* ends and begins is that, since the words we use to describe "dear ones" embrace both of these meanings simultaneously, we can never decide whether our love for them is primarily a nostalgia for what is old and familiar or an eagerness for what is yet unattained. For Cicero, the theory of *oikeiōsis* explains why love both returns to the past and looks forward to the future, why it is as much a form of nostalgia as anticipation. This is indeed why Laelius can be found to describe love as something that projects a bright ray of hope into the future" (*bonam spem praelucet in postremum*) and equally as a longing that follows upon the memory of friends long deceased (vii.23).

If a compromise can be struck between the promiscuous and monogamous views of human nature, then surely it can be found in Cicero. A relationship should last, but an old companion is not, simply by virtue of being familiar, inherently good. How and when to dissolve a friendship is a question referred to the need to preserve the continuity of friendship—without which one cannot derive its full benefits—and the equally important need to make sure that past ties do not stifle and thwart the pursuit of future virtue.

Love as Abundance

The most important question is simply in what sense we may be said to *need* or *desire* another. For Aristophanes, the loved one was once near and close at hand, but is now lacking. For Socrates, the other may possess something that we presently possess *in some measure*, but that we seek to secure for the future. But it must be proposed that if the Stoics have an intellectual forebearer it is neither Socrates nor Aristophanes; it is Agathon, or rather Agathon *before* he is compelled by Socrates to admit that the desirer "must have desire for what it lacks, and again, have no desire if he has no lack" (*Sym.* 200b2).

The Stoics believe what Socrates forces Agathon to deny, that the strong have a desire for the strong, the virtuous for the virtuous. They assert that, while we all desire virtue, those who are most virtuous most eagerly put themselves at the service of another and give of themselves in a way that manifests *true* love. This is what is meant by describing love as neither the offspring of poverty nor want, but of abundance and self-sufficiency. For Cicero, those who are most abundant in virtue and those who find the most resources for it in themselves are those most capable of true love.

But lest this self-sufficiency, which is at the root of love, be taken for what it is not, we must distinguish it from emotional distance. Cicero is absolutely clear that we cannot root out from our hearts the *humanitas* that binds us to other people. Even though emotional ties can sometimes become strained in a way that causes emotional upset, that pain we feel as a result "has no more power to banish friendship from life than it has to cause us to reject certain cares and annoyances" (xiii.48). "For," as he argues, "it is inconsistent not to undertake any honorable business or course of conduct, or to lay it aside when undertaken, in order to avoid anxiety. Nay, if we continually flee from trouble, we must also flee from virtue, who necessarily meets with some trouble in rejecting and loathing things contrary to herself" (xiii.47). Thus, he says that "if we flee care and worry, then virtue too is to be fled" (*si curam fugimus, virtus fugienda est*: xiii.47).

In Laelius we find an example of this self-sufficiency. We have in him a man who "finds all his belongings in himself" and who therefore finds complete contentment in exercising his own virtue. Able to exercise his virtue contentedly and without being distracted by externals or the pull they exert upon him, he is able to continue in that direction without interference from exterior events. Laelius' ties to Scipio were strengthened through their exchange of favors given and received. Indeed, this is how each came to regard the other, not just as a part of *his life*, but a part of *himself* with whom his own well-being became intertwined. Of course, the ties binding them together *could* be strengthened because at no point in the process of their strengthening did one friend ever abandon virtue, an event that would have called the process of unification to an abrupt halt, not just because it would have destroyed the source of their mutual attraction, but because, if one friend had strayed from the path of virtue, it would have destroyed that harmony of *mores* that is the basis of friendship. For "difference of *mores* is attended by difference of desires or pursuits" (*dispares enim mores disparia studia sequuntur*), and Cicero says that it is this *dissimilitudo* or "difference" that dissolves friendships (xx.74). Meanwhile, Laelius and Scipio were able to live in close and lasting union because they "enjoyed that wherein lies the whole essence of friendship—the most complete agreement in policy, and in pursuits, and opinions" (iv.15).

With the intertwinement of two mutually sustaining lives comes a kind of mutual reliance, but while, for the Stoics, our lives become deeply intertwined with another's, we are not reduced to a state of "dependency." According to Cicero, we come to "depend" upon friends in the certain limited sense of habitually relying upon them to do for us what we might do for ourselves. There is nothing wrong with this state of "dependency"—so long as it remains a state of dependency in name alone. But if we really do come to "depend" upon friends to provide us with what we cannot provide ourselves, then that very dependency will be the friendship's demise. For when we admit that we depend on friends for things we cannot provide ourselves, we admit that there exist things so valued that friendship can come second in importance to them. As Cicero says in *De Finibus*, the very externals for which friendship is sought will be its undoing (*Fin.* III.xxi.70).

The same would hold if virtue were like an external end. If virtue were merely the external end to which the friend was an external means, then the loved object's failure to provide a direct means to that end would make the claims of friendship dispensable. Every time a conflict arose, and one was forced to choose between pursuing virtue and attempting to meet the needs of a friend, the friend could be neglected as easily as Socrates neglects Alicibiades.

However, if the virtue the lover seeks is something he is already *completely self-sufficient to realize himself* whenever he chooses to actualize his own *inner* potential, then virtue does not have the status of an external end to which the friend is merely a convenient but dispensable means. With virtue being a desired end, the resources for the attainment of which lie *within ourselves*, the friend is saved from being a means to an end.

Friends contribute to our virtue, but insofar as they do so, they come to be regarded, not as a tool, but as an intrinsic part of our being. They literally become a *part* of ourselves in a way that makes it possible to say that "one who looks on a friend looks on an image of himself" (vii.23). Curiously, what this means is that, even when the friend's urges are base and nonvirtuous, we still feel them with the same urgency as our own. Such blurring of the lines between ourselves and others becomes striking in the following lines: "For everyone loves himself, not with a view to acquiring some profit from himself from his self-love, but because he is dear to himself on his own account; and unless this same feeling were transferred to friendship, the real friend would never be found; for he is, as it were, another self" (xxi.80). The passage shows that, though the friend is a part of us, as Aristophanes says, we cannot draw the conclusion that the beloved is desired as the external compensation for some internal lack. If we needed the beloved to "complete" us, the other would still serve us in a merely instrumental capacity, as something that "completed" us by giving us what we could not give ourselves. It is actually because we love the other as though he were ourselves that we cannot be said to instrumentalize our friends any more than we could ever be said to instrumentalize ourselves. Friends do not complete us in the way that Aristophanes suggests, by supplying us with that of which, when removed, we feel the lack. If it were otherwise, then with Scipio's death, Laelius would be left wanting, incomplete, and lacking. As we know, he does not feel any of these emotions.

In what sense then may we be said to want or need others? In a certain sense, we cannot be said to "need" our friends at all as long as we can exercise our virtue independently, as indeed we must before we come to truly love them. If what we needed friends to supply us were anything but the virtue we already possessed, then our love for them would never become true *benevolentia*.

Meanwhile, if a relationship is to last long enough to become true love it must be based on something that is not likely to change, and since virtue is, by definition, the only thing synonymous with constancy and firmness in the face of external change, it alone serves as the only constant and firm foundation for a friendship. In other words, it is precisely because virtue is defined as a stable character of mind, unlikely to be destabilized by externals, that it becomes the only stable basis for friendship.

In conclusion, both Socrates' and Aristophanes' positions are misguided insofar as they rest upon the assumption that love and desire are born of a kind of lack that the object of attachment is supposed to fill, while love is actually born of an internal abundance of the very thing we seek outside ourselves in another—virtue.

Such a conclusion, in turn, enables us to grasp the difference between Stoic friendship and romantic love. Lovers like Aristophanes usually believe they are incomplete without each other, a suspicion borne out when the relationship ends and each discovers that he or she has depended upon the other to supply something without which he or she is incomplete. Stoic friendship, as I hope to have shown, involves all of the erotic components of romantic love, but without its shortcomings and imperfections. A perfect friendship is one in which each friend relies upon the other to give something, but neither quite depends upon the friend to give what is lacked. Characterized by the dynamic of love without need, desire without want, this more perfect friendship becomes a model for all human relationships in Stoicism. This is not to say, however, that romantic infatuation cannot give way to friendship nor to deny that many of the important favors exchanged between friends are sexual in kind.[30] The Stoics would undoubtedly agree that the test of a friend is his ability to provide for physical needs and that Alcibiades was owed more favors than he received.

I have concluded, in sum, that the Stoics did not describe desire as arising from a lack that the desired object needed to fill. This explains why Laelius appears to contradict himself in several instances. The contradiction is merely apparent in each case. First, he says that we are attracted to those who are similar to ourselves and then says that we are attracted to the virtuous. Both are true if we recall the Stoic doctrine of *oikeiōsis*: Since we are attracted to those who appear as the means by which our own virtue may actualize itself, we are initially attracted to those who *are* similar to ourselves, and then to those who have begun to *be* a part of the virtuous person we are becoming. But since the only person who can continuously foster our virtue, rather than impede it, is a virtuous person, it would be correct to say that those to whom we remain *most* attached *in the long term* are those who are *most* virtuous. Second, Laelius remarks that friends need each other, and then again, that they do not need each other at all. Again, on the Stoic theory of *oikeiōsis,* both are true: we desire our friends because they appear as necessary parts of the virtuous person we are becoming, but on the other hand, we should desire them without needing them. Third, Laelius sometimes speaks as though we must refuse friends no favors and maintain friendship at all costs. At others, he speaks as though we must put conditions on friendship and break ties when, instead of helping us to attain virtue, friends interpose between us and virtue. Here again, both positions have their truth: all we can do is strike a compromise between the two since, according to the Stoic conception of desire, we desire friends neither solely as other selves nor merely as a means to virtue. Fourth, Laelius sometimes tells us to dispense with old friends for more promising new ones, while at other times, he tells us that we should not abandon the old for the new. Again, both statements have their truth insofar as what a friend is is what he or she becomes over time, so that we can neither treat friends as dispensable nor hesitate to dispense with them when they hold us back. In sum, neither Socrates nor Aristophanes has the whole truth.

Notes

1. This is even less a surprise because to *philon* was yet another way of speaking of whatever was near and dear to one, *hoi philoi* being those one considered one's "nearest and dearest." Homer could even use the same word to describe a man's legs as *phila guia*, that is, as "his *own dear* limbs" (*Illiad* 13.85).
2. For Pembroke, the *Lysis* is a dialogue in which Plato shows of how little use it is to say that we love the *oikeion*. Pembroke, "Oikeiosis," in Long 1971, 116.
3. In his chapter entitled "*Philia* in Plato," El Murr avers that Plato *is* able to reconcile both views by advancing the claim that those who desire the good

attract others who desire the good as well. Since we are attracted to those who are similar to us with regard to virtue, it then becomes possible to say that we are attracted both (1) to what is good and (2) to what is similar to ourselves. In what follows, we will see to what extent the Stoics reconciled these two positions in a similar fashion.

4. Cicero's thoughts on friendship are admittedly very Aristotelian in inspiration, and the parallels between them and Aristotle's discussion of friendship in books VIII and IX of the *Nicomachean Ethics* will be apparent to anyone who considers them alongside *De Amicitia*. We know that these ideas may also have come down to Cicero through Aristotle's successor, Theophrastus. He wrote his own book called *De Amicitia*, and Aulus Gellius would later remark, in *Noctes Atticae*, that it "appears to have been read by Cicero." He continues, "What other things he thought proper to borrow from Theophrastus, he transposed, as was the nature of his genius and his taste, most happily and most pertinently" (I 3.11).

5. Our Laelius is none other than Laelius the Wise, so called because of his knowledge of philosophy, particularly Stoic philosophy. He not only studied with Diogenes, but also joined with Scipio in taking lessons from Panaetius while he lived at Scipio's home (*Fin.* II.vii.24). Laelius, however, sometimes disassociates himself from formal Stoic doctrine in this dialogue, a fact which may be accounted for by his apparent desire to convince his audience of a point without requiring of his audience an adherence to the more difficultly swallowed aspects of Stoic doctrine.

6. The Stoics also say that friendship is "a sharing in the things of life, when we treat our friends as we do ourselves" (*DL* vii.124).

7. A concise account of social behavior as described by Cicero and its antecedents in the texts of earlier Stoics can be found in Graver, 2007, 175–78.

8. Readers familiar with Stoicism will recognize this claim as a potentially controversial one in an ongoing debate about Stoic end, or *telos*, the terms of which are best explained in overview by Gill, 2006, 144–66. Briefly put, the question of what the Stoics considered their *telos* to be turns upon the precise nature of a shift Cicero describes individuals to undergo at some point over the course of their development (*Fin.* III.vi.20). The transformation heralds a new appreciation for virtue as one's *telos* in life. But there are at least two competing ways of understanding the new way in which individuals feel motivated to attain this *telos,* once they have realized that they are striving after it. "One which we may call "self-realizationalist," explains the shift in motivation by reference to the idea of realizing, through virtue and knowledge of the good, one's human nature as a rational creature. The other, which we may call "cosmic," stresses, rather, the importance of patterning oneself on the order embodied in the natural universe and of seeing virtue as a way of expressing this order in one's own life and character" (146). But my "self-realizationist" assertion that the Stoics are essentially Aristotelians who believe that we are striving after the full actualization of our human potential, and with it, the full development of our rational faculties, should not be misunderstood to foreclose the further possibility that Stoicism demands of an individual the adherence to an external standard.

9. This applies to friends as well according to Seneca. The virtuous person is so skilled at friend-making that when he loses a friend he is able to find another to substitute in his place (*Ep.* ix.5). For further comment on this passage, see Bernard Collette-Dučić, "Making Friends," in this volume. See further Graver 2007, 183–185.

10. See further Bernard Collette-Dučić, "Making Friends," in this volume.

11. For example, in *De Abstinentia* (III.25, trans. mod.), Porphyry cites Theophrastus as making the following argument: "We define as naturally akin (*oikeious phusei*) those who are born of the same father and mother; next we also consider akin those tracing their descent to the same ancestor; and furthermore, the citizens of the same city because of their sharing the same society and country." Porphyry goes on to argue that animals are akin to us because "their bodies are developed from the same beginnings (*archas*); and by 'beginnings,' I do not mean elements (*stoicheia*), for they are found in plants also, but in such matter as skin, flesh, and the constituent fluids of human beings." See Brink, 1956, 126, for an account of the relationship between *oikeious* and *suggenēs* (cf. kinship and relationship). Goldin 2011, 266, also draws our attention to the way in which, in the *Republic*, one is either *othneios* and *allotrios* (foreign and alien) or *oikeios* and *suggenēs* (akin and related) (470b6–7).

12. The Stoics use the love between parent and child as a model for all love. As Reydams-Schils, 2005, 115–144, has noted, this already seems to set them apart from a dominant strain in the Platonic tradition, which tends to demean loving one's biological kin when one could love one's "spiritual kin" instead.

13. Cicero does not appear to have chosen a single Latin equivalent for this Greek term. He chooses instead to employ turns of phrase which allow him to speak, for example, of those with whom we *congruere*, and therefore to exploit the full range of significance contained in a verb that can denote belonging, suiting, fitting, agreeing with, or corresponding to (viii.27).

14. According to Reydams-Schils, 2005, 160, the crucial difference between the Stoics and Platonists, who also believe that love for family members is to be extended beyond the family, to others, for the benefit of the community at large, is that Platonists claim that, in the *Republic*, "Plato proposes abolishing the ties between spouses and parents and children and replacing them with surrogate community ties."

15. This is Cicero's Latin rendering of the Greek *antiphilein*, which Plato uses in a famous passage in the *Phaedrus* (255c), as well as throughout the *Lysis*.

16. Thus, the other is a literal part of the virtuous man, but a part he can nonetheless lose. Seneca compares the loss of the friend to the loss of a hand or eye: "[I]f an accident cost him an eye, or even both eyes, the remaining parts of him would be sufficient for him; he would be as happy with his body diminished as he would be with it whole" (*Ep.* ix.4).

17. El Murr will have shown us that Plato does not finally dispute the idea that like is attracted to like. He merely doubts, in the *Lysis*, that the bad will be attracted to the bad, making it impossible to say that the principle "like will be

attracted to the like" holds unless the two individuals in question are good (*Lys.* 214d5). For Plato, "like is attracted to like" because two friends will be drawn to each other if they have an identical desire for the good. See further El Murr's chapter entitled "*Philia* in Plato." For Cicero, however, "like attracts like" still holds as a universal law of nature even when it is interpreted in a conventional way. First, "like attracts like" because we are attracted to those who have similar dispositions and interests, and this similarity is the reason why friendships are initiated in the first place. Second, similarity of disposition is also the reason why friends remain bound to each other. The more like our friend we become, the less our desires conflict, and the more it becomes possible to say that the person most similar to us is the person who attracts us most.

18. Until one becomes a sage, according to Seneca, one needs friends in order to become happy. Once one becomes a sage, one no longer needs friends to be happy (*Ep.* ix.15).

19. This problem arises in Plato. If the good have no need of the good, it is they who must least want friendships with good men (*Lys.* 215a).

20. She has the art of making friends described at length in the chapter by Collette-Dučić in this text. For virtue, as the pursuit of choice-worthy ends, always entails the exercise of an art for the Stoic; a special species of this art is the art that pursues the most choice worthy of all ends—friendship. Like the art of life itself, its whole value likes in its exercise rather than in the results it achieves, a fact which explains why Seneca could say that "it is pleasanter to make than to have friends" (*iucundium esse amicum facere quam habere*: *Ep.* ix.7). See Collette-Dučić, "Making Friends."

21. In Plato, it is still difficult to distinguish the philosophic friendship from that in which the friend has merely instrumental value as the means to what the other is internally lacking. There is no doubt that Plato tries to draw this distinction, as we learn from El Murr. But Plato only succeeds in distinguishing the philosophic friendship from the instrumental friendship by claiming that it does not arise from any of the bodily desires that could lead one friend to make the other a means to his own ends. It comes, then from a pure and disinterested love for the other's soul. Plato does not do enough to convince us that this love is not instrumental, or that the friend is only wanted as long as he can give us what we have not got. The Stoics therefore aim to explain what Plato does not—how true friendship differs from the instrumental variety.

22. When Cicero speaks of the value of friendship in the *Tusculan Disputations*, it is also with reference to the friends' "natural harmony and agreement of sentiments throughout the conduct of life" (IV.xxv).

23. The question of whether to put justice before friends or friends before justice seems to have been the most important one that Cicero inherited from Theophrastus' treatise on friendship. Aulus Gellius, however, faults Cicero for not having treated the matter with the same subtlety as his predecessor: "He has omitted to borrow what Theophrastus wrote with equal labor and reflection, and leaving

the more complex and subtle part of the dispute, has given but a few words on the nature of the thing itself" (I.3.20).

24. If Cicero can be criticized for not clearly and consistently dictating how to handle individual situations in which we must weigh friendship against other concerns, his failure to do so is in a way similar to that for which Gellius faults Theophrastus. He does not give us clear enough *praecepta* (I.3.23). But, as Griffin (1997, 86–109) avers, Cicero is writing in 44 to show that there are no easy answers to questions that were on everyone's mind at the time, questions about the competing claims of justice and friendship—the "need" to betray friends for the sake of the *res publica*.

25. Here too, is an answer to a question raised by Bernard Collette-Dučić: Why would a perfectly virtuous man bother to initiate a friendship with a young man of lesser virtue? Collette-Dučić emphasizes the difference in motives between the nonvirtuous and the virtuous when they enter into a new friendship. But Cicero emphasizes the similarity of motives. The non virtuous must have some incentive to do the first favor because it is impossible for us to give without expectation of return. For Cicero, things are not much different for sages. They, like us, pursue a choice-worthy end that can only help them to further increase their virtue. The only difference is that because the virtuous *need* nothing, they are all the more willing to initiate friendship since they see no reason not to give, even when they cannot be sure the gift will be returned. If anything then, the virtuous have *more* reason to initiate a friendship. It matters not whether the virtue of the friend-to-be is merely potential when the relationship is formed. The sage can wait until the seeds he plants bear fruit. It is, one might then suppose, the ability of the nonvirtuous to befriend the virtuous that is in greater need of explanation.

26. In De *Academica* Cicero portrays Chrysippus as responding in the following way to the question of how he will restrain himself from asserting an untruth: "[L]ike a clever charioteer, before I get to the end, I shall pull up my horses, and all the more so if the place they are coming to is precipitous" (*Ac.* II.xxix.94).

27. Arguably, this false belief that lies at the root of erotic passion is concomitant with the belief, described by Brad Inwood 1997, 62, that the beloved is an unconditional and irreplaceable good.

28. The discussion of emotion in chapter 4 of the *Tusculan Disputations* provides Cicero with an opportunity to distinguish the love bearing the Stoic seal of approval and that love which can only be condemned: "All that which is commonly called love (and believe me, I can find no other name to call it by), is of such a trivial nature (*tantae levitatis est*) that nothing, I think, is to be compared to it" (V.xxxiii.70). This kind of lust is inseparable from the erotically charged atmosphere of the Greek gymnasium in which it takes hold, but designating these loves as *libidosos*, Cicero mentions the sanction Plato and the Stoics give to other forms of love. The Stoics specifically sanction love that is a *conatum amicitiae faciendae*, an "attempt to form a friendship." He continues by saying that "provided there is any one in the nature of things without desire, without care, without a sigh, so

be it; for he is free from all lust: but I have nothing to say to him." His quarrel is with a love a little short of *insania* because that arises, like *pertubationes animi,* from the confusion of an apparent with a real good (V.xv).

29. Even the virtuous, we may surmise, are goaded on by the promise of future friendship with the untutored young men they approach, for "having many friends is a good" (*DL* vii.124).

30. That marriage offered the perfect setting for *philia* between men and women was a commonly held view among the Stoics. For a full discussion, see Reydams-Schils, 2005, 148–76.

Bibliography

Aulus Gellius. 1927. *Attic Nights.* Translated by J. C. Rolfe. Cambridge: Loeb Classical Library, Harvard University Press.

Aristotle. 1984. *The Nicomachean Ethics.* Translated by W. D. Ross. In *The Complete Works of Aristotle: The Revised Oxford Translation.* 2 Vols., ed. Jonathan Barnes. Princeton NJ: Princeton University Press.

Brunt, P. A. 1965. "*Amicitia* in the Roman Republic." *Proceedings of the Cambridge Philological Society* 11: 1–20.

Brink, C. O. 1956. "*Oikeiōsis* and *Oikeiotēs*: Theophrastus and Zeno on Nature in Moral Theory." *Phronesis* 1: 123–145.

Cicero. *De Finibus.* 1914. Translated by H. Rackham. Cambridge, MA: Harvard University Press, Loeb Classical Library.

———. *De Officiis.* 1914. Translated by Walter Miller. Cambridge, MA: Harvard University Press, Loeb Classical Library.

———. *De Senectute. De Amicitia. De Divinatione.* 1923. Translated by W. Falconer. Cambridge, MA: Harvard University Press, Loeb Classical Library.

———. *Letters to Atticus,* 5 vols. 1999. Translated by D. R. Shackleton Bailey. Cambridge, MA: Harvard University Press, Loeb Classical Library.

———. *Tusculan Disputations.* 1927. Translated by J. King. Cambridge, MA: Harvard University Press, Loeb Classical Library.

———. *De Natura Deorum. Academica.* 1933. Translated by H. Rackham. Cambridge, MA: Harvard University Press, Loeb Classical Library.

Diogenes Laertius. 1925. *Lives of Eminent Philosophers,* 2 vols. Translated by R. D. Hicks. Cambridge MA: Harvard University Press, Loeb Classical Library.

Endberg-Penderson, Troels. 1990. *The Stoic Theory of Oikeiosis.* Arhuss: Arhuss University Press.

Fortenbaugh, W. 1983. *On Stoic and Peripatetic Ethics: The Work of Arius Didymus.* New Brunswick: Rutgers University Press.

Gadamer, Hans-Georg. 1999. "Friendship and Self-Knowledge: Reflections on the Role of Friendship in Greek Ethics." In *Hermeneutics, Religion and Ethics,* ed. J. Weinsheimer. New Haven: Yale University Press.

————. 1980. "*Logos* and *Ergon* in Plato's *Lysis.*" In *Dialogue and Dialectic: Eight Hermeneutical Studies on Plato,* translated by Christopher Smith. New Haven: Yale University Press.

Gill, Christopher. 2006. *The Structured Self in Hellenistic and Roman Thought.* Oxford: Oxford University Press.

Glidden, D. K. 1981. "The *Lysis* on Loving One's Own." *The Classical Quarterly,* New Series, 31, no. 1: 39–59.

Goldin, Owen. 2011. "Conflict and Cosmopolitanism in Plato and the Stoics." *Apeiron* 44: 264–286.

Graver, Margret. 2007. *Stoicism and Emotion.* Chicago: University of Chicago Press.

Griffin, Miriam. 1989. "From Aristotle to Atticus: Cicero and Matius on Friendship." In *Philosophia Togata: Essays on Philosophy and Roman Society,* ed. M. Griffin and J. Barnes, 86–109. Oxford: Oxford University Press.

Inwood, Brad. 1997. "Why Do Fools Fall in Love?" In *Aristotle and After,* ed. Richard Sorabji, 55–69. London: Institute of Classical Studies.

Keith, Arthur. 1929. "Cicero's Idea of Friendship." *The Swanee Review* 37, no. 1 (Jan.): 51–58.

Long, Anthony, and David Sedley (ed. and trans). 1987. *The Hellenistic Philosophers,* 2 Vols. Cambridge: Cambridge.

Laurand, Valéry. 2007. "L'érôs pédagogique chez Platon et les stoïciens." In *Stoic Platonism, Platonic Stoicism,* ed. Mauro Bonazzi and Christoph Helmig. Leuven: Leuven University Press.

Lesses, Glenn. 1993. "Austere Friends: The Stoics on Friendship." *Apeiron* 26: 57–75.

Pembroke, Simon. 1971. "Oikeiōsis." In *Problems in Stoicism,* ed. Anthony Long, 114–49. London: University of London, Athlone Press.

Plato. 1925. *Lysis, Symposium, Gorgias.* Translated by W. Lamb. Vol. III. Cambridge MA: Harvard University Press; Loeb Classical Library.

Porphyry. 1823. *On Abstinence from Killing Animals.* Translated by Thomas Taylor. London: J. Moyes, Granville Street.

Price, A. W. 1989. *Love and Friendship in Aristotle.* Oxford: Clarendon Press.

————. 2002. "Plato, Zeno, and the Object of Love." In Martha Nussbaum and Juha Shivola, *The Sleep of Reason: Erotic Experience and Sexual Ethics in Ancient Greece and Rome,*170–190. Chicago: The University of Chicago Press.

Reydams-Schils, Gretchen. 2005. *The Roman Stoics: Self, Responsibility, and Affection.* Chicago: University of Chicago Press.

Schofield, Malcolm. 1991. *The Stoic Idea of the City.* Chicago: University of Chicago Press.

Seneca. 1917–1925. *Epistles.* 3 vols. Translated by Richard Gummere. Cambridge, MA: Harvard University Press, Loeb Classical Library.

Vogt, Katja. 2008. *Law, Reason, and the Cosmic City.* Oxford: Oxford University Press.

PART 3

PATRISTIC AND
MEDIEVAL PHILOSOPHERS

7

FRIENDSHIP IN LATE ANTIQUITY

THE CASE OF GREGORY NAZIANZEN AND BASIL THE GREAT

John Panteleimon Manoussakis

Τῷ ἐμῷ Βασιλείῳ,
Σεβ. Μητροπολίτη Προύσης

—κ.κ. Ἐλπιδοφόρῳ.

1. Introduction: Classical and Christian Friendship

One thing we should expect to find unchanged when we look at the new world that emerges during the Christianization of the Greco-Roman Empire is the fact that people continue to form friendships and continue to consider and reflect on the nature of friendship as such. Even so, there is some justification in expecting that the rise of Christianity might effect some kind of change on the institution of friendship, as indeed it did on many other institutions borrowed from the classical world. One might indeed expect that such a change in communing with friends might have taken two possible, seemingly antithetical, directions: either toward a *diminution* of friendship's importance, especially when compared to other evangelical virtues—most notably love—insofar as friendship establishes particular attachments, or rather attachments that are limited to a few individuals, whereas Christianity had proclaimed and demanded the universality of such affections—or toward the *intensification* of friendship's meaning so as to become commensurate with Christian universality. In other words, in a Christian perspective, the benefits and duties of friendship are no longer limited to my friends, as it might have been in antiquity, but are to be extended to everyone, to every fellow Christian, insofar as every Christian is a member of the newly emerged community, and to the extent that the Gospel is addressed to "all nations," to every man and woman.

It is the balance between, or rather the mutual upholding of, these two antithetical ways that constitutes the paradox of Christian friendship. From the historiographical point of view Christian authors maintained both.[1] Some saw in the bonds of friendship the danger of exclusion of the broader Christian community—in essence, nothing less than a camouflaged, yet amplified, selfishness; while others extended *philia* to all humanity, as *philanthropia*, a term that occurs in Christian literature with a frequency unparalleled in the classical period.

Furthermore, one could introduce a (seemingly pseudo-) historical distinction between classical antiquity and Christianity, a distinction drawn on the basis of the assumption that the former was oriented towards *philia* and *erōs*, while the latter placed itself under the banner of the notion of *agapē* of which the classical world knew little or nothing.[2] Yet the Gospel seems to imply a different hierarchy, where friendship (*philia*) ranks even higher than *agapē*.

In the famous exchange between Jesus and Peter in John 21:15–17, Jesus asks Peter whether he loves Him (*agapan*), to which Peter replies affirmatively by employing the more emphatic, we presume, verb *philein*. For it would make little sense indeed to imagine, with the view that takes *philein* to be a lesser declaration of love than *agapan*, that Jesus asks Peter if he loves Him, to which Peter replies that he "likes" Him. Pavel Florensky reads this exchange, particularly the use of the verb *agapan*, as a way of indicating to Peter that he is prepared to be loved even as an enemy is loved (see Luke 6:31–36). Peter's reply with *philein* indicates, on the other hand, that he loves the Teacher in the way of *philia*, that is, the way that one can love only a friend and never an enemy: "By the twice-uttered question, the resurrected Christ indicates to Peter that he violated friendly love—*philia*—for the Lord and that henceforth one can demand of him only universal human love, only that love which every disciple of Christ necessarily offers to every person, even to his enemy."[3] We need to remind the reader that the command to love one's enemy in the Gospel is always rendered with the verb *agapan*.

Taking inspiration from this exchange between Jesus and Peter, I will attempt a presentation of the friendship between two of the most illustrious ecclesiastical authors who have had, without any doubt, a long and lasting influence on Christian letters: St. Basil the Great, archbishop of Cappadocia's Caesarea, and St. Gregory the Theologian.[4] To describe their friendship is to tell a story similar to that of the concluding chapter of St. John's Gospel— that is, a story structured around three betrayals and an equal number of reconciliations. The second part of this chapter is arranged in three "acts," as it were, each corresponding to a movement of friendship from *agapan* to *philein* in their relationship, and appending, at the end, a third part as a conclusion. But first, some general remarks on the particularities of Christian friendship are in order.

In the friendship between Basil and Gregory we will find still something of the Old World, namely, a friendship that at times takes the form of *hetaireia* or *xenia*, that is, the societal institution that connects individuals of equal status for the purpose of their mutual advancement.[5] As such, friendship is "historically and logically"[6] prior to politics (and the "politics of friendship" as Jacques Derrida puts it[7]) and often acts as a force of subversion to the established political order. Its prepolitical nature makes friendship more suitable for, or more understandable within, a Christian context, since the Church, and the bonds of communion amongst its members, ought to stand in a similar idiosyncratic position vis-à-vis the political order—"for our citizenship is in heaven" (Phil. 3:20). At the same time, we see in the friendship between Basil and Gregory something new emerging, something that is particularly Christian, or rather, some characteristics that belong specifically to their identity as Christians. Let us summarize the characteristics proper to Christian friendship.

First, in terms of *ethics*: Christian friendship appears to be a-causal, that is, free from an economy of ends as it is so often found in classical treatments of the topic.[8] To put it differently, it is not the "object" that defines the nature of the love, but rather the nature of the love itself that defines what or who the recipient of that love is.[9] Friendship, thus, does not serve anymore the ends of personal *eudemonism* (such as it was), nor is it subordinated to *rationality* in accordance with which one had to select one's friends, and for the sake of which friendship, especially what counts as its higher form in Aristotle's treatment, in which "friendship is the source of considerable cognitive benefits which could not otherwise be secured."[10] Selection as such, the possibility of selection, which was largely the defining characteristic of classical friendship, does not play that crucial role any more, insofar as a friend is not so much chosen, inscribed, as it were, within an economy of calculation or equality of virtue, but rather given as a gratuitous, and perhaps even unmerited, gift.

Second, in terms of ontology: the Trinitarian model, which affirms the consubstantiality of the divine Persons while respecting and preserving at the same time their distinct personal characteristics, and which thereby shows the ability of Christian thought to uphold sameness *and* otherness, challenges most decisively the classical ontology of friendship, for which the starting point is *oikeiotēs* (as in Plato's *Lysis*), and which seeks its perfection in narcissistic *homoiōsis* (the friend as another self, alter ego, mirror image, double).[11] As above, the Christian redefinition of the friend as a gift points to the Trinitarian model of reciprocal donation, where *to-be* is tantamount with *to-be-given*.

Third, in terms of *epistemology*: Christian friendship differentiates itself from classical friendship with respect to the question on which antiquity insists, the question of preference between loving or being loved—reminding the reader that the Greek for the verb "to befriend," *philein*, can also mean "to love," and friendship is a form of love. For classical treatments of friendship, such as Aristotle's, the question "to love or to be loved" is decided in terms of Greek metaphysics, that is, in terms of act over potency, form over matter, knowledge over ignorance.[12] Friendship is based on knowledge, most fundamentally on knowing that one loves the beloved (which cannot be said about the recipient of love, who might be loved without his or her knowledge). Thus, to love is preferred over being loved, the lover over the beloved, for the lover knows. Thus, with Greek metaphysics we have the priority of knowledge. Love in Christianity, however, is blind with respect to the beloved, whom one is commanded to love regardless of that person's qualities or virtues (the sinner as much as the saint), and regardless of whether that love is reciprocated (the enemy as much as the friend), but also blind with respect to one's own doing, not knowing what one is doing or whether one is doing anything at all (cf., Mt. 6:3). Even the possibility of loving rests upon the condition of having been loved *before*, before knowing it, even before the foundation of the world (Eph. 1:4)—who could have known it then?—and having been loved *first*, "for God loved us first" (1 John 4:19), before one could have known it or known how to love back. If we know love now—know how to love—this is because we were loved with a love prior to any knowledge or act: "[I]n this is love, not that we loved God, but that he loved us" (1 John 4:10).

However, the difference between the two worlds that emerges most noticeably in the material presented here is the fact that neither Gregory, who dedicates a considerable part of his work to his relationship with his friends and in particular to Basil, his best friend, nor Basil, who avoids writing about the subject, in line, we presume, with his more reserved character, are interested in constructing a theory of friendship. Abstract discussion of friendship is thoroughly lacking in their work. What one finds instead is a preoccupation with the concrete and the specific cases of particular friends, particular affections, and particular episodes that seemed to betray those friendly affections. In short, they are interested in their friends, not in friendship in general. Given, then, that their orientation is *historical*—they present us with the history of their friendship—we should not be surprised that they adopt their medium accordingly, that is, narrative over analysis, particularly autobiographical (we could say "confessional" with a nod to St. Augustine) narrative. Indeed, the documents most pertinent to our discussion are precisely Gregory's so-called autobiographical poems, his funeral oration for Basil, and their letters. Unlike earlier philosophers, Gregory talks about their friendship, not about friendship as such. Here the willingness of Christians to focus on their concrete experience is underlined, the best example being that of St. Augustine's *Confessions*.

It is far from accidental then, that when St. Augustine wished to speak about the same topic, even though he was much more systematic an author than either of the Cappadocians, he chose precisely the same method, namely, narrative, as well as the same orientation, that of giving preference to particular friends—although in one famous case he prudently withheld the friend's name—over some abstract notion of friendship.[13] On the other hand, it should be a matter of interest, as well as of perplexity, to observe that, for all his detailed analysis of friendship, Aristotle never felt the need to enter the autobiographical mode; that is, he never felt the need to speak about his friends, or, as we would say, to speak from experience.

There is, we suspect, a good reason for this change of emphasis between, on the one hand, the approach of the philosopher and, on the other, that of the Christian thinker. The incarnation of the eternal Logos in Jesus of Nazareth has focused attention on the historical (see, for example, with what detail the circumstances of Jesus' birth are recorded in the Gospel of Luke) as well as on the particular. The result was a slow but irrevocable reversal of the old priority of theory's universality over history's particularity.[14] Thus, when St. Augustine wishes to speak in his *Confessions* of God's dramatic intervention in human affairs, he was able to do so only by recounting the "minute particulars," to recall Blake's phrase, of his personal life. The lesson of those *Confessions*, demonstrated in so many ways, is the newly felt conviction that for God the history of the one individual is as worthy and important as the history of the whole human race.

I could think of only one example from the pre-Christian philosophical literature where there is similar emphasis on the autobiographical and the confessional: Alcibiades' speech in Plato's *Symposium*. When asked to speak about love, Alcibiades did not provide an oration on *erōs* or turn his eye to the lofty yet fleshless Form of the beautiful, but spoke of a particular and personal relationship with a particular person, Socrates, *this* Socrates; as his interruption of the philosophical discussion on the good (*to agathon*) was marked by his demand to see, not the Form, but the person, Agathon himself.[15]

We shall return to Plato's *Symposium* at the very end of this chapter, when the question of a literary parallel between Plato's dialogue and Gregory's last letter to Basil will give us the opportunity to draw some concluding remarks. For now, however, retaining the *Symposium*'s tone, we shall speak of friendship, not in a series of abstractions, speculatively as it were, but phronetically, by following the very narrative that brought Gregory and Basil together, by recounting the episodes, no matter how episodic they might seem to us, of their friendship.

2. A Story of Friendship in Three Acts: From *agapan* to *philein*

2.1 First Betrayal: Friendship between Students

Away from home and free from the cares that would come to burden them later in life, two young men might rejoice in the paradisiac life that is a student's. By studying together and, even more eagerly, by studying each other through their common endeavors, they come to learn about themselves. And it is the same Arcadian experience that Gregory would recall with a reasonable nostalgia in his late autobiographical poems[16] and in the funeral oration for his friend, Basil.[17] It was Athens that brought them together, and their years of study alongside each other forged a friendship that not only lasted their lifetime, but also became one of the most celebrated examples of Christian friendship for generations to come.[18]

The year is 348, and Gregory is nineteen years old. He arrives in Athens after a long and stormy journey by sea from Alexandria—an experience that, when he recalls it later in life, allows him to cast himself as both Ulysses and St. Paul.[19] Is Athens, then, his Ithaca? Not without Basil, who arrives shortly afterward. Gregory in his *Funeral Oration* for Basil[20] indicates that he knew him, or at least knew of him, before Athens.[21] It was in fact such knowledge that helped them become friends, for Gregory had arranged that the Cappadocian newcomer be exempted from paying his due penalty as a freshman in Athens by being subjected to a raucous rite of initiation. That was the "spark," as Gregory puts it, of their friendship. But there was another event which set that first spark ablaze.[22] A group of Armenian[23] students had challenged Basil to a public debate. The challenge might have been provoked by the fact that he had escaped the initiation harassment on account of the rumors of his intelligence which, such was the presumption, would have been offended by an exhibition of sophomoric puerility (but wasn't that the point?). So the Armenian students wished to check for themselves whether Basil was worthy of the special treatment that he had received. Gregory recounts how, to begin with, he took their side, blinded by their pretensions of friendship, and hoping, perhaps, to see Basil triumph over their arguments. Soon, however, he came to realize that this *agōn* was nothing other than a setup that would have subjected Basil to a different form of harassment, possibly more humiliating than the earlier one. He therefore turned against their Armenian colleagues, exposed their plans, and, in doing so, won the victory for Basil.[24]

Here then is the story of a friendship initiated by a missed initiation, of a friend showing his fidelity to his friend by betraying other friends. Was Gregory a little overprotective of someone who had not befriended him yet, someone who, by all accounts, did not need his protection? Gregory rescued Basil, so he tells us, from the humiliation of the initiation. Why? On account of the seriousness of Basil's character (*tou ēthous stasimon*). But it is a man with precisely such character who has nothing to be afraid of and who could therefore have endured the silliness of the ritual. Gregory averted the Armenians' plan to engage Basil in some debate. And where was the risk for Basil in that? If he was the prodigy that Gregory describes him as being (in *Orat. 43* XXIII–XXIV), why wasn't Gregory confident in his future friend's abilities?

The two episodes that Gregory chose to recall several years later, anxious to remind his audience of his friendship with the late Archbishop of Caesarea, especially since the fidelity of this friendship had been brought under question in the last years, reveal a great deal more about that friendship and about Gregory himself than he might have been ready to admit. One suspects that they must have been staples in a stock of such stories idealizing their common life in Athens. He repeats them here as he must have done on several other occasions before.[25] It is the third episode in this series of memories that sheds light on the preceding ones:

> He moreover, according to that human feeling, which makes us, when we have all at once attained to the high hopes which we have cherished, look upon their results as inferior to our

expectation, he, I say, was displeased and annoyed, and could take no delight in his arrival. He was seeking for what he had expected, and called Athens an empty happiness. I however tried to remove his annoyance, both by argumentative encounter, and by the enchantments of reasoning; alleging, as is true, that the disposition of a man cannot at once be detected, without a long time and more constant association, and that culture likewise is not made known to those who make trial of her, after a few efforts and in a short time. In this way I restored his cheerfulness, and by this mutual experience, he was the more closely united to me.[26]

Basil's disillusionment with Athens was a potentially threatening situation for Gregory's dreams. It could have forced upon him the dilemma of choosing between Basil and Athens. Yet, Gregory wanted Basil with Athens and Athens with Basil. Either alone wouldn't do. Indeed, when Basil departed from Athens (and in the way that he did), Athens meant nothing to Gregory. As Gregory's modern biographer aptly puts it, "Gregory continued to live in Athens, but the lights had gone out in Arcadia."[27] Under this extinguished light, one can understand more clearly Gregory's actions in the first two episodes that he narrated. It was not that Basil needed Gregory's protection during his first days of his student life in Athens. Rather Gregory's motives seem to have been to secure for himself, through such a series of calculated moves, the possibility of Basil's friendship. For that, he needed both Basil and the city (*Orat. 43* XVII, 23). Had Basil found the initiation rite a little too distasteful or the Armenian challenge a little too disrespectful, he might have changed his plans and decided to leave Athens. Such an early departure would have robbed Gregory of the bliss he describes in his oration, a bliss whose mere memory elicits some of the most daring language in his corpus.[28]

Of course, the plan was inevitably doomed, and Gregory's happiness could not but be short lived. One cannot perpetuate an Arcadian sojourn indefinitely. So Basil left Athens soon afterward since he could not bear to "be seen any more in that miserable state or being in the position to explain to everyone the reasons of their separation."[29] The separation was a painful one: "A thing incredible, before it happened. For it was like cutting one body into two, to the destruction of either part, or the severance of two bullocks who have shared the same manger and the same yoke, amid pitiable bellowings after one another in protest against the separation."[30] There are no attempts here on Gregory's part to hide the real sting of his pain.

Basil had led him to believe that he would not leave Athens without him. How could he? Were they not one soul living in two bodies?[31] When he did leave, abandoning both friend and friendship, Gregory therefore rightly felt betrayed.[32] It was only the first blow that his friendship with Basil would cause him. Gregory's pain in finding that Basil had betrayed him, apart from the betrayal itself, was caused by a degree of blindness caused by projecting on Basil's actions some of his own hopes and expectations. Under the wishful language of "one soul/two bodies," Gregory had seen for too long too much of himself in his friend. Basil's departure from Athens—a real possibility that became a reality—seems to have remained for him purely imaginary, due to the trust vested in the image of their undivided selfhood. That image seems to have become for Gregory a regulatory concept for understanding the friendship, but it was, at the same time, a remnant of the classical *homoiotēs* (likeness), according to which a friend with a different viewpoint or following a different course of action, is hard to justify. It is very much the same condition that would cause a great deal of pain and elicit very similar reactions from St. Augustine upon hearing about his friend's death.[33] One could say that by leaving Athens with such a bruised self, Gregory also left behind him a narcissistic conception of friendship, more Greek than Christian.

After their Athenian sojourn was over, they never managed to recapture the carefree happiness of the time of their common studies. Gregory's decision to join Basil in his monastic seclusion in Pontus (Annesoi, 359–60) must be read as a brief and unsuccessful attempt to return to their former Arcadia. Basil's new life, however, was not fit for Gregory, who had a rather different understanding of what it meant for a Christian to live the philosophic life.

The passage from *agapan* to *philein* is marked by the interruption of an infantile desire to see the friend as an extension of oneself, an interruption that is occasioned by the emergence of the friend as other than oneself. The friend's otherness allows him to appear with his own distinct characteristics, which may contradict or even challenge the assumptions that we sought to impose upon him.

2.2 SECOND BETRAYAL: FRIENDSHIP AND THE PHILOSOPHIC LIFE

The first letters[34] exchanged between the two friends record for us the beginnings of a disagreement concerning the proper way of living what usually goes by the name of *philosophia*. When Gregory writes, remembering those early days in Athens, that philosophy became their study,[35] he means only loosely and incidentally the discipline we call by that name today. As it becomes clear in the rest of the oration, philosophy for him meant something more. He goes on to explain how they embarked upon the study of *philosophia* more systematically when they had both left Athens and were no longer students[36] (suggesting, perhaps, the time when Basil was touring the monastic communities of Egypt and Palestine) and how Gregory's care for his parents became a hindrance on his own way to *philosophia*.[37] With the same aim at pursuing the philosophic life, Basil had established his study[38] at Pontus, following Elijah (the prophet) and John (the Baptist), "the first among the philosophers."[39] In his first letter to Basil, Gregory admits to having betrayed his promise to follow him in what he calls *sumphilosophēsein*. The same terminology is used in *De Vita Sua* (270 and 321). *Philosophia*, for him, therefore, is clearly not a branch of knowledge, but a way of life—a life lived in introspection, away from the clamor of worldly affairs. The change that Christianity had brought about to the goal and purpose of human life effected a similar change, as noted above, not only in the understanding of *philia*, but also in the understanding of *philosophia*, insofar as it is a form of *philia* as well. Even though we read that the model for such a philosophical life was already set by the example of Plotinus and the Neoplatonic ascetics,[40] it was Christian monasticism, which was just at this time reaching its first bloom, that fully embodied all the nuances that the term *philosophia* conveyed to the Christian mind of that time.

Yet—and here lies the root of Gregory's disagreement with Basil—monasticism, especially in the form which has been known ever since and of which Basil himself is considered to be founder,[41] did not fully coincide with what Gregory was envisioning as the proper philosophic life.[42] He clearly explains how he felt toward the simple monasticism of his time when he writes:

> But when I actually considered the divine ways
> It was hard to decide which path was definitely the better.
> Each thing seemed good or bad depending on the arguments,
> As is often the case when action needs to be taken.
> (. . .)
> I admired Elijah the Tishbite
> And the great Carmel or the strange food,
> The property of the Precursor, the desert,
> And the simple way of life of the sons of Jonadab.
> Then again a desire for the Holy Scriptures got the upper hand
> As did the light of the spirit in the contemplation of the word—

Practices not suited to the desert or a life of calm.
After swinging to and fro between these positions many times,
I at last reconciled my desires in the following way,
And giving each position its due, checked the vacillations of
    my mind:
I realized that those who enjoy a practical life
Are useful to others who are in the thick of things
But do not benefit themselves; they are distracted by the wicked,
    too,
Who disrupt their calm disposition. On the other hand,
Those who have withdrawn are in some way more stable
And with a tranquil mind can keep their gaze directed towards
    God,
But they only benefit themselves, for their love is a narrow one
And strange and harsh is the life they lead.
So I chose a middle path between solitude and involvement,
Adopting the meditative ways of the one, the usefulness of the
    other.[43]

Basil's ideas of the philosophic life were closer to the monasticism introduced by the heretical Eustathius of Sebaste, with whom Basil was then connected in friendship and admiration. Eustathius' monasticism was radically ascetical: in addition to other regulations one might expect to find prescribed to monks—such as regular prayer, fasting, and continence—it also incorporated hard manual work, a demand that the noble Gregory found intolerable since "the tools of his ascesis were books, enquiring conversation, and reflection in simple solitude."[44] The middle path of the scholar-monk, paved by Gregory in the lines quoted above, became a royal way to be followed by other luminaries of that age, most notably St. Augustine during his retirement at Cassiciacum, and St. Paulinus of Nola, as well as by many other sensible men ever since. Eustathian monasticism, on the other hand, was condemned as radical by the Synod of Gangra (340), and Eustathian theology was condemned at the Second Ecumenical Council in Constantinople (381), over which Gregory presided briefly.

Like Athens, however, *philosophia*, and the debate of how one should best live according to it, became an issue that brought the two friends together as much as it kept them apart. In Athens, the philosophical life was what had brought them together and kept them united "as two bodies are by one soul." Although the first ominous clouds had already begun to appear on the horizon of their friendship, *philosophia* became in Pontus the promise of reinventing their friendship at a higher level, by placing it in the service of the Church. In Caesarea, however, after Basil's election to the see of that city, an election that made him ecclesiastically superior to Gregory, who now had to submit to his friend's authority, *philosophia* takes on a different role: instead of providing the common ground for the friendship between the two men, it now protected friend from friend and offered a defense where their very friendship had left them unequal and vulnerable. Thus, when Basil complains, as friend and superior, that Gregory has left him alone by refusing to pay him a visit, Gregory is delighted to appeal to his engagement with the philosophic life (*philosophoumen, Ep.* 46) as the reason that kept him away from his friend and his newly assumed duties at the helm of the local Church. And when Basil writes alarmed by Gregory's indifference in showing any care for his own episcopal see at Sasima, he boldly retorts that leisure (*apraxia*)—in his eyes the chief characteristic of the philosophical life—has been the great work and accomplishment of his life (*emoi de megistē praxis, Ep.* 49).

While Basil, as Archbishop of a Metropolitan See, had a wide range of means at his disposal by which he could bring Gregory to do what he thought of as the right course of action (Gregory's ordination as bishop of Sasima, for instance), Gregory was left with only one tactic to protect himself from Basil's directives: the epistolary deferral of his expected engagement with Church affairs, an engagement which, at times, took the more explicit form of promising to join in person the Archbishop of Caesarea, a promise that was never kept.[45] The first and the last of Gregory's letters addressed to Basil (*Ep.* 1 and 60) are good examples of this tactic, as is *Ep.* 45: "I didn't come immediately, nor will I come, don't demand that even yourself. . . . You may ask me 'when will I come and until when will I retreat?' Until God commands me." Gregory invoked two major reasons for denying Basil his presence: his duty to his parents and his duty to his vocation to lead a philosophic life, a vocation which they both had, after all, chosen as their common goal in life. Thus, in Gregory's eyes, Basil's elevation to an archbishopric had proven to be a double betrayal: a betrayal of his friendship with true wisdom (*philo-sophia*), since his active engagement with Church affairs could not be reconciled with a quiet life of study, and a betrayal of his friend with whom the philosophical life would have been pursued and, hopefully, realized:

So much for Athens and our common efforts for education . . .
So much for our pledges to cast the world aside
And live a shared life dedicated to God,

Devoting our skill for words to the Word who alone is wise:
All this has been scattered, dashed to the ground,
And the winds carry off our former hopes.
Where was I to wonder? Wild beasts, will you not welcome me?
For there is more loyalty among you, it seems to me.[46]

On the other hand, Gregory, too, set one friendship against another by placing his friendship with wisdom over and above his friendship with Basil. As he concludes in a letter to Basil (*Ep.* 46): "Are you, therefore, taking offense at my devotion to philosophy? Allow me, then, to say that it is this alone which ranks higher even than your words."

Following the first "betrayal," when the friend refuses to be subsumed under one's categories, this second "betrayal" demands that one casts a critical eye on oneself; it demands that one realizes a truth about oneself, a truth that one is not willing to ignore anymore in the hope of preserving a more idealized and less authentic friendship. Meeting the Other beyond the generalized love denoted by *agapan*, in the more personal space of *philein*, requires that one affirms one's own being over that of the friend.

2.3 THIRD BETRAYAL: FRIENDSHIP AMONG THEOLOGIANS

Inevitably, their friendship became entangled with the Church politics of the day. The see of Caesarea became vacant with the death of Eusebios,[47] and Basil seemed to have immediately moved to position himself as the successor. As a priest of Eusebios, Basil did not always enjoy the favor of his old bishop. As Gregory's letters 16, 17 18 (to Eusebios), and 19 (to Basil) indicate, Basil withdrew to Pontus for a second time a little after his ordination to the priesthood as a result of his growing alienation from Eusebios, hoping that reinforcing his image as a monastic would check Eusebios' episcopal authority—a strategy similar, as seen above, to the one that Gregory would later use against Basil himself. Gregory's interventions on behalf of his friend, however, succeeded in reconciling the two parties. Basil returned from his monastic retreat in time for the two friends to face the emperor and his Arian theologians. This they did quite successfully at the time of Valens' first visit to Cappadocian Caesarea in 365. The feat was repeated once more when Valens paid a second visit in 372, by which time Basil was on the Caesarean Church's throne. The funeral oration that Gregory wrote for Basil provides us with some unforgettable images of that second encounter between the two defenders of Nicean orthodoxy and their heretical emperor. Much less is known about the emperor's first visit, except that it provided Eusebios with a good motive for putting aside his hostility toward Basil and convinced Basil to act less stubbornly toward his bishop. When the faith of the local Church emerged victorious, Basil remained on the side of his bishop, organizing every aspect of the diocese's life. So when Eusebios died in September 370 it was fitting that Basil should see himself as his uncontested successor. He did not think that his friend Gregory might have the same aspirations.

Whether intentionally or not, Basil led Gregory to believe that he was near death. Basil's letter is lost, but we know the reaction it caused thanks to Gregory's response. Gregory's vividness of language makes it worth citing at some length his description of these events:

> You pretend to be very ill, indeed at your last breath, and to long to see me and to bid me a last farewell. . . . I started in great grief at what had happened; for what could be of higher value to me than your life, or more distressing than your departure? And I shed a fountain of tears; and I wailed aloud; and I felt myself now for the first time unphilosophically disposed. What did I leave unperformed of all that befits a funeral? But as soon as I found that the Bishops were assembling at the City, at once I stopped short in my course; and I wondered first that you had not perceived what was proper, or guarded against people's tongues, which are so given to slander the guileless; and secondly, that you did not think the same course to be fitting for both yourself and myself, even though our life and our rule and everything is common to us both, who have been so closely associated by God from the beginning. Thirdly, for I must say this also, I wondered whether you thought that such nominations are worthy of the more religious, and not, as it is the case, of the more powerful, and of those most in favor with the multitude. For these reasons then I backed water, and held back. Now, if you think as I do, determine to avoid these public turmoils and evil suspicions. I shall see your Reverence when the matters are settled and time allows, and I shall have more and graver reproaches to address to you.[48]

Since Gregory was not yet a bishop—in which case he would have had a vote in the election of the primate of the local church—Basil's motives for calling him so urgently, and therefore his motives in employing such a ruse—if indeed it was one—remain unclear. Perhaps he was relying on his friend's oratorical skill and diplomatic acumen to secure for himself the bishops' support. If that was the case, Gregory's earlier negotiations between Eusebios and Basil could provide Basil with a precedent, together with the hope that Basil would again intervene on his behalf.

Indeed, the next four letters in Gregory's epistolary corpus were written by him on behalf of his father, Gregory the elder, bishop of Nazianzus, in support of Basil's candidacy for the Metropolitan see of Caesarea. Whether Gregory might have desired the position for himself, (or whether his father might have thought that his son would make as good a candidate as Basil) is not clear. Yet these suspicions find some ground in certain expressions, left intentionally ambiguous, or so it seems to me, in the documents before us. In a letter after Basil's enthronement, for instance, Gregory justifies his decision to stay away at that hour of his friend's glory by the desire to keep himself "in calmness and free from jealousy."[49] As McGuckin rightly observes, Gregory avoids specifying "whether it is the envy of outsiders . . . or the bad feelings he still nurtures inside himself. The master orator is never ambivalent in his meanings without reason."[50]

Thanks to the support rallied by Nazianzus, Basil was elected archbishop of Caesarea. Gregory the elder and his son had done their duty, as their association and friendship with Basil demanded. It was now time for Basil to do his. There is no doubt that both Gregories expected Basil to return the favor. So when he finally did, two years later in 372, Gregory felt betrayed by his friend for a second time. For it was nothing like what Gregory had imagined. Yes, he was made a bishop, but of a town that would become for him his lifelong embarrassment. He would describe the "glorious Sasima,"[51] as he calls it with no reservation of irony, as:

A place without water, without vegetation, completely uncivilized,
An utterly dreadful and cramped little settlement.
It is all dust and noise and chariots,
Cries and groans, officials, instruments of torture and shackles,
A population consisting only of visitors and vagrants.[52]

For Basil, this was a political move. Valens had divided Cappadocia into two administrative districts, Cappadocia Prima with Caesarea, Basil's see, as its capital, and Cappadocia Secunda, with Tyana, as a capital rivaling Caesarea.[53] In the East, ecclesiastical jurisdictions tended to conform to, and reflect, changes made in the civic structures of the empire. Basil naturally saw Cappadocia's restructuring as a threat to his influence over the region and quickly moved to secure that influence by placing friends (like

Gregory) and relatives (like his brother, also Gregory) to suffragan dioceses (Sasima and Nyssa respectively). Gregory resisted this ordination, too, as much as he could, and refused to assume pastoral responsibility over Sasima as its new bishop, thus causing Basil's anger. The damage, however, was done. Years later, a fraction of the bishops gathered in Constantinople for the Second Ecumenical Council would protest Gregory's appointment as archbishop of the empire's capital on account of his previous appointment at Sasima, forcing him thus to resign.[54] Until then, though, his pain was over a broken friendship:

> This was what he appointed me to, he who was surrounded
> By fifty suffragan bishops—what magnanimity on his part![55]

Having been betrayed by his best friend, he now became disillusioned with friendship in general. He, therefore, concludes a letter to Basil, written in that same year, with these bitter words: "As for me, I have gained this from your friendship: learning not to trust friends."[56]

The break from *agapan* to *philein* (to the possibility of genuine *philia*) is now complete. Painful changes have affected both friends, and the changes have been occasioned by the actions of both. Here, then, comes the moment of decision: would one continue to stand next to one's friend in spite of differences in viewpoint and character, would one continue to stand next to one's friend in spite of spatial and mental distance, or would one revert to the generalized well wishing of *agapan*?

3. Friendship Redeemed: Gregory's Final Achievement

At some point Gregory must have realized that his celebrated oratorical skills put him in charge, not only of crowds and congregations, but also of something far more important, namely, history. His works—to which at the end of his life he devotes all his energies, polishing, editing, copying, and publishing—are his real legacy; they can shape and, if need be, reshape, the way history is told. Basil is very much a part of that history, and although Gregory was powerless to control any change in what had become of their friendship, he was nevertheless successful in transforming his friend. The transformation he effected was not only in Basil's image, though a great deal of Gregory's work was concerned with that, but also with Basil himself and in particular with his opinions on what was at the time a highly controversial issue, an issue that defined the theological agenda of the so-called Neonicene party, namely, the divinity of the Holy Spirit.

Throughout most of his life, Basil had been unable to call the Holy Spirit clearly and explicitly "God," stopping one step short of a fully Trinitarian confession, such as Gregory's *Five Theological Orations* would achieve.[57] Yet, around the year 375, Basil would begin to compose one of the first treatises on the subject, seeking to demonstrate precisely the equality between the Holy Spirit, God the Father, and God the Son. One of the reasons that might have prompted him to embark upon this project was, I believe, Gregory's cunning solicitation of such a work, evidence of which we can find in Gregory's letter 58, addressed to Basil a few years earlier.

Letter 58 is an extraordinary document, unique among Gregory's letters, as it narrates and, when it breaks into direct dialogue, re-enacts a scene that is supposed to have taken place shortly before the composition of the letter. The event was a symposium to which some "distinguished friends" were invited, among whom was a "philosopher." There was no drink, only talk, or talks, not about *erōs,* but *philia,* in particular the friendship between Basil and Gregory. I suspect that the letter was composed in a more or less conscious imitation of Plato's *Symposium.*[58] If I am right, it becomes exceedingly interesting to read, with Gregory, what he would have intended his reader to read between the lines. The above-mentioned "philosopher," who is a monk, assumes Alcibiades' position by first interrupting the praise of friendship that was unfolding in the name of Basil and Gregory and, secondly, by turning praise into blame, accusing Basil of impiety and Gregory of tolerating Basil's error by not speaking up: " 'What is this, gentlemen?' he said, with a very mighty shout, 'what liars and flatterers you are. You may praise these men for other reasons if you like, and I will not contradict you; but I cannot concede to you the most important point, their orthodoxy. Basil and Gregory are falsely praised; the former, because his words are a betrayal of the faith, the latter, because his toleration aids the treason.' "[59] Gregory engages in an examination of the monk's accusations—a mock Socratic *elenchus*—without refuting any of the charges. Instead, he closes the letter by referring the matter to his addressee: "[B]ut you, O divine and sacred head, do teach me up to which point one should advance concerning the divinity of the Spirit, and what words should one use, and how much of the economy should one apply." There is nothing in the tone of this apostrophe that would justify reading it in any other way than sarcastic: the Homeric appellation and the pretensions of Socratic ignorance are all the more incredible that they come from a man who was already acknowledged as an expert on the subject. Yet, Gregory delights in his mockery. He opened the letter by assuming for himself, not the place of a friend, but that of a pupil: "I have taken you from the very beginning as my teacher and professor both in life and in faith." Such reinvention of roles was necessary for the Platonic *mise-en-scène* to work. Like Plato in the *Symposium*, Gregory manipulates and, one could even say, undermines his teacher insofar as he forces Basil, the learned teacher addressed in his letter, into a position that he had very carefully and for very long time avoided.

Basil dies in 379. The celebrated *Funeral Oration* gives Gregory, quite literally, the last word on their friendship. It is in this momentous document that he builds a splendid memorial to unite the two friends forever and overshadow whatever residue of imperfection history had left on Basil's image. Basil's long association with the heretical Eustathios of Sebaste is unmentioned; Basil's own initial hesitations on matters of dogma are passed over in silence; what is more, he is immortalized as the pioneer of the Holy Spirit's consubstantial divinity. As has been well said, "If Basil had once violently pressed Gregory into his service, Gregory now presses Basil into his."[60] At long last Gregory has the friend he had dreamed of since their common days of study in Athens. Basil is the friend whom Gregory rediscovers only now, over his grave, posthumously, the friend Gregory bequests to eternity: Basil the Great.

If Aristotle, by his cryptic remark that the friend is another self (*allos autos*),[61] meant to say, *not* that in our friend we find an image of our own self, but rather that we find our true self by means of, and through, friendship with others,[62] then his remark holds true for the two Cappadocian friends. As a result of their friendship, each emerges transformed at the end. However, it is not so much that they have changed by becoming someone else, different from the person they were at the beginning of their friendship; rather, they have changed by staying the same, by becoming who they always were. It is only now that the identity which lay latent in them, beneath their thoughts and actions, has become fully actualized and therefore recognizable as such, thanks to both the confrontations that took place in the intervening years and the confrontations that tested their friendship as well as their character. It is the nature of genuine friendship to move by means of such interplay of betrayal and reconciliation. In contrast, then, to Aristotle's speculation that virtuous friends would not quarrel and that friends should spend their time together, Basil and Gregory remain friends despite their disagreements and the distance from each other in which they lived their separate lives.

Notes

1. For general background on the Christian conception of friendship, see Clark and Clark 1989.

2. Such is indeed the argument that Nygren makes in *Agape and Eros*, 1982. That Christian authors made an unapologetic use of the terms and the concepts of *philia* and *erōs* does not need to be demonstrated here. That they had no reservations in applying the term *erōs* even to the Godhead is attested by the works of Dionysius the Areopagite and Augustine of Hippo. The latter thinks that even friendship (*amicitia*) can be used in describing the communion of the Holy Trinity's Persons. He stops short from doing so in *De Trinitate* ("So the Holy Spirit is something common to Father and Son, whatever it is, or is their very commonness or communion, consubstantial and coeternal. Call this friendship, if it helps, but a better word for it is charity" VI.7.209), but the step is undertaken by Aelred of Rievaulx who writes, paraphrasing 1 John 4:16, "Deus amicitia est" (*De Spirituali Amicitia* 1. 69–70, as cited by White 1992, 236, n. 21.)

3. Florensky 1997, 291.

4. St. Gregory was elected bishop of the small town of Sasima, a see that, as he never fails to remind us, he never assumed. Instead he exercised his episcopal office as archbishop of Constantinople during his brief sojourn (379–381) in the Capital City. He is known, especially in the West, as "Nazianzen" because of Nazianzus, his hometown in Cappadocia, where his father, also a bishop, had his see.

5. It is this type of friendship that John McGuckin seems to prefer, perhaps not without reason, when attempting to understand Gregory's friendship for Basil in his biography of St. Gregory (McGuckin, 2001).

6. Herman, Gabriel, "Friendship, Greece," *Oxford Classical Dictionary*, 1996.

7. Derrida 1997. The first chapter of this work becomes quite relevant when the details of the friendship between the two church fathers are taken into account.

8. See, for example, the "*heneka tou kai dia ti*" of *Lysis* (218d7).

9. See, Kierkegaard, *Works of Love*, 1995, where his whole analysis of the command to "love one's neighbor" is based upon this principle, thus it is not the neighbor whom we should love as oneself but rather the kind of love that transforms everyone, even one's enemy, into the neighbor. Kierkegaard's insight might have been proven helpful in solving Freud's difficulties with the command "thou shalt love thy neighbor." For those difficulties, see his *Civilization and Its Discontents*, 1961, 65ff.

10. Stern-Gillet 1995, 50.

11. For examples of the friend as a mirror image of oneself, see Aristotle, *Nicomachean Ethics*, IX 4, 1166a31, and Cicero, *Laelius de Amicitia* VII.23 ("verum enim amicum qui intuetur, tamquam exemplar aliquod intuetur sui"). For a more nuanced reading of these passages see Gary Gurtler's essay "Aristotle on Friendship: Insight form the Four Causes" in this volume as well as Arthur Madigan 1985. Even though by "the friend as another self" Aristotle seeks to underline the

intersubjective character of friendship, an element of *homoiōsis* is inescapable even by the most sophisticated readings. See, for example, Stern-Gillet's conclusion that "we can now infer that those whom primary friendship binds together, '*become*' each *other's self* in the act of apprehending each other's moral excellence" (Stern-Gillet, 53–54, my emphasis).

12. See, for example, *NE* VIII 8, 1159a and IX.7, 1168a.

13. On Augustine and friendship, especially the friendship with the anonymous friend of the *Confessions* IV, 4, see "*Inimica Amicitia*: Augustine's Critique of *Amicitia* in *Confessiones* 1–4" in this volume. The same argument is made by Wetzel 2003. See also Nawar's contribution to the present volume.

14. An allusion to Aristotle's hierarchy in *Poetics* 1451b 5–7.

15. For a discussion on Alcibiades' speech in the *Symposium* and its importance for the whole dialogue, see Martha Nussbaum 1986, 165–99.

16. Most notably, *De Vita Sua*, in *Gregory of Nazianzus: Autobiographical Poems*, ed. and trans. Caroline White, 1996. The numbers following the title of the work refer to the lines of the poem in the Greek original.

17. *Oration 43* in *Grégoire de Nazianze: Discours funèbres*, ed. F. Boulanger 1908, 58–230, as reprinted in vol. 60 of the *Bibliotheke hellenon Pateron kai ekklesiastikon syggrapheon*, 1980. Hereafter abbreviated as *Orat. 43*, followed by chapter number in Roman numerals and, when necessary, the line number.

18. If one were to believe Gregory, their friendship was known throughout Greece already during their lifetime so much so as to eclipse the classical standard of Orestes and Pylades. See *Orat. 43* XXII, 4–5, and *De Vita Sua*, 228.

19. *De Vita Sua*, 101–210.

20. *Orat. 43* XIV, 19–20 (delivered three years after Basil's funeral, most probably on the memorial of his death in 382).

21. *Orat. 43* XIV, 19–20.

22. *Orat. 43* XVII, 37–8. The term "spark" (*spinthēr*) is of Stoic provenance (see de Andia 2008, note 6) and denoted the part of the divine that dwells in humans (therefore, the highest part of the human mind, in terms of dignity). The fact that Gregory chooses precisely this term to speak of the inception of his friendship with Basil suggests that he understands that friendship as providential. The divine spark continued its traveling through the history of ideas: when we find it again it has been transformed into the *lumen naturale* that gives its light to the Enlightenment.

23. What Gregory says at this point about Armenians in general ("I find the Armenians to be not a simple race, but very crafty and cunning": *Orat. 43* XVII, 14–15), might be his way of reminding his audience, consisting mostly of Basil's friends, of Basil's devastating friendship with Eustathios of Sebaste, whose hometown and episcopal see was the metropolis of Armenia. For Basil's friendship with Eustathios, see below.

24. *Orat. 43* XVII, 32.

25. See for example the evidence of Letter 58 (to Basil) where Gregory recounts how stories about their "friendship and [their] Athens and the common

agreement and unanimity in everything" were narrated in a "symposium," as he calls it, of monks gathered around him. We will return to this letter below. For bibliographical information on Gregory's and Basil's letter, see the notes below.

26. *Orat. 43* XVIII, 1–11.

27. McGuckin 2001, 80.

28. "And when, as time went on, we acknowledged our mutual affection, and that philosophy was our aim, we were all in all to one another, housemates, messmates, intimates, with one object in life, or an affection for each other ever growing warmer and stronger. Love for bodily attractions, since its objects are fleeting, is as fleeting as the flowers of spring. For the flame cannot survive, when the fuel is exhausted, and departs along with that which kindles it, nor does desire abide, when its incentive wastes away. But love which is godly and under restraint, since its object is stable, not only is more lasting, but, the fuller its vision of beauty grows, the more closely does it bind to itself and to one another the hearts of those whose love has one and the same object. This is the law of our superhuman love." *Orat. 43* XIX, 12–23.

29. *Orat. 43* XXIV, 30–31.

30. *Orat. 43* XXIV, 26–29.

31. "One soul living in two bodies": *Orat. 43* XX, 40; "one soul uniting two separate bodies": *De Vita Sua*, 229–30.

32. *Orat. 43* XXIV, 25.

33. *Confessions* IV, 4–7.

34. For Gregory's letters I use Paul Gallay's edition *Gregor von Nazianz, Briefe* (1969) as reprinted in volume 60 of the *Bibliotheke hellenon Pateron kai ekklesiastikon syggrapheon* (1980). For Basil's letters I used the two-volume bilingual edition of *Les Belles Lettres*, edited by Yves Courtonne (volume I: 1957; volume II: 1961). In both cases, the letter is denoted by the abbreviation "*Ep.*," followed by the number of the letter cited.

35. *Orat. 43* XIX, 13.

36. *Orat. 43* XV, 38–39.

37. *Orat. 43* XXV, 4.

38. This settlement must have been closer to what is known in the West as an oratory than a monastery proper. Gregory likes to use the term *phrontistērion* (*Orat. 43* XXIX, 40; *Ep. 4*), rather playfully, as this term was coined by Aristophanes in order to describe Socrates' "thinkery" (*Clouds*, 94).

39. *Orat. 43* XXIX, 42.

40. Hadot 1995.

41. In the absence of monastic orders in the Eastern Church, the West has considered all Eastern monks and nuns "Basilians." This is on account of Basil's two sets of Rules (*regulae fusius et brevius tractate*, PG 31), which have largely defined the monastic life in the East.

42. "[I]t is clear that the two men [Basil and Gregory] had different understandings of spirituality and monasticism alike." McGuckin 2001, 97.

43. *De Vita Sua*, 284–86 and 292–311 (trans. White 1992, 32–33).

44. McGuckin 2001, 97.

45. Basil, naturally, notices that Gregory has been avoiding him and cites distance as the cause of all misunderstandings between them (*Ep.* 71).

46. *De Vita Sua*, 476 and 480–5 (trans. White, 1992, 45–47, modified).

47. Not to be confused with the renowned Church historian of the same name whose episcopal see, also Caesarea, was located in Palestine (Caesarea Maritima).

48. *Ep.* 40. The translation has been modified.

49. *Ep.* 45.

50. McGuckin, 2001, 177, n. 26. McGuckin finds another such instance in the encyclical letter Gregory wrote on behalf of his father to the synod of bishops (*Ep.* 41). He writes that "the elder Gregory's scribe, the ghostwriter son, now touched ever so lightly on the fact that there were indeed others who were worthy of the post, though Basil was their chosen candidate. With what exquisite acid he etched his testimonial for his friend, acknowledging that he was the 'best of those who were willing to stand' " (175).

51. *Ep.* 48. 1.

52. *De Vita Sua*, 441–45 (trans. White 1992, 43).

53. *Orat. 43* LVIII, 29–38.

54. *De Vita Sua* 1797–1918.

55. *De Vita Sua*, 447–48 (trans. White 1992, 43).

56. *Ep.*, 48.

57. "Unlike Basil, who did not in fact say the word, Gregory Nazianzen explicitly stated that the Spirit *is* God." Congar 2005, 3:33. Italics in the original.

58. Such Christian appropriation by imitation of Plato's work was not entirely new at this time: another church father, Methodios of Olympus, had written a dialogue called *Symposium* after the Platonic one.

59. *Ep.*, 58.

60. McGuckin 2001, 374.

61. *NE* IX 4,1166a31.

62. See the discussion of this well-known and often misunderstood maxim by Stern-Gillet 1995, 51ff., as well as Madigan 1985.

Bibliography

de Andia, Ysabel. 2008. "L'amitié de Grégoire de Nazianze et de Basile de Césarée." *Contacts, Revue française de l'orthodoxie* 221: 26–46.

Augustine. 1991. *De Trinitate* Translated by Edmund Hill, O.P. New York: New City Press.

Saint Basile (Basil of Caesarea). 1957, 1961. *Lettres* Edited by Yves Courtonne, vols. I and II. Paris: *Les Belles Lettres*.

Clark, G., and S. R. L. Clark. 1989. "Friendship in the Christian Tradition." In *The Dialectics of Friendship*, ed. R. Porter and S. Tomaselli. London: Routledge.

Congar, Yves. 2005. *I Believe in the Holy Spirit.* Translated by David Smith. New York: The Crossroad Publishing Company.

Derrida, Jacques. 1997. *Politics of Friendship.* Translated by George Collins. London and New York: Verso.

Florensky, Pavel. 1997. *The Pillar and Ground of the Truth.* Translated by Boris Jakim. Princeton, Princeton University Press.

Freud, Sigmund. 1961. *Civilization and Its Discontents.* Translated by James Strachey. New York and London, W. W. Norton.

Gregory of Nazianzus. 1996. *De Vita Sua,* in *Gregory of Nazianzus: Autobiographical Poems.* Edited and translated by Caroline White. Cambridge, Cambridge University Press.

———. 1908. *Oration 43* in *Grégoire de Nazianze: Discours funèbres* Edited by F. Boulanger, Paris. Reprinted in vol. 60 of the *Bibliotheke hellenon Pateron kai ekklesiastikon syggrapheon* (Athens, 1980).

———. 1894. *Oration 43, Letter 40* in *Nicene and Post-Nicene Fathers.* Translated by Charles Gordon Browne and James Edward Swallow, Second Series, vol. 7, eds. Philip Schaff and Henry Wace. Buffalo: Christian Literature Publishing.

———. 1969. *Gregor von Nazianz, Briefe.* Edited by Paul Gally. Berlin. Reprinted in vol. 60 of the *Bibliotheke hellenon Pateron kai ekklesiastikon syggrapheon* (Athens, 1980).

Hadot, Pierre. 1995. *Philosophy as a Way of Life: Spiritual Exercises from Socrates to Foucault.* Translated by Michael Chase. New York: Blackwell.

Kierkegaard, Sören. 1995. *Works of Love.* Translated by Howard and Edna Hong. Princeton: Princeton University Press.

Madigan, Arthur. 1985. "*EN* IX 8: Beyond Egoism and Altruism?" *The Modern Schoolman* 63.1: 1–20.

McGuckin, John. 2001. *Saint Gregory of Nazianzus.* Crestwood: St. Vladimir's Seminary Press.

Nussbaum, Martha. 1986. *The Fragility of Goodness: Luck and Ethics in Greek Tragedy and Philosophy.* Cambridge: Cambridge University Press.

Nygren, Anders. 1982. *Agape and Eros: The Christian Idea of Love.* Translated by Philip S. Watson. Chicago: University of Chicago Press.

Stern-Gillet, Suzanne. 1995. *Aristotle's Philosophy of Friendship.* New York: SUNY Press.

Wetzel, James. 2003. "The Trappings of Woe and Confession of Grief." *A Reader's Companion to Augustine's Confessions.* Edited by Kim Paffenroth and Robert P. Kennedy. Louisville and London: Westminster John Knox Press, 53–69.

White, Caroline. 1992. *Christian Friendship in the Fourth Century.* Cambridge, Cambridge University Press.

8
———

ADIUTRIX VIRTUTUM?

AUGUSTINE ON FRIENDSHIP AND VIRTUE*

Tamer Nawar

I

Among ancient philosophers who gave attention to friendship (φιλία, *amicitia*), Aristotle and Cicero have special significance. Aristotle, articulating a seemingly common intuition, points out that friendship seems to require a noninstrumental concern for the friend: a concern for the friend *for his own sake* (e.g., *Rhet.* 1380b35–1381a1). At the beginning of his discussion in the *Nicomachean Ethics*, he writes that friendship "is virtue of a sort, or involves virtue; further, it is most necessary for life" (*NE* 1155a3–5).[2] Such remarks are indicative of the important role that friendship played in ancient ethical thought: it was typically envisaged as an aid to virtue (it encourages and nourishes virtue) or else was itself seen as constitutive of virtue.[3] Friendship often seems to be a necessary condition of happiness, and for Aristotle, it is friendship (above even justice) that legislators are said to aim at instituting in a city (*NE* 1155a22–4). On Aristotle's view, our natural sociability indicates that friendship is good for us (*NE* 1169b16–19), and he points out that the young need friends to keep them from error (*NE* 1155a12–13) while drawing attention to the role of shared activity and deliberation in friendship and its contribution to the pursuit of the good (*NE* 1155a14–16, 1169b30–1170b19, 1172a1–13; cf. 1112b10–11).

In his *De Amicitia*, Cicero also gave substantial attention to the benefits of friendship. While often giving practical advice on the usefulness of friendship (in advancing one's career or maintaining one's reputation), Cicero (like Aristotle) emphasizes the ethical importance of friendship and its role in virtue and the good life. Friendship was, Cicero emphasizes, given by nature not as a companion of vice, but as a handmaid to the virtues (*Amic.* 83).[4]

In classical antiquity, the value of friendship was widely appreciated;[5] however, with the coming of Christianity, its importance is often thought to have diminished.[6] The Christian scriptures have little explicit to say about friends or friendship.[7] Further, even where classical notions of friendship are invoked, explicit mentions of friendship are often not forthcoming.[8] We find little or no attention to those features deemed important in classical thought, for example, the role of friends in keeping us from error, how friends can inspire each other to virtue or help each other accomplish tasks that they could not complete singly, or the role of friendship in shared deliberation and agency. In the Christian scriptures, love of neighbor is privileged over love of friends, and friendship does not seem to play a significant role in the good and righteous life.

The late fourth century saw the influx of the western Roman aristocracy into Christianity.[9] It also saw the appearance of friendship as a significant theme in Latin Christian literature and thought, notably in the writings of Ambrose, Paulinus of Nola, and Augustine. Ambrose's treatment of friendship comes primarily in the final chapter of his *De Officiis*. Throughout the work, Ambrose largely follows Cicero's *De Officiis*; however, in the final chapter (3.22), Ambrose's model becomes Cicero's *De Amicitia*.[10] Ambrose gives advice to the clergy, telling them how they should go about preserving *amicitia* among themselves and follows Cicero on many of the relevant details.[11] While Ambrose's ability to supply biblical examples of friendship is curtailed by the relative absence of the theme in scripture, he is able to muster a considerable number of biblical examples when called to and supplies the language of classical *amicitia*.[12] Ambrose praises faithful friends as a *medicamentum vitae* (*Off.* 3.129) and extols the splendors of friendship (*nihil est in rebus humanis pulchrius*, *Off.* 3.132). Like Aristotle and Cicero (and unlike earlier Christians), Ambrose explicitly names friendship a virtue (*virtus est enim amicitia*: *Off.* 3.134). Although Ambrose does not seem to work out the details of these notions in any great detail, he does note that friendship brings ethical improvement in various ways insofar as it may, for instance, act as a remedy against arrogance (*Off.* 3.138).

Paulinus of Nola offers a contrasting case. Having renounced his wealth and position in order better to live a Christian life, he also seems to have turned his back on Cicero and the pagan classics, and in his writings we do not find a significant role for *amicitia* in the good life. Further, whereas Ambrose often uses the terms "*caritas*" and "*amicitia*" interchangeably, for Paulinus it is *caritas* and not *amicitia* that joins the members of the body of Christ together (e.g. *ep.* 4.1, 11.2).[13] Paulinus seems to use "*amicitia*" primarily of worldly, non-Christian, friendships and criticizes *amicitia* as being characterized by flattery and as being generally deficient in comparison with the neighborly love of Christianity. Although the relation between friendship and virtue is not explicitly given much in the way of attention by Paulinus, his hesitation in using the term "*amicitia*" of the relation that obtains (or should obtain) among Christians is notable.[14]

II

Unlike, for example, Cicero, Augustine wrote no treatise on friendship.[15] His earliest discussion of friendship (which extends beyond a line or two) comes in his treatment of virtue (*virtus*) in his early *De Diversis Quaestionibus Octoginta Tribus*.[16] In this work, Augustine follows Cicero's account in *De Inventione* (2.166) incredibly closely, often to the extent of copying Cicero almost word for word.[17] Like Cicero, Augustine divides virtue into four parts: prudence (*prudentia*), justice (*iustitia*), fortitude (*fortitudo*), and temperance (*temperantia*).[18] He goes on to note that goodwill (*gratia*), seemingly an aspect or element of justice,[19] requires keeping in mind friendships and a desire to repay good deeds rendered (*div. qu.* 31.1).[20] Thus, not defaulting in the duties owed to a friend seems to be a part of justice (which itself is a part of virtue).[21] Augustine goes on to note that there are a number of things that might be sought as much on account of their value or standing (*dignitas*) as because of their enjoyment (*fructus*) (*div. qu.* 31.3).[22] Among these he names the following four: glory (*gloria*), dignity (*dignitas*), grandeur (*amplitudo*), and friendship (*amicitia*).[23] Augustine goes on to say that friendship is "a desire for good things for someone for his own sake, along with an equal desire on his part" (*div. qu.* 31.3).[24] While suggestive of a positive role for friendship in the good life, Augustine's remarks in *De Diversis Quaestionibus Octoginta Tribus* are brief and show no signs of original thought.[25] In his earliest work, *Contra Academicos* (completed by 387), his reliance on Cicero was similarly in evidence (though there he had the grace to reveal he was citing the thought of another). There, in a tangential remark, Augustine cited Cicero in order to seemingly agree with him in defining friendship as "agreement on human and divine affairs combined with good will and charity" (c. Acad. 3.6.13;[26] cf. Cic. Amic. 20).

It is only several years later, when writing an epistle to Marcianus (perhaps around 395),[27] that Augustine attempts to provide something like his own thoughts on friendship. In ep. 258, though he praises the account of friendship offered by Cicero in De Amicitia (ep. 258.1), Augustine emphasizes that Cicero's definition of friendship was deficient and required amending. He stresses that in order for true friendship to obtain, the agreement (consensio) on human and divine matters, which Cicero seemed to have taken as necessary and sufficient for amicitia, must be based "in Jesus Christ our Lord and our true peace" (ep. 258.4; cf. conf. 4.4.7). In this short epistle, which offers one of Augustine's more detailed discussions of friendship, Augustine addresses Marcianus as his oldest friend (antiquissimus amicus) but stresses that he did not have him as a true friend until he adhered to him in Christ (in Christo [. . .] tenebam; ep. 258.1). Augustine initially says that before their conversions, they were friends in a certain way but that they are now true friends (ep. 258.2).[28] However, although in their earlier lives Marcianus may have been filled with perseverante benevolentia toward Augustine (ep. 258.2), nonetheless, in wishing well for Augustine by the lights of the world (hoping he would attain wealth, success, and so forth), Augustine reveals that Marcianus in fact wished ill for him (ep. 258.2–3). It is only now that, being Christians, they are agreed on divine matters and human matters.[29] Against the earlier claim that in their youth they were friends in a certain way, Augustine concludes that, in fact, he and Marcianus were not then (before their conversions) friends even in part.[30]

Although this short letter strongly invokes the classical language of amicitia by means of learned allusions,[31] it does not seem to offer us much in the way of an account of Christian friendship. Rather, what seems to be offered is an account of neighborly love: the relationship between Augustine and Marcianus does not seem to go beyond the germanitas and caritas that obtains between all Christians in virtue of their being Christian. Revealingly, precisely at that point in the letter in which Augustine talks of the true friendship that now obtains between himself and Marcianus, he appeals to the great commandment: to love one's neighbor as oneself (diliges proximum tuum tamquam te ipsum, ep. 258.4). That is to say, he invokes not the friend (to whom, perhaps, preferential duties are owed) but the neighbor. Further, Augustine signs off the letter by referring to Marcianus no longer as his friend, but as his frater (ep. 258.5). It has been observed that Augustine's employment of the language of amicitia seems to recede after the Confessiones, and this preference for talking of caritas, amor, germanitas and the like (over amicitia) seems to be observable even within this one letter.[32]

III

It is in the *Confessiones*, written between 397 and 401 (probably not long after the letter to Marcianus), that Augustine offers his most extended and detailed thoughts on *amicitia*.[33] Although friendship is a significant theme throughout the narrative of the *Confessiones*, it is especially in the first four books (when discussing his wayward youth) that *amicitia* receives the greatest attention. In the early books, Augustine's account is notable for how it marks a departure from earlier, more Ciceronian, reflections (both his own and those of Ambrose) on *amicitia*.[34] In focusing on friendships among those who are less than good, Augustine offers several keen observations on the role that friendship may play not (as per Cicero) as a handmaid to the virtues, but rather as a companion to vice. First impressions are important, and the first use of the term "*amicitia*" sets the scene, I believe, for much of what follows. Addressing himself to God, Augustine notes: "[I]ndeed, friendship of this world is fornication against you" (*amicitia enim mundi huius fornicatio est abs te: conf.* 1.13.21; cf. James 4:4, Psalms 72:27). However, friendship first comes to the fore only at the beginning of the second book when treating of the intense friendships of adolescence:

> For a time, in my adolescence, I burned to be satisfied with hellish things and I recklessly ran wild with changing and shadowy loves. My splendor wasted away and by pleasing myself and desiring to please human eyes, in your eyes I became putrid. And what was it that delighted me but to love and be loved? But the measure was not maintained from soul to soul as far as the bright trail of friendship is. Instead, clouds arose from the muddy lust of the flesh and from the springs of youth and clouded and darkened my heart so that I could not distinguish the tranquil brightness of love from the mist of lust. (*conf.* 2.1.1–2.2)[35]

Much could be said about this passage,[36] but for our purposes it suffices to note: first, that Augustine saw his desire for the approval of his fellows as a source of sin; and second, that this is Augustine's first discussion of *concupiscentia carnis*, one of the three lusts discussed in 1 John 2:16. What becomes clear in Augustine's subsequent discussion is how the three lusts of 1 John 2:16 (*concupiscentia carnis, conscupicentia oculorum*, and *superbia vitae*), which are the main sources of wickedness (*capita iniquitatis*) for Augustine in the *Confessiones* (*conf.* 3.8.16; cf. Plotinus, *Enn.* 3.3.6, 3.5.9), are intertwined in earthly *amicitia*.

A central focus of the second book of the *Confessiones* is, notoriously, the episode involving the theft of the pears. The allusions to *Genesis* and the Fall are clear, and the question that preoccupies Augustine here is why he committed that theft:

> Why did that which I would not have done on my own delight me? [. . .] Alone I would not have committed that theft, in which what delighted me was not that which I stole but the theft itself; because had I been alone it would not have pleased me to do it and neither would I have done it. Oh exceedingly unfriendly friendship! Inscrutable seduction of the mind, from games and jests arises an appetite for hurting another without even personal benefit or a desire for revenge; it is enough when someone says: "come on, let's do it" for one to feel shame at not being shameless. (*conf.* 2.9.17)[37]

Thus, reflecting back on this early episode, Augustine raises several important points: he loved the theft for its own sake; friendship acted as an *inscrutable seduction of the mind,* and seemingly spontaneously evil can come about from friendly activities. What is striking about Augustine's own case is that he opted to steal the pears even though he recognized that the pears held no attraction for him and that he knew the theft was wrong. This, Augustine thinks, is mysterious: no one commits a crime without a cause (*conf.* 2.5.11). In cases of sin, the relevant goal of the action is usually considered under the guise of some good: one pursues something that one has some reason to pursue. For instance, adultery might be pursued under the guise of attaining pleasure, theft under the guise of acquiring wealth, murder under the guise of doing justice, and so on. However, Augustine reveals that he did not love the putative good which he acquired, but the theft itself. That is to say, he loved the theft, a wrongful act, *for its own sake.* As it is presented here, this seems to be a case of loving sin *qua* sin: of loving sin while recognizing it as sin and recognizing the damage it does and how it distances one from happiness (*conf.* 2.4.9).[38] This, Augustine thinks, is puzzling; he sees no reason for the theft: no attraction in it for his young self.[39] Insofar as the agent acted with no reason for action, Augustine is faced with a conundrum: seeking to explain an action without a reason is like seeking to explain an effect without a cause.[40] Accordingly, Augustine considers a number of possible vices from which the sinful act might have arisen (*conf.* 2.6.13): *superbia, ambitio, saevitia, curiositas, ignorantia, ignavia, luxuria, avaritia, invidentia,* and *ira.* He seems (though this is not entirely clear) to favor that vice which would later preoccupy his attention the most: a perverse desire to imitate God that is characteristic of *superbia* (*conf.* 2.6.14; cf. *civ. Dei* 12.1).

Augustine does not here provide a comprehensive analysis of such cases of sin, and the discussion seems to end in *aporia*. However, although Augustine does not seem to provide an explicit or detailed resolution of the issue, he does provide a diagnosis which sheds some light on what has gone wrong on such occasions. Saliently, he gestures towards the fact that he was "seduced" by friendship and that the sin was occasioned by friendship in some way. Augustine emphasizes that alone he would not have committed the sin and that he was seduced by peer pressure into wrongful action (cf. *conf.* 2.8.16). The invocation of friendship in order to explain the sin and the offering of friendship as a necessary condition for the sin finds parallel in Augustine's later analysis of the sin of Adam and Eve in *De civitate Dei* (14.11). There, Augustine tells us that in his effort to corrupt humanity, Lucifer began with Eve (*civ. Dei* 14.11).[41] Putting aside that Augustine thinks that Eve was weaker because she was a woman and that Lucifer began with her for that reason, we may observe that Augustine perceives that in the case of Adam and that of Aaron, the agent's freedom and judgment were somehow constricted or curtailed owing to the presence of his friends. In these cases the agent perceives the sin *qua* sin (he is not taken in) and yet does it anyway. Just as Aaron did not consent to making the idol because he was convinced, but rather yielded to compulsion, so too Adam sinned *not* because he was deceived "but because of the bond of fellowship" (*sed sociali necessitudine: civ. Dei* 14.11).

It seems then that Augustine thinks that friendship can somehow override conscience or practical reasoning and lead us to sin. The mechanism of friendship's *seductio* is not entirely perspicuous, and Augustine considers whether it might have been because company is a necessary condition of laughing and taking pleasure in certain activities (*conf.* 2.9.17). He does not take up that option, but the relevant point seems to be that which Augustine raises in elaborating: "from games and jokes arises an appetite for hurting another without even personal benefit or a desire for revenge; it is enough when someone says: 'come on, let's do it' for one to feel shame at not being shameless" (*conf.* 2.9.17). This element provokes puzzlement (*conf.* 2.10.18)[42] but is most plausibly linked to *superbia* (which was highlighted earlier), and Augustine here hints at how friendships wrongly cultivate our sense of pride and shame (a prominent theme of these early books). For Augustine, human concern for the opinion of others (friends, in particular) does not restrain men from immoral behavior, but rather seems to make them commit greater evils than they would normally. Augustine had earlier dwelt upon how his desire for praise by his friends led him to evil acts (and the pretense of evil acts) so that he might be accepted (*conf.* 2.3.7).[43] He established a link between *honor temporalis* (which can give rise to *vindictae aviditas*) and *amicitia hominum*. It is, Augustine says, "on account of all these [*honor, aviditas, amicitia*], and the like, that sin is committed" (*conf.* 2.5.10). He does not give great attention here (or elsewhere) to explicating the relation between *honor, aviditas,* and *amicitia* (e.g., which might ground the other); however, it does seem that certain activities that manifest pride, such as boasting, are facilitated by one's friends being present. Similarly, many of the activities that friends regularly engage in, such as paying each other compliments, might be seen (from Augustine's perspective) to exacerbate pride. Even in *ep.* 258, which does not dwell upon the ills of friendship, Augustine had drawn attention to how friendships inflated his pride (*ep.* 258.1).[44] Man being corrupted by the Fall,[45] popular opinion is likely to mislead and corrupt (*conf.* 3.5.9, 4.14.21–23).[46]

What lesson then are we to draw from all this? The following: when unredeemed people gather together, the vile desires in each of us serve to feed off and egg on those of the others. Even if there are few of us, we coalesce into a mob. Seeing our evil desires reflected in our friends seems to sanction our will to enact them. Our nature being corrupted by the Fall, friendship seems to magnify and strengthen our evil desires; it shows the faults of humanity writ large and leads us into error. One might offer Aristotle as a contrast: where Aristotle invokes the role of shared activity and deliberation in friendship and its contribution to the pursuit of the good, Augustine instead focuses on how friendship obstructs moral reasoning. The mechanism by which it does so is not examined in great depth, but it seems that the presence of friends impairs our conscience and our moral deliberation. When friends gather, ill desires become manifest, and concern for the esteem of our friends leads us to pursue an action even when we see that, all things considered, it is worse. In focusing on the ills of pride and reputation and the manner in which friendship fosters these and serves to habituate us, not toward the good, but toward evil, Augustine shows himself to have departed radically from the classical tradition's depiction of friendship and his own earlier Ciceronian inclinations.[47]

IV

The second book of the *Confessiones* focuses on a circle of friends of unclearly delineated number (*conf.* 3.3.6) and explores how such friendships might serve to cultivate pride (and other vices) and obstruct right action. However, could friendship not serve as an aid to the virtues? Concern for another for his own sake is, as Aristotle says (*Rh.* 1380b36–1381a1), commonly deemed to be an essential feature of friendship, and while it is not a central feature of his account, it sometimes seems that, for him, even friendship among the less than good can play a role in the development of virtue (or at least the inhibition of vice).[48] Could friendship then not aid in the development of other-directed concern or of some virtue or part of virtue, for instance, *caritas*? In contrast with what has gone before, in the fourth book of the *Confessiones* Augustine dedicates his attention to the relation between two close friends: the sort of friendship that was especially prized by the classical tradition (cf. Arist. *Nic. Eth.* 1171a14–15). One might think to find in this fourth book a depiction of the sort of friendship that could nourish virtue and perhaps even act as a locus for a robust concern for the other for his own sake; however, this would, I think, be a mistake. In recounting this friendship with his unnamed friend, Augustine instead gives an account of how such close friendship among those unredeemed by grace was lacking in charity or godly devotion and was instead motivated by a sinister form of egoism and pride. Augustine's friendships in the second book acted as an "inscrutable seduction of the mind," and something similar emerges with regard to the close friendship of the fourth book.

The relationship between Augustine and his unnamed friend was intimate. Taking into account the prism of earthly lusts through which Augustine structures the narrative in these early books (see above), the account of this friendship makes one think that both *concupiscentia carnis* and *concupiscentia oculorum* were involved, especially when he tells us that this friendship had been especially sweet (*suavis: conf.* 4.4.7).[49] The account is notoriously suggestive,[50] but what deserves special attention is that the friendship, not yet a year long, was a shallow one. Augustine tells us right away that this friendship had its origin not in a shared regard for virtue or character but simply in shared interests (*conf.* 4.4.7). This becomes clearest when we examine what Augustine has to say about how he considered his friend to be *another self.* In antiquity there was a significant tradition of talking of a close friend as *another self*,[51] in its common use, "another self" and cognate phrases are employed to indicate a friend for whom one has a robust concern. The concern in question is meant to be for the friend *for his own sake*, which means that it should arise independently, in some sense, of egotistic concerns *and* that the concern should be a significant one, to the extent that one cares for the friend as one cares for oneself.[52] Although Augustine does not here use the phrases "alter ego" or "alter idem," he does employ cognate locutions which are part of the tradition (e.g. *conf.* 4.6.11;[53] cf. Arist. *Mag. mor.* 1213a12)[54] and goes on to speak of his friend as half his soul (*dimidium animae*) or himself and his friend as one soul in two bodies (*conf.* 4.6.11;[55] cf. Arist. *Mag. mor.* 1211a32–33).

While Augustine knowingly evokes this ancient tradition of treating the friend as another self by means of learned allusions, it does not seem that Augustine could be said to have treated his friend as another self in the ordinary sense: by showing the same level of concern for his friend as he did for himself or for showing a concern for the friend *for his own sake*. Even a weaker form of other-directed concern seems to require, at the very least, recognizing the other person *as* another person, one with her own desires, goals, and crucially, as an agent within her own right. This, in turn, requires, for instance, desiring goods for them (*vera rel.* 46.87). However, at least as it is depicted in the *Confessiones*, Augustine's concern for his friend fails to meet such a threshold. Thus, we find that when his friend lay dying, Augustine rejected his friend's desire to return to Christianity; instead he hoped that his friend would recover so that he "could do with him what he willed" (*conf.* 4.4.8).[56] Augustine thus seems to have viewed his friend as a mere tool and not as an agent or a person in his own right at all. Further, in the course of the narrative it becomes apparent that Augustine viewed the friend as a sort of vessel for his various enthusiasms: one to be molded as Augustine saw fit. When telling us how he had turned his friend away from Christianity (*conf.* 4.7.7) we find Augustine saying that he had then hoped that his "friend's soul would retain what it had received" from Augustine (*conf.* 4.4.8).[57] Talk of molding the friend (or the beloved) finds precedent in the Platonic tradition (notably *Phdr.* 252d5–e1; Plotinus, *Enn.* 1.6.9; cf. *NE* 1172a11–14). However, whereas for Plato, the talk of molding the friend seems to have been aimed at making the friend better and instilling virtues in him, in Augustine's account it is clear that what he was aiming to inculcate in his friend were vices and false religion. When the friend, after having been baptized while unconscious, takes issue with Augustine's derision, he acts for the first time as his own person, and this shocks Augustine. Augustine tells us he was *stupefactus* at his friend's *mirabilis et repentina libertas* (*conf.* 4.4.8). This show of independence, immediately prior to the friend's death, seems to have marked the end of their friendship: no longer being a tool in Augustine's hands but a free agent in his own right, the (putative) friendship seems to have evaporated.

Augustine equally reveals his concern for his friend to have been egotistic (in a narrowly conceived manner) and to be driven by base motivations *after* the friend's passing. While the unnamed friend's death greatly grieved Augustine (*quo dolore contenebratum est cor meum*: *conf.* 4.4.9), such grief should not be considered as evidence for a robust form of altruism or any charitable feelings. At the friend's death, Augustine does not dwell on, or even mention, the fact that his friend had died while not having achieved things he wished to achieve, or else that he died while accepting the Christian faith (which Augustine at that time took to be false), or any number of other issues. Instead, Augustine focuses solely on his own pain in a profoundly selfish manner; further, he notes that he would not have given his life for his friend (in the manner of Orestes and Pylades, *conf.* 4.6.11). Immersing himself, indeed wallowing, in grief, he tells us that his life of misery was in fact dearer to him than his friend: (*conf.* 4.4.9,[58] 4.6.11).[59]

What becomes apparent here is that now dead, the friend served as an occasion for grief just as he had earlier served Augustine as an occasion for other enthusiasms. Such grief should be seen as similar in kind to Augustine's earlier affectations where he describes himself as happy to be sad at the stories of Virgil (*conf.* 1.13.21; cf. 3.2.2–4). In this respect, Augustine's friendship with the unnamed friend seems significantly similar to those described by Rousseau, in whose *Confessions* (and indeed other works) *imagination* and *enthousiasme* (the projection of qualities onto the beloved object) play such a large role. In an influential paper, Gregory Vlastos argued that Platonic love is necessarily selfish and turns upon objectification of the beloved. In elucidating the deficiencies of Plato's account, Vlastos invoked Rousseau, noting of Rousseau's love for Madame D'Houdetot that "she served him only as a mannequin to wear his fantasies."[60] Whatever one makes of Vlastos' thesis with regard to Plato,[61] for Rousseau at least the remark seems apt, and as we have seen here, it seems apt also for Augustine. For Augustine, as for Rousseau, the object of affection, in this case the unnamed friend, served primarily as a model for one's fantasies rather than a colleague in virtue or the object of other-regarding concern.[62]

V

The friendship of book IV is thus revealed by Augustine to have lacked concern for the friend for his own sake (at least on Augustine's part) and to have been driven by base desires. Regarding this last, something in the way of further comment is required. In the first book of the *Confessiones*, Augustine tells us that the instincts implanted in him by God were good and pushed him toward truth and self-preservation (*conf.* 1.20.31), but this comes with an admonitory remark: that one should not love the creature to the point of neglecting the creator (*conf.* 1.20.31).[63] This theme—the manner in which inappropriately delighting in the creature distracts one from appropriately delighting in the creator—is also prominent in the treatment of the close friendship of the fourth book.

For Augustine, the desire to know and to love God is strongly grounded in the human desire for happiness. Augustine takes it to be a fact of human psychology that humans seek to always possess happiness, and since possessing happiness eternally requires eternal life, humans desire eternal life.[64] This desire for eternal life finds its complement in an aversion to prospective extinction: fear of death (*c. Faust* 21.3–7; *lib. arb.* 3.7.20–8.23). The desire for eternal life and fear of death may be seen as a primary (two-part) motivational impetus insofar as they are crucial to the ultimate explanation of many of our actions.[65] Thus, humans are deficient and have a fundamental lack within themselves; being conscious of this and that we are unable to secure eternal possession of happiness we are meant to search for the means to do so; realizing that we cannot do so through our own efforts, we are meant to come to the Church and to God. On such an account, fear of death and perceiving our own inadequacy are crucial indicators to man that he should seek God. The *Confessiones* begins, famously, by describing this: "Man: a small piece of your creation, divulging his mortality, desires to praise you. [. . .] You stir [man] to delight in praising you because you made us to be oriented towards you and our heart is restless until it finds peace in you" (*conf.* 1.1.1).[66]

At the beginning of the third book of the *Confessiones*, a link is made between loving to be loved, as was Augustine's habit in his friendships, and the inner lack that humans feel: "I did not yet love, but I loved to love, and out of a hidden lack, I hated myself for lacking less. Loving to love, I sought after what I might love, and I hated safety and the path without snares. For I had a hunger within for intimate food: Thyself, my God" (*conf.* 3.1.1).[67] This more hidden lack (*secretiora indigentia*)—a hunger for inner food—was in fact (as Augustine sees while writing) a desire for eternal happiness—an eternal life of knowing and loving God. As Augustine reveals throughout these early books of the *Confessiones*, he felt the hunger but mistook its object. Taking the object of such a lack to be other than it was, he focused his attention not on God, but rather on human friendships and sought to fill the void within him with human *amicitia*. This is one way then in which *amicitia* can mislead: feeling a lack within ourselves, we focus our delight on our friendships and do not seek God as we should (*conf.* 2.5.10, 4.7.12–8.13).

One might think it arbitrary that *amicitia* should be singled out for attention as an obstacle to righteousness in this way; delight in one's career, family, wealth, or a multitude of other things might seem equally capable of impeding spiritual progress (cf. Matthew 10:35–9, 19:41–4; Luke 14:26). Augustine does have things to say about such matters in the *Confessiones*,[68] but there does seem to be something special about the potential for *amicitia* to mislead. While other putative goods might seem to fill the God-shaped hole that is meant to point toward the spiritual life, Augustine seems to think that *amicitia* deserves special attention insofar as it is especially adept at alleviating the symptoms of the human predicament and distracting one from the seriousness of one's condition. The fourth book gives attention to the errors of Manichaeism as a false religion, but it emerges that *amicitia* also provides a distinctive delight and has the potential to act as a substitute for the love and worship of God.

We have seen above how Augustine sought delight in the *suavitas* of his friend rather than that of God (in whom Augustine should have delighted).[69] It is also his unnamed friend's death that gives Augustine occasion to remark on the errors of misplacing love, and he notes the misery caused by having a mortal thing as the object of one's delight (*conf.* 4.6.11). To love mortal things in such a way is, Augustine observes, to be pierced by sorrows (*ad dolores figitur, conf.* 4.10.15).[70] Such love and delight should not be focused on something mortal, but rather on something eternal, which cannot be so lost, namely, God (*conf.* 4.8.13).[71] In focusing on the beauty of creatures, Augustine forgot to seek the beauty of the creator that such earthly beauty was meant to point him toward (*conf.* 4.10.15).[72]

Aristotle notes that "wicked men seek for people with whom to spend their days, and shun themselves; for they remember many a grievous deed, and anticipate others like them, when they are by themselves, but when they are with others they forget" (*NE* 1166b13–17).[73] This seems eminently applicable to the young Augustine. Augustine notes that at his friend's death he should have placed his trust and hope in God (*conf.* 4.5.9); however, he once again sought out earthly friendships to fill the void in his life and focused on false religion. Talking, making jokes, reading books, and debating with friends all served to distract Augustine from his condition (*conf.* 4.8.13); his friendships drew Augustine away from the lesson he should have learned concerning taking a mortal thing as the object of one's love (cf. *conf.* 4.6.11). Rather than accept his shortcomings and seek refuge in God, Augustine sought to forget the state of his soul and looked instead to the comfort of other earthly friendships.

VI

The first four books of the *Confessiones* show Augustine progressing ever further in his *exitus* from God (before attempting a *reditus* in the later books). In the latter books of the *Confessiones*, once Augustine is (more or less) set on the right path, a less negative view of friendship seems to be offered. This is especially evident in Augustine's friendship with Alypius in the sixth book. In contrast with the earlier friendship with his unnamed friend, Augustine's friendship with Alypius was long-standing and he indicates right away that his affection for Alypius grew out of regard for his character rather than shared pleasures or interests (*conf.* 6.7.11).[74] In a further (and telling) contrast with his previous friendships, Augustine notes that he loved Alypius and his other friends at that time *for their own sakes* (*conf.* 6.16.26).[75] In what follows, a nuanced account of the role of friendship among those dedicated to the pursuit of wisdom (as Augustine and his friends were at this time) emerges.

Despite Alypius' virtuous character, Augustine notes that Alypius' other friends brought him to grief. Dragging him to the circus, they instilled in him a damaging vice: a delight in cruel spectacles. As was the case for Augustine in the second book of the *Confessiones*, it is emphasized that Alypius would not have fallen into sin had it not been for his friends (*conf.* 6.8.13). However, through Augustine's intervention, Alypius gives up his damaging addiction to the games (*conf.* 6.7.12). One might think that this shows how friendship can fulfill an edifying role (perhaps so long as the friends are dedicated to the pursuit of wisdom) but, in the same breath, Augustine evidences his ambivalence on this score by noting that their friendship brought Alypius into the grip of the Manichees.[76] In a similar vein, Augustine notes the pleasure that he derived from conversing with his friends while at the same time lamenting the loathsome things they discussed (*conf.* 6.16.26).[77] Equally, while they lived together (*conf.* 6.10.17, 12.21), Alypius, Augustine, and Nebridius made plans for a contemplative life, namely one of a community of friends with no private property (*conf.* 6.14.24),[78] but the plans came to nothing. Finally, with Alypius and Nebridius, Augustine discussed the ends of good and evil (*de finibus bonorum et malorum*: *conf.* 6.16.26).[79] While the sort of joint philosophical inquiry that is hinted at here might be seen as important to ethical improvement, Augustine tells us little of its positive results. Furthermore, in the next book he reveals that, when he had previously inquired into the origin of evil (presumably meaning to include the kinds of inquiries conducted among friends, as discussed in the sixth book), he had inquired poorly (*et quaerebam unde malum, et male quaerebam*: *conf.* 7.5.7).

That Augustine is ambivalent about the role of friendship in fostering virtue even among those who are more or less on the right path emerges most clearly from a closer consideration of Augustine's discussion of his friendship with Alypius. In discussing this particular friendship, Augustine begins by right away making clear that there are limits to the role that friendship could play in ethical improvement: he notes that his friendship with Alypius did not mean that he could steer the latter away from vice (*conf.* 6.7.11).[80] Further, it was not just that the bond of friendship has limited power in this regard, but also, as Augustine reports, that the well-being of Alypius was not even at the forefront of his mind at the time (*conf.* 6.7.12).[81]

It is in elaborating how, through Augustine's intervention, Alypius came to give up his damaging addiction to the circus, that Augustine draws attention to an important feature of his thought; whatever good comes of friendship is to be credited neither to friendship nor to the friends themselves, but to God. This point requires something in the way of elaboration, and Augustine provides it in explaining why he deserves no credit for Alypius' moral improvement. In giving his lessons, Augustine happened one day to castigate the circus games (*conf.* 6.7.12) and this brought Alypius, who happened to be in the audience, to his senses. What Augustine goes on to say here is interesting: "to you [God] should be credited his improvement; though you worked it through me, I was unaware [. . .] you know, our God, that I had not then thought about saving Alypius from that sickness, but he took it to heart, and believed I had said it only on his account" (*conf.* 6.7.12).[82] Thus, in hearing Augustine castigate the circus, Alypius took the words as a personal rebuke and amended his behavior as a result *even though this was not what Augustine had intended.* That is to say, correcting Alypius' error was not the reason why Augustine said what he said. Accordingly, he stresses that Alypius' improvement should not be credited to his friendship with Augustine or to Augustine himself because the benefit came about accidentally as an unintended result (what we might regard as a side effect) of Augustine's actions.[83] In fact, Augustine wants to say that the true cause was not Augustine (or Augustine's words) but God who used him (namely, Augustine) as an instrument of his will. As Augustine immediately tells us here: "but You [God] use all, both those who know and those who are unaware" (*sed utens tu omnibus et scientibus et nescientibus: conf.* 6.7.12).

Such a sentiment is further elaborated in the seventh book with regard to Augustine's rejection of astrology, brought about by conversing with a friend: Firminus. As with Augustine's improvement of Alypius, Augustine emphasizes that it was not Firminus' primary intent to break Augustine's penchant for astrology (*conf.* 7.6.8),[84] and here it becomes similarly clear that Augustine does not credit his friends or their actions for turning him from vice; rather, these were merely occasions by means of which God acted as a cause. It was God, he emphasizes, who brought his ethical improvement about: "[I]t was you [God], wholly you" (*tu enim, tu omnino*: *conf.* 7.6.8).

However, surely this does not mean that *any* good that comes out of a friendship is not to be credited to either friendship or the friends? Surely, Augustine is focusing only on cases of unintended benefit to draw attention to God's role in these particular circumstances for the sake of certain theological considerations in his *Confessiones*? Perhaps so, but Augustine does not directly tell us of any goods that might come of friendship that may in fact be credited either to friendship itself or the friends and his thoughts here are reflective of a dominant (and unattractive) feature of his later thinking: that when it comes to virtuous action God is to be credited, but when it comes to wrongdoing man is to blame. Elaborating the details of such views concerning agency, praise, and blame is beyond my remit here; however, it is interesting to note that, in emphasizing the limited role of *amicitia*, Augustine shows considerable agreement with the ideas of Paulinus and his emphasis on predestination and God working through man (e.g., *ep.* 3.1ff).

VII

When Augustine discusses *amicitia* in later writings outside of the *Confessiones*, he does give some attention to the pleasure that friendship brings (e.g., *ep.* 130, *Trin.* 8.3.4), but (unlike Aristotle or Cicero) he does not dwell upon its role in the virtuous life (and we have already seen, with regard to the earlier books of the *Confessiones*, the capacity that such pleasure has for distracting us from love of God).[85] Neither does he have much to say about issues that would greatly exercise more recent Christian thinkers, such as whether there is some possible tension between the demands of an *amor caritatis* which the Christian should feel toward all (*qua* neighbors) and the *amor amicitiae* which may be borne only towards a few.[86] Rather, what seems to occupy his greatest attention is the volatile nature of friendship and the obscurity of the human heart. Augustine emphasizes that professions of friendship, like much else in this life, must be taken on trust (*util. cred.* 8.20, 10.24, 11.26; *f. invis.* 1.2–2.4; *conf.* 6.5.7; *civ. Dei* 11.3). While one can directly perceive the (putative) friend's acts, one cannot directly perceive their character or will (*voluntas*, e.g., *f. invis.* 1.2–2.3); thus one cannot (Augustine thinks), strictly speaking, *know* whether true friendship obtains between oneself and another. It is in the light of these considerations that Augustine typically emphasizes the fragility of friendship; characters are prone to change, and we cannot be fully confident even of what we will ourselves be like in the future, let alone someone else. Here, the estrangements he observed between even eminent Christians of his acquaintance (such as Jerome and Rufinus)[87] seem to have impressed themselves upon him: "In sum, which friend might not be feared as a future enemy if there could arise that lamentable [division] between Jerome and Rufinus? Oh pitiful and pitiable [human] condition! Oh treacherous is the knowledge of the wills of present friends when there is no foreknowledge of their future characters" (*ep.* 73.3.6).[88] In this letter, Augustine goes on to say that these uncertainties may be put aside, and he praises friendship as a consolation in times of hardship and grief (*ep.* 73.3.10). However, the uncertainties of friendship recur in other writings (e.g., *ep.* 130.2.4) and even when praising the consolation offered by friendship (which is the main positive effect that emerges from friendship in these discussions), in the same breath Augustine typically emphasizes the anxieties that it produces (*civ. Dei* 19.8). Even though we turn to friends to ease our worries, we nonetheless worry over their safety and spiritual health.

VIII

In *De Civitate Dei*, Augustine tells us that a brief but accurate account of virtue is that it is the correct ordering of love (*definitio brevis et vera virtutis ordo est amoris*: *civ. Dei* 15.22). His counsel is thus to apportion one's love to the value of its object: we should not love things more or less than they deserve.[89] Part of Augustine's problem in his early life was that he failed to heed this counsel: he did not love wisely (in that he did not apportion the degree of his love to its object) and he did not love well (in that his love was vicious and driven by *cupiditas* rather than *caritas*). In discussing the friendships of his adolescence and young adulthood, Augustine's account shows us the many ways in which friendship, rather than serving as an impetus to virtue, may lead us astray. This focus on friendship among those less than good is unusual, and the account of friendship with which we are presented in the early books of the *Confessiones* shows the consequences of disordered love; however, it shows not only how friendship *manifests* various vices but also how it *fosters* and *encourages* them. Thus, friendships can act as a *seductio* of the mind, constricting our practical reasoning and leading us to sin on occasions (like that of the theft of the pears) where we would otherwise persevere on the right course of action; this seems to be connected to how friendships influence our sense of shame and pride. Further, Augustine also shows how, even within a close friendship of the sort especially prized by the classical tradition, friendship may lack the sort of robust, noninstrumental and other-directed concern often attributed to it and how it may act as a locus for *concupiscentia* and *superbia*. Finally, he also points toward how the distinctive delight provided by *amicitia* might assuage some of the symptoms of man's fallen condition in such a way that he no longer seeks God as he ought.

This is not to say that Augustine thinks friendship is a vice or exclusively acts to foster vice: he does not.[90] In the later books of the *Confessiones*, something in the way of an account toward how friendship might foster virtue is provided. However, even here, when discussing friendship among those dedicated to the pursuit of wisdom, Augustine takes care to note that friendship may not only point us toward virtue, but also towards vice. He also takes substantial care to emphasize that whatever good comes of friendship should not be credited to the friends, but to God. In later writings (after the *Confessiones*), Augustine gives some attention to how friendship may act as a consolation in times of grief. However, unlike Aristotle or Cicero, he has little to say about the role of friendship in aiding us to be virtuous and typically draws attention to the fragility of friendship and the fact that friendship may produce as many anxieties as it assuages.

Augustine remarks that the friendship portrayed in the early books of the *Confessiones* was not true friendship as it was not bound by the *caritas* of the Holy Spirit (*conf.* 4.4.7). However, even when talking of friendships among those who are Christians or are otherwise dedicated to the pursuit of wisdom, he shows himself keenly aware of its dangers. It is striking that he does not anywhere in his voluminous writings discuss *vera amicitia* in any detail or how *amicitia* may play a significant role in a good Christian life. Whereas much of the classical philosophical tradition focused emphatically on the place of friendship in the good life and its role as an aid to virtue (or even as constitutive of virtue), Augustine offers a more nuanced account which gives pronounced emphasis and shows special sensitivity to the dangers of *amicitia*.

Notes

*I would like to thank the following: the editors, especially Professor Suzanne Stern-Gillet for all her work on this volume, inviting me to contribute, and her kind encouragement in correspondence; an anonymous reader who made a number of very helpful suggestions and constructive criticisms; the copy-editor; and, especially, Naomi O'Leary for reading this piece (several times!). Two final notes. First, this chapter grew out of an essay I wrote for my M.Phil. Despite the long gestation period of this volume, my piece no doubt still bears many marks of callowness. Second, it covers some of the same issues as (but is nonetheless significantly distinct from) another piece which also grew out of that work (provisionally entitled 'Augustine on the Dangers of Friendship').

1. In the last few hundred years a robust form of noninstrumental other-directed concern (i.e., altruism) has often been taken to be a prerequisite of morality. The eudaemonism of the ancients, with its emphasis on the agent's pursuit of his or her own happiness, has sometimes been taken to lack such an other-directed concern. Much recent scholarship aims to save the ancients from such a charge and friendship typically receives substantial attention in this regard. For discussion see, for instance, Madigan 1985, 1–20; Kraut 1989, 78–154; Annas 1993, 223–90.

2. Except where noted otherwise, all translations are my own. Note that for the *Confessiones*, I have followed the Latin text of O'Donnell 1992. For other ancient authors (e.g., Aristotle, Cicero) I have followed the most recent standard editions.

3. I take Aristotle's initial hesitation as to whether friendship is itself a virtue, a constitutive part of virtue, "involves" virtue, or else an aid to the development of virtue and a necessary condition of happiness, to be a feature of a number of the ancient discussions. Here I will focus primarily on the role of friendship as an aid to the development of virtue.

4. *Virtutum amicitia adiutrix a natura data est, non vitiorum comes.*

5. For a general treatment of friendship in the ancient world, see Konstan 1997. The classical tradition did dedicate some attention to the dangers of false friends and of flattery, but by and large the focus was on the positive role of friendship in the good life. On the dangers of friendship, see especially the essays in Fitzgerald 1996.

6. An often iterated thought; see, for instance, Smith Pangle 2003 as well as Manoussakis' contribution to the present volume.

7. While the term "φίλος" (usually rendered as "*amicus*") does appear a number of times in the New Testament, sometimes with positive connotations (most notably at John 15:13–14), "φιλία" (usually rendered as "*amicitia*") in fact explicitly appears only once and does so in a negative context where what is spoken of is the friendship of this world which is hostile to God: *amicitia huius mundi inimica est Dei* (James 4:4).

8. Thus, for instance, it is the multitude of believers (*multitudo credentium*) who are said to share one heart and one soul and who hold all things in common (Acts 4:32; cf. Acts 2:44). The believers are not there described as friends, nor is the relation that obtains between them described as one of friendship.

9. For discussion of the context, see Konstan 1996, 87–113.

10. Ambrose's treatise, like the relevant material in Cicero, seems to be primarily practical and hortatory in character and we find little in the way of explicit argument or analysis.

11. However, unlike Cicero, Ambrose sees friendship among the poor as superior to that among the rich (*Off.* 3.135) for it is free of the danger of flattery.

12. Ambrose will also often say something as to how these biblical examples outdo those offered by the pagans (e.g., *Off.* 3.80).

13. This *caritas* obtains between Christians even though the Christians in question may not know each other, a fact Paulinus stressed to Augustine upon making his acquaintance through correspondence (*ep.* 4.1, 6.1–2). Members of the Church are joined together by the common bond of the love of Christ in both senses of that phrase: the love toward Christ and Christ's love (*ep.* 11.1–3, 51.3).

14. See, for instance, *ep.* 40.2. For Paulinus' denigration of *amicitia* in general, see Fabre 1949, 142–52, and White 1992, 158–59. While White rightly observes that Fabre overstates the case somewhat, Fabre's general analysis is, I think, sound. For agreement and discussion, see Konstan 1997, 157–60; 1996, 97–101.

15. The most substantial treatment of friendship in Augustine is McNamara 1958. However, probably the best up-to-date treatment is the brief, but very helpful, encyclopedia entry of Lienhard 1999, 372–73.

16. The diverse questions were posed (and responded to by Augustine) between 388 and 396. The order is often taken to be chronological, but several questions, such as number 31, have often been thought difficult to date. I assume that the differences in the treatment of friendship between what we find in *div. qu.* 31 and *ep.* 258 (which I take to have been written around 395, but which is itself not absolutely certain in date) are to be explained by *div. qu.* 31 being written earlier. Notice that all abbreviations employed follow the conventions of Fitzgerald 1999. The same applies for dates except where noted otherwise.

17. As far as I can tell, the extent of Augustine's dependence on Cicero here is rarely raised in the scholarship.

18. Augustine here writes that "virtue is a disposition of the soul in harmony with the way of nature and reason" (*virtus est animi habitus naturae modo atque rationi consentaneus: div. qu.* 31.1). For other early accounts of virtue, compare *mor.* 1.19.35ff; *mus.* 6.15.49ff; *vera rel.* 15.28. In his later works, Augustine seems most often to regard virtue as correctly ordered love (*civ. Dei* 15.22).

19. Note that Augustine treats goodwill (*gratia*) under justice (*iustitia*) but does not explicitly say that it is a part of justice (the other virtues are more explicitly treated in terms of their constitutive parts). For an illuminating explanation of how, when *A* is a *part* of *B*, predicating something of *A* affects predications of *B*, see Reinhardt 2003, 217–20 ad Cic. *Top.* 13–14.

20. *Gratia in qua amicitiarum et officiorum alterius memoria et remunerandi voluntas continetur.*

21. This is not, of course, to say that friendship is itself a part of, or necessary for, virtue, merely that justice (itself a part of virtue) requires recognizing the duties to and good turns performed by a friend.

22. *Sunt igitur multa quae nos, cum dignitate, tum fructu quoque suo ducunt.* Notice that this seems to mark the first hints of the distinction between *usus* (use)

and *fruitio* (enjoyment) which would occupy Augustine greatly in some others works (notably *De doctrina Christiana*).

23. The first three, it must be emphasized (especially on the Ciceronian account that Augustine gives of them here), are not especially consonant with the Christian life and its emphasis on humility and its repudiation of pride; in later works Augustine will be far more cautious on this score (e.g., *civ. Dei* 5.12ff).

24. *Amicitia voluntas erga aliquem rerum bonarum illius ipsius causa quem diligit cum eius pari voluntate.* Cf. Cic. *Inv.* 2.166.

25. Unlike Ambrose, Augustine does not here even attempt to adapt Cicero; he merely repeats what he finds (without mentioning his source).

26. *Siquidem amicitia rectissime atque sanctissime definita est, rerum humanarum et divinarum cum benevolentia et caritate consensio.*

27. See A. Mandouze 1982, 691–92.

28. *Eum quem quoquo modo habui diu amicum, habeo iam verum amicum.*

29. In fact, Augustine seems to think both that agreement on human affairs follows from agreement on the divine (*ep.* 258.2) and that those who do not share agreement on divine affairs cannot be agreed on human affairs either. *Ita fit ut inter quos amicos non est rerum consensio divinarum, nec humanarum plena esse possit ac vera* (*ep.* 258.2). The assumptions motivating this line of thought are not entirely perspicuous.

30. *Proinde non dico, nunc mihi plenius amicus es, qui eras ex parte; sed quantum ratio indicat, nec ex parte eras, quando nec in rebus humanis mecum amicitiam veram tenebas. Rerum quippe divinarum, ex quibus recte humana pensantur, socius mihi nondum eras; sive quando nec ipse in eis eram, sive posteaquam ego eas utcumque sapere coepi, a quibus tu longe abhorrebas* (*ep.* 258.2). In fact, as Augustine goes on to stress, he (Augustine) was not even a friend to himself at that point in his life (*nec ipse mihi amicus eram, sed potius inimicus: ep.* 258.3).

31. Lucan (*Bellum Civile* 7.62–3), Cicero (*Amic.* 20), Terence (*An.* 189), and Virgil (*Ecl.* 4.13–14) are all cited in this short letter.

32. Concerning the usage of *amicitia*, Konstan 1997, 161, has it right in saying that "*amicitia*" in Augustine sometimes "designates friendship in the strict sense i.e., the bonds uniting two persons in mutual sympathy" (e.g., *ep.* 84.1), but this usage seems most frequent in the *Confessions*, where Augustine is characterizing relationships formed prior to his conversion." See also Konstan 1996, 103; Lienhard 1999, 373.

33. The helpful entry of Lienhard 1999 lists the significant passages discussing *amicitia* as follows: *sol.* 1.2.7–1.12.22; *div. qu.* 71.5–7; *f. invis.* 2.3–5.8; *cat. Rud.*, passim; *Trin* 9.6.11; *ep. Jo.* 8.5; *c. ep. Pel.* 1.1; *civ. Dei* 19.8; *ep.* 73, 130.6.13–7.14, 192, 258. To these we might add others: for instance, *vera rel.* 47.91 and *s.* 336.2. It is difficult to summarize all these intricate discussions in a way that does them justice, especially if one considers, as one should, how these discussions fit into the framework of his views on *usus* and *fruitio* and *amor* and *caritas*. Notice, however, that while in later works, Augustine speaks more of *amor*

than he does of *amicitia*, he does not (at least not explicitly) seem to depart too far from the amended Ciceronian definition of friendship that he accepted in *ep.* 258. Thus, for instance (invoking Greek discussions of *eunoia* in his discussion of the sermon on the mount) he strongly associates friendship with benevolence: *ubi enim beniuolentia, ibi amicitia* (*s. dom. mon.* 1.11.31).

34. Much of the relevant scholarship focuses on the role Augustine gives to friendship in the virtuous life; however, there is little in Augustine's texts to go on. While he has much to say about the love of neighbor and its importance, he has, as I argued above, less to say about *amor amicitiae* in this regard. Contrast my own treatment (in what follows) with, for instance, Paffenroth 2005, 53–65.

35. *Exarsi enim aliquando satiari inferis in adulescentia, et silvescere ausus sum variis et umbrosis amoribus, et contabuit species mea, et computrui coram oculis tuis placens mihi et placere cupiens oculis hominum. et quid erat quod me delectabat, nisi amare et amari? sed non tenebatur modus ab animo usque ad animum quatenus est luminosus limes amicitiae, sed exhalabantur nebulae de limosa concupiscentia carnis et scatebra pubertatis, et obnubilabant atque obfuscabant cor meum, ut non discerneretur serenitas dilectionis a caligine libidinis.*

36. For detailed discussion, see O'Daly 2007, 211–23.

37. *Cur ergo eo me delectabat quo id non faciebam solus?* [. . .] *Solus non facerem furtum illud, in quo me non libebat id quod furabar sed quia furabar: quod me solum facere prorsus non liberet, nec facerem. o nimis inimica amicitia, seductio mentis investigabilis, ex ludo et ioco nocendi aviditas et alieni damni appetitus nulla lucri mei, nulla ulciscendi libidine! sed cum dicitur, 'eamus, faciamus,' et pudet non esse impudentem.*

38. "My wickedness had no cause but wickedness; it was loathsome yet I loved it. I loved being corrupted, I loved my fall, not that for which I had fallen, but the fall itself" (*et malitiae meae causa nulla esset nisi malitia. foeda erat, et amavi eam. amavi perire, amavi defectum meum, non illud ad quod deficiebam, sed defectum meum ipsum amavi: conf.* 2.4.9).

39. In speaking of reasons for action, Augustine often couches his discussion in terms of *pulchritudo, delectatio, decorum,* and *species.* Thus, for instance: *quid ego miser in te amavi, o furtum meum*[?][. . .] *quaero quid me in furto delectaverit, et ecce species nulla est* (*conf.* 2.6.12).

40. Sometimes Augustine is attracted by the thought that paradigmatic sins, being the sort of evil that they are, have no cause (*lib. arb.* 2.54; *civ. Dei* 12.6–9); however, he does seem to think that all events, including sins, have causes (e.g. *ord.* 1.11–15); that is precisely why he seeks to explain the sins of Adam and Lucifer.

41. Lucifer decided to send the snake to Eve "not thinking that the man would be so credulous nor able to err by being deceived so easily but rather that he would fall by the error of another. Just as it was with Aaron while the people were in error, he didn't consent to the making of the idol because he was convinced, *but he yielded to compulsion*" (*non existimans virum facile credulum nec errando posse decipi, sed dum alieno cedit errori. Sicut enim Aaron erranti populo ad idolum fabricandum non consensit inductus, sed cessit obstrictus: civ. Dei* 14.11).

42. *Quis exaperit istam tortuosissimam et implicatissimam nodositatem?*

43. *Quoniam audiebam eos iactantes flagitia sua et tanto gloriantes magis, quanto magis turpes essent, et libebat facere non solum libidine facti verum etiam laudis. quid dignum est vituperatione nisi vitium? ego, ne vituperarer, vitiosior fiebam, et ubi non suberat quo admisso aequarer perditis, fingebam me fecisse quod non feceram, ne viderer abiectior quo eram innocentior, et ne vilior haberer quo eram castior* (conf. 2.3.7).

44. *Tu autem, mi carissime, aliquando mihi consentiebas in rebus humanis, cum eis more vulgi frui cuperem, et mihi ad ea capessenda quorum me poenitet, favendo velificabas, imo vero vela cupiditatum mearum, cum caeteris tunc dilectoribus meis, inter praecipuos aura laudis inflabas* (ep. 258.1).

45. Whereas Epicureans and Stoics had discussed whether infants were initially impelled by nature toward pleasure or self-preservation, Augustine inaugurates a far more pessimistic view wherein humans seem directed primarily toward *concupiscentia* and pride; he portrays the infant as a little tyrant viewing others as subjects who should obey its will and not wanting to share even when this means that its own portion will not be diminished (*conf.* 1.6.8, 1.7.11).

46. Augustine notes how, in his early life, he loved people on account of popular opinion and forcefully condemns the affection he developed for an orator he had never met based on his reputation (*conf.* 4.14.21–3). Similarly, the desire for a fine writing style, so highly praised, proved an obstacle to Augustine accepting the truth of scripture (*conf.* 3.5.9; cf. 1.18.28–29). The account of how his mother's desire to see him do well by worldly lights (having a prestigious career, etc.) was in tension with the demands of a Christian life (*conf.* 2.2.4; 2.3.8; 5.8.15; 8.12.30) might also be read in such a way.

47. Though Cicero's *Hortensius* may have served as the impetus that sparked Augustine's search for wisdom (*conf.* 3.4.7–8; cf. 8.7.17), Augustine read many of Cicero's works, and Cicero's influence on Augustine was pervasive, the difference between Cicero and the Augustine of the *Confessiones* is stark, especially in their treatment of *honos, laus,* and the like. Cicero typically emphasizes the positive role of praise and fame (e.g., *Tusc.* 1.2.4, *Inv.* 2.166, etc.), and in writing on friendship, he emphasizes that reputation is paramount. The value of friendship is confirmed by the esteem in which it is held by people and that one can obtain *maxima gloria* through having it (*Amic.* 23, 25); defense of one's reputation, or that of a friend, makes an otherwise illicit deed permissible (*Amic.* 61). For discussion of Augustine's relation to Cicero, see Testard 1958.

48. Aristotle does seem to think that genuine care for the friend for his own sake can be present even in the lower forms of friendship, which are dedicated, not to the good, but primarily to utility or pleasure. For discussion of these features, see Cooper 1980, 301–40.

49. *Suavi mihi super omnes suavitates illius vitae meae.*

50. That many of the celebrated friendships of antiquity had a homosexual element is fairly clear. For judicious remarks on whether Augustine's friendship here had such an element, see the remarks of O'Donnell 1992, 2:108–110 ad *conf.* 2.2.2.

51. The phrase "another self" finds its origin, at least in philosophical discourse, in Aristotle (e.g., *NE* 1166a31–2; cf. *MM* 1213a12). For discussion of the notion in Aristotle's account, see Schollmeier 1994; Stern-Gillet 1995; Whiting 2006, 276–304.

52. Aquinas offers an admirably concise summary of the ordinary sense: "when someone loves someone through the love of friendship, he desires the good for him just as he desires the good for himself; on account of this, he apprehends him as another he in as much as he desires the good for him just as much as for himself. And that is why the friend is said to be another self" (*cum aliquis amat aliquem amore amicitiae, vult ei bonum sicut et sibi vult bonum: unde apprehendit eum ut alterum se, inquantum scilicet vult ei bonum sicut et sibi ipsi. Et inde est quod amicus dicitur esse alter ipse: ST* I–II, 28.1). For Aquinas' views on friendship, see Kerr's chapter in the present volume.

53. Thus, Augustine writes: *mirabar enim ceteros mortales vivere, quia ille, quem quasi non moriturum dilexeram, mortuus erat, et me magis, quia ille alter eram, vivere illo mortuo mirabar* (*conf.* 4.6.11). Notice that "other self" is often used in English translations here. Thus, "for he was my 'other self'" (Chadwick 1991, 59), "I his other self living still" (Sheed 2006, 61), "for I was his second self" (Pine-Coffin 1961, 77).

54. This is noticed by Aquinas (*Summa Theologiae* I–II, .28.1). Augustine does use the phrase *alter ego* on one occasion (*ep.* 38.1; cf. Ovid *Am.* 1.7.31). In Cicero one finds the following: *quicum ego cum loquor nihil fingam* (*Att.* 1.18.1); *me enim ipsum multo magis accuso, deinde te quasi me alterum et simul meae culpae socium quaero* (*Att.* 3.15.4); *ego tecum tamquam mecum loquor* (*Att.* 8.14.2). Cicero, however, does use *alter idem* (*Amic.* 80).

55. *Ego sensi animam meam et animam illius unam fuisse animam in duobus corporibus.*

56. *Distuli omnes motus meos, ut convalesceret prius essetque idoneus viribus valetudinis, cum quo agere possem quod vellem.*

57. *Baptizatus est nesciens, me non curante et praesumente id retinere potius animam eius quod a me acceperat.*

58. *Solus fletus erat dulcis mihi et successerat amico me in deliciis animi mei.*

59. *Sic ego eram illo tempore et flebam amarissime et requiescebam in amaritudine. Ita miser eram et habebam cariorem illo amico meo vitam ipsam miseram.*

60. See Vlastos 1973, 29.

61. For discussion (and repudiation) of Vlastos' charge, see, e.g., Sheffield 2012, 117–41.

62. For Rousseau's *Confessions* as being influenced by Augustine (a controversial thesis), see Hartle 1999, 263–85.

63. "My sin was this: I sought pleasures, exaltation, and truths not in God but in his creatures: in myself and others" (*hoc enim peccabam, quod non in ipso sed in creaturis eius me atque ceteris voluptates, sublimitates, veritates quaerebam: conf.* 1.20.31).

64. This is a perpetual theme in Augustine from early works such as *De moribus ecclesiae catholicae* (e.g., 1.3.4–11.19) and *De beata vita* (e.g. 2.11) to later works such as *De civitate Dei* (e.g. 14.4) and *De Trinitate* (e.g., 13.7.10): *sed non est mortalitatis huius haec [beata] vita, nec erit nisi quando et immortalitas erit*. While the eudaemonist tradition at large took it as a given of human psychology that we all aim at happiness (e.g. *Euthydemus* 278e3–6, 280b5–6, 282a1–2; *Symp.* 204e1–205d9; Arist. *Rh.* 1360b4–7), the emphasis that we seek to possess *eternal happiness* might seem distinctively Platonic (e.g. *Symp.* 206a). That humans seek eternal happiness is most often interpreted by Augustine as a psychological claim, addressing what agents do (rather than a normative claim, addressing what agents *should* do). For Augustine, as for much of the eudaemonist tradition, the good person differs from the bad insofar as they better appreciate how to successfully secure their happiness: by being good and desiring the right things (e.g., *NE* 1169a3–6). For Augustine, we all seek happiness; what we *should do* is pursue this eternal happiness by living a Christian life (e.g., *s.* 150.4).

65. Augustine even attempts to explain suicide on the basis of a desire for continued life: the agent desires to "live on" by means of fame and renown (*lib. arb.* 3.8.22–3).

66. *Et laudare te vult homo, aliqua portio creaturae tuae, et homo circumferens mortalitatem suam [. . .] tu excitas, ut laudare te delectet, quia fecisti nos ad te et inquietum est cor nostrum, donec requiescat in te* (*conf.* 1.1.1). The first sentence of the translation above is loose as I have cut the Augustine off mid-sentence in the Latin.

67. *Nondum amabam, et amare amabam, et secretiore indigentia oderam me minus indigentem. quaerebam quid amarem, amans amare, et oderam securitatem et viam sine muscipulis, quoniam fames mihi erat intus ab interiore cibo, te ipso, deus meus.*

68. Augustine does give some attention to these, noting the evils of pagan literature and how his career as a rhetor had to be given up in order to get closer to God (*conf.* 1.16.26–18.29, 3.3.6, 4.1.1ff), and even how his mother's love for him *qua* mother came in the way of her love for him *qua* Christian. In this regard, it was her desire for grandchildren or his having a wife that were problematic (*conf.* 2.2.4, 2.3.8, 5.8.15, 8.12.30).

69. *Et quis est hic nisi deus noster, suavitas et origo iustitiae,* (*conf.* 4.3.4). Augustine elsewhere attributes *suavitas* to God (e.g., *conf.* 2.9.13, 9.1.1, 10.17.26); however, its invocation here, shortly before his discussion of the *suavitas* of his friend (*conf.* 4.4.7) is pointed and indicates, I think, the manner in which that friendship sought to supplant a closer relation with God.

70. *Laudet te ex illis anima mea, deus, creator omnium, sed non in eis figatur glutine amore per sensus corporis. eunt enim quo ibant, ut non sint, et conscindunt eam desideriis pestilentiosis, quoniam ipsa esse vult et requiescere amat in eis quae amat. in illis autem non est ubi, quia non stant: fugiunt* (*conf.* 4.10.15).

71. "For why had that grief pierced me so easily and deeply other than my pouring my soul into the sand by loving someone who would die as if he would

not die?" (*nam unde me facillime et in intima dolor ille penetraverat, nisi quia fuderam in harenam animam meam diligendo moriturum acsi non moriturum:? conf.* 4.8.13).

72. On how the beauty of sensible things is meant to lead us to God, see also *conf.* 10.6.9–8.12; Augustine's remarks on this issue seem to parallel the discussion of the *scala amoris* that we find in the *Symposium* (210a6–c6). Note however that Augustine explicitly remarks (in *conf.* 4.10.15) that we should not become too attached to mortal things as this seems to impede our ascent.

73. The translation used is that of Ross, revised by Urmson 1984.

74. "And he loved [me] greatly because I seemed to him to be good and learned and I [loved] him on account of his great innate virtue which was sufficiently evident when he was of no great age" (*et diligebat multum, quod ei bonus et doctus viderer, et ego illum propter magnam virtutis indolem, quae in non magna aetate satis eminebat, conf.* 6.7.11).

75. "I loved them for their own sake and I felt that they in turn loved me for my own sake" (*quos utique amicos gratis diligebam vicissimque ab eis me diligi gratis sentiebam, conf.* 6.16.26).

76. *et audire me rursus incipiens illa mecum superstitione involutus est, amans in manichaeis ostentationem continentiae, quam veram et germanam putabat* (*conf.* 6.7.12).

77. *Nec considerabam miser ex qua vena mihi manaret quod ista ipsa foeda tamen cum amicis dulciter conferebam.*

78. Significantly, neither the community in Acts (4:32–37) nor the emerging monastic movement was an influence: Augustine does not cite Acts and later we learn that he and his friends were completely ignorant of the monastic movement (*conf.* 8.6.14–15). Augustine remarks that, when reading Cicero's *De Finibus*, Epicurus appealed to him the most (*conf.* 6.16.26); this may reveal that Augustine and his friends took the Epicurean garden as their model.

79. A clear reference to Cicero's work of the same title.

80. "But there was no warning him and holding him back by some restraint neither by the goodwill of friendship nor by the command of a teacher" (*sed monendi eum et aliqua cohercitione revocandi nulla erat copia vel amicitiae benivolentia vel iure magisterii: conf.* 6.7.11).

81. "But what to do with him so that his blind and violent zeal for empty games should not extinguish so great a talent had fallen from my mind" (*sed enim de memoria mihi lapsum erat agere cum illo, ne vanorum ludorum caeco et praecipiti studio tam bonum interimeret ingenium: conf.* 6.7.12).

82. *tibi tribueretur eius correctio, per me quidem illam sed nescientem operatus es [. . .] scis tu, deus noster, quod tunc de Alypio ab illa peste sanando non cogitaverim. at ille in se rapuit meque illud non nisi propter se dixisse credidit.*

83. When I say "accidentally" I do not mean by luck; for, as Augustine emphasises, it was not luck, but God's hand at work.

84. "Yet he knew something [about astrology] which he said he had heard from his father: but he was ignorant of what value it would have for the overturning of belief in that art" (*et tamen scientem aliquid quod a patre suo se audisse dicebat: quod quantum valeret ad illius artis opinionem evertendam ignorabat: conf.* 7.6.8).

85. In fact, at one point he notes that enemies may be better at chastising and reproving than friends who are afraid to offend us (*ep.* 73.4).

86. Some see this as the principal issue that any Christian giving ethical consideration to friendship should consider. Kierkegaard, in his Kantian vein, was particularly preoccupied with this question. He emphasises that a Christian should have only neighbors, not friends. He focuses upon the absence of friendship in the scriptures and decries friendship as pagan, erotic and egotistic (1998, IX, 21–200 especially 32).

Augustine occasionally offers some truisms about *amor* and *amicitia* (e.g., *Quid est enim aliud amicitia, quae non aliunde quam ex amore nomen accepit et nusquam nisi in Christo fidelis est, in quo solo esse etiam sempiterna ac felix potest? c. ep. Pel.* 1.1.1) but insofar as he actually touches upon the issue in a meaningful way (e.g., *ep.* 130.6.13; *doc. Chr.* 1.59–62; *ver. rel.* 49.91) he does not seem to see it as too great a worry. Thus, he emphasises: "All people should be loved equally. But you cannot do good to all people equally, so you should take particular thought for those who, as if by lot, happen to be particularly close to you in terms of place, time, or any other circumstances" (*Omnes autem aeque diligendi sunt. Sed cum omnibus prodesse non possis, his potissimum consulendum est qui pro locorum et temporum vel quarumlibet rerum opportunitatibus constrictius tibi quasi quadam sorte iunguntur, doc. Chr.* 1.61). "And since he cannot do good to all people: who he loves equally, unless he prefers to do good to those to whom he is more closely united, there will be injustice. The unity of souls is greater than that of [e.g.] place or time which comes about while we live in this [earthly] body, but that unity which prevails over these is greatest of all" (*Cum itaque omnibus, quos pariter diligit, prodesse non possit, nisi coniunctioribus prodesse malit, iniustus est. Animi autem coniunctio maior est, quam locorum aut temporum quibus in hoc corpore gignimur, sed ea maxima est quae omnibus praevalet. ver. rel.* 47.91).

87. See Kelly 1975; White 1992, 129–45.

88. *Quis denique amicus non formidetur quasi futurus inimicus, si potuit inter Hieronymum et Ruffinum hoc quod plangimus exoriri? O misera et miseranda conditio! O infida in voluntatibus amicorum scientia praesentium, ubi nulla est praescientia futurorum!* Augustine immediately goes on to say that this is hardly surprising given that we do not know what we ourselves will be like in the future: *sed quid hoc alteri de altero gemendum putem, quando nec ipse quidem sibi homo est notus in posterum? Novit enim utcumque, vix forte, nunc qualis sit; qualis autem postea futurus sit, ignorat* (*ep.* 73.3.6; cf. *ep.* 130.2.4).

89. Elsewhere, whether things are to be enjoyed or loved for their own sake is discussed in terms of whether *fruitio* or *usus* is appropriate to the object of one's love (e.g., *doc. Chr.* 1.22.20); however, discussion in such terms seems to be absent from the *Confessiones*. For discussion of *usus* and *fruitio*, and whether one's fellow humans are to be used or enjoyed, see O'Donovan 1982, 361–397; Canning 1993, 79–115.

90. A more difficult question is whether Augustine thinks that all friendships among the unredeemed lead astray. The prospects for *amicitia* among the unredeemed depend in part upon the extent to which pagans are capable of virtue. In *De civitate Dei*, Augustine seems to tell us that the putative virtues of the ancient

Romans were not in fact virtues, but vices (*civ. Dei* 5.19, 19.25; cf. *retr.* 1.3.2 [ad *ord.* 1.11.31]). For discussion see Irwin 1999, 105–27.

Bibliography

Annas, J. 1993. *The Morality of Happiness*. Oxford: Oxford University Press.

Bowery, A. M. 1999. "Plotinus, *The Enneads*." In *Augustine through the Ages*, ed. A. Fitzgerald. Michigan: Eerdmans, 654–57.

Brown, P. 2000. *Augustine of Hippo: A Biography—New Edition with an Epilogue*. London: Faber.

Canning, R. 1993. *The Unity of Love for God and Neighbor in St. Augustine*. Heverlee-Leuven: Augustinian Historical Institute.

Cooper, J. M. 1980. "Aristotle on Friendship." In *Essays on Aristotle's Ethics*, ed. A.O. Rorty. Berkeley: University of California Press, 301–340.

Fabre, P. 1949. *Saint Paulin de Nole et l'amitié chrétienne*. Paris. Paris: E. de Boccard.

Fitzgerald, J. T. (ed.). 1996. *Friendship, Flattery, & Frankness of Speech: Studies on Friendship in the New Testament World*. Leiden: Brill.

Hartle, A. 1999. "Augustine and Rousseau. Narrative and Self-Knowledge in the Two Confessions." In *The Augustinian Tradition*, ed. G. B. Matthews. Berkeley: University of California Press, 263–285.

Irwin, T. 1999. "Splendid Vices? Augustine for and against Pagan Virtues," *Medieval Philosophy and Theology* 8: 105–127.

Kelly, J. N. D. 1975. *Jerome: His Life, Writings and Controversies*. London: Duckworth.

Kierkegaard, S. 1998. *Works of Love*. Edited by H. V. Hong and E. H. Hong,. Princeton NJ, Princeton University Press.

Konstan, D. 1996. "Problems in the History of Christian Friendship." *Journal of Early Christian Studies* 4: 87–113.

———. 1997. *Friendship in the Classical World*. Cambridge: Cambridge University Press.

Kraut, R. 1989. *Aristotle and the Human Good*. Princeton: Princeton University Press.

Lienhard J. T. 1999. "Friendship, Friends." In *Augustine through the Ages*, ed. A. Fitzgerald. Michigan: Eerdmans, 372–373.

Madigan, A. 1985. "*EN* IX 8: Beyond Egoism and Altruism?" *The Modern Schoolman* 63: 1–20.

Mandouze, A. 1982. *Prosopographie chrétienne du Bas-Empire I: Afrique (303–533)*. Paris: C.N.R.S.

McNamara, M. A. 1958. *Friends and Friendship for Saint Augustine*. Friburg: The University Press.

O'Daly, G. 2007. "Friendship and Trangression: *Luminosus Limes Amicitiae* (Augustine, *Confessions* 2.2.2) and the Themes of *Confessions* 2." In *Reading Ancient*

Texts Volume II: Aristotle and Neoplatonism, ed. S. Stern-Gillet and K. Corrigan. Leiden and Boston: Brill, 211–223.

O'Donnell, J. J. 1992. *Augustine Confessions: Volume 1: Introduction and Text.* Oxford: Oxford University Press.

———. 1992. *Augustine Confessions: Volume 2: Commentary, Books 1–7.* Oxford: Oxford University Press.

O'Donovan, O. 1982. "*Usus* and *Fruitio* in Augustine, *De Doctrina Christiana* I," *Journal of Theological Studies* 33: 361–397.

Paffenroth, K. 2005. "Friendship as Personal, Social, and Theological Virtue in Augustine." In *Augustine and Politics*, ed. J. Doody, K. L. Hughes, K. Paffenroth. Lanham, MA: Lexington Books, 53–65.

Price, A.W. 1990. *Love and Friendship in Plato and Aristotle.* Oxford: Oxford University Press.

Reinhardt, T. 2003. *Cicero's Topica: edited, with a translation, introduction, and commentary.* Oxford: Oxford University Press.

Schollmeier, P. 1994. *Other Selves: Aristotle on Personal and Political Friendship.* Albany: SUNY Press.

Sheffield, F. 2012. "The Symposium and Platonic Ethics: Plato, Vlastos, and a Misguided Debate." *Phronesis* 57: 117–141.

Smith Pangle, L. 2003. *Aristotle and the Philosophy of Friendship.* Cambridge: Cambridge University Press.

Solignac, A. (trans. et ed.). 1962. *Les Confessions (Livres I–VII): Bibliothèque Augustinienne 13.* Paris.

Stern-Gillet, S. 1995. *Aristotle's Philosophy of Friendship.* Albany: SUNY Press.

Stern-Gillet, S., and K. Corrigan (eds.). 2007. *Reading Ancient Texts: Aristotle and Neoplatonism. Essays in Honour of Denis O'Brien.* Brill.

Testard, M. 1958. *Saint Augustin et Cicéron.* Paris: Études augustiniennes.

Vlastos, G. 1973. "The Individual as an Object of Love in Plato." In *Platonic Studies,.* Princeton: Princeton University Press, 3–42.

White, C. 1992. *Christian Friendship in the Fourth Century.* Cambridge: Cambridge University Press.

Whiting, J. 2006. "The Nicomachean Account of *Philia*." In *The Blackwell Guide to Aristotle's Nicomachean Ethics*, ed. R. Kraut. Oxford: Blackwell, 276–304.

9

AELRED OF RIEVAULX
ON FRIENDSHIP

John R. Sommerfeldt

1. Introduction

Aelred of Rievaulx was born about 1110, the son and grandson of married priests. When Aelred was fourteen or fifteen, he was sent to the court of King David of Scotland (1124–1153), where he spent some nine years and where he deepened his knowledge of both Latin and vernacular literature. In 1134, David sent Aelred to York on a diplomatic mission. On his way back Aelred stopped to survey the new Cistercian monastery of Rievaulx in North Yorkshire and committed himself to the life he found there. In 1147, Aelred was elected abbot, in which role he served until his death in 1167.

Scholars and lay folk alike have been attracted to Aelred by the discovery of his teaching on friendship. This is really a rediscovery, for, as early as 1934, Bede Jarrett had written with enthusiasm: "The beauty of his [Aelred's] life is the beauty of his friendships; for him they made his life, they helped him to understand life, they gave life the only value it had for him."[1] Appreciation of Aelred's teaching on friendship still motivates students of Aelred's thought. Recently, Bernard McGinn has written that Aelred's "*amicitia spiritualis*" (spiritual friendship) takes its place alongside Bernard's *amor sponsalis* (bridal love) as the main contributions to the Cistercian mysticism of love."[2] Aelred's treatise on friendship has been judged by many others too as the most sophisticated exposition of friendship in Western literature[3]—an exposition that is also an extensive and appreciative reading of the Roman rhetor Cicero's treatise on the subject. To appreciate

227

fully Aelred's teaching on his and Cicero's topic, friendship, it is necessary to gain some understanding of Aelred's anthropology.

2. Aelred's Anthropology

Human beings, Aelred affirms, "were created with the highest dignity,"[4] a dignity derived from the Creator in whose image and likeness they are made.[5] Although humans share with all other creatures the derivative and dependent nature of their existence,[6] as rational beings, they are given a greater share in God's being.[7] Aelred's view of human nature, both its dignity and dependence, leads him to affirm that happiness is possible for humans, "for, in the creation of all things, [God] gave humans not only being and not only some good or beautiful or well-ordered being—as he gave to other creatures—but beyond these, he granted humans happiness in being."[8] Human beings, then, are capable of happiness, and this is because human nature is good.[9]

The dignity of human beings is enhanced, Aelred believes, by their composite unity. Human beings are "composed of a body and of a soul."[10] The high level of awareness, the consciousness, or, as Aelred puts it, the rationality of the soul and the corporeality of the body are both necessary to being human.[11] A human being is thus an entity; in humans rationality and physicality are conjoined.[12]

The human body provides services essential to life as a human and thus assumes for Aelred a dignity not often associated by moderns with the thought of medieval monks. The influx of sensations from the body provides the mind information necessary for the direction and control of that body.[13] The body also supplies through the senses the raw material for thought,[14] and thus knowledge of the whole of creation is made available to the human mind.[15] For Aelred, then, the body is good, the body's very limitations are natural and thus good, and the body will be perfected in beauty and immortality in the happiness of heaven.[16]

As Aelred rejoices in the dignity and dynamics of the body, he also urges his audience to "consider the great dignity of the rational soul."[17] Perhaps the adjective, "rational," is more useful than the noun, "soul," for our understanding of Aelred's position, for by "soul" he understands human rationality, human consciousness, human thought processes.[18] "There are three components comprising the nature of the rational soul," says Aelred. "[T]hey are memory, reason, and will."[19] Because the soul is made in the image and likeness of God, it is able to discover him in itself,[20] and thus reflection on the triune soul leads Aelred to a knowledge of the triune God.[21] But, like the triune God of which the soul is an image, it exists in unity.[22] This is so because "the soul is a simple being, not made up of parts."[23] Reason, will, and memory are, then, merely three ways of expressing the powers which the soul possesses, the ways in which the soul functions.[24]

Thought is the function, the activity, of the intellect.[25] The rational soul does not simply think; it is capable of "recognizing the truth."[26] And because this is so, the intellect can provide necessary guidance in choosing the good.[27] Aelred asserts that "to distinguish between what is just and what unjust is impossible without reason."[28] But the soul possesses "a still higher power" than the discernment of truth and justice, "and that is to see God."[29] Indeed, for Aelred, knowledge of truth and justice and knowledge of God are, on the highest level, the same knowledge.[30]

The power, and hence dignity, of the human will is equally impressive, as Aelred sees it. That power is the power of choice, which the will exercises in absolute freedom, "subject to no necessity."[31] But, in order to choose, one must know what one is choosing, and so the will requires the intellect's assistance in its choices.[32] The action to which the will is directed by the intellect can—and most often does—involve activity by the body, which must be directed by the will. The result is the accomplishment of deeds which respond to God's will for the right ordering of the universe. As the body receives its perfection in beauty and immortality, as the intellect is perfected by knowledge, the perfection of the properly choosing will is justice.

The third power of the human mind or soul is memory, a power, simply put, "by which it remembers."[33] But Aelred's memory possesses powers beyond the obvious; it also expresses the human powers of perception and imagination. Perception, as Aelred sees it, is the process by which the mind becomes aware of the data provided by the body's senses.[34] Through imagination the mind arranges the perceived data into a pattern comprehensible to the intellect.[35] Implicit in Aelred's description of the essential role of the memory as mediator is an affirmation of the close association, the mutual dependence, the continuous interaction of mind and body.[36]

There is more to Aelred's reading of the structure of the human nature. He sees the soul gifted with a faculty or power which goes beyond the traditional Augustinian[37] triad of intellect, will, and memory. To the rational, volitional, perceptive, and imaginative powers of those faculties, Aelred adds the powers of emotion and of feeling made possible by a faculty he calls the *affectus*. The word "*affectus*" admits no single definition or translation, but one of the ways in which Aelred uses the word conveys the meaning of "attachment." Aelred explains that "attachment is . . . a sort of spontaneous inclination of the mind toward someone—an inclination accompanied by delight."[38]

Human beings, Aelred firmly believes, are properly filled with delight—with emotions and attachments. To prove his point Aelred offers the example of Jesus of Nazareth, for "the God become man delighted in the human pleasure of attachment."[39] And Aelred excuses his emotions at the death of his friend Simon by pointing to the tears shed by Jesus at the death of his friend Lazarus.[40] Even unpleasant or aggressive feelings are not necessarily evil; though Aelred can speak of being "besotted by anger,"[41] he can also speak of "wholesome anger."[42] Both "good" feelings and "bad" feelings are natural and human, and thus, these emotions can be morally good. Like perception, the emotions have their origin in the body's senses and are felt in the soul.[43] As the sensations provided by the body affect one's feelings, so too the feelings are properly expressed exteriorly by the body.[44]

The fulfillment, the happiness, of the whole person, which Aelred seeks, requires the interaction of body and soul. For its part, the soul vivifies the body; it is active in the whole body "in something of the same way that God acts in the universe."[45] For its part the body provides the raw materials, sense data, for the soul's perception, recollection, imagination, discernment, and decision[46]—a decision then carried out by the body.[47]

The ideal human is, for Aelred, the natural human in that she or he has a body and a soul with natural powers. This ideal, natural human being is symbolized, as Aelred sees it, by the prelapsarian Adam. Aelred advises all human beings to

> consider the dignity of the first human condition, the dignity in which God created humans. You can see this dignity is threefold: in liberty, in power, in happiness. Adam was free, full of power, and happy . . . Before him stood good and bad, . . . death and life, happiness and wretchedness . . . He chose what he wished, as much as he wished, and as he wished. He [likewise] had freedom in activity, for he made use of the world to amass delights, to increase his happiness.[48]

Aelred's enthusiastic appreciation of human dignity is a result of his optimistic analysis of human nature. A complementary but more dynamic view of the human condition emerges from Aelred's consideration of the social character of humans. Again, Aelred's model is Adam, now in conjunction with Eve: "When God created [the first] human, in order to commend the goodness of social life he said: 'It is not good for the man to be alone; let us make for him a helper like himself [Genesis 2:18].' It was from no similar stuff, nor even from the same matter, that the divine power formed this helper. Rather, as a more pressing incentive to love and friendship, he brought forth the woman from the very substance of the man."[49] Thus from the beginning of human existence, Aelred affirms, the social nature of the species was affirmed. His admiration for this pattern is clear: "How beautiful is it that the second human being was taken from the side of the first [see Genesis 2:21–22], so that nature might teach that all humans are equal—side by side, so to speak—and that there should be no superior or inferior in human affairs. . . . Thus, from the very beginning, nature imprinted the desire for friendship and love in the human heart—a desire that an interior capacity for loving soon urged on with a certain taste of sweetness."[50] Humans are thus by their very nature physical, rational, and social animals, and for Aelred, these constitute a nature of wondrous dignity.

3. Friendship as the Perfection of Attachment

Although Aelred is sure that true love brings delight and joy, peace and serenity, to the affective powers of humans,[51] he also sees the *affectus*—and thus the whole human—fulfilled in friendship. Friendship requires love, but it is not the same thing as love—not even true love. Aelred does make an attempt to relate friendship and love by etymological derivation: " 'Friend' [*amicus*] comes from 'love' [*amore*], the nourishment of which is wisdom, and wisdom, as it 'reaches powerfully from one end to another' by its strength, so, by true love, 'disposes all things delightfully [Wisdom 8:1].' "[52] But, though they are related linguistically—and in the order of reality— Aelred is convinced that love and friendship are distinct.

In Aelred's treatise *On Spiritual Friendship*, he has Ivo, one of the participants in the dialogue, ask: "Are we to believe that there is no difference between true love and friendship?"[53] Aelred answers:

> By no means! Not at all! Divine authority ordains that many more must be received in to the bosom of true love than into the embrace of friendship. For we are compelled by true love's law to receive into the embrace of love not only our friends but also our enemies [see Matthew 5:44; Luke 6:27–35]. But we call friends only those to whom we do not fear to entrust our heart

and whatever is in it, to those who, in turn, are bound to us by the same law of faith and freedom of fear.[54]

Though quite different in the existent of their embrace, friendship necessarily proceeds from love: "The fountain and source of friendship is love. Though there can be love without friendship, friendship without love is impossible."[55] But all whom one loves are not friends, not even all those to whom reason and attachment direct one: "We embrace many with great attachment, but we still do not admit all of them to the intimacy of friendship, which consists above all in the revelation of our inmost thoughts and plans."[56]

The core of Aelred's complex, and sometimes confusing, concept of friendship is intimacy, itself a notion perhaps more easily described than defined. And Aelred does indeed describe its components:

> Four things seem especially to pertain to friendship: love and attachment, freedom from anxiety and delight. We see love in the benevolent giving of service, attachment in the delight which somehow springs forth from within, freedom in the revelation, without fear or suspicion, of all confidences and concerns, delight in the pleasant and amicable sharing of everything that happens, whether joyful or sad, the sharing of all thoughts, whether harmful or useful, the sharing of everything taught or learned.[57]

The attachment of the *affectus* is clearly a major component of the intimacy associated with friendship, but it is not the only element.

There are many sorts of attachment, Aelred says, some spiritual, some rational, some irrational, some dutiful, some natural, some physical.[58] Although attachments are in themselves good, each of them can have good or bad consequences:

> There is a [sort of] spiritual attachment which comes from the devil, a [kind of] irrational attachment which fosters vice, a [sort of] physical attachment which leads to vice. Not only should these [kinds of] attachment not be pursued, they must not be allowed. Still more, they must be uprooted from our hearts as much as possible. But the spiritual attachment which comes from God must not only be allowed but stimulated and increased in every way . . . Even our actions should surely be stimulated by this [sort of] attachment, but those actions ought not to be ordered according to this attachment.[59]

Attachments, then, need ordering, and the actions that spring from attachments need some moderating influence. This is because an attachment "very often ignores moderation, does not properly gauge human strengths, consumes physical passions, rushes blindly and impetuously toward the object of its desire, thinks only of that for which it longs and disdains everything else."[60] Because the *affectus,* the passionate, emotive faculty, "in undertaking some burdensome, arduous, and impossible task as if it were a slight and effortless work . . . does not sense the troublesome afflictions to its outward person because of the delight of its interior attachment . . . So that we might not overstep the bounds of physical capabilities, we must be restrained by the moderating influence of reason."[61] Thus, reason must regulate the *affectus* and allow the will to choose what is best for the whole human being. The intimacy of friendship can thus be ordered toward human happiness. "For that reason," Aelred writes, "the beginnings of spiritual friendship must have, first of all, purity of intention, the instruction of reason, and the restraint of moderation."[62]

4. Becoming a Friend

Because friendship and intimacy are such elusive constructs, listing their necessary components is not enough. Perhaps the best way to understand Aelred's teaching on friendship is to follow his description of the process by which one becomes a friend. In that process, the attachment of the *affectus* plays an initiatory role: "The inclination of the soul which we call attachment sometimes results from sight, sometimes from hearing, and sometimes from dutiful service. When we see persons with cheerful faces, a pleasant manner, delightful speech, we are immediately inclined toward them by an agreeable attachment. We sense in them some praiseworthy virtue and holiness. The same occurs in us when we anticipate some mutual service."[63] The resultant inclination toward friendship, Aelred is sure, should not always be pursued: "Granted that attachment most often precedes friendship, still it ought not to be followed unless reason leads it, integrity regulates it, and justice rules it."[64] In this triad Aelred finds the principles by which he and his hearers can select some for friendship from all those whom they must love, and from the smaller body of those whom attachment suggests: "Not all whom we love should be received into friendship, for all are not found suitable for it. 'Since your friend is the comrade of your soul, to whose spirit you unite, devote, and so share your spirit that you become one instead of two; and since you entrust yourself [to your friend]' as if 'he or she were another you,' from whom you keep nothing secret, 'from whom you fear nothing,' you should surely first consider whether he or she is suitable for all this."[65] Having found someone so suited to friendship, "then he or she must be tested and at last finally admitted."[66]

Aelred's testing process is rigorous and demanding—understandably so, given the degree of intimacy Aelred associates with friendship: "The friend's loyalty, integrity, and patience must be tested. Little by little should occur the sharing of confidence, the serving of common concerns, and a certain conformity in outward expression."[67] Clearly, Aelred thinks that the conformity of friends' minds is suitably expressed in the external, physical likeness of both. It is equally clear that the unity he seeks is primarily spiritual. Thus "intention too must be tested. This is especially necessary since there are many who see nothing good in human affairs save that which eventually brings profit. These folk . . . lack genuine and spiritual friendship, which ought to be sought for its own and God's sake."[68]

5. How to Be a Friend

Given cautious choice and testing of a friend, one maintains the friendship, Aelred teaches, by a joyful though exacting service that is extraordinarily beneficial to both friends:

> How salutary is it then [for friends] to grieve for one another, to toil for one another, to bear one another's burdens [see Galatians 6:2], while each considers it delightful to forget oneself for the sake of the other, to prefer the will of the other to one's own, to minister to the other's needs rather than one's own, to oppose or expose oneself to misfortunes. How delightful friends find it to converse with one another, to reveal their concerns to each other, to examine all things together and come to one decision on all of them.[69]

This self-revelation, which is such a major component of friendship, requires, Aelred is sure, a relationship based on equality.[70]

And, of course, the knowledge of another's inmost thoughts requires a friend to exhibit dedicated loyalty.[71] To loyalty, Aelred adds generosity—both material and spiritual.[72] Underlying Aelred's list is a concern for the friend's physical and spiritual well-being—and a great sensitivity for the feelings of the friend: "You ought so to respect the eye of a friend that you do nothing shameful or undertake anything of which it is unbecoming to speak. When you fail yourself in any way, the failure so overflows to your friend that you alone do not blush and grieve interiorly, but your friend too, who sees or hears of the failure, reproaches herself or himself as if she or he had failed."[73] Respect, concern, and sensitivity can be expressed in many ways. And indeed, Aelred teaches that one must support one's friend in all possible ways:

> There are other benefits in spiritual love, through which friends can be present and of advantage to one another. The first is to be solicitous for one another, then to pray for one another, to blush for one another, to rejoice for one another, to grieve for one another's faults as for one's own, to consider each other's progress as one's own. By whatever means in one's power, one ought to raise up the faint-hearted, support the feeble, console the sorrowful, restrain the wrathful.[74]

Although prayer for one's friends is passed over quickly in this statement, in another passage Aelred makes clear the importance of prayer for friendship. There he underscores the efficacy of prayer for both the person praying and the one for whom the prayers are offered:

> Added to these [practices of friendship] there is prayer for one another, which, in remembering the friend, is more efficacious the more lovingly it is sent to God with flowing tears brought forth by fear or awakened by attachments or evoked by sorrow. Thus, one praying to Christ for her or his friend, and for the friend's sake hoping to be heard by Christ, directs her or his attentions earnestly and longingly to Christ. Then it sometimes happens that, speedily though imperceptibly, the one attachment carries over into the other, and, as if coming into close contact with delight in Christ himself, one begins to taste how sweet and sense how pleasant he is [see Psalm 33:9; Psalm 99:5].[75]

The practice of friendship thus leads one from an exalted human relationship to intimacy with the divine Source of friendship.

"Among the advantages [of friendship] are counsel in doubt, consolation in adversity, and other benefits of like nature."[76] But, Aelred adds: "Let us also correct one another, knowing that 'wounds from a friend are better than an enemy's deceitful kisses [Proverbs 27:6].' "[77] Correction, however, must be done in the right spirit; "the desire to dominate" must never be the corrector's motivation.[78] It is so important to friendship that correction be given without overbearing domination that Aelred makes his guidelines explicit. He first details the approaches to be avoided: "Beware of anger and bitterness of spirit in correction, so that you can be seen to desire the improvement of your friend rather than the satisfaction of your own irritation. I have seen some who, in correcting their friends, cloak their up swelling bitterness and boiling rage sometimes with the name of zeal, sometimes with the word candor. Following impulse not reason, they do no good by such correction, but rather cause great harm. Among friends there is no excuse for this vice."[79] Rather, Aelred admonishes,

> A friend ought to have compassion for the friend, ought to reach out to the friend, ought to think of the friend's fault as his or her own, ought to correct the friend humbly and compassionately. Let a somewhat troubled countenance or saddened word make the reproof. Let tears take the place of words, so that the friend may not only see but also feel that the reproof comes from love rather than rancor. If the friend should reject your first correction, surely you must correct him or her a second time.[80]

The friend who corrects must also possess a sensitive insight into the personality and character of a friend, for there are some friends "who benefit from blandishment and quite readily and favorably respond to it. There are others who cannot be so guided and are more easily corrected by verbal chastisement. So conform and adapt yourself to your friend that you may respond appropriately to your friend's state of mind."[81] Finally, because correction must serve the truth, the corrector must not deceive a friend in the mistaken belief that this might serve their friendship: "A friend owes truth to her or his friend, without which the name of friendship can have no value."[82]

This is indeed a demanding program, though Aelred insists it is far more rewarding than burdensome. But the heavy demands that friendship imposes surely bring with them the possibility of failure, and Aelred recognizes this. When one has wronged a friend, Aelred's remedy is humble effort at reconciliation: "If it should happen that we neglect the law of friendship in some way, let us shun pride and seek to win back our friend's favor by some humble service."[83] If one has been wronged, Aelred urges the same sort of response: "A friendship is proven more excellent and virtuous in which the one who has been hurt does not cease to be what he or she would be, loving the other by whom he or she is no longer loved, honoring the other by whom he or she is rejected, blessing the other who has spoken badly of him or her, and doing good to the other who has contrived evil against him or her."[84]

Intimacy is at once the way in which friendship is best expressed and the joyful fruit of friendship: "Let those who are united to us in the innermost and most secret recesses of our heart, be bound ever more tightly to us, and be more and more fondly cherished."[85] The delight, the joy, in this intimate relationship is, for Aelred, a means to the delight and joy experienced in an intimate relationship with God himself: "Surely our desire should be directed toward this: that in God we delight in one another, as is fitting, and that we delight in the God who is in both of us."[86]

6. The Foundation of Friendship

For Aelred, friendship is not merely a pleasant adjunct to human life; it is a reflection of a fundamental aspect of the ordering of the cosmos. Friendship is found among inanimate beings, among plants and animals, and among angels.[87] From the first moment of their existence on earth, human beings have been so constituted by God that they need the intimate companionship of one another to be truly human. For Aelred, the first models of friendship were Adam and Eve; in their natural, pristine state, humans exhibit the happy intimacy of husband and wife.[88] "As I see it," writes Aelred, "nature first impresses on the human mind the desire for friendship, then experience encourages it, and finally the authority of law regulates it."[89]

For Aelred, then, "it is evident that friendship is natural, as are virtue, wisdom and the like—and it should be sought and preserved for its own sake as a natural good."[90] Without the intimacy of friendship, happiness is impossible for humans. As Aelred puts it: "Truly, even in those in whom wickedness has obliterated every sense of virtue, reason, which cannot be extinguished in them, has left a desire for friendship and fellowship, so that, without fellow human beings, riches can hold no charm for the avaricious, or glory for the ambitious, nor pleasure for the licentious."[91] Aelred is sure that "without friends absolutely no life can be happy,"[92] and he offers the doubter this challenge:

> Let us suppose that the whole human race were removed from
> the world, leaving you as the sole survivor. Now behold before
> you all the delights and riches of the world: gold, silver, precious

stones, walled cities, lofty castles, spacious buildings, sculptures and paintings. And now consider yourself re-formed into that ancient state in which all [creatures] are subject to you, "all sheep and cattle, all the beasts of the field as well, the birds of the air and fish of the sea which swim through the waters [Psalm 8:8–9]." Tell me now, I ask you, whether without a companion you could be happy with all these.[93]

Even in this world—a world inhabited by great numbers of people—happiness is impossible unless one reaches out to some one of them in friendship: "If you were to see a person living among many others, suspecting all, fearing all as ambushers lying in wait to injure him or her, cherishing no one and thinking himself or herself cherished by none, would you not judge such a person wretched indeed?"[94]

This conclusion Aelred sees as so obvious, so grounded in nature and reason, that it is accessible to all who, through reason, recognize the natural order: "Even the philosophers of this world have ranked friendship not among matters casual or transitory but among those virtues which are eternal"[95] Perhaps the most forceful statement of Aelred's position is this: "I should call them beasts, not humans, who say that one ought to live without being a source of consolation to anyone. Beasts even those who say that one ought not be a source of burden or grief to anyone. Beasts too, those who take no delight in the good fortune of another or bring before no other their own bitterness of misfortune, caring to cherish no one and be cherished by none."[96]

7. The Perfect Friendship of God

In Jesus of Nazareth, God shows himself as friend, and, in return, Jesus must be loved as "a most intimate friend."[97] Aelred demonstrates his response to his own admonition in a sermon for Christmas: "At other times my office [as abbot] compels me to speak; today attachment provides the necessity. But from where will the words come to me? Surely, if my whole body were transformed into a tongue, I could not satisfactorily express my attachment [for Christ]. No wonder! I have seen how great is he who comes for the salvation of all people."[98]

Aelred teaches that friendship for Christ is possible only because of Christ's friendship for his sisters and brothers. Indeed, their friendship with each other is informed by Christ's friendship and thus leads to friendship with him: "In friendship are joined honesty and delight, truth and enjoyment, charm and good-will, attachment and action. All these are begun by Christ, are advanced through Christ, are perfected in Christ. So the ascent does not seem too steep or unnatural, the ascent from Christ, who inspires the love by which we love our friends, to Christ, who offers himself to us as a friend to love—so that delight might follow on delight, enjoyment on enjoyment, attachment on attachment."[99] Aelred offers a concrete and scriptural example of Christ's friendship for human beings in the case of a family who lived at Bethany, "where the most holy bond of friendship was consecrated by the authority of the Lord. For Jesus loved Martha and Mary and Lazarus [see John 11:5]. No one can doubt that this was because of the special privilege of friendship by which they are said to have clung to him. Evidence for this is the kind tears that Jesus shed with those who were crying [over the death of Lazarus]—the tears that all the people interpreted as a sign of love: 'See,' they said, 'how much he loved him [John 11:36].' "[100] For Aelred, then, "friendship is a step bordering on perfection, which consists in the love and knowledge of God, so that a human, from being a friend of a fellow human, becomes a friend of God, as the Savior says in the gospel: 'I shall now not call you servants but my friends [see John 15:15].'"[101] And thus Aelred can say that, long before that gospel passage was written, "Moses spoke with God as a friend with a friend."[102]

Aelred thus affirms God's intimate relationship with humans, and the possibility of God's leading humans to friendship with him. And this leads Aelred to a statement that he acknowledges is daring. In the dialogue *On Spiritual Friendship*, Aelred has one of the participants ask: "What is this? Should I say of friendship what John, the friend of Jesus, says of true love [see 1 John 4:16]; that God is friendship?"[103]

Aelred answers: "[T]hat would be unusual and does not carry the authority of Scripture. Still, what is true of true love I do not really doubt can be said of friendship, since those who abide in friendship abide in God, and God in them [see 1 John 4:16]."[104]Aelred clearly sees friendship as "a step toward the love and knowledge of God."[105]

Friendship leads one to the contemplation of God in this world[106] and to union with him in the next.[107] And all these glorious fruits are, for Aelred, the product of God's initiative, often beginning in a conversation between potential friends. At the very beginning of Aelred's dialogue *On Spiritual Friendship*, he states simply: "See, here we are, you and I—and, I hope, a third, Christ, in our midst."[108]

Notes

1. Jarrett 1933, 87.
2. McGinn 1994, 323.
3. *Sermo in dominica in kalendis Novembris* [hereafter *Kal Nov*] 78.1; in *Corpus Christianorum Continuatio Mediaevalis* [hereafter *CCCM]* 2B:302. A far more detailed presentation of Aelred's anthropology and cosmology can be found in chapter 2 of Sommerfeldt 2005, 10–27. See, too, Sommerfeldt 2006, 3–7.
4. See, for example, *Sermo de onerous* [hereafter *Oner*] 16; in *Patrologia latina* [hereafter *PL*] 195:423D, in which Aelred sees God stamping his image and likeness on the rational soul, as one might stamp an image in striking a coin.
5. See *Oner* 2; *PL* 195:363AB.
6. *Kal Nov* 78.18; *CCCM* 2B:307–08
7. *De speculo caritatis* [hereafter *Spec car*] 1.3.8; *CCCM* 1:16.
8. For Aelred, the ultimate testimony to the goodness of human nature is the fact that the Second Person of the Trinity assumed that nature. See *Sermo in assumptione sanctae Mariae* [hereafter *Asspt*] 20.4; *CCCM* 2A:155.
9. *Spec car* 3.22.52; *CCCM* 1:130. See *De anima* [hereafter *Anima*] 1:28; *CCCM* 1:693. See also *Sermo in adventu Domini* [hereafter *Adv*] 2.24; *CCCM* 2A:22.
10. See *Anima* 1:63; *CCCM* 1:705.
11. See *Anima* 1:40; *CCCM* 1:696; and *Anima* 2.60; *CCCM* 1:730.
12. *Anima* 1:25–26; *CCCM* 1:692.
13. See *Sermo de ieiunio* [hereafter *Ie*] 53.18; *CCCM* 2B:63.
14. See *Sermo in nativitate sanctae Mariae* [hereafter *Nat M*] 75.47; *CCCM* 2B:281.
15. See *Sermo in die pasco* [hereafter *Pasc*]; CCCM 2A:325–26. See also *De institutione inclusarum* [hereafter *Inst incl*] 3.33; *CCCM* 1:678.
16. *Sermo in festivitate omnium sanctorum* [hereafter *OS*] 46.13; *CCCM* 2A:369.
17. See *Anima* 1.10–11; *CCCM* 1:687–88.
18. *Sermo in die pentecostes* [hereafter *Pent*] 67.9; *CCCM* 2B:183.
19. *Anima* 1.5; *CCCM* 1:686.
20. *Anima* 2.16; *CCCM* 1:711–12.
21. *Anima* 2.1; *CCCM* 1:707.
22. *Anima* 1.43; *CCCM* 1:697–98.
23. See *Sermo in synodo ad presbyteros* [hereafter *Syn pres*] 64.12; *CCCM* 2B:165.
24. See *Sermo in ramis palmarum* [hereafter *Palm*] 35.10, *CCCM* 2A:289; and *Sermo in nativitate Domini* [hereafter *Nat*] 3.20; *CCCM* 2A:31, in which thoughts are pictured as hairs springing forth from the head, that is, from the intellect.
25. *Anima* 7.55; *CCCM* 1:702.
26. *Anima* 2.20; *CCCM* 1:714.
27. *Anima* 1.31; *CCCM* 1:694.

28. *Sermo in purificatio sanctae Mariae* [herafter *Pur*] 34.18; *CCCM* 2A:283.
29. *Anima* 2:18; *CCCM* 1:712–13.
30. *Anima* 2.29; *CCCM* 1:717.
31. See *Spec car* 3.8.22; *CCCM* 1:115.
32. *Anima* 2.15; *CCCM* 1:711.
33. See *Anima* 3.9; *CCCM* 1:735.
34. See *Anima* 3.9; *CCCM* 1:735; *Pent* 67.9–10; *CCCM* 2B:183; and *Oner* 20 (*PL* 195:440D).
35. See *Anima* 3.10; *CCCM* 1:735.
36. The triad of intellect, will, and memory—and the images of the Trinity in that triad—constitute a recurring theme in Aelred's treatise *On the Soul* and are manifestly derived from Augustine's *On the Trinity*. See Connor 1992, 277 and n. 6.
37. *Sermo in ypapanti Domini* [hereafter *Yp*] 51.5; *CCCM* 2B:41. See too *Spec car* 3.11.31; *CCCM* 1:119.
38. *Sermo in annuntiatione dominica* [hereafter *Ann dom*] 57.14; *CCCM* 2B:102.
39. See *Spec car* 1.34.112; *CCCM* 1:63.
40. *Spec car* 2.14.35; *CCCM* 1:83.
41. *Inst incl* 2.22; *CCCM* 1:655. Aelred clearly approves of the wrathful reaction of King Edmund of England to the Danish invasion. See *Genealogia regum Anglorum*, *PL* 195:732B.
42. Aelred offers an example in *De sanctis ecclesiae Hagulstadensis*, prologus; ed. Raine, 1864, 174.
43. See *Ann dom* 58.20; *CCCM* 2B:112.
44. *Anima* 1.4; *CCCM* 1:686.
45. See *Anima* 1.4; *CCCM* 1:698.
46. See *Sermo in natali sanctorum apostolorum Petri et Pauli* [hereafter *Nat PP*] 18.18; *CCCM* 2A:144.
47. *Sermo in ascensione Domini* [hereafter *Asc*] 65.5; *CCCM* 2B:171.
48. See *Sermo in natali Benedicti* [hereafter *Nat Ben*] 6.2; *CCCM* 2A: 53; and *Spec car* 1.1.2; *CCCM* 1:13.
49. *Ann dom* 58.13; *CCCM* 2B: 110.
50. *Spir amic* 1.31; *CCCM* 1:294.
51. *Spir amic* 1:32; *CCCM* 1:294.
52. *Spir amic* 3.2; *CCCM* 1:317.
53. *Spir amic* 3.83; *CCCM* 1:334–35.
54. *Spir amic* 3.51; *CCCM* 1:327.
55. See *Spec car* 3.11.31; *CCCM* 1:119.
56. *Spec car* 3.23.53; *CCCM* 1:130.
57. *Spec car* 3.23.54; *CCCM* 1:130.
58. *Spec car* 3.23.54; *CCCM* 1:130–31.
59. *Spir amic* 2.59; *CCCM* 1:313.
60. *Yp* 51.5; *CCCM* 2B:41–42.
61. *Spir amic* 2.57; *CCCM* 1:313.

62. *Spir amic* 3.6; *CCCM* 1:318.

63. *Spir amic* 3.6; *CCCM* 1:318.

64. *Spir amic* 3.130; *CCCM* 1:348.

65. *Spir amic* 3.68; *CCM* 1:330–31.

66. *Spir amic* 3.132; *CCCM* 1:349.

67. See *Spir amic* 2.11; *CCCM* 1:304. See too *Spir amic* 3.84; *CCCM* 1:335, where the self–revelatory character of friendship is given as a reason for caution in the choice of a friend. More on equality between friends can be found in *Spir amic* 3.96–97; *CCCM* 1:339.

68. See *Spir amic* 3:88–89; *CCCM* 1:336.

69. See *Spir amic* 3.102; *CCCM* 1:340.

70. *Spir amic* 3.101–02; *CCCM* 1:340.

71. *Spir amic* 3:133; *CCCM* 1:349.

72. *Spir amic* 2.61; *CCCM* 1:313.

73. *Spec car* 3.40.112; *CCCM* 1:161.

74. *Spec car* 2.26.75; *CCCM* 1:102.

75. *Spir amic* 3.106–07; *CCM* 1:341.

76. *Spir amic* 3.107; *CCCM* 1:341–42.

77. *Spir amic* 3.108; *CCCM* 1:342.

78. *Spir amic* 3.109; *CCCM* 1:342. See also *Spir amic* 3.109–12; *CCCM* 1:342–43.

79. *Spir amic* 3.26; *CCCM* 1:322.

80. *Spir amic* 3.49; *CCCM* 1:326.

81. *Spec car* 3.38.106; *CCCM* 1:157.

82. *Spec car* 3.22.52; *CCCM* 1:130.

83. See *Spir amic* 1.54–56; *CCCM* 1:298.

84. See *Spir amic* 1.57–58; *CCCM* 1:298–99.

85. *Spir amic* 1.51; *CCCM* 1:297.

86. *Spir amic* 1.61; *CCCM* 1:299.

87. *Spir amic* 1.60; *CCCM* 1:299.

88. *Spir amic* 3.76; *CCCM* 1:333.

89. *Spir amic* 3.77; *CCCM* 1:333.

90. *Spir amic* 3.81; *CCCM* 1:334.

91. *Spir amic* 1.21; *CCCM* 1:292.

92. *Spir amic* 2.52; *CCCM* 1:312.

93. *Adv* 1.14; *CCCM* 2A:6.

94. *Nat* 49.1: *CCCM* 2B:22.

95. *Spir amic* 2.20; *CCCM* 1:306. See *Spir amic* 3.127; *CCCM* 1:348.

96. *Inst inclu* 3.31; *CCCM* 1:667.

97. *Spir amic* 2.14; *CCCM* 1:305. See *Spir amic* 3.87; *CCCM* 1:336.

98. *Sermo in festivitate apostolorum Petri et Pauli*, 70.19; CCCM 2B:213.

99. *Spir amic* 1.69; *CCCM* 1:301.

100. *Spir amic* 1.70: *CCCM* 1:301.

101. *Spir amic* 2.18; CCCM 1:306. See *Spir amic* 2.14; *CCCM* 1:305.
102. See Sommerfeldt 2005, 133–34.
103. Ibid., 115–16.
104. *Spir amic* 1.1; *CCCM* 1:289.
105. *Spir amic* 2.18; *CCCM* 1: 306; See *Spir amic* 2.14; *CCCM* 1:305.
106. See Sommerfeldt 2005, 133–34.
107. Ibid., 115–16.
108. *Spir amic* 1.1.; *CCCM* 1:289.

References

I. PRIMARY SOURCES

Aelred of Rievaulx. 1864. *De sanctis ecclesiae Hagulstadensis*, prologus, in *The Priory of Hexham: Its Chronicles, Endowments and Annals* 1, ed. James Raine, Surtees Society 44. Durham, Andrews & Co.

The following works ("Opera") of Aelred of Rievaulx are contained in the *Corpus Christianorum Continuatio Mediaevalis* [hereafter *CCCM*], 1, 2A, 2B, 2D, Turnhout, Brepols Publishers, 1971, 1983, 2001 and 2005.:

Sermo in dominica in kalendis Novembris [hereafter *Kal Nov*]
De speculo caritatis [hereafter *Spec car*]
Sermo in assumptione sanctae Mariae [hereafter *Asspt*]
De anima [hereafter *Anima*]
Sermo in adventu Domini [hereafter *Adv*]
Sermo de ieiunio [hereafter *Ie*]
Sermo in nativitate sanctae Mariae [hereafter *Nat M*]
Sermo in die pasco [hereafter *Pasc*]
De institutione inclusarum [hereafter *Inst incl*]
Sermo in festivitate omnium sanctorum [hereafter *OS*]
Sermo in die pentecostes [hereafter *Pent*]
Sermo in synodo ad presbyteros [hereafter *Syn pres*]
Sermo in ramis palmarum [hereafter *Palm*]
Sermo in nativitate Domini [hereafter *Nat*]
Sermo in purificatione sanctae Mariae [herafter *Pur*]
Sermo in ypapanti Domini [hereafter *Yp*]
Sermo in annuntiatione dominica [hereafter *Ann dom*]
Sermo in natali sanctorum apostolorum Petri et Pauli [hereafter *Nat PP*]
Sermo in ascensione Domini [hereafter *Asc*]
Sermo in natali Benedicti [hereafter *Nat Ben*]

Sermo in festivitate apostolorum Petri et Pauli,
Migne's *Patrologia latina* [hereafter *PL*] contains the following works:
Sermo de honoribus [hereafter *Oner*]
Genealogia regum Anglorum

2. SECONDARY SOURCES

Connor, Elizabeth. 1992. "Saint Bernard's Three Steps of Truth and Saint Aelred
of Rievaulx's Three Loves." In *Bernardus Magister*, ed. John R. Sommerfeldt.
Cistercian Studies Series 135. Kalamazoo, Michigan: Cistercian Publications;
Saint-Nicolas-lès-Cîteaux, Commmentarii Cistercienses.
Dutton, Marsha L. 2005. "Friendship and the Love of God: Augustine's Teaching
in the *Confessions* and Aelred of Rievaulx's Response in *Spiritual Friendship*."
American Benedictine Review 56.
Jarrett, Bede. 1933. "St. Aelred of Rievaulx (110–1166)." In *The English Way*, ed.
Maisie Ward. New York: Sheed and Ward.
McGinn, Bernard. 1994. *The Growth of Mysticism, the Presence of God: A History of
Western Christian Mysticism II*. New York, Crossroad.
Sommerfeldt, John. 2005. *Aelred of Rievaulx: Pursuing Perfect Happiness*. New York/
Mahwah, NJ: The Newman Press.
———. 2006. *Aelred of Rievaulx: On Love and Order in the World and the Church*.
New York/Mahwah, NJ: The Newman Press.

10

THOMAS AQUINAS

CHARITY AS FRIENDSHIP*

Fergus Kerr, OP

1. The Thirteenth-Century Reception of Aristotle's *Ethics*

"What is one to make of a man who, at sixty years of age, conscious though he was of declining powers of memory, took up the study of Greek and established an atelier for the production of translations, and who was learning Hebrew in his eighties? Late development is generally reckoned, after all, to have its limits."[1] Robert Grosseteste the man in question, having taught theology at Oxford for many years, was elected bishop of Lincoln in 1235. As the largest diocese in England at the time it demanded a great deal of attention, and the record amply shows how energetically he fulfilled his responsibilities. He was, for all that, able to continue, and even to extend, his already manifold scholarly activities. He presided over a team which produced revisions and fresh versions of Latin translations of much Greek Christian literature, including the Dionysian corpus. About 1240 they turned to Aristotle. Fragments of an earlier translation survive, but as Herman the German noted at the time, Grosseteste's version of Aristotle's *Nicomachean Ethics*, available by 1246–47, was the first complete edition.[2] Its appearance was certainly one of the great intellectual events of the century. It survives in almost three hundred manuscripts. It has been published by the Dominican scholar R. A. Gauthier, using a good late thirteenth-century text discovered in 1972 in Trinity College, Dublin.[3]

Albert the Great was among the first to make use of Grosseteste's translation of the *Ethics*. He moved from Paris to Cologne in the summer of 1248 in order to set up the first Dominican study house in Germany. It is possible that Thomas Aquinas, then about twenty-four years of age, accompanied him. There is no doubt that Thomas attended Albert's course on the *Ethics*, sometime between 1248 and 1252, because a copy of the notes that he took has survived.[4]

The date of Thomas' own study of the *Ethics*[5] remains obscure largely because its purpose is disputable. The traditional story, following the memorandum of Tolomeo of Lucca, his *socius*, ascribes the work to the early 1260s, when Thomas was probably conventual lector in the Dominican priory in Orvieto. This smallish Umbrian town, splendidly sited on an isolated rock, had just become an important administrative and intellectual center because the newly elected Pope Urban IV was to spend his short pontificate there. Albert the Great, for instance, having just rid himself of episcopal office, came for the winter of 1262–63. Urban certainly commissioned Thomas to produce his *Expositio* of the four gospels—the *Catena aurea* as it has been called since the fourteenth century: an immediate success and one of his most widely diffused works in the Middle Ages. Containing not one word written by him, it is an anthology of passages from Latin and Greek patristic texts. At Urban's request Thomas also wrote his *Contra errores Graecorum* at this time, without apparently ever trying to learn any Greek, though still only in his late thirties.

His principal duty in Orvieto, as conventual lector, would have been to expound the scriptures to the Dominican community. It was up to the lector to choose the text, and Thomas expounded the book of Job. The result, no doubt considerably written up, contains many references to Aristotle's *De partibus animalium*, a translation of which was completed on December 23, 1260 by the Flemish Dominican William of Moerbeke, later to become archbishop of Thebes.

Thomas' exposition of the *Ethics* is little more than a paraphrase, so elementary and pedestrian that it seems likely enough that he undertook it at this period as part of the internal course of studies for the less bright young friars in the community in Orvieto who were not going to be sent to any university.

R. A. Gauthier, however, a formidable authority in these matters, ascribes Thomas' *Sententia libri Ethicorum* to 1271–72, when he was back teaching in Paris: Weisheipl concurs.[6] The argument is that the *secunda secundae* of the *Summa Theologiae*, begun early in 1271, shows signs of fresh study of certain sections of the *Ethics*. The famous Socratic thesis that one cannot knowingly do wrong (*Ethics*, VII) appears, however, in the *prima secundae* (*ST*. Ia IIae, 77, 3) and is first discussed in a set of disputations (*De Malo*, q.3) which Gauthier dates to the winter of 1266–67, when Thomas was in Rome, setting up the study house of his own province. The relevant passage in Thomas' commentary on the *Ethics* certainly reads more like a preparation for that disputation than anything written after the discussion of the Socratic paradox in the *prima secundae*. It is also difficult to believe, as V. J. Bourke notes,[7] that, back in Paris, with Grosseteste's notes and Albert's commentary readily accessible, Thomas needed to embark on his own paraphrase of the *Ethics*.

It does not matter very much. According to Harry Jaffa, Aristotle's ideas are more lucidly expressed in Thomas' commentary than they are in the original.[8] Gauthier is surely on stronger ground when he judges that Thomas' commentary on the *Ethics* is of little help to the student of Aristotle. It is greatly excelled, as Bourke says,[9] "except in humility," by the work of Gauthier and Jolif, the standard modern commentary.[10]

What matters, of course, is what happened to Aristotle's *Ethics* in the *secunda pars* of the *Summa Theologiae*. Over a million words long, it must have been composed at the rate of a thousand words a day if it was completed in the twenty-seven months that the bio-bibliographers allow. It has been described as "Thomas' most original contribution to theology"[11] and as "Aquinas' greatest work."[12] It may, with more precision, also be described as one of the great texts in the history of moral philosophy as well as of Catholic theology—and, in both respects, still largely unexplored territory. It advances on Aristotle in many ways, not counting questions affected by Thomas' theological interests (where improvements may not always be obvious to non-Christian readers). But I want to concentrate here on a central topic in Christian theology which is interestingly and decisively illuminated by an idea Thomas took from the *Ethics*: namely, his well-known thesis that charity is a kind of friendship—on analogy with Aristotle's conception of friendship.

2. Aquinas' Change on Friendship and Charity

Considering how often he covers the same ground in one work after another, with little or no substantial change in the argumentation, it is surprising to find that Thomas discussed the nature of charity only twice in his career, and interesting that his approach changed dramatically. Something happened between the discussion in his *Scriptum* on the *Sentences* of Peter Lombard, dated about 1256, and the discussion in the *secunda pars* of the *Summa* and the closely associated disputed question *De Caritate*, both dated to 1269–72. What happened, clearly, was that Thomas reread Aristotle's *Ethics*.

In the *Scriptum*,[13] for a start, Thomas deals with the nature of charity in the context of Christology: "Did Christ have faith, hope and charity?" In the *Summa*, of course, Christology is held over to the *tertia pars*, and the discussion of the theological virtue of charity becomes the centerpiece (almost literally) of the newly independent *secunda pars*. The consideration of Christian love is no longer embedded in questions about the human nature of Christ; the placing of charity becomes a decisive move in a radically theocentric description of human beings as moral agents. Focused by happiness and virtue, Aristotle's *eudaimonia* and *aretē* (human flourishing and human excellence), the *secunda pars* inaugurates a style of Christian ethics which has not yet borne fruit in many people's lives. Thomas introduces Aristotle's theory of friendship so incisively when he comes to consider charity in the *Summa* that one cannot help sharing his relief at being able to leave behind the ruminant account in the *Scriptum*.

In the *Scriptum* the discussion naturally starts from Peter Lombard's definition of charity as a certain *dilectio*: "a love in which God is loved for his own sake and one's neighbor for or in God." Thomas first lists seven other terms which might seem to offer a better clue than *dilectio* to the place of charity: it might be envisaged with Augustine as *concupiscentia*, desire (for God); with Dionysius as *amor* (*eros* in Greek); as *benevolentia*, wishing eternal life for oneself and for others; as *concordia*, unifying the church; as *beneficentia*, doing good; as *pax*, the bond that unites souls; and as *amicitia*, friendship, since, as Aristotle says, "Friendship resembles an overflowing of love." (This text will not reappear in the *Summa*, presumably because Thomas checked the original and found that Aristotle is saying something quite different.)

Thomas is going to opt for friendship, but he now has to list five serious objections to doing so: friendship is between people who love one another, and charity extends to one's enemies; friendship involves being together, and charity brings us into contact with transcendent beings like angels; friendship is public, and charity is absolutely hidden; friends try to see one another as much as possible, while Jerome says that this is not true in regard to charity; and finally, friendship is possible only with a few people, and they have to be of good character, while charity extends to everybody, including wicked people.

Thus Thomas places himself between seven plausible glosses on the nature of charity, incidentally showing that thirteenth-century Christians had a much richer range of associations than most people have today, and

a set of five objections to seeing it as a kind of friendship, all of them suggested no doubt by Aristotle's *Ethics* although only two are referred explicitly
to that source. Thomas' *responsio*, his solution to the problem, unfolds in
four steps. Taking up the immediately preceding discussion of the nature
of *amor* in terms of some fulfillment of desire, "quieting of appetite," he
isolates the desire which rational beings have: since it includes an element
of rational choice, *electio*, it is appropriately called *dilectio*: a love that selects
one person out of a crowd. Thus Peter Lombard's definition is vindicated,
if on what seems to be merely etymological or even assonantal grounds.

Next, Thomas argues very schematically that charity thus understood
as *dilectio* includes elements of desire for God, wishing well to one's neighbor, concord, doing good, and peace, while *amor* adds that extra something:
namely, desire's coming to rest in possession of the beloved.

Third, the hitherto unmentioned notion of *amatio* comes into the
story, adding to *amor* a certain *intensio* and *fervor* (straining and burn-
ing). The concept of friendship (*amicitia*) adds two further elements to
the picture: this love has to be reciprocated, friends know that they love
one another; and secondly, neatly rounding the discussion off, friendship is
rooted "not only in feeling (*passio*)" but also in choice, *electio*.

Thus, in the fourth step, Thomas can conclude: "Friendship is the
most perfect among the kinds of love, since it includes all that we have
mentioned; charity is obviously to be placed in the category of the most
perfect kind of love; it is therefore the friendship between man and God
in which man loves (*diligit*) God and God man, and thus an association
exists between them: If we walk in the light, as he is in the light, then we
have fellowship (*koinonia*) with one another."

The terms with which Thomas started are thus all included, in one
way or another, in the notion of friendship. Thomas now adds that "charity,
caritas, supplements friendship by specifying that the friend is God, thus
more precious and more dear, *carior.*"

The five difficulties in the way of seeing charity as a kind of friendship are dealt with in the following way. As to the problem of being friends
with your enemies, it may be suggested that a friend loves his friend's sons,
brothers, and the like, even though they may not return this love: it is God
whom we love by charity, men only to the extent that they belong to God.
Second, we rise to having conversation with God and the angels because by
charity we become *deiformes*. Third, friendship is said to be visible and public
but your friend's love is known *per signa probabilia*, not *per certitudinem*,
which goes for charity also: there are signs from which one can judge that
a person is charitable. Fourth, as to Jerome's objection, Thomas replies that

Jerome wants only to cut out the idea that the friendship which is charity is principally for one's fellow human beings whereas it is "joined by Christ's glue, *Christi glutino copulata*"—a striking phrase from a letter to Paulinus which has nothing whatever about charity in the context, although Jerome elsewhere speaks of *glutino caritatis haerens*. The fifth difficulty goes with the solution to the first one.

In contrast with all that, the discussion of charity in the *Summa* is remarkably sure-footed, elegant, and condensed. Notions such as *amor* and *concupiscentia* have been, or are to be, redistributed to other places in the *secunda pars*, thus lightening the argument. The atmosphere is also cleared of the imagery of longing and yearning, of being hot and sticky. It is as if the mutual absorption of two lovers in one another had been abandoned in favor of the model of colleagues engaged in a common adventure. The etymological considerations have been replaced by an argument, and the source of that argument is plainly Aristotle's *Ethics*. The text goes as follows:

> According to Aristotle not all love has the character of friend-ship, but only that which goes with well wishing [*benevolentia*], namely when we so love another as to will what is good for him. For if what we will is our own good, as when we love wine or a horse or the like, it is a love not of friendship [*amicitia*] but of desire [*concupiscentia*]. It makes no sense to talk of somebody being friends with wine or a horse. Yet goodwill alone is not enough for friendship for this requires a mutual loving [*mutua amatio*]; it is only with a friend that a friend is friendly. But such reciprocal good will is based on something in common [*communicatio*].
>
> Now there is a sharing [*communicatio*] of man with God by his sharing his happiness with us, and it is on this that a friendship is based. St. Paul refers to it, God is faithful by whom you were called into the fellowship [*koinonia*] of his Son. Now the love which is based on this sort of fellowship [*communicatio*] is charity. Accordingly it is clear that charity is a friendship of man and God. (IIa IIae, 23, 1)

In other words: for friendship to exist we have (1) to wish our friend well for his own sake; (2) the well-wishing has to be reciprocated; and (3) it has to be rooted in a certain community of life. The object of friendship-love has to be someone with a separate and intrinsic value. It cannot be a chattel or any extension of the one who is loving, as a bottle of wine or a horse would be. One wishes the other well, that is to say, beginning from acknowledgment of that person's independence and otherness. You cannot be friends, in the appropriate sense, with somebody who is your slave, infatuated with you, or one-sidedly dependent upon you in some other way. Friendship is a kind of loving that respects and fosters the independent worth of the other person. Second, for there to *be* friendship of the relevant kind, the parties have to have this attitude to one another: each has to be able to let the other be, so to speak. Third, they have to have something in common which gives rise to and sustains this relationship. On Aristotle's view, friendship of this kind exists only between persons who resemble each other in being virtuous. The relationship is grounded on shared goodness of character. This is a daring model for charity. It has had little success in Christian theology and spirituality. But to begin to measure its audacity we have to recreate Aristotle's picture of friendship in some more detail. That will help to explain why this model attracted Thomas, and perhaps also why his account of charity has never been widely accepted. First, then, we have to look briefly at the idea of love which Aristotle's picture is designed to correct.

3. Platonic Love in the *Symposium*

In 367 BC, when he was seventeen, Aristotle joined Plato's circle in Athens. Plato was then about sixty, with twenty years ahead of him. It could not have been long before the young philosopher read the *Symposium*, the dialogue about love and friendship which Plato had composed some years earlier, perhaps even about the time that Aristotle was born.

The climax of the *Symposium* no doubt comes in the lengthy speech in which Socrates recounts the theory of love that he learned from Diotima of Mantinea, his "instructress in the art of love." In the dialogue, then, we have Diotima's lesson in *ta erotika* retailed by Socrates—which already shows how far Plato himself is from endorsing her doctrine. What has happened, for historical reasons we have no space to examine here, and for psychological reasons that will become evident in due course, is that Diotima's program long came to be regarded as "the Platonic theory of love." It certainly voices a deeply and understandably attractive view. It has had fateful effects in the development of Christian spirituality and asceticism. In the *Symposium* itself, however, by the device of having Diotima's doctrine quoted by Socrates, who admittedly makes it his own, Plato distances himself from it. Then, by bringing on the drunken Alcibiades, in what is often disregarded as a ribald anticlimax, Plato exposes Socrates to raw but searching criticism. (For that matter, the entire conversation is supposedly being repeated by a certain Apollodorus, who had in turn heard an account of it many years before from one of the original participants.)

The dramatic date of the banquet is January 416 BC. Agathon, the host, a tragic poet (of whose work less than forty lines survive), is celebrating his success in the Dionysiac festival. He is in his late twenties; Socrates is fifty-three; and Alcibiades, the legendarily handsome, able, and doomed military leader, is thirty-four. He is passionately in love with Socrates, who, by now bald, potbellied, and twice married, has loved Alcibiades for about twenty years. By the time Plato composed the *Symposium* it was at least fifteen years since Socrates had drunk the hemlock, and twenty years since the murder of Alcibiades. In a complete interpretation of the dialogue we should have to reconstruct a good deal of the political and intellectual background as well as flesh out the personal relationships among the participants. The dialogue is not just a string of set speeches: on the contrary, one line of thought is extended or undercut by another, and it is important to know who is speaking and with what interests. But we shall have to be content with a brief account of the two final speeches.[14]

Pausanias, one of the earlier speakers, has defended *paiderastia* and the practice of philosophy and virtue in general. Aristophanes, the future comic poet, in a riotously funny fantasy, traces the pain of erotic desire to our each being half of an original globular androgyne. Agathon praises the god of love, the youngest and tenderest of the gods, "of flexile form" (Jowett), dwelling in a place of flowers and scents, and so on, and "the cause of what is fairest and best in all other things." Thus the way is prepared for Socrates' speech.

"Human beings love the good," Diotima eventually tells him. What are people doing, then, who show "all this eagerness and heat which is called love?" It turns out that, to enter the greater and more hidden mysteries of love, one must begin young to seek the company of corporeal beauty—"to love one beautiful body only." The beautiful thoughts that this experience will generate soon make you realize that the beauty of one body is the same as that of another—which abates your violent love of the first individual (which you will now "despise and deem a small thing"). You will now become a steadfast lover of *all* beautiful bodies. At the next stage beautiful *souls* will come to seem more precious to you than beautiful *bodies*. Then you will be "compelled to contemplate and see the beauty in institutions and laws, and to understand that the beauty of them all is of one family, and that personal beauty is a trifle." By this time you are well away, so you "cease to be like a servant in love with one beauty only, that of a particular youth or man or institution." Thus, "using these as steps only," you at last come to see "the divine beauty, pure and clear and unalloyed, not infected with the pollutions of the flesh and all the colors and vanities of mortal life."

That is where Diotima's lesson concludes. *People*, or rather *young men*, already reduced to the status of "beauties," as though they might not rather be interestingly and attractively intelligent, humorous, kind, loyal, kooky, and a thousand other things, are finally treated as the lowest rungs on the individual's climb to the secure vision of that which is absolutely and immutably beautiful. The very idea of loving a man for himself, never mind a woman for herself, has no place in this program. To let flesh-and-blood men and women be such objects of affection would be to stop on the bottom step of the ascent to the vision of the beautiful. We are to love one another as place holders for absolute beauty. What we love in another human being is the (necessarily very partial and flawed) presence of the transcendental form of the beautiful in him or her. All along it is his beauty, not the man himself, that is loved; and his beauty is homogeneous with the beauty of poetry writings, legislation, and suchlike. If a man had eyes to see the divine beauty, Diotima tells Socrates, he would then be immune to the attractions of gold, garments, and fair boys.

Desire thus becomes so exclusively and absorbingly focused on the Form of the Beautiful that the erotic attractions of human beings disappear. By concentrating one's desire solely on the Idea of Beauty one becomes invulnerable to the beauty of any particular human being. Since their beauty is all the same, other people become intersubstitutable; they lose their refractory particularity. Diotima's program trades on an understandable inclination in any passionate man or woman to transcend the risks of love. You can never be let down or betrayed or rejected by the Idea of the Beautiful. Diotima's course in erotics would secure immunity against all the pain and the uncertain pleasures of being in love with human beings.

Just as Socrates finishes his "encomium of love" a great knocking at the door announces the late arrival of Alcibiades, very drunk, roaring and shouting, supported by a flute girl and some companions, with his head garlanded with ivy and violets. Socrates, as soon as Alcibiades recognizes him, appeals to Agathon for protection: "[S]ince I became his admirer I have never been allowed to speak to any other beauty. . . . If I do, he goes wild with envy and jealousy, and not only abuses me but can hardly keep his hands off me," and so on. Alcibiades, invited by the company to make a speech in praise of love, insists that he will "speak the truth." He makes an embarrassing confession of his passionate desire for Socrates, which he

offers as praise of the older man's magnificent self-control. At great length
he describes how he once tried to seduce Socrates but ended lying the
whole night long, "having this truly superhuman wonder in my arms"—and
"nothing more happened." He goes on to tell of Socrates' extraordinary
powers of endurance: he can go without food, he can drink wine endlessly
without ever getting drunk, he can walk barefoot on ice, he has been seen
standing motionless in thought, for twenty-four hours on end, and so on.

When Alcibiades finishes the company laugh—"for he seemed to be
still in love with Socrates." Socrates now asserts that the whole speech was
got up to make the handsome young Agathon transfer his affections from
him (Socrates) to Alcibiades. Agathon moves closer to Socrates: "I must
move instantly, that I may be praised by Socrates." "The usual way" Alcibiades comments wryly. "[H]ow readily he has invented a specious reason for
attracting Agathon to himself."

The discussion now ends, a large party of revelers breaks in, everybody
drinks enormous quantities of wine, Socrates keeps on arguing and compels
Agathon, the tragic poet, and Aristophanes, the comic poet, to agree that
there is no difference between tragedy and comedy—but they are too sleepy
to argue and eventually, at dawn, Socrates puts them to bed and goes off
to have a bath.

The comic and the tragic poets are put to bed by the philosopher
whom neither drink nor drowsiness nor the warmth of a man's naked body
can touch. Alcibiades, laughed at and rejected, leaves the room without anyone's noticing. Diotima's formula for dealing with the risks of passion has,
in various transformations, shaped the European imagination from Plotinus
to Dante. Socrates is portrayed in the *Symposium* as a successful practitioner
of the ascent to divine Beauty—or so readers commonly think. With the
appearance of Alcibiades the dialogue is thought to drift into frivolity: his
speech seems like a comic turn, which lowers the metaphysical tone. Philosophers, of course, often regard the *Symposium* as "literature," as if it did
not contain enough philosophical content for them to explore. But there
is another way of reading the text. The dialogue as a whole, and certainly
the final confrontation between Socrates and Alcibiades, surely touches on
ethical issues of great importance. Plato leaves us to decide whether Alcibiades' embarrassingly naked vulnerability is satisfactorily treated by the icy
control that Socrates displays—which, in any case, does not stop him from
getting Agathon to sit beside him. If equating tragedy and comedy is as
profound a thought as many commentators on this passage seem to think,
then no doubt the wisdom of Socrates is the last word. But surely Plato is
leaving us free to regard it as an absurd thesis, sprung from the mind of

a philosopher who understands neither comedy nor tragedy. The "success" of Diotima's system is perhaps to be measured by the sight of the hurt and rejected Alcibiades. Plato himself, after all, is the author of the *whole* dialogue.

4. Aristotle's Early Ethical Writings

What Aristotle made of the *Symposium* when he first encountered it we cannot determine. The student of the *Nicomachean Ethics* learns much more from the text if it is seen as a deliberate and critically informed response to certain Platonic doctrines. But the discussion of friendship in the *Ethics* must be dated to 334–322 BC, when Aristotle had reached his maturity as a thinker. We cannot reconstruct what he thought at earlier stages. His apparently numerous dialogues have not survived, except for some fragments. They were famous in antiquity for their style: Cicero, in the first century BC, admired them, while David the Invincible, the fifth-century Armenian Christian writer, speaks of them as "overflowing with controlled eroticism."[15] One would not say so much of the works that have come down to us.

Interestingly enough, however, Aristotle's dialogues included his own *Symposium*, though our sources speak of it more often as his "book on drunkenness" (*Peri Methes*).[16] The surviving fragments mostly appear in the amazing writings, of Athenaeus of Naucratis (fl. c. AD 200). They do not add up to anything very significant. They do not even inspire much confidence that Aristotle wrote them. Consider, for example, the following fragment: "The liquor made from barley called beer has a certain peculiarity; people who are intoxicated by other liquors fall in all sorts of directions—to the left, to the right, on their knees, on their backs; only those who are intoxicated with beer always fall backwards and lie on their backs." Plutarch, in another fragment, says that, in his *Peri Methes*, Aristotle noted that "old men are overtaken most easily, and women least easily, by drunkenness": Plutarch expresses his surprise that Aristotle did not work out the reason for this circumstance—"a thing he was not wont to fail to do."

Aristotle wrote another dialogue called the *Eroticus*. It might have had more bearing on our subject here but, perhaps fortunately, very little of it survives.[17] Athenaeus makes the following claim: "Aristotle says that lovers look at no other part of the body of their beloved than the eyes, in which modesty dwells." Sixth-century vase paintings of men wooing boys perhaps lend some support to this unlikely thesis, but such remarks do not remind us of Aristotle at his best. Athenaeus has an incomparable nose for trivia, but the evidence does not allow us to decide whether the fragments that survive show the crassness of his readers or the fatuity of Aristotle's dialogues.

5. Friendship in Aristotle's *Ethics*

Two of the ten books of the *Nicomachean Ethics* are devoted to discussing friendship. Aristotle is, among other things, out to show how a man who loves the good nevertheless loves his friends—and not just as stand-ins for the Idea of the Good but for their own sake.

Attempting to deal with one's desire for others by concentrating on something higher results in treating them as counters. Friendship, on Aristotle's view, is absolutely indispensable for life: "For no one would choose to live without friends, but possessing all other good things" (*NE* VIII, 1155a). The rich need friends on whom to practice beneficence, the poor turn to friends for succor, the young need friends to protect them, the elderly to tend them. "Even when traveling abroad," Aristotle notes, "one can observe that a natural affinity and friendship exist between human beings everywhere." Friendship is the bond of the community. Indeed, justice seems to involve friendship at a certain point. But, above all, Aristotle says, "friendship is not just a necessity, it is also beautiful" (1155a).

It is a much debated question, so Aristotle tells us, whether friends are necessary for one's happiness: "People say that the supremely happy are self-sufficing, autarkic, and so have no need of friends: for they have the goods of life already, and therefore, being complete in themselves, require nothing further" (*NE* IX, 1169b). They have reached that radical independence of other people which Diotima's program of erotic exercises is intended to secure. Such a man becomes so self-sufficient that he becomes indifferent to the presence of other people. There is nothing for them to do for him—but the deeper motivation of this ideal of an autarkic condition surely lies more in the absence of other people's threatening and exciting qualities than in the redundance of their practical skills. The good man cannot be harmed, so Socrates argued: what is of supreme value, that is to say, is an internal condition that can no longer be affected by the outside world. The lesson of Diotima is the only way to escape the torments of erotic passion and all the other wounding and bewildering elements in the surrounding world.

This interest in cultivating self-sufficiency shows how intense and often violent people's emotional life was: the whole point is to get one's feelings under the management of *reason*. It is no coincidence that Socrates sought to get people to agree that a man cannot do wrong *knowingly*—that one can do wrong only through lack of knowledge. Nor is it a coincidence that, in book VII of the *Ethics*, Aristotle goes to great lengths to make room, between virtuous and vicious conduct, for the moral phenomenon of weakness of will. Socrates seems to deny even the possibility of such behavior, on the grounds that, once a man had the truth about the situation, it would be monstrous to suppose that anything could distract him from doing the right thing. "This theory," Aristotle comments, "is manifestly at variance with plain facts; and we need to investigate the state of mind in question more closely" (*NE* VII, 1145b). There is no use in wielding mere theory to deny the existence of inner moral conflict; it is more reasonable to attend to the facts ("Don't think, but look," as one might say). Aristotle's reaction to Socratic intellectualism reveals its depth and audacity only if we allow ourselves to appreciate its horror at the presence in ourselves of something that eludes rational control. Such intellectualism has had to work so hard to differentiate rational behavior from emotional reaction that it simply cannot entertain the possibility that a man of reason might nevertheless act against his better judgment. Aristotle, however, feels relaxed enough about the claims of reason to look calmly at the existence of moral dilemmas by showing that however clear one' reason may be, it may be no more effective than an actor's lines in overcoming the pull of emotion, echoing, as he recognizes, Socrates' own critique of "Socratic" intellectualism.

In a similar way, in the next two books of the *Ethics*, Aristotle feels free to investigate the nature of friendship, attending patiently to the complexity of the phenomenon rather than subjugating it to the yoke of theory. He gestures briefly in the direction of Hesiod, Euripides, Heracleitus, Empedocles, and proverbial wisdom in general on the cosmic dimensions of love, before inviting us, characteristically, to "look at the human side of the question"—to attend, that is to say, to "character and emotions" (*NE* VIII, 1155b). For example: is everyone capable of friendship, or does the very possibility rest on one's having a certain *character*? Again: is there only one form of friendship? Is *philia* as uniform and homogeneous, and therefore as potentially impersonal and intersubstitutable, as Diotima's *eros*? Here Aristotle makes his first criticism of Platonist doctrine: "Those who hold that all friendship is of the same kind because friendship admits of degree, are relying on an insufficient proof, for things of different kinds can also differ in degree." In effect, that is to say, he resorts once again to that perception of the analogical behavior of certain concepts which is perhaps his most decisive contribution to philosophy.

When you listen to what we say, so Aristotle goes on, you find that *philia* is not mentioned in connection with inanimate objects. The concept always involves a return of affection and wishing the other's good. Bottles of wine may head ineluctably in a certain man's direction, but this is not because they have the feelings toward him that he has for them. In the second place, "it would be ridiculous to wish well to a bottle of wine: at the most one wishes that it may keep well in order that one may have it oneself."

Thus the crucial insight is introduced: "[I]n the case of a friend we necessarily say that we wish the good to him for his sake, *ekeinou heneka*" (1166b). That final phrase runs like a refrain throughout Aristotle's discussion. It marks the world of difference between loving a man for the sake of the good and wishing the good for a man *for his sake*. Aristotle must have known what he was doing. The phrase embodies a polemic against any theory of personal relationships which effectively empties the other person of intrinsic worth and particularity. Aristotle has begun his long campaign to remind his readers that friends are considered to be "the greatest of external goods" (1169b). Although the *spoudaios* possesses a type of self-sufficiency, Aristotle is quick to show that this is within the context of our social nature, where one's moral and contemplative virtues are known and cherished in relation to friends, honoring the essential value of these external attachments. What comes "from outside" is the greatest of his goods. *Philia*, that is to say, is necessarily a relationship with somebody else—who is allowed to retain his separate existence. Friendship, then, includes an other-relatedness which is inevitably also a source of great vulnerability. Friends die. The very possibility that Diotima's erotic ascent seeks to exclude from the life of the happy man is thus recognized as indispensable to it.

To do justice to our humanity Aristotle rehabilitates our vulnerability. He cannot admire men who have trained themselves to be indifferent to any particular mundane joys: "[S]uch *anaisthesia* is simply not human" (*NE* III, 1119a). Indeed, he goes on to say, every animal prefers to eat one thing rather than another: "[I]f there is a creature to which one thing feels just like another, it must be very far removed from humanity." His respect for humanity comes out again and again. It would be eccentric, he says, to picture the happy man as a singular and solitary figure: "Nobody would choose to have all possible good things on the condition that he must enjoy them alone, for human beings are social beings and naturally live together" (*NE* IX, 1169b). Whatever the problems of living with other people, Aristotle cannot conceive of a kind of human life that would transcend them. He certainly does not want us to become radically different: "No one would choose to possess every good in the world on condition of becoming somebody else, but only while remaining himself, whatever he may be" (1166a).

You might be tempted to think it desirable for your friend to have what would surely be the greatest gift of all—to become divine; but if a friend in the proper sense wishes his friend's good for that friend's own sake, *ekeinou heneka*, then that friend would have to remain *himself*, in his separate otherness—"so that [one] will really wish him only the greatest goods compatible with his remaining a human being" (1159a). Finally, in a palpable hit at Plato, "you could not endure even the Absolute Good itself forever, if it bored you" (1158a).

It may seem a noble prospect to cultivate self-sufficiency by radically exclusive attachment to the Idea of the Good: one might become impervious to the vicissitudes and vulnerabilities of life. Independence of the beauties around one, with their overwhelming and ever-changing attractions, may seem the higher way to happiness. For Aristotle, however, friendship itself is "the beautiful thing" (1155a).

Philia is not uniform and homogeneous, like Platonic *eros*: Aristotle has an analogical vision of the world. We may leave aside purely exploitative relationships, in which the parties each aim at using, or having enjoyment out of, the other, one treating the other as a horse or a bottle of wine. Such relationships do not count as friendship at all. But we may genuinely want the best for one another in some relatively limited enterprise—for instance as business partners or as theologians. One might lose by doing so: the other may make the faster buck or find the way, with humiliating ease, to refute one's pet theory. The other man's good is what one wishes; his separate independence is respected; but he is wearing a certain hat—our acquaintance with each other as business partners or as theologians. Look around you, Aristotle seems to say: friendship occurs on that kind of basis. Such friendships, according to Aristotle, "seem to occur most frequently between the old, as in old age men do not pursue pleasure but profit. . . . Friends of this kind do not indeed frequent each other's company much, for in some cases they are not even pleasing to each other" (1156a). With these friendships he somewhat curiously classes "family ties of hospitality with foreigners"— but at the time *xenia*, guest-friendship, counted as one of the deepest and most essential expressions of our humanity. To place it here only shows how highly Aristotle regards the mutuality of genuine well-wishing for the other person's sake, even when both parties meet on relatively limited ground.

Friendships may also arise on the basis of enjoying one another's jokes: we find one another's company pleasant. Each wants the best for the other if the singing and the crack are to be memorable. Here, among friendships that are founded on people's pleasure-giving qualities and qualifications, Aristotle locates the mutual well-wishing of lovers qua lovers. In one paragraph he notes the problems of fickleness and jealousy that dominate the discussion in Plato's *Symposium*—"the young are prone to fall in love," and so on, but nothing is said or even hinted about the fevered eroticism among the middle-aged intellectuals at Agathon's party.

Friendship in the richest sense, however, is grounded, not on people's supportive or pleasure-giving qualities, but on their goodness: "[S]uch friends are both good in themselves and, so far as they are good, wish the good of one another. But it is those who wish the good of their friends for their friends' sake, *ekeinou heneka*, who are friends in the fullest sense, since each loves the other for what the other is in himself and not for something he has about him which he need not have" (1156b). Each loves the other, not on the basis of any inessential personal quality such as some relevant expertise or delightful skill, but for what the other person most deeply is as a moral agent. Such friends are of course a help to one another; they also delight in one another's presence. But the relationship rests on something more radical than these relatively transient and incidental qualities. One may, after all, lose the relevant competence or become distressingly wasted by disease. The stability in love that Aristotle envisages is open only to those who are, in a tricky Greek phrase, "alike, or at one, at the level of goodness, moral excellence, or humanity" (*kat' aretēn homoioi*: 1156b). Long before Aristotle's time the key word *aretē*, etymologically connected with Ares (Mars), god of war, had ceased to mean prowess, valor, "being a man," bravery, and the like, and come simply to mean human excellence as such. It is thus in their humanness at its finest that friends in the richest sense ground their relationship. "Hence their friendship lasts," Aristotle observes, "as long as they continue to be good; and *aretē* is durable."

Virtue endures. We may have the stability in love that people who are at one on this level of radical humanity can achieve: no less, but also no more. It is quite astonishing, and surely very moving, to watch Aristotle describing a kind of loving that no voice in Plato's *Symposium* could name. For there, particularly in Socrates' great speech but also elsewhere in the dialogue, it is assumed that the desire to possess and control is characteristic of all love—which, in any case, is of only one kind. Jealousy, anger at one's vulnerability, fear of instability, and so on, could be defeated only by submitting to the discipline of training one's love exclusively upon objects less fickle, unreliable, and imperfect, than human beings. Over against all that, Aristotle reminds us that there is a kind of human love that really respects and enhances the separate good of the other person. It is a love which includes other kinds of love, which arise on more limited and unstable grounds. The open-endedness and stability of this kind of love cannot compete with that ascent to secure vision of "the divine beauty, pure and clear and unalloyed, not infected with the pollutions of the flesh and all the colors and vanities of mortal life," like the Platonic *eros*; but in its acceptance of the human condition Aristotle's *philia* certainly has its own beauty.

6. The Influence of the *Ethics* on Aquinas

Now for the speculation.[18] We do not know why Aristotle's account of love appealed so much to Thomas Aquinas that he went back to study the *Ethics* much more carefully, at some indeterminable point between 1256 and 1272, with the result that he radically revised his approach to the nature of charity. We certainly know that he never read Plato's *Symposium*. He clearly knew that Aristotle was often polemicizing against Platonic doctrines. When he gave such prominence to Aristotle's model of friendship in the first question about charity in the *Summa*, did he realize that he was taking sides in a debate that was already sixteen hundred years old? If that is unlikely, did he turn to Aristotle by a kind of instinct to disengage himself from a certain neo-Platonic mysticism of love, present even in the Augustinian tradition?

As we saw, the discussion in the *Scriptum*, if it does not exactly reek of sublimated eroticism, nevertheless has a certain neo-Platonic redolence. It is a good deal more interesting, however, to find a completely new question in the *Summa*, paralleled only in exactly contemporary writings: namely, whether it is God alone who is loved in the case of charity (IIa IIae, 25, 1). That is to say: Do we love our neighbor, in charity, or is it God alone whom we love? Why did Thomas set himself this hitherto undiscussed question? Who ever doubted that "he who loves God should love his brother also"? Why should Thomas want to discuss whether charity's love does or does not have any other object than God—unless he suspected that we might be tempted to think that love of God and love of neighbor were radically different in kind? Or perhaps that the object of charity's love for our neighbor was not the neighbor himself but really only God in the form of our neighbor? Are we merely "channels" for the circulation of divine love, such that God in me would love God in you, and we should both disappear from the scene? After all, it seemed to Peter Lombard, a great authority in Thomas' day, that charity was the Holy Spirit in the believer's soul, and not something human (IIa IIae, 23, 2). The difficulties in the way of practicing Christian love may well give rise to the idea that it must be something in which human beings have no part. Charity, thus envisaged, perhaps begins to remind us of that vision of an invulnerable and impersonal love such as Socrates describes in the *Symposium*.

Again, did Thomas detect, in a certain spirituality, a determination to love everyone so impartially that one actually loved no one in particular? Why does he go into such detail about the *ordo caritatis* (IIa IIae, 26), arguing that we are bound to love certain neighbors more than others (art. 6), that our charity should be directed to those who are nearer to us more than to those who are better (art. 7), that we ought to love our kindred more than other people (art. 8), and so on? Who needed to be persuaded of such banalities? Whose problems was Thomas attempting to resolve with these arguments? Whose distress at finding charity towards some people much easier than towards others required to be thus assuaged? What theory of spirituality needed the therapy of these considerations?

Spiritual success has often seemed to require detachment from particular circumstances and people, including even oneself. Our neighbor becomes an "occasion" for the exercise of charity—very much as the first beautiful boy in Diotima's system is a place holder for the Idea of the Beautiful. Charity can be understood as, ideally, making people inter-substitutable. Charity reduced to doing good, to well-meaning "do-goodism," is evidently common enough to have become proverbial. Worse still, however, and much more likely to be in Thomas' sights, is a whole style of Christian spirituality, no doubt afflicting clergy and the religious most of all, in which something very like Diotima's ascetic exercises, suitably transformed, has flourished like blight. It is surely significant, for example, that, discussing the priorities to be observed in loving objects out of charity, Thomas resists the thesis that our own body has either a low or indeed no place in the *ordo caritatis*: "Our bodily nature, far from issuing from an evil principle, as the Manichees imagine, is from God" (IIa IIae, 25, art. 5). Manes, a Gnostic Christian who lived in Persia in the third century, produced a system that struck people at the time as a "Pauline heresy." How much connection it had historically with the doctrines and practices associated with the Cathari and the Albigenses that posed by far the greatest internal threat to the Catholic Church in the thirteenth century need not be discussed here. Indeed, if there was no direct influence at all, that would only confirm the case for the perennial vitality of a spirituality that seeks to cope with the vulnerabilities and vicissitudes of human life, against a spirituality practicing a detachment that denies the intrinsic value of anything belonging to this world.

As so often, it is a recurrent temptation in Christian doctrine and piety that Thomas wants to expose and eradicate—and, again as so often, it is to Aristotle that he instinctively turns to help him to articulate the sane alternative. It should not be concluded that he thus bypasses the traditional Christian sources. On the contrary: in the very years that he was transforming the *Nicomachean Ethics* into the *secunda pars* of the *Summa* he was also lecturing on the fourth Gospel, which resulted in the finest of his scripture commentaries. In his last years he seems to have become more and more passionately committed to the works of Aristotle and St. John the Evangelist. It is not just that Aristotelian emphases enabled Thomas to detect Christian deviations; they also allowed him to make breathtakingly audacious theological assertions.

Perhaps I should note at this point that Thomas does not always have everything well worked out. He was not out to produce a mathematically consistent system, whatever some readers fear and others would like to think. He sometimes betrays his best insights. Like any great thinker— starting with Plato and Aristotle—his creative advances occasionally leave pools of earlier ideas overgrown or untrained. To my mind at least, when he argues that the companionship of other human beings is not *de necessitate* in heaven—"Were there but one single soul enjoying God it would be happy though without a neighbor to love"—he would have done better to think a little harder about what Aristotle is saying in the text that he cites (IIae, 4, art. 8). The reader may well feel, as Thomas Gilby remarks at this point in his translation, "that this article marks a relapse into a primness of the *Nicomachean Ethics*." While the question—one of the few that Thomas never discussed elsewhere but apparently invented as he worked on the *secunda pars*—would have been quite unintelligible to Aristotle or anyone else in the fourth century BC, is it so clear that this lamentable "primness" is fairly attributed to the *Ethics*?

The syndrome in theology and piety that attracted Thomas' criticism over the years, as everyone knows, was a certain supernaturalism that effectively devalued our humanity and our world. Christology, for example, is for Thomas predominantly a confrontation with docetic temptations.[19] Indeed, in one of the extremely rare first-person remarks in all his millions of words, he corrects his earlier docetic understanding of how Jesus acquired knowledge (IIIa, 9, art. 4). It is no surprise to find that it was reflecting on Aristotle's philosophy of mind that enabled Thomas to catch himself out. We have already noted that the Catholic Church in his day had scarcely recovered from the deep internal trauma of Albigensianism. The great external challenge in the thirteenth century came from Islam: how much Thomas owed, and knew that he owed, to that source need not be detailed here. It was, for a start, the main conduit of the works of Aristotle. But he also feared that some Islamic theologians spoke of the power of God in such a way as to deprive human beings of their intrinsic reality: "To make the creature almost nothing in the sight of the Holy One, far from respecting the divine majesty, only reduces it" (*Summa contra Gentiles* III, 69, freely translated). Since God is an omnipotent agent and so responsible for everything in the world, how can we understand the human act as something for which we are responsible? It was to elucidate this question that Thomas turned to Aristotle's account of causality.

It is not surprising, then, that when at last he had to reconsider the topography of charity, Thomas instinctively appropriated Aristotle's criticism of the Platonic theory of love that is voiced in Socrates' speech in the *Symposium*. He did not, of course, know what he was doing: having no access to the relevant Platonic texts he could not have made the comparison or located the radically different approaches to love in the *Symposium* and the *Ethics* respectively. Indeed, given his customary reverential exposition of texts which he is often correcting and even rewriting, it might be asked whether he had enough idea of the modern way of taking up a critical stance to a text to be able to see how different the two approaches are. His intuition, at any rate, drew him to the Aristotelian side in the profound conflict that I have tried to identify.

One way, for emotionally fragile creatures such as we human beings are, to cope with the wonderful but bewildering and often wounding realities of the world, is to immunize ourselves against them all by uniting ourselves with the one totally reliable and stable reality which will by definition never desert or betray us, or in some other way get out of control. In the end, paradoxically enough, one becomes rather like Aristotle's notion of God: *chroristheis*, separate, uninvolved, apart in oneself (*NE* VIII, 1159a).

But if one's conception of God runs rather in a direction that is illuminated by the doctrine of the Incarnation, including of course a proper doctrine of the Church, after the fashion which Thomas adumbrates in the *tertia pars* of the *Summa*, an entirely different perspective opens out. If God has shared his own goodness with human beings, so that this love is reciprocal, then they have become *good*: lovable, desirable, beautiful, intrinsically valuable. Each partner in the relationship loves the other for his or her *character*—for what the other most deeply and radically is in himself or herself. In such love neither partner is lost in, or enslaved by, the other. On the contrary: each loves the other precisely for the sake of his or her *otherness*. In such mutual respect for the separateness of each partner it is therefore at last possible for us to let God be *God* in the knowledge that God lets us be *us*. But this means, of course, that we have to live with each other—and God is no more securely in our control than we are in his, at least if by that we desire to be his favorite doll.

As so often, however, since Thomas' theology is certainly "systematic" in the sense that the very nature of the investigation compelled him to travel criss-cross over the ground in every direction, memories of many other tractates or "treatments," in the *Summa* and elsewhere, crowd in. What he ventures about charity as friendship illuminates, and is in turn illuminated by, things that he says on a string of other matters. But such explorations must be left for another occasion.

To sum up, then, we may say this: when Thomas reread Aristotle's *Ethics* he found a new depth to the idea of charity as a kind of friendship. In charity we are friends with God. There can be no friendship, in the fullest sense, except between equals—but God has made us his equals. This kind of friendship, according to Aristotle, is based on each partner's acknowledging the other's goodness. Second, they let one another be: each delights in the other's existence, and the freer the one allows the other to be the more fully and truly they are revealed to each other. What is crucial, I think, is that there is no question of one partner's losing his or her identity in the other. The lover is not infatuated with the beloved. There is no annihilation of self in submission to, or submersion in, the absolute other. The relationship is modeled on the kind of "space" that friends accord one another: *koinōnia*, conversation, even a kind of "symposium." For Thomas, as for Aristotle and Plato, what is defining about human beings is that we find ourselves in language. Even in that divine way of loving which is charity we neither are nor want to be struck dumb. We are friends with God. We do not lose ourselves in that self-hating spirituality that has afflicted so many people's lives nor in some ascetical detachment that would save us from the vulnerabilities of love.

In thus rethinking the nature of charity in the light of Aristotle's analysis of love with the incisiveness and clarity that he shows in the *Summa*, Thomas must surely have thought that he had opened up a new theological perspective that his followers would develop. In fact, however, as happened with nearly all his most original and characteristic insights, this proposal was soon distorted out of all recognition or simply consigned to oblivion.[20] It was explicitly rejected by Durand de Saint-Pourçain, the leading Dominican thinker in Paris by the second decade of the fourteenth century, but then he objected to all the essential Thomist insights and escaped being silenced by Dominican censorship only by becoming a bishop. Dominicans, alas, no doubt unwittingly, did more than anyone else to bury Thomas' idea. In

Germany, again by the first years of the fourteenth century, in the teachings of such Dominican luminaries as Helwic the Teutonic and Johannes Korngin von Sterngassen, the idea of friendship with God had become assimilated into those currents of piety that bloomed in the mystical writings of Tauler and others. The network of mystics in the Rhineland and Switzerland who took the name of "friends of God," with their emphasis on the personal union of their souls with God, not to mention their tendency to attack certain aspects of ecclesiastical life for "externality," had effectively diverted the idea of charity as friendship into the solitary merging of the individual with the absolute which, if I am right, Thomas was instinctively rejecting. As a result, such thoughts as Catholics have about the nature of charity would now be captured perfectly well by the account Thomas offered in the *Scriptum*. A moralistic notion of "doing good" is the sole runner, except perhaps in the case of special cloistered souls, for whom ascetical loss of self in disinterested and impartial love may still be conceivable. What Thomas, and Aristotle before him, was out to free us from still seems to be the natural thing to think.

Notes

*This chapter is a lightly revised version of "Thomas Aquinas: Charity as Friendship," which initially came out in Brian Davies OP (ed.), *Language, Meaning and God: Essays in Honour of Herbert McCabe* (London: Geoffrey Chapman, 1987). It was subsequently reprinted under the same title by Wipf and Stock (London, 2010), who generously gave us permission to reprint it in the present collection free of charge, a rare thing these days amongst publishers.

1. McEvoy 1982, viii.
2. Callus 1955, 62.
3. *Aristoteles Latinus* XXVI, 1–3.
4. Pelzer 1922.
5. *Sententia libri Ethicorum.*
6. Weisheipl 1974, 380.
7. Bourke 1974, 1: 239–59, esp. 254.
8. Jaffa 1952, 6.
9. Bourke 259.
10. Gauthier and Jolif 1958–59.
11. Weisheipl 1974, 256.
12. Kenny 1980, 24.
13. *Scriptum, super libros Sententiarum*, III, 27.2.1.
14. Discussion of the *Symposium* took a new turn with the well-known essay by Vlastos 1973, chapter 1; but readers who know Nussbaum 1986 will easily see how deeply I am indebted to it in the rest of this chapter.

15. Cited by Nussbaum 1986, 503.
16. *The Works of Aristotle* 1952, 8–14
17. Ibid., 25–26.
18. I am indebted here to lectures given at le Saulchoir, Paris, in the winter of 1962–63, by Jacques Pohier.
19. The term "docetic" (Greek *dokein*, to seem; *dokesis*, apparition, phantom) is applied in Christology when the doctrine that Jesus Christ is truly divine is emphasized so strongly that he is no longer considered to be really human; he only looked like a human being: in some early gnostic Christian heresies Jesus did not genuinely suffer or really die.
20. Egenter 1928.

Bibliography

Aquinas, Thomas. 1975. *Summa Theologiae*, Blackfriars ed., vol. 34 (Charity). Translated by R. J. Batten. London and New York: Eyre & Spottiswoode.

———. 1969. *Sententia libri Ethicorum*. Leonine ed. Rome.

———. *Scriptum, super libros Sententiarum*, critical ed. in progress.

Aristoteles Latinus Database, Brepols.

Aristotle. 1952. *The Works of Aristotle*. Translated and edited by Sir David Ross, vol. 12, Select Fragments. Oxford: Oxford University Press.

Bourke, Vernon J. 1974. "The *Nicomachean Ethics* and Thomas Aquinas." In *St. Thomas Aquinas 1274–1974, Commemorative Studies*. Toronto: Pontifical Institute of Mediaeval Studies.

Callus, Daniel A. 1955. "Robert Grosseteste as Scholar" In *Robert Grosseteste: Scholar and Bishop*, ed. D. A. Callus. Oxford: Clarendon Press.

Egenter, R. 1928. *Die Lehre von der Gottesfreundschaft in der Scholastik und Mystik des 12. und 13. Jahrhunderts*. Augsburg, Dr. Benno Filser Verlag.

Gauthier, R. A., and J. Y. Jolif. 1958–59. *L'Ethique à Nicomaque, Introduction, traduction et commentaire*. 3 vols. Louvain and Paris.

Jaffa, Harry V. 1952. *Thomism and Aristotelianism: A Study of the Commentary by Thomas Aquinas on the* Nicomachean Ethics. Chicago, University of Chicago Press.

Kenny, Anthony. 1980. *Aquinas*. Oxford: Oxford University Press.

McEvoy, James. 1982. *The Philosophy of Robert Grosseteste*. Oxford: Oxford University Press.

Nussbaum, Martha Craven. 1986. *The Fragility of Goodness: Luck and Ethics in Greek Tragedy and Philosophy*. Cambridge: Cambridge University Press.

Pelzer, A. 1922. "Un cours inédit d'Albert le Grand sur la Morale à Nicomaque, recueilli et rédigé par saint Thomas d'Aquin." *Revue néo-scolastique* 23.

Vlastos, Gregory. 1973. "The Individual as Object or Love in Plato." *Platonic Studies*, Princeton: Princeton University Press.

Weisheipl, James A. 1974. *Friar Thomas d'Aquino*. Oxford: Blackwell.

PART 4

ENLIGHTENMENT THINKERS

11

ARISTOTLE AND KANT ON SELF-DISCLOSURE IN FRIENDSHIP·

Andrea Veltman

1. Introduction

Among the common elements in the accounts of friendship offered by Aristotle and Kant is the notion that the highest form of friendship makes possible a mutual knowing of another. Both note that in the course of spending time together friends come to know and to be known by each other. Aristotle names this activity "joint perception" in the *Eudemian Ethics* (1245b24), where Kant speaks of "disclosing" or "revealing" ourselves to another in friendship in the *Lectures on Ethics* and the *Metaphysical Principles of Virtue*. Inventively, Aristotle argues that knowing another person in friendship enables friends of like virtue to know themselves. By knowing another person who resembles ourselves, we are able to overcome the difficulties normally involved in self-perception and, in effect, see ourselves in seeing someone whose character mirrors our own. Kant similarly characterizes the highest friendship as one that allows friends to jointly know each other, but instead of identifying a benefit of self-knowledge in the activity of mutual knowing, Kant notes that the highest friendship permits an intrinsically valuable self-disclosure unachievable through any other venue. In revealing themselves to a trusted friend, people in the highest friendships become known by another person, thereby connected to another person, and no longer remain alone.

In this chapter, I consider Aristotle's treatment of knowing another in friendship in the context of Kant's claim that the highest friendships allow

271

an intrinsically valuable self-disclosure. Viewed next to Kant's treatment of self-disclosure in friendship, Aristotle's account of knowing a friend appears both less attractive than Kant's account and puzzling in itself, given Aristotle's emphasis on the social dimension of human beings. Although both Aristotle and Kant identify the mutual knowing involved in friendship as a reason for cultivating friendships with others of good virtue, Kant understands self-disclosure in friendship to be valuable in itself, whereas Aristotle regards joint perception in friendship as a means to self-knowledge.

In addressing Aristotle's argument that character friendships enable self-knowledge, scholars of Aristotle's ethics have not only tried to interpret Aristotle's cryptic remarks on contemplating others but have also argued that friendships, in spite of their utility in securing self-knowledge, have an intrinsic value for Aristotle.[1] The literature on Kant's account of friendship has centered less around his remarks on self-disclosure in friendship and more around issues of impartiality and friendship, but some attention has been given to his notorious admonition in his earlier work that we hold back from revealing ourselves to our friends, lest we be harmed by the improbity, untrustworthiness, or sheer clumsiness of our friends.[2] However, while Aristotle's and Kant's accounts of self-knowledge and self-disclosure in friendship have been treated within their respective literatures, comparative analyses of Aristotle and Kant on friendship have neglected the similarities and differences in these aspects of their accounts of friendship. Here I suggest that, at the same time that Aristotle and Kant emphasize complimentary aspects of the mutual knowing involved in friendship, Kant gives a comparatively more attractive account of self-disclosure as an inherently valuable activity.

Although Kant's account of self-disclosure in friendship represents an advance over Aristotle's account, Aristotle's account of friendship as a whole is nevertheless more developed and more firmly grounded in human sociability than Kant's account of friendship. Aristotle establishes a more prominent place for friendships in a good life, since on his account the need to cultivate relations with others flows from our make-up as social creatures, and friendships are integral in human happiness. Kant, in contrast, determines friendship to be a duty and human nature an "unsocial sociability."[3] In his earlier remarks on friendship, Kant also mars his otherwise appealing picture of self-disclosure in friendship with an admonition to beware of the ultimate untrustworthiness of friends, whereas Aristotle notes that friends develop trust only in time in the course of sharing activities. Given that Aristotle's account of friendship retains several advantages over Kant's, it is not the case that Kant advances a superior account of friendship; rather, he advances a superior account of self-disclosure in friendship.

2. Aristotle on Knowing Another Person in Friendship

In the course of supplying reasons why the happiest life includes friend-ships, Aristotle observes that the highest form of friendship between people of good character allows friends to achieve self-knowledge. Time spent in shared activities in the course of being together enables friends to know each other, and the similarity between friends of good character, in turn, enables friends to know themselves in knowing each other. As Gary Gurtler aptly summarizes in his chapter in the present volume, "There is a sense in which we come to know ourselves and see the depths of our own nature in that peculiar mirroring that the other provides for us, especially in friend-ship. . . . The friend is essential, precisely as another self who facilitates this awareness."[4] A friend whose virtue mirrors one's own reflects one's self, and thus beholding one's friend permits one to see oneself and to achieve a component of self-knowledge, although, to be sure, the self-knowledge of the virtuous person likely extends beyond "the particularities of his own person and situation"[5] to include, for example, knowledge of the normative standards of his community, as Suzanne Stern-Gillet argues in her chapter in the present volume.

Aristotle's argument for the importance of character friendships in achieving self-awareness and in living well appears in each of the Aristotelian treatises on friendship in the *Nicomachean Ethics*, the *Eudemian Ethics*, and the *Magna Moralia*.[6] Whereas the *Nicomachean* and *Eudemian Ethics* present the argument in a manner both convoluted and truncated, however, the *Magna Moralia* gives the most clear and concise treatment of the argument. In the *Magna Moralia*, Aristotle summarizes the argument as follows:

> If, then, when one looked upon a friend one could see the nature and attributes of the friend, . . . such as to be a second self . . . as the saying has it, "Here is another Hercules, a dear other self." Since then it is both a most difficult thing, as some of the sages have said, to attain a knowledge of oneself, and also a most pleasant (for to know oneself is pleasant)—now we know we are not able to see what we are from ourselves (and that we cannot do so is plain from the way in which we blame others without being aware that we do the same things our-selves, . . . and there are many of us who are blinded by these things so that we judge not aright); as then when we wish to see our own face, we do so by looking into the mirror, in the same way when we wish to know ourselves we can obtain that

> knowledge by looking at our friend. For the friend is, as we
> assert, a second self. If, then it is pleasant to know oneself, and
> it is not possible to know this without having someone else for
> a friend, the self-sufficing man will require friendship in order
> to know himself. (*MM* 1213a10–26.)

The first premise of the argument is that self-knowledge is a highly desirable but elusive good. Because it is pleasant to contemplate ourselves, Aristotle reasons, "self-perception and self-knowledge is most desirable to everyone" (*EE* 1244b25). He similarly notes in the *Nicomachean Ethics* that it is pleasant not just to live well but to perceive our living well, adding that the purpose of the happy man is to contemplate his own virtuous actions (*NE* 1170a2–3; 1170b1–10). Knowledge of ourselves, however, is difficult to obtain given that human beings cannot readily see who we are for ourselves. Aristotle himself addresses the reason we cannot easily perceive ourselves only briefly in the *Magna Moralia*, in which he suggests that the tendency to exaggerate our virtues and distort our faults prevents us from accurately seeing ourselves (*MM* 1213a16–20).

In the *Nicomachean Ethics*, Aristotle fills out the notion that we cannot perceive ourselves well with the notion that we can, in contrast, perceive others. Giving the second major premise in his argument that character friendships enable self-knowledge, Aristotle remarks that "we can contemplate our neighbors better than ourselves and their actions better than our own" (*NE* 1169b34–35). This premise remains without further explanation in the *Nicomachean Ethics* or elsewhere and has primarily two possible interpretations. First, as John Cooper has suggested, Aristotle may mean simply that we have a degree of objectivity in relation to others that allows us to see others as we cannot see ourselves.[7] To its advantage, this interpretation conforms with the suggestion in the *Magna Moralia* that self-knowledge ordinarily remains elusive because of the human tendency to inflate our virtues and downplay our shortcomings. The lack of objectivity human beings have in relation to ourselves may be one reason for the overly generous self-assessments that, according to the *Magna Moralia*, prevent us from knowing ourselves.

Alternatively, Aristotle may be referring to a human inability to step back and contemplate ourselves in the course of exercising virtue in action. We can adequately appreciate a characteristic or virtue, Richard Kraut has argued, only when observing it exercised by another.[8] Someone exercising courageousness in war, for example, would be far too engrossed in courageous activity to step back and behold the courageousness of his action.

Likewise, a statesman acting or speaking in the political arena may be focused on the political issues at hand and cannot simultaneously contemplate her virtues as a politician. It is, rather, only an onlooker observing courageousness or political skill in another who can readily observe and appreciate the realization of virtue in the actions of others. Aristotle himself, in fact, underscores that it is in contemplating actions that human beings can see others better than we see ourselves. In the *Nicomachean Ethics*, he fills out the premise that we can contemplate others better than ourselves by noting that friends of good character know each other by contemplating their actions: "[T]he supremely happy man will need friends of [the best kind] since his purpose is to contemplate worthy actions and actions that are his own, and the actions of a good man who is his friend have both these qualities" (*NE* 1170a1–4).

Interpreting Aristotle's remark on contemplating others as an inability to step back may appear more attractive given that it has some ground in the *Nicomachean Ethics*, whereas the interpretation concerning objectivity only loosely falls into place with the *Magna Moralia*. Another reason to prefer the interpretation favored by Kraut is that it is supported by Aristotle's account of virtue as a disposition toward performing right action. Aristotelian virtue requires more than a good state of character: it requires realization through performing virtuous deeds, for the good life is one of activity (*NE* 1105a26–b13; 1114b28–9).[9] A person of good virtue thus engages in activities that give realization to virtue but cannot, apparently, behold herself performing such actions.

The interpretation concerning objectivity, however plausible, does not rule out the first interpretation that we see others better than ourselves because we have a degree of objectivity in relation to others that we lack in relation to ourselves. It can be the case both that we contemplate others through their virtuous actions and that the objectivity we have in relation to them allows this perception. Far from being mutually exclusive, these two explanations may work together. The distance we have vis-a-vis another person may be a basic reason why we can see virtuous character realized only in another person's actions. Indeed, insofar as Kraut also notes the difficulty of stepping back and seeing ourselves in action, both interpretations effectively credit the proximity we have to ourselves as a reason why self-knowledge is not possible without a friend like ourselves.

If the meaning of Aristotle's premise that we can contemplate others better than ourselves is indeed that we can best behold or appreciate the virtues when we see them in the actions of others, then Aristotle's self-knowledge argument also keeps from collapsing into to a paradox concerning self-knowledge. In the absence of Kraut's interpretation, it may appear that in order to achieve self-knowledge by contemplating our friends, we must already possess at least some self-knowledge. Unless we know ourselves prior to contemplating our friends, or prior to choosing our friends, we cannot know that our friends resemble ourselves, in which case we cannot rely on the mirroring dimension of friendship to achieve self-knowledge. Since we must know ourselves to know that we resemble our friends, it appears that self-knowledge must be possible without the contemplation of friends, and the mirroring of virtuous friendship thus appears unnecessary in the achievement of self-knowledge.

However, Kraut's interpretation of Aristotle's remark on contemplating others lends itself to a distinction between knowing that we possess a certain virtue or characteristic and beholding or appreciating the virtues or characteristics we possess. Once we make this distinction and interpret Aristotle's second premise in terms of appreciating what we possess, this apparent paradox of Aristotelian self-knowledge dissolves. We frequently know that we possess certain virtues or characteristics prior to contemplating our friends, and we do not need the mirroring of virtuous friendship to achieve the knowledge that we possess certain virtues. We do, however, need to perceive the virtuous actions of our friends in order to behold or appreciate what such virtues look like on ourselves, because our proximity to ourselves prevents us from beholding our virtue in our own actions. Although we do occasionally need a friend to point out that we possess a certain virtue or characteristic, it is the beholding and appreciating of our virtue that we require the mirroring dimension of friendship to provide.

The second premise of Aristotle's self-knowledge argument, however, is not sufficient to entail the conclusion that virtuous friendships enable self-knowledge. Contemplating someone else's character does not in itself enable self-knowledge, since two unlike individuals would not, given their dissimilarity, achieve self-knowledge by contemplating each other. It is only on the condition that the contemplated person resembles the self that contemplating another person enables self-knowledge. The third key premise in the argument is thus that friends of good virtue resemble each other in character. The friend whose virtue matches our own functions as "a second self" who closely resembles ourselves in character, pursuits, tastes, and aims (NE 1166a29, 1170b7; EE 1245a30).[10] Because they see a second self, friends of good virtue are able to achieve self-knowledge by beholding someone whose character mirrors their own. This premise together with the first two premises warrants the conclusion of the argument: "[T]o perceive a friend must be in a way to perceive one's self and to know a friend is to know one's self" (EE 1245a35–36).

While the argument that self-knowledge can be achieved through character friendships thus hinges on the similarity between friends, it is a fair question whether friends of good character always closely resemble each other. It is not difficult to believe that affinity often draws friends to each other, but it is also the case that people cultivate friendships with others whom they do not closely resemble. If friendships generally exist between people who do not mirror each other, knowing another person in friendship does not always enable self-knowledge.

On Aristotle's account, however, friendships of the highest sort exist only between people of similarly high moral characters, and friends of good virtue therefore share at least some virtues common to all good people (*NE* 1156b7–14; *EE* 1236b2–4). Character friendships will thus allow good people to contemplate their virtuous characters, although friendships between those who do not possess good characters will not always enable self-knowledge, given the inconsistency of character found among people who lack virtue. However, since it is not Aristotle's aim to supply reasons why an unhappy life may include friendships, it is not a compelling objection against Aristotle's account of self-knowledge in friendship that friendships between nonvirtuous individuals do not always produce self-knowledge.

Although it is not a problem on Aristotle's account that many friends, generally speaking, do not closely resemble each other, it may indeed be a problem that even friends of good character rarely mirror each other exactly. Even if friends of good character share a large repertoire of virtues, seldom do two people share all the characteristics that define themselves. Since they are not identical individuals, even friends of good virtue will differ from each other at least in possessing qualities which are not virtues. While one friend may be more sociable than the other, the other friend may possess a greater amount of industriousness, for example. Unless it is the case that people of virtue uniformly possess identical characters, friends of good virtue will have some variation in character between each other.

Considering that friends of good virtue, as any two people, would likely not be identical to each other in character, it appears that the most Aristotle may claim is that by contemplating a friend, a person can come to see some of her friend's qualities. He cannot claim, however, that by contemplating a single friend a person can know herself, since herself comprises at least all her characteristics and virtues, not all of which will be mirrored in a single friend. It may be this consideration that leads Aristotle to note in the *Eudemian Ethics* that "the characteristics [of friends] are scattered" and to appear to maintain that groups of friends share salient characteristics with each other (*EE* 1245a31).[11] Although a single friend cannot enable self-knowledge, we can gain sight of some of our characteristics by contemplating one friend and other characteristics by contemplating other friends, in order to secure self-knowledge from a cohort of friends of similar virtue.

In short, Aristotle notes that self-knowledge is a highly desirable good that friends of like virtue can achieve by contemplating each other. The activity of joint perception in friendship enables friends to overcome the lack of objectivity they have in relation to themselves and, in effect, to behold their own virtuous characters. Joint perception in friendship thus serves the purpose of attaining self-knowledge and is not for Aristotle, as it is for Kant, worthwhile because it makes possible an inherently valuable disclosure of ourselves to another person. We engage in joint perception in friendship, rather, because "it is pleasant to know oneself, and it is not possible to know this without having someone else for a friend" (*MM* 1213a24–25).

3. Kant on Self-Disclosure in Friendship

Whereas Aristotle argues that knowing a friend of like virtue allows us to know ourselves, Kant differs primarily in maintaining that moral friendships permit an intrinsically valuable self-disclosure. In his work on friendship in the *Metaphysical Principles of Virtue*, Kant writes that the highest form of friendship enables friends of good character to rise above the reticence and anxiety that plagues most social interaction and to open themselves up to each other "even without thereby aiming at anything."[12] Kant's earlier remarks on friendship in the *Lectures on Ethics*, in contrast, reflect an indecisiveness on Kant's part concerning self-disclosure in friendship, since in this early treatise Kant extols the virtues of self-disclosure but also advises against fully revealing ourselves even to our most intimate friends. Thus, we must make a distinction between Kant's earlier and later work on friendship. Maintaining that Kant improves over Aristotle in treating self-disclosure in friendship requires taking his later work on friendship as representative of his view.

In both his earlier and later work on friendship, Kant writes that we simultaneously desire to reveal ourselves to others and yet hold back from doing so out of fear that others might abuse our self-disclosure.[13] We feel an impulse to share our thoughts, dispositions, and judgments with another and to achieve a communion with another in revealing ourselves. Ordinarily, however, we conceal the greater part of ourselves, lest those to whom we would reveal ourselves use our self-revelation to their advantage or harm us in their indiscretion concerning what bears repeating and what does not. Human beings thus interact with each other while wary of the possible damaging consequences of candidly revealing ourselves, reticent and covertly distrustful in our interactions with others. Summarizing this predicament of a social but prudential creature, Kant writes of the human animal that "in the cultivation of the social state he strongly feels the need to open himself up to others. . . . But, on the other hand, he is also constrained and admonished by his fear of the abuse which others might make of this disclosure of his thoughts. . . . [H]e must not risk it because others. . . . might make use of his remarks to his own detriment."[14] In the protection of our own long-term good, we therefore live among others but imprisoned within ourselves, alone with our thoughts.

A friendship between two people of good virtue, however, offers a sanctuary from the constraints of normal social intercourse. When two people who are honest rather than duplicitous, caring and not self-serving, cultivate a friendship marked by love and respect, they can transcend the worry and distrust of most human interaction and reveal themselves completely to each other:

> If we can free ourselves from [our mistrust of others], if we can unburden our heart to another, we achieve complete communion. That this release may be achieved, each of us needs a friend, one in whom we can confide unreservedly, to whom we can disclose completely all our dispositions and judgments, from whom we can and need hide nothing, to whom we can communicate our whole self. . . . [Friendship] is man's refuge in this world from his distrust of his fellows, in which he can reveal his disposition to another and enter into communion with him.[15]

Because moral friendship rests on a trust cultivated between principled friends, in moral friendship we can finally reveal ourselves to another without reserve. Friends of integrity are unencumbered by anxiety over whether the other person will misuse their self-disclosure, and they are thus able to achieve the sort of candid disclosure of themselves to another which is, Kant remarks, "the whole end of man, through which he can enjoy his existence."[16]

Although Kant presents the highest form of friendship as a forum for candidly revealing ourselves to another person, in works other than the *Metaphysics of Virtue* Kant advises adopting a reticence even in moral friendships that works against his picture of self-disclosure in friendship. Even a trusted friend, Kant warns in the "Lecture on Friendship," can one day turn into an enemy or, even, if not an enemy, possibly ruin us by spreading around our shared confidences to our peril. Even in the friendship of disposition: "We must so conduct ourselves towards a friend that there is no harm done if he should turn into an enemy. We must give him no handle against us. . . . [I]t is very unwise to place ourselves in a friend's hands completely, to tell him all the secrets which might detract from our welfare if he became our enemy and spread them abroad."[17] It is this possibility that friends may turn our vulnerabilities against us that should motivate prudent friends to reveal themselves only guardedly:

> There is in man an element of improbity, which puts a limit on such candor. . . . Even the sages of old complained of this obstacle to the mutual outpouring of the heart, this secret distrust and reticence, which makes a man keep some part of his thoughts locked within himself, even when he is most intimate with his confidant: "my dear friends, there is no such thing as a friend!" And yet the superior soul passionately desires friendship, regarding it as the sweetest thing a human life may contain. Only with candor can it prevail.[18]

Friendship rests on a candid disclosure of ourselves to another person, but the "secret distrust" that lies behind even the closest friendships should prevent any cautious and far-sighted individual from revealing himself to his friend wholeheartedly.[19] The moral friendship, in which we can candidly reveal ourselves to another person, appears unattainable given the ultimate untrustworthiness of human beings. Kant's praise of moral friendship as a reprieve from the guardedness of most human interaction is thus dampened in this earlier work on friendship by the improbity he considers human beings to have and by the maxim of prudence he advises adopting in friendships.

In contrast to his earlier writings on friendship, however, Kant's treatment of friendship in the later *Metaphysical Principles of Virtue* does not depict close friends as ultimately untrustworthy. Here the candid self-disclosure that moral friendship permits is unmitigated, and Kant gives no admonition to remain on guard against revealing anything potentially damaging. It is in ordinary social interaction alone that we hesitate to reveal ourselves, but when we find a friend of good disposition we can finally and unhesitatingly open ourselves up to another person. By definition, moral friendship "requires an understanding and trusted friend."[20]

Kant's *Metaphysical Principles of Virtue* represents an advance over his earlier writings on friendship not only in depicting self-disclosure unfettered with distrust but also in acknowledging that an open self-disclosure is valuable in itself. In moral friendships, Kant writes, an individual may "open himself up to others (even without thereby aiming at anything)."[21] Having no end beyond itself, self-disclosure in moral friendship has an intrinsic value in this later work. In the "Lecture on Friendship," in contrast, Kant identifies a further benefit of self-disclosure in friendship. Disclosing our true judgments and thoughts to a friend often enables the friend to correct our mistakes, thus furthering our intellectual and personal improvement.[22] But when Kant writes the *Metaphysical Principles of Virtue* roughly twenty years later, he omits any mention of a further end beyond self-disclosure and notes instead that self-disclosure in moral friendship is worthwhile for its own sake. In his final work on friendship, Kant thus jettisons the dim view of human trustworthiness that underlies his earlier work on friendship at the same time that he regards self-disclosure as an end-in-itself.

4. Aristotle and Kant on Mutual Knowing in Friendship

If we take Kant's depiction of self-disclosure in moral friendship in the *Metaphysical Principles of Virtue* as representative of his view, his depiction reveals not just a different focus on the activity of knowing a friend, but also a more attractive account of this activity. Although both Kant and Aristotle highlight the mutual knowing involved in friendship as a virtue of the highest form of friendship, Kant's emphasis lies not on knowing another person but on being known by another person, since it is in being known by another person that we become connected to someone else. In contrast, Aristotle's interest lies in knowing another person rather than in being known by another person, since it is only through knowing another person that we can come to know ourselves. The value of joint perception in friendship for Kant is that it allows another person to perceive himself, whereas for Aristotle joint perception allows us to perceive ourselves through another person. In short, Aristotle's identification of self-knowledge as a benefit of friendship directs his attention to the activity of knowing another person, through which self-knowledge is achieved. Kant, however, notes that human beings desire to reveal themselves to someone, to be known by someone, and thus concerns himself with being known by another person rather than with knowing another person. Furthermore, the instrumental value Aristotle assigns to knowing another in friendship becomes especially apparent viewed next to Kant's treatment of being known by another. For Aristotle, we contemplate our friends not because doing so makes possible an intimate connection to our friends but because it is pleasant to behold our virtuous character, and it is not possible to do this without a friend who mirrors us.

In light of Aristotle's larger argument in the *Nicomachean* and *Eudemian Ethics* that happiness requires developing connections with others in friendship, his construal of joint perception as an instrumental good appears misplaced. The mutual knowing that occurs in friendship is a major avenue through which friends become connected to each other, as Kant recognizes, yet Aristotle overlooks this fact and instead points to the personal good of self-knowledge secured by knowing another person. Aristotle appears to overlook that it is precisely in the activity of knowing each other that friends become bonded to each other as friends, whereas Kant articulates an impressively sentimental picture of the "complete communion" friends achieve in self-disclosure in spite of his tortured characterization of human nature as distrustful and "unsocially sociable."[23] The connection that arises through self-disclosure in friendship is something so "sweet" and "tender," Kant remarks, that it "approximates a fusion into one person" and enables friendships to transcend the aim of mutual advantage.[24] Yet, while Kant recognizes that the reciprocal knowing involved in friendship binds friends to each other, Aristotle lacks this recognition even with an account of human sociability superior to Kant's.

Although the mutual knowing involved in friendship is, for Aristotle, a means to achieving self-knowledge, character friendships are not themselves merely means to self-knowledge on Aristotle's account. It has been widely acknowledged that Aristotle considers character friendships both instrumentally and intrinsically valuable in a blessed life.[25] Friends of good character enable each other to perform virtuous activities more continuously and pleasantly, help each other in contemplating truth, and make the best subjects for beneficence, in addition to enabling contemplation of our own virtue (*NE* 1169b11–17; 1170a4–9; 1177a35–1177b1). In spite of its instrumental value, however, character friendship is nevertheless "desirable in itself" as well as the greatest of the external goods (*NE* 1099b1–4; 1159a27). The social nature of human beings alone makes us creatures whose well-being requires living in common among friends (*NE* 1169b17–21). Friendships are indeed so integral to good living that, as Aristotle comments at the outset of his treatise on friendship, "without friends no one would choose to live, though he had all other goods" (*NE* 1155a5–6).

It is therefore necessary to make a distinction between the mutual knowing involved in friendships and friendship per se: although knowing a friend who mirrors us has merely instrumental value in the Aristotelian treatises on friendship, friendship itself does not. It is possible to make this distinction given that mutual knowing is an integral part of friendship,

but it is not the entirety of friendship. Friendship requires several activities other than mutual contemplation: shared hours, joint projects, mutual
beneficence, and good will are, as Aristotle notes, but some of the elements
that comprise friendships. To be precise then, it is the mutual contemplation
of another person in friendship, which is necessary for friendship but not
equivalent to it, that Aristotle treats as merely an instrumental good in the
acquisition of self-knowledge.

It may initially appear that, in like manner as Aristotle regards contemplating friends as a means to self-knowledge, Kant also regards self-disclosure
as a means to achieving a communion with another in friendship. At a key
juncture in his "Lecture on Friendship," Kant suggests that the end of moral
friendship is not the disclosure of ourselves to another but the "complete
communion" with another that this disclosure achieves.[26] Contrasting the
openness of moral friendship with the constraint of ordinary social interaction, he writes, "if we can free ourselves of this constraint, if we can
unburden our heart to another person, we achieve complete communion."[27]
The language of achieving a complete communion may appear to indicate
that it is communion or fusion with another person in friendship, rather
than self-disclosure itself, that is truly the intrinsic good for Kant. If self-
disclosure and communion with another are indeed understood as discrete
occurrences, then a case can be made that Kant regards joint perception in
friendship as a good which is useful for achieving some further end.

However, whereas self-knowledge is a further end apart from self-
disclosure in friendship, communion with another person in friendship
is achieved in the activity of self-disclosure. Once friends candidly reveal
themselves to each other, they therein transcend their isolation as discrete
individuals and become more connected with each other than with others.
As Kant notes, communion with another person in friendship cannot be
achieved without showing our real selves to someone else, since it is in
the very activity of revealing ourselves to another person that we become
known by the other person and therein connected with the other person.[28]
Self-disclosure is therefore intrinsic to communion with a friend, whereas
self-knowledge is a possible consequence of perceiving a friend. Even if
our friends resemble ourselves in virtue, we may observe our friends and
need not use such an observation to imagine what such virtues look like
on ourselves. It is at least possible that we contemplate our friends simply
for the sake of contemplating our friends, without performing an act of
reflection in which we achieve self-knowledge.

Presumably, complete communion with another person in friendship requires not only a context of moral friendship but also a mutual or
reciprocal self-disclosure. Although asymmetrical self-disclosure exists both

inside and outside the bounds of friendship, asymmetrical self-disclosure can destabilize intimate friendships. If we reveal more of ourselves to our friends than they reveal to us, we are prone to wonder why our friends are holding back, whether they trust us as friends, or whether our friendship is as intimate as we believe. We confront doubts and instabilities that undermine friendships. Furthermore, friends cannot achieve a complete communion with each other if only one friend candidly reveals herself while the other holds back. For this reason, therapists and their patients, like celebrities and their admirers, are not friends. Even though one party knows the other, the other is not known in return.

Although the self-disclosure of which Kant speaks requires the trustworthiness of a virtuous friend, the mirroring dimension of friendship itself is available to both virtuous and nonvirtuous individuals. Even bad individuals and individuals of mediocre virtue have it within their power to see others more objectively than they can see themselves, inasmuch as our ability to perceive others better than ourselves is not a virtue or limited to the perception of virtues. This ability, which is discussed by Aristotle in the second premise of his self-knowledge argument, arises from the distance we have in relation to other people as separate individuals. Aristotle himself limits his discussion of self-knowledge in friendship to friendships among virtuous individuals perhaps not simply because his aim is to show that virtue friendship is desirable in a happy life, but also because people of good virtue possess a similarity to each other that enables self-knowledge. Individuals who lack virtue or are vicious do not always perceive themselves through their friends given the inconsistency of character found among nonvirtuous individuals, the instrumental nature of their friendships, and their disinclination to examine themselves. However, if bad or ordinary individuals do make an effort to contemplate others who resemble themselves in vice or lack of virtue, they can presumably behold their viciousness or lack of virtue, which may, in turn, motivate their own moral development. Self-perception through perception of the characteristics of others, however, does not itself require the context of a virtuous friendship based upon trust. Unlike Kantian self-disclosure, it does not involve the sharing of private information but only the contemplation of the characteristics of other individuals.

Finally, we should note that although Aristotle does not acknowledge the inherent value of joint perception in friendship, he does have an account of trustworthiness which is superior to Kant's account. The candid sharing of thoughts and dispositions, Kant recognizes, rests on a mutual trust between friends. His earlier comments on friendship differ from his comments in the *Metaphysical Principles of Virtue* primarily in the skepticism they reveal about the possibility that friends can be trusted with a candid self-disclosure. In both his earlier and later work on friendship, however, Kant identifies "trust in the mutual confidences" of friends as a necessary condition of candid self-disclosure.[29] In spite of acknowledging that self-disclosure rests on trust between friends, Kant devotes little attention to the issue of earning trust.[30] He accordingly teeters between admonishing friends not to reveal themselves to each other and maintaining that some friendships achieve enough trust to permit a full self-disclosure.

Aristotle, in contrast, appreciates as Kant does not that the trust that allows friends to be honest with each other develops only in time. Noting that "there is no stable friendship without confidence, but confidence needs time," Aristotle effectively anticipates Kant's definition of moral friendship as a type of friendship that presupposes trust and observes that such trust cannot be supposed present at the start (*EE* 1237b13–14). Since the highest friendships unfold during time spent together during which friends come to know each other's characters, this type of friendship is unequivocally a type in which "trust and the feeling that 'he would never wrong me' . . . are found" (*NE* 1157a23–4). Kant, in contrast, is concerned about the deceit that may lie behind the face of a trusted friend, warning of the possibility that a trusted friend will misuse our self-disclosure for his own gain.[31] Insofar as Aristotle considers friends to build trust through time, his remarks on trust establish a stronger ground than Kant has for the mutual knowing involved in friendship.

Aristotle therefore has the sort of basic account of building trust that Kant needs but conspicuously lacks, and his account of trust in friendship stands as one advantage over Kant's account of friendship. Kant's later characterization of self-disclosure as intrinsically valuable, however, is one advantage that Kant's account of friendship has over Aristotle's. Whereas contemplation of a friend serves the purpose of achieving self-knowledge for Aristotle, Kant regards self-disclosure in friendship as not only valuable in itself but also, indeed, as "the whole end of man, though which he can enjoy his existence."

Notes

*This chapter is a lightly revised version of "Aristotle and Kant on Self-disclosure in Friendship," published in *The Journal of Value Inquiry* 38 (2004): 225–39. It is reprinted here with kind permission of Kluwer Academic Publishers/ Springer Science+Business Media. I would also like to thank Paula Gottlieb, Jean

Keller, Jeff Johnson, Thomas Magnell, Carol Caraway, Madeleine Arseneault, Sara Gavrell, Tasia Persson, and an anonymous referee for the *Journal of Value Inquiry* for helpful comments on earlier drafts. This chapter has been presented at the 2002 Central Division Meetings of the American Philosophical Association and at a Philosophy Department Colloquium at the University of Wisconsin-Madison, and I would also like to thank those present at both sessions for helpful comments and lively discussion.

1. Pangle 2003; Kraut 1989; Cooper 1980.
2. See Wood 1999; Langton 1992; Maucucci 1999.
3. Kant "Idea for a Universal History from a Cosmopolitan Point of View." See Sherman 1997.
4. Gurtler, p. 44.
5. Stern-Gillet, p. 57.
6. *NE* 1169b28–1170a4; *EE* 1244b25–1245a10,1245a29–36; *MM* 1213a10–26.
7. Cooper 1980, pp. 320–322.
8. Kraut 1989, pp. 131–142.
9. Cf. Kosman 1980.
10. For an analysis of Aristotle's concept of the virtuous friend as a second self, see, e.g., Stern-Gillet 2005.
11. For this point, I am indebted to Jeff Johnson.
12. Kant, *Metaphysical Principles of Virtue*, §47, 138.
13. Kant, *Lectures on Ethics*, 205, and *Metaphysical Principles of Virtue*, §47, 138.
14. Kant, *Metaphysical Principles of Virtue*, §47, 138.
15. Kant, *Lectures on Ethics*, 205–06.
16. Ibid., 206.
17. Ibid., 208.
18. Kant, "Letter to Maria von Herbert," 188.
19. Cf. Kant, *Religion within the Limits of Reason Alone*, 28–29.
20. Kant, *Metaphysical Principles of Virtue*, §47, 139; cf. Christine Korsgaard, 1996, 199–200.
21. Kant, *Metaphysical Principles of Virtue*, §47, 138.
22. Kant, *Lectures on Ethics*, 205–06.
23. Kant, *Metaphysical Principles of Virtue*, §47, 138.
24. Ibid., §47, 137.
25. See Pangle 2003, 183–93; Sherman 199, *passim*; Cooper 1980, 331–33.
26. Kant, *Lectures on Ethics*, 205.
27. Ibid.
28. Ibid.
29. Kant, *Religion within the Limits of Reason Alone*, 28.
30. See Sherman 1997, 230–31.
31. Kant, *Lectures on Ethics*, 217, and *Religion within the Limits of Reason Alone*, 28–29.

Bibliography

Aristotle. 1984. *Eudemian Ethics* in *The Complete Works of Aristotle*, vol. II. Translated by J. Solomon and edited by Jonathan Barnes. Princeton: Princeton University Press.

———. 1941. *Nicomachean Ethics* In *The Basic Works of Aristotle*, trans. William David Ross, ed. Richard McKeon. New York, Random House.

———. 1966. *Magna Moralia*, in *The Works of Aristotle*. Translated by George Stock, edited by William David Ross. Oxford: Oxford University Press.

Cooper, John. 1980. "Aristotle on Friendship." In *Essays on Aristotle's Ethics*, ed. Amelie Rorty. Berkeley: University of California Press.

Kant, Immanuel. 1963. "Lecture on Friendship." In *Lectures on Ethics*, trans. and ed. Louis Infield New York: Harper and Row.

———. 1994. *Metaphysical Principles of Virtue*. In *Immanuel Kant: Ethical Philosophy*, 2nd ed., trans. James Ellington. Indianapolis: Hackett.

———. 1963. "Idea for a Universal History from a Cosmopolitan Point of View." In *Kant on History*, trans. and ed. Lewis Beck. Indianapolis, Bobbs-Merril Co.

———. 1967. "Letter to Maria von Herbert." In *Kant: Philosophical Correspondence, 1759–1799*, trans. Arnulf Zweig. Chicago: University of Chicago Press.

———. 1960. *Religion within the Limits of Reason Alone*. Translated by Theodore Green and Hoyt Hudson. New York: Harper and Row.

Korsgaard, Christine. 1996. *Creating the Kingdom of Ends*. Cambridge, Cambridge University Press.

Kosman, Aryeh. 1980. "Being Properly Affected: Virtues and Feelings in Aristotle's Ethics." In *Essays on Aristotle's Ethics*, ed. Amelie Rorty. Berkeley: University of California Press, 103–116.

Kraut, Richard. 1989. *Aristotle on the Human Good*. Princeton, N.J.: Princeton University Press.

Langton, Rae. 1992. "Duty and Desolation." *Philosophy* 67: 481–505.

Maucucci, Silvestro. 1999. "Moral Friendship in Kant." *Kant-Studien* 90.4: 434–441.

Pangle, Lorraine. 2003. *Aristotle and the Philosophy of Friendship*. Cambridge: Cambridge University Press.

Rorty, Amelie. 1980. *Essays on Aristotle's Ethics*. Berkeley: University of California Press.

Sherman, Nancy. 1997. "The Shared Voyage." In *Making a Necessity of Virtue*. Cambridge: Cambridge University Press, 187–238.

Stern-Gillet, Suzanne, 2005. "Des Deux Conceptions du «Soi» chez Aristote." In *Cosmos et Psychè. Mélanges offerts à Jean Frère*, ed. Eugénie Végleris. Hildesheim, Zürich. New York: Georg Olms Verlag, 229–250.

Wood, Allan. 1999. "Desire and Deception" and "Friendship." In *Kant's Ethical Thought*. Cambridge: Cambridge University Press.

12

THE PLATONIC ROOTS OF HÖLDERLIN'S CONCEPT OF FRIENDSHIP IN *HYPERION**

Sandra Dučić-Collette

To Ana Eunyoung Ju, beloved friend, *in memoriam*.
Erōs creates friendship.

—*Symposium*, 182c3–4

Introduction

The importance of ancient concepts of friendship in German idealism is a topic that is yet to receive the attention it deserves in modern scholarship. In this chapter, my aim is to show how Plato's ideas about love and friendship helped Hölderlin[1] to present his own views on idealism, particularly in *Hyperion*, his epistolary novel.[2]

Hölderlin's *Hyperion* is generally taken to be a hymn to love. However, one may be justified, as I shall argue, in seeing it as also a hymn to friendship.[3] Although the two notions are intertwined, they are nevertheless distinct and, in *Hyperion*, they refer to two different ages of the world and humanity:[4] "Love brought to birth millenniums filled with living men; friendship will give birth to them again."[5] While love is associated with the childhood of the world, a kind of state of nature out of which man has now emerged, friendship points to a new, ideal, age, rejuvenated and still to come, governed by "the harmony of spirits" (*die Harmonie der Geister*):

"Once upon a time the people set forth from the harmony of childhood; the harmony of spirits will be the beginning of another history of man."[6] Between the two ages, there is the current state of the world, corresponding to the state of maturity and moral consciousness of humanity in general, a state characterized by chaos or lack of harmony: the garden of the world is now dried up, apparently barren, beauty having left nature to seek refuge in spirit. True love, it seems, has irremediably passed away; as for friendship, it is a long time coming.

The sources, direct and indirect, as well as the underground influences that bore on Hölderlin's thoughts as he wrote *Hyperion*, are multiple and varied. In this chapter, I focus on the Platonic imprint on *Hyperion*, an imprint that is often palpable but at the same time difficult to pinpoint. Joseph Claverie, in *La jeunesse d'Hölderlin jusqu'au roman d'Hypérion*, a study that remains valuable to this day, well says: "It seems that Hölderlin erased the outline of the ideas he received."[7] Hölderlin's references are never specific, and his references to Plato are no exception. However, in the case of the relationship between love and friendship, as described in his "letter on friendship" (I, 2. 15)[8], it is possible to discern the influence of a properly Platonic motif,[9] that of age transforming itself into a new youth. This motif is found in the condensed expression of "return" or *Rückker*, which refer to the reversing of the course of the world and its rejuvenation into a new and original form.[10]

The interpretation of the "letter on friendship" in *Hyperion* is made particularly difficult by the eponymous hero of the novel himself, Hyperion, who deliberately speaks to the select few, who alone are capable of understanding the deep truth that he is unearthing. The essentials are presented in an extremely compact form that can nevertheless be unfolded if one relates them to the content of an earlier letter (cf. I, 1, 7), where it is recounted how Hyperion and Alabanda first met, how they became friends, and how they eventually parted. This letter, set up explicitly under the patronage of Plato, lays down the frame that can help us to shed new light onto the relationship between love and friendship in *Hyperion*.

As we shall see, this Platonic frame presents itself in the form of a dialectical movement comprised of three distinct moments: life, death, and the return of life again. These moments are at the heart of the Platonic conception of *erōs* in the *Symposium*. However, it is not directly the *Symposium* that Hölderlin is referring to, but rather the famous myth of the *Politicus* about the different ages of the world. So much, at least, I would like to suggest here. But before getting into the *Politicus* proper, we need first to look into the context of the first encounter of the two friends, in which the above mentioned Platonic motif is already at play.

1. Aging and Rejuvenating

Hyperion is in Smyrna, a city he is considering leaving soon. His heart, he writes, is each day wearier. Summer has just gone and *Nature*, "which had surged up into every plant and tree like a foaming fountain, now stood before my darkened apprehension fading and closed and turned in upon itself, just as I was."[11] After the exuberant eruption (*emporgedrungen*) of the first seasons of the year, it is now time for withdrawal and waning (*das Schwinden*), and this external, general, and cosmic movement is analogous to the one governing the very heart and life of Hyperion himself, a life that, so he writes, "*refused to renew itself.*"[12] Knowing that he will soon be gone, that "*the recurring year*"[13] will not find him any more among the trees and the mountains of the region, he starts gathering in him all the external things he got attached to and, in particular, goes out in the nearby forest and tries to meet with a mysterious man, whom he had seen only fleetingly. That man is Alabanda, whom he eventually meets.

The two young men become friends immediately. In his letter to Bellarmin (his main confidant throughout the novel), Hyperion recalls in particular one memorable day, when the two of them sat down and began to read Plato: "We had gone to the country together and were sitting with our arms trustfully around each other in the dark shade of an ever green laurel, *looking at our Plato—the passage where he speaks with such wondrous sublimity of aging and rejuvenation*, and from time to time we rested, looking out over the mute, lifeless landscape, where the sky, plain with clouds and sunlight, was more than ever beautiful among the autumnally sleeping trees."[14] In his commentary, Jochen Schmidt noted the importance of the theme of aging and rejuvenating in Hölderlin, not only in *Hyperion* but also in *Der Tod des Empedokles*.[15] According to him, the Platonic passage that Hyperion is referring to is the myth about the *palingenesis* of the souls in the *Meno* (cf. 81a sqq). He bases his claim on the fact that Hölderlin must have been familiar with this dialogue since he not only refers to it in his poem *Menons Klagen um Diotima*, but the cycle of death and rebirth (i.e., what the palingenesis consists in) is also very much present in letter I, 1. 7. However, this particular reference to the *Meno* seems to me dubious. First of all, if it is not incorrect to characterize the set of themes in our text in terms of palingenesis, one should notice that Hyperion is actually speaking of a particular passage in which Plato is dealing with "*Altern und Verjüngen*," words that are not used in the myth of the *Meno*. Besides, nowhere in the *Hyperion* letter is there any mention of any cycle of death and rebirth of *souls*, or, for instance, of reminiscence, the very myth introduced in the *Meno*. These objections might perhaps be of little weight if there were not in fact a better candidate in the *Dialogues* matching more precisely the indications provided in Hölderlin's text. We shall return to the issue presently.

First, let us try to define more precisely the content of Hölderlin's reference to Plato. The quoted passage does not say what exactly it is that ages and rejuvenates. It would be surprising to see Hölderlin introduce such a reference to Plato simply by way of digression, without coming back to it elsewhere. And indeed, one finds another passage in the same letter that seems to recall it. This second text is found—and this is of much significance for its interpretation—after the friendship between Hyperion and Alabanda has ended. Because of an argument, as we shall see later, the two men find themselves separated, being carried away in anger into opposite directions, each incapable of reaching out to the other. Hence these words of Hyperion: "If the life of the world consists in an alternation between opening and closing, between going forth and returning, *why is it not even so with the hearts of men?*"[16] In this excerpt, the world (*der Welt*) is the object of which one affirms the alternation (*Wechsel*) of blooming (*Entfalten*) and closure (*Verschließen*), of going out (*Ausflug*) and returning to oneself (*Rückkehr zu sich selbst*). The idea of alternation shows that it is a *continuous* movement that goes from life to death, and then from death to life again. In other words, the opposition between the blooming and the closing principles is *not sterile*, but remains open to a constant renewal and the coming of a new cycle, a "new age" as Hölderlin will characterize it later.

It seems rather likely that the first passage quoted is about the world too and therefore that it is of the world that one affirms the alternation of aging and rejuvenation. In that case, there is an obvious reference in Plato matching these indications: the famous myth of the *Politicus*,[17] where the Stranger narrates how the world started all at once to rejuvenate. In this myth, it is explained that the world is sometimes governed by god and sometimes left to itself, and how this change, which is caused by the presence or absence of the divine, has the world turning upon his pivot and moving backward:

> The only remaining alternative is what I suggested a little while ago, that the universe is guided at one time (*tote men*) by an extrinsic divine cause, acquiring the power of living again (*to dzēn palin epiktōmenon*) and receiving renewed immortality from the Creator, and at another time (*tote d'*) it is left to itself and then moves by its own motion, being left to itself at such a moment that it moves backwards (*anapalin*) through countless ages, because it is immensely large and most evenly balanced,

and turns upon the smallest pivot. (Plato, *Politicus* 270a2–8, tr. H. N. Fowler)

One finds here again the idea of alternation (*tote men . . . tote d'*) put forward by the second quoted passage of *Hyperion*, as well as that of contrary movements and inversion. Now, this movement of reversion is illustrated in the *Politicus* precisely in terms of rejuvenation, as shown by the next excerpt, in which the Stranger explains what "wonderful and strange" affections the few human survivors experience once the course of the world has been put in the reverse direction:

> The survivors have many experiences wonderful and strange, the greatest of which, a consequence of the reversal of everything at the time when the world begins to turn in the direction opposed to that of its present revolution, is this. (. . .) First the age of all animals, whatever it was at the moment, stood still, and every mortal creature stopped growing older in appearance and then reversed to the opposite direction and became, as it were, younger and more tender (*neōteron kai hapalōteron*); the hoary locks of the old men grew dark, and bearded cheeks grew smooth again as their possessors reverted to their earlier ages, and the bodies of young men grew smoother and smaller day by day and night by night, until they became as new—born babes, to which they were likened in mind and body; and then at last they wasted away entirely and wholly disappeared. (Plato, *Politicus*, 270d1–e9, tr. H. N. Fowler)

This passage in the *Politicus* and the one cited previously are the likeliest to have been those that, in *Hyperion*, Alabanda and Hyperion sat and read together. One finds in them, as just noted, the ideas of aging and rejuvenation, of cyclic alternation and opposite movements. Furthermore, all these changes are caused by the presence or absence of God, an idea that is also fully espoused by Hölderlin himself. We will see in the next two sections how he depicts the world as a garden now dried up, desperately longing for *der Regen vom Himmel* (the rain from heaven) so that it may return to life again (cf. *Hyperion* 40, 10 Schmidt). One may suggest also that the reading of the *Politicus* was initially prompted by the issue the two friends were debating and which would eventually lead them to break off their friendship, namely the role that laws and State should play in the spiritual renewal of mankind[18] (on which, see next section).

If the *Politicus* appears to be a better candidate than the *Meno*, it is also
relevant to suggest another, additional, possible reference: Plato's *Symposium*.
In this dialogue, too, one finds the idea, now familiar, of an alternation of
blooming and withdrawing, this time understood as being inherent to the
very nature of *erōs*: "His nature is neither that of an immortal, nor that of
a mortal, but on the same day, now he flourishes and lives, when he finds
resources, and now he dies, but then come back to life again (*palin de
anabiōsketai*), because of his father's nature, and what he gets for himself is
always slipping away from him so that Love is neither resourceless at any
moment, nor rich, and again is in the middle between wisdom and ignorance" (Plato, *Symposium* 203d–e, translation by C. Rowe). Because of his
special ancestry (son of a god, *Poros*, Resource, and a mortal, *Penia*, Poverty)
erōs finds himself to be by nature in an intermediary state, never completely
satisfied, never completely resourceless. His natural movement is the one
that goes from life (or having) to death (or missing), and then to life again
(cf. *palin de anabiōsketai*). Like the cosmic alternation in the *Politicus*, it is
a three—moment motion that is characteristic of love according to Plato
(or, at any rate, Diotima), in which the third moment is always marked by
regeneration and restoration. Now it is the same movement that Hölderlin,
in his *Hyperion*, attributes to hearts (*das Herz*), at least to loving hearts. To
see that, we need to look again at the second excerpt, quoted above, from
letter I, 1. 7. There, Hyperion, observing the cosmic alternation of going
forth and withdrawing, of opening and closing, asks himself why such movement is not active also in the hearts of men.[19] This must be understood
within the context of the passage: Alabanda and Hyperion have just had
a violent argument and allowed themselves to drift away from each other.
Hyperion especially has let himself overcome by resentment (*der Unmut*)
and pride (*der Stolz*), so much so that the two friends cannot "return" to
their former union: "Now anger raged uncontrolled in me, too. We did
not rest *until any turning—back was well—nigh impossible.* We violently
destroyed the garden of our love, often we stopped and stood silent, and
oh so gladly, so joyously would we have fallen on each other's necks; but
accursed pride stifled every tone of love that rose from our hearts."[20] Hearts,
which until then had been full of love (*Herz voll Liebe*, cf. *Hyperion* 34,
27 Schmidt), have become impoverished and weak like a dried garden; the
passions that now assail them make impossible (or nearly so, cf. *fast*) any
return (*Rückkehr*), that is, any *restoration*. Only true love enables the movement of blooming and drying up to start again and maintain its continued
alternation, as in the case of the love between Hyperion and Diotima. The
comparison—and the gap it reveals—is striking: "Is it not true, dear one!

It is not too late for me to return even now! And you will take me back and can love me again, as before! Is it not true that the happiness of past days is not lost to us?"[21]

Contrary to what was the case with Alabanda, return is never too late when love is true, as it is indeed the case with Diotima, who in *Hyperion* is being characterized in terms clearly reminiscent of the Diotima of Plato's *Symposium*.[22] This shows that the Platonic pattern of permanent alternation of life and death, where life always presents itself as a return or rebirth, is fully taken up by Hölderlin. And he takes the theme at precisely the same two levels identified by Plato, one that is general (the world), and one that is particular (the hearts of men).

2. Death Is a Messenger of Life

The homology between the world and the human heart is essential to Hölderlin and his hero, Hyperion, who from the beginning blames knowledge (*Die Wissenschaft*) for getting him (i.e., his heart) isolated from the world. What Hyperion is blaming, however, is not knowledge as such—for his love for Diotima will turn out to be philosophical—but a knowledge that might be described as "all too human" since it makes man a stranger to the world.[23] It is only when knowledge is reconciled with the human heart,[24] and thus with love, that man shall again "be one with all."[25] Then, and only then, shall man "return in blessed self—forgetfulness into the All of Nature."[26]

Returning to the world and being able to understand it again implies, for man, an acknowledgment and acceptance of the two contradicting desires that are inherent in him. These two desires (*Triebe*) and their possible unification are described in a remarkable passage from an earlier version of *Hyperion*, the *Prosa—Entwurf zur Metrische Fassung*. The Platonic complexion of the text is unmistakable and its reference to Plato's *Symposium* obvious:

> Now we deeply feel the limitation of our nature, and the impeded force rises up against its fetters. And yet there is something in us that likes to keep these fetters—since were the divine in us not be limited by any resistance, then we would not know about anything outside of us, and thus also nothing about ourselves; and to know nothing about oneself, to have no feeling, and to be reduced to nothingness, is, for us, all one and the same thing.

We cannot deny the desire to free ourselves, to improve, to progress endlessly. That would be bestial. But we cannot deny either
the desire to get defined, to receive. That would not be human.
We should perish in the strife of those antagonistic desires. But
Love unites them. She strives endlessly for the highest and the
best, since her father is Abundance. She does not either disown
her mother, Indigence. She hopes for assistance. To love in this
way is human. (My translation)[27]

This text[28] reminds us of how deeply influential the *Symposium* was on
Hölderlin, particularly its description of *erōs*. In the dialogue, we find the
recurring opposition between life and death, having and missing, which, as
we saw, is characteristic of Platonic love. But here, the idea of alternation,
which Hölderlin used as a leitmotiv in the final version of *Hyperion*, is missing, and it is the contrariety of the two desires that is underlined (cf. *dieser
widerstreitenden Triebe*). Man is governed by a desire to free and ennoble
himself, to endlessly progress. But he is also, at the same time, powerless,
a cripple in need of help, who finds himself humbled by the limitedness of
his mortal condition. Man is, like *erōs*, an in-between, and the antagonistic
desires that come through him would end up quartering him, dislocating
him completely, were not love to unite them.

Hölderlin's theme of a double contrary aspiration to unlimitedness and
limitation finds also its source in the famous epitaph of Ignatius of Loyola:
"Not to be confined by the greatest, yet to let oneself be encompassed by
the smallest, is divine" (*Non coerceri maximo, contineri minimo, divinum est*),
which Hölderlin chose as an epigraph to his novel.[29] The fusion of the two
sources, Platonic and Christian, has left visible marks, as we shall soon see,
in Hölderlin's conception of friendship in *Hyperion*.

The excerpt from the *Prosa—Entwurf zur Metrische Fassung* enables us
to shed light on the reasons that led Hyperion and Alabanda to part. Hence
it helps us also to understand what conditions Hölderlin considered to be
necessary for the development of a true friendship, which shall govern a new
age of the world. To see how and why this is so, we must compare the two
characters in their respective conceptions of the world and, in particular,
their desire to rejuvenate it.

Alabanda represents force and action. But what we must understand
is his motivation. With Hyperion, he shares the view that there is "a god in
us,"[30] thus that man has a divine side in his nature.[31] Contrary to Hyperion,
however, he seems to ignore the limitations inherent in human nature:

The god in us, for whose road infinity lies open—shall he stand and wait until the worm crawls out of his way? No! No! We do not ask if you are willing, you slaves and barbarians! You are never willing! Nor will we try to make you better, for that is useless! We will but make certain that you get out of the way of humanity's victorious career! Oh! let someone light a torch for me, that I may burn the weeds from the field, let someone lay me the mine with which I can blow the dull clods from the face of the earth! When possible, we should but gently push them aside, I interrupted.[32]

Alabanda's man is the paradigm of conqueror who, like the sons of the Sun, "lives by victory."[33] All that is lacking force (the cripple, the weak) is conceived by him as slaves and barbarians (*Knechte und Barbaren*) that it is vain trying to help improve, let alone emancipate. On the contrary, serfs and barbarians are in his eyes like this stump that the foot is stumbling over and, for that reason, deserve nothing but being pulled out of the earth. One can see here the thinly veiled tyranny of this character, in which the self-centered "unlimited trust"[34] leads to consider men that are not up to their inner divinity as vermin (*Wurm*).

From this passage on, Hyperion himself starts having doubts about his friend's apology of action and force. This can already be seen from the last sentence of the text where he is trying, still timidly, to temper Alabanda: one must not destroy what is in one's way, only gently move it away. But soon dissensions are growing between the two men, until this animated discussion on the role of State and human laws, where Hyperion now openly criticizes Alabanda:

You accord the State far too much power. It must not demand what it cannot extort. But what love gives, and spirit, cannot be extorted. Let the State leave that alone, or we will take it its laws and whip them into the pillory! By Heaven! He knows not what his sin is who would make the State a school of morality. The State has always been made a hell by man's wanting to make it his heaven. The State is the coarse—husk around the seed of life and nothing more. It is the wall around the garden of human fruits and flowers. But is the wall around the garden of any help when the soil lies parched? Only the rain from Heaven helps then.[35]

Through his criticism of Alabanda for giving too much power to State and laws, Hyperion seeks to show the flaws in the conception of man on which Alabanda bases his account. State is the expression par excellence of human action and government. To conceive, as Alabanda does, of man as a god is to make the State a heaven on earth. In other words, by his excessive divination of man, Alabanda induces a lowering of the divine in general. This issue is first addressed at the beginning of the novel, where Hyperion is blaming men for forcing the divine to lower itself and "become like them."[36] State, on the contrary, has, and in his view should have no other function but to protect the garden of which it is the wall.

To believe that man can renew the world by himself alone is to display the kind of unbound smugness that can only lead the paradise of the world to turn into hell. Of course, the world is like a dried up garden that longs for restoration, but only can *divine* rain (*Regen vom Himmel*) make it bloom again. For that to happen, it is necessary, not to lower the heaven until it reaches human soil, but, on the contrary, to raise humankind with the help of God. In other words, it is to a complete reversal of perspective that Hölderlin-Hyperion is appealing. The striking text, quoted below, has man (this time, Hyperion's man) compared to a sleeping invalid in a hospital:

> O rain from heaven! O inspiration! You will bring us the spring time of peoples again! The state cannot command your presence. But let it not obstruct you, and you will come, come with your almighty blissfulness, you will wrap us in golden clouds and carry us up above mortality; and we shall marvel and wonder if this is still we, we who in poverty asked the stars if a spring bloomed for us among them—do you ask me when this will be? It will be when the most beloved of Time, the youngest, loveliest daughter of time, the new Church, will arise out of these pol-luted, aged forms, when the awakened feeling of the divine will bring man his divinity, man's heart his beautiful youth again—I cannot prophesy it, for my eyes are too dim to surmise it, but it will come, that I know for certain. Death is a messenger of life, and that we now lie asleep in our infirmary testifies that we shall soon awaken to new health. Then, and not till then, shall we exist, then, then will our spirit's element have been found![37]

The description of man that comes out of this passage is almost the opposite of the one endorsed by Alabanda: to the proud, awe-inspiring and victorious man, for whom there are no limits or possible resistance, Hyperion opposes the image of a bedridden man in a deep sleep. Yet the opposition is not total since, as already noted, Hyperion also believes that there is a god "in us." However, this god has left the hearts of men from the moment they forgot the limitations built into their nature. The divine in us, according to the *Prosa—Entwurf zur Metrische Fassung*, does not make man a god. It is only a force leading us "to free ourselves, to ennoble, to endlessly progress" (*zu befreien, zu veredlen, fortzuschreiten ins Unendliche*), provided that (and insofar as) man acknowledges his own finiteness, hence also his powerlessness. Hyperion's man is not abandoned by God; rather, it is he who, willingly, gives himself to the divine, in the full awareness that it is superior to him.

Man's renouncement and powerlessness reveal, negatively, the vacuity and futility of human action as well as the kind of arrogance that it produces. From the start, Hyperion was recalling the sententious characters who "haunt your Germany" and who, by way of advice, were saying to him: "Do not complain, act!" (*klage nicht, handle!*) Alas, he cries, "that I had never acted! By how many hopes should I be richer!" (*hätt ich doch nie gehandelt! um wie manche Hoffnung wär ich reicher!*)[38] Hyperion has learned at his expense that human action can be illusory. One may suspect that another Platonic or Neoplatonic[39] influence is here at work, to the effect that action is a form of bewitchment of the soul by the body. But we must remember that while Platonists oppose contemplation to action, Hyperion, in a more decidedly Christian attitude, opposes action with self-abnegation and humility.[40] So, here again, we find the double influence of Plato and Christianity, which we had noted earlier of the excerpt from the *Prosa— Entwurf zur Metrische Fassung*.

It is remarkable to observe how Hölderlin merges the two influences within this single phrase: *Der Tod ist ein Bote des Lebens*. On the one hand, one can see in it the thinly veiled Platonic thesis of alternation of opposites or, to use the words of the *Phaedo*, of "double becoming":[41]

—First, you say that "being dead" is opposed to "being alive," right?—Yes, of course!—And that they are generated one from the other?—Yes.—So, from the living, what is it that is generated?—The dead, he says.—Very well, says Socrates. And what from the dead?—We have to admit, he said, that it is the living.—But then, Cebes, it is from the dead that the living, whether things or persons, is generated?—That is clear, he replied. (Plato, *Phaedo* 71d–e)

It is a law of nature, a cosmic law, which requires opposites to be generated out of one another, and this law holds also of life and death. Hence, one must admit, like Cebes had to concede to Socrates, that "it is from the dead that the living, whether things or persons, is generated," or, as Hölderlin would say, that death is "a messenger of life."

In addition to this Platonic reference, however, there is also the Christian idea according to which it is through his lowering himself, his finiteness and mortality, that man and the world with him, shall find regeneration. This vital revival is associated in *Hyperion* with a New Church "arising out of polluted, aged forms," when "the awakened feeling of the divine will bring man his divinity, man's heart his beautiful youth again." It is not in spite of these aged forms (*veralteten Formen*), but through them (by their means) that such a renewal shall happen. This is why, against Alabanda, Hyperion refuses to sacrifice the weak and the cripple. Actually, he is himself the symbol of the humble, the spoiled: "And now it was all over, now I was nothing, now I had been so irremediably deprived of everything, had become the poorest men, and did not myself know how."[42] Hyperion's humbling, however, is not hopeless, for death is a messenger of life, and the invalid shall wake up healed.

3. Love Bore the World, Friendship Will Bear It Again

The analysis of the encounter between Hyperion and Alabanda and of the reasons for the failure of their friendship shows the vividness of the Platonic motif of world renewal, in which rejuvenation follows aging and death gives way to life. This motif reappears again in the famous "letter on friendship," to which we now turn.[43] The links between this letter and the one analyzed earlier are many, starting with the setting of the discussion: Hyperion is relating a conversation that took place in Diotima's garden.[44] The garden was the metaphor used by Hölderlin to represent the human heart: it is this garden, the center of love between Hyperion and Alabanda, that has been wrecked once the breakup had taken place.[45] It is also this garden that in the eyes of Hyperion represents the city of the world, which laws and State have to protect instead of besieging or governing by force.[46]

Whatever the nature of Hyperion's views on action, there is at least one cause for which he is willing to stand up and act, namely, freedom, when it is threatened by tyranny. We have seen the tyrannical dimension of Alabanda's ideal man. Now, this dimension is similarly at work in his political views that the State is ready to extort by force the fruits of love and spirit. As mentioned earlier, these tyrannical laws represent the human will of secularizing the divine, of bringing God to the level of man. Against this expression of arrogance—Hölderlin speaks of *hüberheben*—Hyperion cries out: "*Das laß er unangetastet, oder man nehme sein Gesetz und schlag es an den Pranger!*"[47] If, contrary to what Alabanda thinks, human laws are unable by themselves to bring about a spiritual renewal of mankind, they can nonetheless hinder it,[48] as they do in the case of tyranny. Thus, to prevent this from happening, Hyperion is ready to stand up, even to resort to force, if necessary.

The theme of overthrowing tyranny is precisely the one that Hölderlin uses to introduce us to his conception of friendship, in the garden of Diotima. He does so by reminding us of the story of two Greek heroes, Aristogeiton and Harmodius:

> When Harmodius and Aristogiton were alive, someone cried at last, friendship still existed in the world. That pleased me too much for me to remain silent. We should twine you a wreath in reward for those words! I cried. "But have you really any notion, any image, of the friendship between Aristogiton and Harmodius? Forgive me! But, by the Ether! One must be Aristogiton to have a sense of how Aristogiton loved, and surely he must not fear lightning who would be loved with Harmodius' love, for I am mistaken in everything if the terrible youth did not love with all the sternness of Minos. Few have come off successfully in such a test, and it is no easier to be the friend of a demigod than, like Tantalus, to sit at the table of the gods. But by the same token there is nothing more glorious on earth than such a proud pair as they are so sovereign over each other.[49]

Aristogeiton and Harmodius, here taken as symbols of friendship,[50] were known in antiquity as the two famous tyrannicides of Athens. According to the accounts of Thucydides and Aristotle, our two main sources on the matter, their love had led them to assassinate the tyrant's brother, Hipparchus, whose overtures Harmodius had previously resisted, before being themselves executed by the tyrant, Hippias. Their act, deemed heroic, led eventually to the fall of tyranny in Athens and the advent of democracy. Hölderlin had translated into German the poem that Callistratus had composed in their honor,[51] a poem in which it is said that the two friends brought *isonomia* or equality to Athens. The association of equality with friendship has a long history in Greece and was widely accepted.[52] According to Diogenes

Laertius, such association dates back to Pythagoras.[53] Friends form a true community or *koinōnia*, in which everything is held in common. It is also this idea that we can see in our passage, where Hyperion speaks of the mutual and equal dependence of Aristogeiton and Harmodius.[54]

In the *Symposium*, Plato, too, relates the story of the two tyrannicides in a passage that cannot have failed to impress Hölderlin. Indeed, one finds in it the idea that friendship and concord are what love most tends to bring about in us:

> I don't think it is convenient for those in power that there should be big ideas about if these belong to their subjects, or for that matter strong friendships and partnerships (*philias iskhuras kai koinōnias*), and *that is just what all the other things, but especially love, most tend to bring about in us* (*ho dē malista philei ta te alla panta kai ho erōs empoiein*). The tyrants here in Athens themselves learned this from experience, because it was Aristogeiton's love for Harmodius, and Harmodius' friendship for him, when both became firm and constant, that brought their regime to an end. (Plato, *Symposium* 182 c1–6, translation by Rowe, adapted)

The passage is part of Pausanias' speech, but its main point is taken up again by Diotima,[55] when she instructs Socrates as to the kind of offspring genuine philosophical love generates:

> For, I imagine, it's by contact with what is beautiful, and associating with it, that he [sc. the lover] brings to birth and procreates the things with which he was for so long pregnant, both when he is present with him [sc. the beloved] and when he is away from him; and he joins with the other person in nurturing what has been born, with the result that such people enjoy a much greater partnership with each other (*polu meidzō koinōnian . . . pros allēlous*) than the one people have in their children, and a firmer friendship (*philian bebaioteran*) between them, insofar as their sharing is in children of a more beautiful and more immortal kind. (Plato, *Symposium* 209 c1–7, translation by Rowe, adapted)

By making friendship the product of love, Plato indicates at the same time the necessity to distinguish between the two: if friendship cannot take place without love, it is not, for all that, reducible to love, which is rather like its origin and cause. Now what makes *erōs* and *philia* different for Plato is that while the latter implies true equality and community—an idea, as said earlier, well established among the Greeks—the former supposes on the contrary some sort of dissymmetry.[56] Indeed, *erōs*, according to Plato, is first of all a desire, and in that sense can only refer to the one who loves or lover (*erastēs, erōn*), *not* to the one who is loved, the beloved (*eraston, erōmenon*). Since *erōs* is, in the final analysis, desire of knowledge (*philo—sophia*), one can see how philosophers only can be lovers, while beloved are rather younger people, naturally well-endowed for virtue,[57] whom the philosophers will seek to educate.[58]

It is not difficult to see that Hölderlin is taking a similar line on the distinction between love and friendship. I have shown that he appears to conceive of friendship as a reciprocal and egalitarian relationship. As to love, he thinks it is divine only when it occurs between two souls of which one is superior and seeks to raise the other: "Do you know how Plato and his Stella loved each other? So I loved, so was I loved. Oh, I was a fortunate boy! It is pleasant when like and like do meet, but is divine when a great man draws lesser men up to him."[59] The loving relationship in question here, for which Plato and his Stella provide the model, is the one between Hyperion and Diotima. In this relation, Hyperion stands as a boy (*ein Knabe*), who is being taught, while Diotima is the teacher, that is, a superior soul that seeks, through love, to instruct and raise him. Only such a love is *göttlich*.[60] Thus one can see that it is the Platonic ideal of a philosophical and pedagogical love (or love for the "unlike") that Hölderlin espouses.[61]

We can now turn to the analysis of the central passage of the letter on friendship, in which friendship represents the rebirth of the world:

> This is my hope, too, my longing and my joy in solitary hours, that such noble tones, yes, and nobler, must yet sound again in the symphony of the world's course. Love brought to birth millenniums filled with living men; friendship will give birth to them again. Once upon a time the people set forth from the harmony of childhood; the harmony of spirits will be the beginning of another history of man. Men began and grew from the happiness of the plant, grew until they ripened; from that time on they have been in ceaseless ferment, inwardly and outwardly, until now mankind lies there in a Chaos, utterly disintegrated, so that all who can still feel and see are dizzied; but Beauty forsakes the life of men, flees upward into Spirit; the Ideal becomes what Nature was, and even though the tree is dried out and

weatherworn below, a fresh crown has still sprung from it and
flourishes green in the sunlight as the trunk did once in its days
of youth; the Ideal is what Nature was. By this, *by this Ideal,
this rejuvenated divinity*, the few recognize one another and are
one, for one thing is in them; and from them, from them, the
world's second age begins—I have said enough to make it clear
what I think. You should have seen Diotima then, springing up
and giving me both her hands and crying: I have understood
it, beloved, much as it means, understood it all. *Love bore the
world, friendship will bear it again.*[62]

Even if Hyperion claims to have said enough to make it clear what he thinks,
the density and profundity of his speech are nevertheless almost disarming.[63]
But I believe that my argument so far has provided us with enough clues
to understand what is at stake here. Indeed, this passage gathers together
a number of Platonic themes and even references to the *Dialogues* which
we have already encountered. First, one finds in it the motif of oldness
transforming itself into new youth, of a movement of alternation going
from life to death, and then back to life again. Second, one can see in it
the demarcation between love and friendship identified earlier as well as
the idea that friendship is somehow a product of love, its last, unexpected,
fruit. Finally, there is again the theme of faith, earlier identified as Christian
in spirit, in the return to life in what normally can no longer bear fruit.

The text distinguishes between two ages: one, now passed, governed
by nature, and another, to come, governed by spirit (*der Geist*, or *das Ideal*).
Between the two, there is the current state of the world, which represents
the state of moral consciousness of mankind, characterized by chaos. We
have seen that Hyperion is longing for a *spiritual* renewal of man: "[W]
hen the awakened feeling of the divine will bring man his divinity, man's
heart his beautiful youth again," he says, "then will our spirit's element have
been found!"[64] By "Spirit" and "Ideal," we should therefore understand the
return of the "feeling of the divine." God seems to have deserted nature
and left man in a near total state of poverty; it is only when the rain from
heaven shall fall again—by which one should understand the return of the
divine *in the heart of men*—that the garden, now dried, shall bloom again.

What is specific in the current chaos or absence of harmony is thus the
fact that God is not present in the world, and does not appear to govern it
anymore. Now, this is precisely the central idea of the myth in the *Politicus*.
In the *Politicus*, Plato, like Hölderlin in *Hyperion*, distinguishes two ages
between which the world is said to be left to itself: God has abandoned the

helm of the world and installed himself at the observation post.[65] Again, as with *Hyperion*, the withdrawal of God, in the *Politicus*, leads the world to chaos: left with its own (sensible) nature, the world forgets little by little "the teachings of the Creator and Father."[66] The more oblivion sets in, the more "the lack of harmony"[67] spreads. In the end, "fearing that it might founder in the tempest of confusion and sink in the boundless sea of diversity [i.e., chaos], he resumed his place as its helmsman, reversed whatever had become unsound and unsettled in the previous period when the world was left to itself, set the world in order, restored it, and made it immortal and ageless."[68] The similarities with *Hyperion* are too obvious not to have been meant. They confirm the profound and underground influence of the *Politicus* on Hölderlin.

In a very original way, Hölderlin identifies the two ages of the world as respectively those of love and friendship. As Plato, Hyperion conceives love as an asymmetrical relationship between unlike beings, one of whom is superior and seeks to raise the other to his own level. Friendship, on the contrary, is a fundamentally egalitarian relation taking place between likes, that is, between beings who are at the same (superior) level of spirituality and morality. Since, as we have just seen, the current state of chaos of the world comes from the dryness of men's hearts, in which God is no longer present, one can see that, according to Hyperion-Hölderlin, it is only with, and through, the love of God and the godlike (in particular, in *Hyperion*, the love of Diotima who, in the novel, is described as a divine being[69]) that the world and humanity will succeed in reviving. This revival, however, does not mean the return of the same, as is the case, for instance, with the Stoic *ekpyrosis*, but rather the advent of a new form of life, namely, the life of spirit. The government of spirit and friendship means that, through the love of God, man has found a way to rise spiritually, to divinise himself, and, somehow, to become immortal. We have here, once again, an illustration of the impassable gap between Hyperion and Alabanda: while the latter believes in the inborn divinity of man and denies his finiteness, thus reducing the divine to the mortal, Hyperion for his part contemplates the salvation of humanity only through the elevation of man's moral and spiritual sense. In the specific case of the love relationship between Hyperion and Diotima,[70] one can say that Hyperion stands for humanity in its poverty, while Diotima is a divine being in charge of instructing Hyperion with true knowledge, the knowledge of how man can be one again with everything. One can think that, once such instruction is completed, their relationship shall transform itself (spring up again) into genuine friendship.

Merged into this Platonic frame—unless it be the other way around— one finds, again, in this passage, some deeply Christian tones. What is here distinctively Christian, to put it succinctly, is the idea that the revival and renewal of the world is happening *contrary to (nearly) all expectations*: it is, in a sense, a cosmic, Platonic law that life shall be born again out of death; however, in another sense, it is probably absurd or, at any case, *not natural* that oldness should still bear fruit. But this is what Hyperion is precisely saying: "[E]ven though the tree is dried out and weatherworn below, a fresh crown has still sprung from it and flourishes green in the sunlight as the trunk did once its days of youth." This, it is important to note, far from being a Platonic, or even a Greek, notion, is a Christian one. It is to be found, for instance, in the parable of the fig tree which, being withered and dried up, is about to be uprooted by its owner, but is saved—for a while at least— by the gardener who still believes it can bear fruit the next year (cf. Luke 13:6–10). One can also remind oneself of these women in the Bible who, although being in their old age, nevertheless eventually brought forth (cf. Sarah, *Gen.* 18:1–16; Elisabeth, mother of John the Baptist, Luke 1:5–26).

That Hölderlin has knowingly and deliberately intermingled the two sources—Platonic and Christian—is suggested by the reading of one of his homilies, written in 1785, namely some seven years before he started work on *Hyperion*. That particular homily presents striking similarities with our passage from the letter on friendship: "The hope and assurance of a better life acts with comparable power on our felicity. The idea, which gives us unutterable courage, is that every force in us, all that we have done and undergone, is still active, that the day the harmony of the inanimate Nature disappears will be the beginning of the much higher harmony of the moral world. All that, we owe to Christ's teaching. Let's follow him, so that one day, we shall like him enter his Glory"[71] (my translation). The passage refers to a now familiar demarcation line, that between the harmony of inanimate nature and the harmony of the moral world. As with *Hyperion*, the two harmonies do, at least implicitly, correspond to two different ages, the moral age being still one to come. Similarly again with what we found in *Hyperion*, it is argued here that it is by following God's teaching (*der Lehre*) that the harmony of nature shall revive in a new, superior, moral form. But in the homily, contrary to what is the case in *Hyperion*, God is named, and his name is Christ.[72]

Conclusion

Hölderlin's conception of friendship in *Hyperion* cannot be fully understood unless it is placed against the background of the Platonic influence that is at work throughout the novel. The very idea of renewal and rejuvenation, of which friendship in *Hyperion* is the symbol, is a motif that Hölderlin took from the *Dialogues*, and, like Plato, used at both a general, cosmic, level and a particular, human, one. I hope to have shown the importance in this respect of the *Symposium* and the description of *erōs*, which served as model to Hölderlin for his depiction of the human nature. It is also in the *Symposium* that Plato spells out the distinction between love and friendship, and how friendship is the product of love. Hölderlin follows similar lines in his letter on friendship, presenting friendship as a fresh crown that blossoms out of the garden of love. But the imprint left by the myth of the *Politicus* may even strike us as more remarkable. It is in this myth that one finds, not only the idea of oldness turning into new youth, but also the idea that it is because of the absence of the divine (and the forgetfulness of the teachings of God) that the world is left to a state of chaos, a situation that is the very starting point of *Hyperion*. The Platonic influence is never present in *Hyperion* without some Christian overtones: *erōs'* poverty becomes in Hölderlin the sign of man's humbleness; the rejuvenation that is taking place after oldness is happening against all expectations, in the manner of an unhoped—for fruit borne by a barren tree. Such a conjunction of Platonic and Christian influences is a perfect illustration of the way Hölderlin received ancient Greece and its wisdom.[73] He never sought simply to reproduce, let alone copy, what the Greeks invented. On the contrary, he tried to revive it in a new and original form, unknown to the Greeks themselves. The result is a masterly work, which we are still trying to understand.

Notes

*I could not have written this chapter without the help of my husband. I am grateful for his continuing love and support.

1. The importance of Hölderlin for the shaping of German idealism is now fully recognized, thanks in particular to studies by Frederick C. Beiser: "While Schelling, Schlegel, and Novalis were still under Fichte's magical spell, and while Hegel was busy applying Kantian ideas to religion, Hölderlin was already a critic of the *Wissenschaftslehre*, striving to move beyond its confines. As early as the spring 1795, Hölderlin had argued against the subjective status of the principle of subject—object identity; he had postulated an aesthetic intuition of the absolute; he had criticized Fichte's concept of nature; and he had given nature a standing independent of the ego. There are good reasons to think that it was Hölderlin who first impressed such views on Schelling and Hegel. For all these reasons, Hölderlin has been considered the father of absolute idealism." Beiser 2002, 375.

2. *Hyperion* is a novel that presents itself in the form of a series of letters written by the eponymous character to his friend Bellarmin. They tell the story of Hyperion's education in Germany, his falling in love with Diotima, his friendship with Alabanda, and his failed attempt to liberate Greece from the Turks.

3. On the importance of friendship in Hölderlin, see Mittner 1962, Böschenstein 1971, Hamlin 1971, Cancik 1990, Berbig 1996, Louth 2004, Thiel 2004, and Heinrichs 2007.

4. In this study, all English translations of Hölderlin's *Hyperion* are by Willard R. Trask (adapted by David Schwarz), from Eric L. Santner's edition.

5. *Hyperion* 73 Schmidt: *Die Liebe gebar Jahrtausende voll lebendiger Menschen; die Freundschaft wird sie wiedergebären.*

6. *Hyperion* 73 Schmidt: *Von Kinderharmonie sind einst die Völker ausgegangen, die Harmonie der Geister wird der Anfang einer neuen Weltgeschichte sein.*

7. *Il semble qu'Hölderlin ait effacé le relief des idées qu'il a reçues.* Claverie 1921, 85.

8. Letters in *Hyperion* are not numbered in modern editions. For the sake of convenience, I shall refer to them starting with the volume (I or II), the book inside the volume (1 or 2), and the place of the letter in the book.

9. On this motif, see again Claverie 1921, 100.

10. It is also possible to link this Platonic motif with the letters that form *Hyperion*, and especially the Elegiac mode Hölderlin uses, since it is the mode par excellence used to recall what is now gone, a lament over the glorious past of the Greeks. However, in Hölderlin, the elegy in question is also a place for hope, hope for the return of the old into a new rejuvenated form. On this issue, see also Thiel 2002, 121 and Heinrichs 2007, 242. On the relationship between friendship and correspondence in Hölderlin, cf. Pankow 1999, 146–48 and Adler and Louth 2009, xxvii–xxix.

11. *Hyperion* 32, 3–7 Schmidt: *die, wie ein schäumender Springquell, emporgedrungen war in allen Pflanzen und Bäumen, stand jetzt schon da vor meinem verdüsterten Sinne, schwindend und verschlossen und in sich gekehrt, wie ich selber.*

12. *Hyperion* 32, 11 Schmidt: *wollte nimmer sich erfrischen.*

13. *Hyperion* 31, 34 Schmidt: *das wiederkehrende Jahr.*

14. *Hyperion* 35, 33–36, 3 Schmidt: *Wir waren zusammen aufs Feld gegangen, saßen vertraulich umschlungen im Dunkel des immergrünen Lorbeers, und sahn zusammen in unsern Plato, wo er so wunderbar erhaben vom Altern und Verjüngen spricht, und ruhten hin und wieder aus auf der stummen entblätterten Landschaft, wo der Himmel schöner, als je, mit Wolken und Sonnenschein um die herbstlich schlafenden Bäume spielte.*

15. Cf. Commentary *ad loc.*, 996–97.

16. *Hyperion* 46, 23–25 Schmidt: *Bestehet ja das Leben der Welt im Wechsel des Entfaltens und Verschließens, in Ausflug und in Rückkehr zu sich selbst, warum nicht auch das Herz des Menschen?*

17. P. Jaccottet and P. Beissner have already suggested the reference to the *Politicus* (see Jaccottet 1967, 1153, and Beissner 3, 450).

18. This question is to be understood against the backdrop of *Hyperion*, a novel relating Hyperion's attempts to liberate Greece which at the time (ca 1770) was under Ottoman occupation.

19. Another parallel passage is found earlier in *Hyperion* that shows how sensitive this issue is for Hölderlin: "All things age and are rejuvenated. Why are we excepted from this beautiful circling of Nature? Or does it rule us too?" (*Alles altert und verjüngt sich wieder. Warum sind wir ausgenommen vom schönen Kreislauf der Natur? Oder gilt er auch für uns?: Hyperion* 25, 13–16 Schmidt).

20. *Hyperion* 45, 28–33 Schmidt: *Nun brach auch mir der Unmut vollends los. Wir ruhten nicht, bis eine Rückkehr fast unmöglich war. Wir zerstörten mit Gewalt den Garten unserer Liebe. Wir standen oft und schwiegen, und wären uns so gerne, so mit tausend Freuden um den Hals gefallen, aber der unselige Stolz erstickte jeden Laut der Liebe, der vom Herzen aufstieg.*

21. Hyperion 145, 33–36 Schmidt: *Nicht wahr, du Teure! noch ist meine Rückkehr nicht zu spät, und du nimmst mich wieder auf und kannst mich wieder lieben, wie sonst? nicht wahr, noch ist das Glück vergangner Tage nicht für uns verloren?*

22. *Liebe Sophistin!* (*Hyperion* 108, 19 Schmidt), to be compared with *hösper hoi teleoi sophistai* (*Symposium* 208c1), and *Die Priesterin* (*Hyperion* 112, 27–28 Schmidt), with *Symposium* 201d. On Diotima and the imprint of the *Symposium* on *Hyperion*, see Dučić—Collette 2010.

23. Cf. *Hyperion* 16, 24–29 Schmidt: "Nature closes her arms, and I stand like an alien before her and no doubt do not understand her. O! had I never gone to your schools! The knowledge which I pursued downs its tunnels and galleries, from which, in my youthful folly, I expected confirmation of all my pure joy—that knowledge has corrupted everything in me." (*Die Natur verschließt die Arme, und ich stehe, wie ein Fremdling, vor ihr, und verstehe sie nicht. Ach! wär ich nie in eure Schulen gegangen. Die Wissenschaft, der ich in den Schacht hinunter folgte, von der ich, jugendlich töricht, die Bestätigung meiner reinen Freude erwartete, die hat mir alles verdorben.*)

24. Cf. *Hyperion* 19, 28–20, 2 Schmidt: "How I hate the Barbarians who imagine that they are Wise because there is no more heart left in them! All the self—important monstrosities who slay and desecrate beautiful youth a thousand times over with their petty, meaningless discipline!" (*Wie haß ich dagegen alle die Barbaren, die sich einbilden, sie seien weise, weil sie kein Herz mehr haben, alle die rohen Unholde, die tausendfältig die jugendliche Schönheit töten und zerstören, mit ihrer kleinen unvernünftigen Mannszucht!*)

25. *Hyperion* 16, 6 Schmidt: *Eines zu sein mit Allem.*

26. *Hyperion* 16, 6–7 Schmidt: *in seliger Selbstvergessenheit wiederzukehren ins All der Natur.*

27. *Prosa—Entwurf zur Metrischen Fassung*, 208, 7–24 Schmidt: *Nun fühlen wir tief die Beschränkung unseres Wesens, und die gehemmte Kraft sträubt sich gegen ihre Fesseln, und doch ist etwas in uns das diese Fesseln gerne behält—denn würde das Göttliche in uns von keinem Widerstande beschränkt, so wüßten wir von nichts außer uns, und so auch von uns selbst nichts, und von sich nicht zu wissen, sich nicht zu*

fühlen, und vernichtet sein, ist für uns Eines. Wir können den Trieb, uns zu befreien, zu veredlen, fortzuschreiten ins Unendliche, nicht verleugnen. Das wäre tierisch, wir können aber auch den Trieb, bestimmt zu werden, zu empfangen, nicht verleugnen, das wäre nicht menschlich. Wir müßten untergehn im Kampfe dieser widerstreitenden Triebe. Aber die Liebe vereiniget sie. Sie strebt unendlich nach dem Höchsten und Besten, denn ihr Vater ist der Überfluß, sie verleugnet aber auch ihre Mutter die Dürftigkeit nicht; sie hofft auf Beistand. So zu lieben ist menschlich.

28. A fuller interpretation of this text is provided in Dučić-Collette 2010, 190–94.

29. On this epigraph, see Ogden 1991, 65–66, and Dučić-Collette 2010, 193–94.

30. Hyperion has been instructed of this truth by his master Adamas. *Hyperion* 25, 5–7 Schmidt: "There is a god in us, he added more quietly, who guides destiny as if it were a river of water, and all things are his element. Above all else, may he be with you!" (*Es ist ein Gott in uns, setzt' er [sc. Adamas] ruhiger hinzu, der lenkt, wie Wasserbäche, das Schicksal, und alle Dinge sind sein Element. Der sei vor allem mit dir!*).

31. Cf. *Hyperion* 37, 2 Schmidt: *Du hast ein herrlich Wort gesprochen, Hyperion! . . . Der Gott in uns.*

32. *Hyperion* 37, 4–13 Schmidt: *Der Gott in uns, dem die Unendlichkeit zur Bahn sich öffnet, soll stehn und harren, bis der Wurm ihm aus dem Wege geht? Nein! nein! Man frägt nicht, ob ihr wollt! Ihr wollt ja nie, ihr Knechte und Barbaren! Euch will man auch nicht bessern, denn es ist umsonst! man will nur dafür sorgen, daß ihr dem Siegeslauf der Menschheit aus dem Wege geht. O! zünde mir einer die Fackel an, daß ich das Unkraut von der Heide brenne! die Mine bereite mir einer, daß ich die trägen Klötze aus der Erde sprenge! Wo möglich, lehnt man sanft sie auf die Seite, fiel ich ein.*

33. Cf. *Hyperion* 37, 27–29 Schmidt: "The children of the sun live by their deeds; they live by victory; their own spirit rouses them, and their strength his their joy." (*Von ihren Taten nähren die Söhne der Sonne sich; sie leben vom Sieg; mit eignem Geist ermuntern sie sich, und ihre Kraft ist ihre Freude.*)

34. Cf. *Hyperion* 43, 24 Schmidt: "He is evil, I cried, yes evil! He feigns unbounded trust and consort with such as these—and hides it from you." (*Er ist schlecht, rief ich, ja, er ist schlecht. Er heuchelt grenzenlos Vertrauen und lebt mit solchen—und verbirgt es dir.*)

35. *Hyperion* 39, 35–40, 10 Schmidt: *Du räumst dem Staate denn doch zu viel Gewalt ein. Er darf nicht fordern, was er nicht erzwingen kann. Was aber die Liebe gibt und der Geist, das läßt sich nicht erzwingen. Das laß er unangetastet, oder man nehme sein Gesetz und schlag es an den Pranger! Beim Himmel! der weiß nicht, was er sündigt, der den Staat zur Sittenschule machen will. Immerhin hat das den Staat zur Hölle gemacht, daß ihn der Mensch zu seinem Himmel machen wollte. Die rauhe Hülse um den Kern des Lebens und nichts weiter ist der Staat. Er ist die Mauer um den Garten menschlicher Früchte und Blumen. Aber was hilft die Mauer um den Garten, wo der Boden dürre liegt? Da hilft der Regen vom Himmel allein.*

36. *Hyperion* 17, 29–34 Schmidt: "But this men cannot bear. The divine must become like one of them, must learn that they, too, are there; and before

Nature drives it out of its paradise, men entice and draw it out into the field of the curse, so that, like them, it shall drudge its life in the sweat of its brow." (*Aber das können die Menschen nicht leiden. Das Göttliche muß werden, wie ihrer einer, muß erfahren, daß sie auch da sind, und eh es die Natur aus seinem Paradiese treibt, so schmeicheln und schleppen die Menschen es heraus, auf das Feld des Fluchs, daß es, wie sie, im Schweiße des Angesichts sich abarbeite.*)

37. *Hyperion* 40, 11–29 Schmidt: *O Regen vom Himmel! o Begeisterung! Du wirst den Frühling der Völker uns wiederbringen. Dich kann der Staat nicht hergebieten. Aber er störe dich nicht, so wirst du kommen, kommen wirst du, mit deinen allmächtigen Wonnen, in goldene Wolken wirst du uns hüllen und empor uns tragen über die Sterblichkeit, und wir werden staunen und fragen, ob wir es noch seien, wir, die Dürftigen, die wir die Sterne fragten, ob dort uns ein Frühling blühe—frägst du mich, wann dies sein wird? Dann, wann die Lieblingin der Zeit, die jüngste, schönste Tochter der Zeit, die neue Kirche, hervorgehen wird aus diesen befleckten veralteten Formen, wann das erwachte Gefühl des Göttlichen dem Menschen seine Gottheit, und seiner Brust die schöne Jugend wiederbringen wird, wann—ich kann sie nicht verkünden, denn ich ahne sie kaum, aber sie kömmt gewiß, gewiß. Der Tod ist ein Bote des Lebens, und daß wir jetzt schlafen in unsern Krankenhäusern, dies zeugt vom nahen gesunden Erwachen. Dann, dann erst sind wir, dann ist das Element der Geister gefunden!*

38. Cf. *Hyperion* 15, 4–6 Schmidt.

39. Cf. Porphyry, *De abstinentia* I 27, §2.

40. One should recall here the very last sentence of letter I, 2, 7: *Und darum, Lieber! überhebe ja sich keiner* (*Hyperion* 48, 15–16 Schmidt).

41. This expression means that opposites "are really generated out of one another, and there is a passing or process from one to the other of them" (*Phaedo* 71a–b).

42. *Hyperion* 47, 22–25 Schmidt: *Und nun war es dahin gekommen, nun war ich nichts mehr, war so heillos um alles gebracht, war zum ärmsten unter den Menschen geworden, und wußte selbst nicht, wie.* One can also recall the image Hyperion is using (to represent himself), when he is leaving Alabanda: "A strange beggar, is he not, Alabanda? I cried; he throws his last penny into the bog! If he does, then let him go hungry! he cried, and left me." (*Nicht wahr, Alabanda, rief ich ihm zu, das ist ein sonderbarer Bettler? seinen letzten Pfenning wirft er in den Sumpf! Wenns das ist, mag er auch verhungern, rief er, und ging.*) *Hyperion* 45, 37–46, 4 Schmidt.

43. For other interpretations of letter I, 2, 15, see Kiefner 1997, Thiel 2004, and Heinrichs 2007.

44. Cf. *Hyperion* 72, 21 Schmidt. Garden might be seen, in Hölderlin, as the homeland of friendship. Cf. "Am Tage der Freundschaftsfeier" vs. 132–133, and Canick 1990, p. 17, n. 29 and 30.

45. Cf. *Hyperion* 45, 28–33 Schmidt.

46. Cf. *Hyperion* 39, 35–40, 10 Schmidt.

47. Cf. *Hyperion* 40, 1–2 Schmidt.

48. Cf. *Hyperion* 40, 12–14 Schmidt: "The state cannot command your presence. But let it not obstruct you, and you will come (. . .)" (*Dich kann der Staat nicht hergebieten. Aber er störe dich nicht, so wirst du kommen . . .*).

49. *Hyperion* 72, 28–73, 9 Schmidt: *Da Harmodius und Aristogiton lebten, rief endlich einer, da war noch Freundschaft in der Welt. Das freute mich zu sehr, als daß ich hätte schweigen mögen. Man sollte dir eine Krone flechten um dieses Wortes willen! rief ich ihm zu; hast du denn wirklich eine Ahnung davon, hast du ein Gleichnis für die Freundschaft des Aristogiton und Harmodius? Verzeih mir! Aber beim Aether! man muß Aristogiton sein, um nachzufühlen, wie Aristogiton liebte, und die Blitze durfte wohl der Mann nicht fürchten, der geliebt sein wollte mit Harmodius Liebe, denn es täuscht mich alles, wenn der furchtbare Jüngling nicht mit Minos Strenge liebte. Wenige sind in solcher Probe bestanden, und es ist nicht leichter, eines Halbgotts Freund zu sein, als an der Götter Tische, wie Tantalus, zu sitzen. Aber es ist auch nichts Herrlicheres auf Erden, als wenn ein stolzes Paar, wie diese, so sich untertan ist.*

50. Some commentators (see Heinrichs 2007, 245 and Thiel 2002, 117–18) have suggested comparing Hyperion and Alabanda with Harmodius and Aristo-geiton. If the suggestion has indeed textual support in *Hyperion* (cf. letter II, 1, 2 in *Hyperion* 107, 31–33 Schmidt), it is nonetheless a misleading analogy. Indeed, the State Alabanda is seeking to establish is potentially as tyrannical as the one he is willing to overthrow, and we have seen that Hyperion and he are parting because of this issue. Hyperion, in the second part of the novel, appears to have forgotten about Alabanda's dark side and finally decides to go and fight with him for the liberation of Greece. But Diotima is not mistaken and warns him: "You will conquer," cried Diotima, "and forget what for; you will, at the most, force the establishment of a free state, and then ask yourself, 'What have I been building for?' Ah! it will be consumed, all the beautiful life that was to have being there, it will be exhausted even in you! The savage fight will tear you to pieces, beautiful soul, you will grow old, blissful spirit! and, weary unto death, you will ask in the end: 'Where are you now, you ideals of youth?'" (*Du wirst erobern, rief Diotima, und vergessen, wofür? wirst, wenn es hoch kommt, einen Freistaat dir erzwingen und dann sagen, wofür hab ich gebaut? ach! es wird verzehrt sein, all das schöne Leben, das daselbst sich regen sollte, wird verbraucht sein selbst in dir! Der wilde Kampf wird dich zerreißen, schöne Seele, du wirst altern, seliger Geist! und lebensmüd am Ende fragen, wo seid ihr nun, ihr Ideale der Jugend?: Hyperion* 108, 29–36 Schmidt). Diotima's words are most telling: she perfectly well foresees that, instead of rejuvenating and reviving, Hyperion "will grow old" (*du wirst altern*) and forget about the ideals of his youth.

51. Cf. "Reliquie von Alzäus," *Sämtliche Werke* ed. Beissner, 1965, 5: 35.

52. Cf. Hamlin 1971, 81–83.

53. Cf. Diogenes Laertius, VIII, 10.

54. In the directly preceding letter, Hölderlin speaks on two occasions of how Hyperion and Diotima "belonged to each other": *Eh' es eines von uns beeden wußte, gehörten wir uns an* (*Hyperion* 71, 15 Schmidt); *Gehörten wir da nicht längst uns an?* (*Hyperion* 72, 14 Schmidt.)

55. On these passages, see the article by Bernard Collette—Dučić in this collection. On how the many discourses in Plato's *Symposium* are all approximations of the truths Diotima is disclosing to Socrates, see Sedley 2006.

56. As Rowe justly notes (cf. commentary *ad loc.*), such a dissymmetry is already at work in Pausanias' speech, which is careful to speak of "Aristogeiton's *love* for Harmodius, and Harmodius' *friendship* for him" (*Symposium* 182c6). As to Hölderlin, he does not seem to make such a distinction, presumably because he takes Aristogeiton and Harmodius as symbol of friendship (which, for him, is a symmetrical relationship).

57. Cf. Plato, *Symposium* 209b6: *euphuei*.

58. Cf. Plato, *Symposium* 209c2: *epikheirei paideuein*. On the philosophical and pedagogical dimension of the Platonic love, see B. Collette—Dučić's contribution to the present volume.

59. *Hyperion* 19, 15–20 Schmidt: *Weißt du, wie Plato und sein Stella sich liebten? So liebt ich, so war ich geliebt. O ich war ein glücklicher Knabe! Es ist erfreulich, wenn gleiches sich zu gleichem gesellt, aber es ist göttlich, wenn ein großer Mensch die kleineren zu sich aufzieht.*

60. One should be wary of interpreting what Hölderlin here says about love for like as somehow implying a form of depreciation of friendship, since the passage is not about friendship, but about two sorts of love (one divine, the other not). This is why the otherwise reliable translation of Willard R. Trask is in this instance, not only unfaithful to the German text ("when like and like meet *in friendship*," italics mine), but also potentially misleading.

61. This point is also confirmed by the rest of the letter that the passage introduces, in which Hyperion is meeting Adamas, a master and a sage. Cf. *Hyperion* 20, 12 Schmidt: *wem du* (sc. Adamas) *begegnest mit deiner Liebe und Weisheit.*

62. *Hyperion* 73, 10–36 Schmidt: *Das ist auch meine Hoffnung, meine Lust in einsamen Stunden, daß solche große Töne und größere einst wiederkehren müssen in der Symphonie des Weltlaufs. Die Liebe gebar Jahrtausende voll lebendiger Menschen; die Freundschaft wird sie wiedergebären. Von Kinderharmonie sind einst die Völker ausgegangen, die Harmonie der Geister wird der Anfang einer neuen Weltgeschichte sein. Von Pflanzenglück begannen die Menschen und wuchsen auf, und wuchsen, bis sie reiften; von nun an gärten sie unaufhörlich fort, von innen und außen, bis jetzt das Menschengeschlecht, unendlich aufgelöst, wie ein Chaos daliegt, daß alle, die noch fühlen und sehen, Schwindel ergreift; aber die Schönheit flüchtet aus dem Leben der Menschen sich herauf in den Geist; Ideal wird, was Natur war, und wenn von unten gleich der Baum verdorrt ist und verwittert, ein frischer Gipfel ist noch hervorgegangen aus ihm, und grünt im Sonnenglanze, wie einst der Stamm in den Tagen der Jugend; Ideal ist, was Natur war. Daran, an diesem Ideale, dieser verjüngten Gottheit, erkennen die Wenigen sich und Eins sind sie, denn es ist Eines in ihnen, und von diesen, diesen beginnt das zweite Lebensalter der Welt—ich habe genug gesagt, um klar zu machen, was ich denke. Da hättest du Diotima sehen sollen, wie sie aufsprang und die beeden Hände mir reichte und rief: ich hab es verstanden, Lieber, ganz verstanden, so viel es sagt. Die Liebe gebar die Welt, die Freundschaft wird sie wieder gebären.*

63. Hyperion is speaking to a small group of initiates (those friends who already live the life of spirit) and is deliberately using cryptic language. On several

occasions in *Hyperion*, Hölderlin is using biblical expressions for parables ("das Gleichnis," or "das Zauberwort," "der *Zaubersprüche*"). Hyperion and Diotima are actually speaking "für die Frommen" (for the pious): "But your words are like snow-flakes, useless, they only make the air darker, and your magic formulas are for the pious, but the unpious do not hear you" (*Aber deine Worte sind, wie Schneeflocken, unnütz, und machen die Luft nur trüber und deine Zaubersprüche sind für die Frommen, aber die Unglaubigen hören dich nicht*; cf. *Hyperion* 107, 21–29 Schmidt). As Heinrichs explains, "the poet will not, nor will he be able in any case to ask the public to pay homage to his declaration. Thus he looks for legendary tales, the names of which are straightforwardly accepted by professors, in order to tell these tales through concealed images and riddles, *so that they may be understood and at the same time not be understood*, as also Jesus calls the Parables" (cf. Heinrichs 2007, 245, my translation).

    64. *Hyperion* 40, 22–24 and 28–29 Schmidt.

    65. Plato, *Politicus* 272e5.

    66. Plato, *Politicus* 273b1–2, tr. H. N. Fowler.

    67. Plato, *Politicus* 273c7–d1.

    68. Plato, *Politicus* 273d5–e4, tr. H. N. Fowler.

    69. Cf. *Hyperion* 62, 22 Schmidt: *O Diotima, Diotima, himmlisches Wesen!*

    70. On this, see Dučić–Collette 2010.

    71. *Predigt über 2. Joh. 7–9* 459, 3–10 Schmidt: *Eben so mächtigen Einfluss auf unsre Glückseligkeit hat die Gewisse Hoffnung eines bessern Lebens. Der Gedanke gibt unaussprechlicher Mut, dass Jede Kraft in uns, alles was wir duldeten und taten, fortwirke, dass wenn einst die Harmonie der seelenlosen Natur aufgelöst ist, die viel höhere Harmonie der sittlichen beginnen werde. Und all dies danken wir der Lehre Christi. Lasset uns ihm nachfolgen, dass wir einst, wie er, in seine Herrlichkeit eingehen.*

    72. The comparison between the two texts suggests a form of underlying Christology in *Hyperion*. On this, see Ogden 1991.

    73. On this issue, see Hamlin 2006.

Bibliography

Adler, J., and Louth Ch. (eds.). 2009. *Friedrich Hölderlin: Essays and Letters*. London and New York: Penguin Classics.

Beiser, F. C. 2002. *German Idealism. The Struggle against Subjectivism, 1781–1801*. Cambridge, MA, and London: Harvard University Press.

Berbig, R. 1996. "Ein Fest in den Hütten der gastlichen Freundschaft: Überlegungen zum Verhältnis von Freundschaft und Heimat bei Hölderlin." *Monatshefte* 88, no. 2: 157–175.

Böschenstein, B. 1971/1972. "Klopstock als Lehrer Hölderlins. Die Mythisierung von Freundschaft und Dichtung ('An Dichters Freunde')," *Hölderlin Jahrbuch*, 30–42.

Cancik, H. 1990. "Freundschaftskult: Religionsgeschichtliche Bemerkungen zu Mythos, Kult und Theologie der Freundschaft bei Friedrich Hölderlin." In *Loyalitätskonflikte in der Religionsgeschichte. Festschrift für Carsten Colpe*, ed. C. Elsass and H. Kippenberg. Würzburg: Königshausen und Neumann, 22–23.

Claverie, J. 1921. *La jeunesse d'Hölderlin jusqu'au roman d'Hypérion*, Paris: Alcan.

Courtine, J.-F. (ed.). 1989. *Hölderlin*, Paris: Editions de l'Herne.

Dučić-Collette, S. 2010. "Turning point in the reception of Plato's *Symposium*: Hölderlin's Diotima in *Hyperion*." In *Conversations Platonic and Neoplatonic: Intellect, Soul, and Nature*, ed. J. F. Finamore and R. M. Berchman. Sankt Augustin: Academia Verlag, 187–200.

Hamlin, C. 1971/1971. "Hölderlin mythos der Heroischen Freundschaft (2. Fassung, 1801)." *Hölderlin Jahrbuch*, 74–95.

———. 2006–07. "Hölderlin's Hellenism: Tyranny or Transformation?" *Hölderlin Jahrbuch* 35, 252–311.

Heinrichs, J. 2007. *Revolution aus Geist und Liebe. Hölderlin, 'Hyperion,'* München, Moskau, Warschau, Varna, London, New York: Steno Verlag.

Hölderlin: Sämtliche Werke. 1946–1985. F. Beissner (ed.), Stuttgart: W. Kohlhammer (8 vols.).

Hölderlin. Oeuvres. 1967. Edited by P. Jaccottet, Paris: Gallimard (Bibliothèque de la Pléiade).

Kiefner, H. 1997. "Ideal wird, was Natur war. Abhandlungen zur Privat Rechtsgeschichte des späten 18. und des 19. Jahrhunderts," Goldbach: Keip Verlag.

Louth, Ch. 2004–2005. "Hölderlins Freundschaftsbriefe," *Hölderlin—Jahrbuch*, 34, 175–179.

Mittner, L. 1962. "Freundschaft und Liebe in der Deutschen Literatur des 18. Jahrhunderts." In *Stoffe, Formen, Strukturen. Studien zur deutschen Litteratur*, ed. A. Fuchs und H. Motekat. München: Hueber.

Mossé, C. 1969. *La tyrannie dans la Grèce antique*. Paris: Presses Universitaires de France.

Ogden, M. 1991. *The Problem of Christ in the Work of Friedrich Hölderlin*. London: Modern Humanities Research Association.

Pankow, E. 1999. "Epistolary Writing, Fate: Hölderlin's 'Hyperion.'" In *The Solid Letter: Readings of Friedrich Hölderlin*, ed. A. Fioretos. Stanford: Stanford University Press.

Plato. 1914. *Phaedo* Translated by H. N. Fowler, Cambridge, MA: Harvard University Press.

Plato. 1998. *Symposium* Edited with an introduction, translation, and notes by C. J. Rowe. Oxford: Oxbow Books (Aris and Phillips Classical Texts).

Plato. 1921. *Statesman* Translated by H. N Fowler. Cambridge, MA: Harvard University Press.

Santner, E. L. (ed.). 1990. *Hyperion and Selected Poems*, New York: Continuum.

Schmidt, J. (ed.). 1992. *Friedrich Hölderlin: Sämtliche Werke und Breife*. Frankfurt am Main: Deutscher Klassiker Verlag.

Sedley, D. 2006. "The Speech of Agathon in Plato's *Symposium.*" In *The Virtuous Life in Greek Ethics,* ed. B. Reis. Cambridge: Cambridge University Press, 49–67.

Thiel, L. 2004. *Freundschafts—Konzeptionen im späten 18. Jahrhundert. Schillers "Don Karlos" und Hölderlins "Hyperion,"* Wurzburg: Königshausen und Neumann.

CONTRIBUTORS

Bernard Collette-Dučić is *professeur adjoint* at Laval University and currently a Humboldt Fellow (Universität zu Köln). After writing a doctoral thesis on Plotinus's metaphysics (Université Libre de Bruxelles), later published under the title *Plotin et l'ordonnancement de l'être* (Vrin, 2007), he was post-doctoral Fellow of the Fonds National de la Recherche Scientifique (Belgium) and of the Wiener-Anspach Foundation (Belgium), Visiting Scholar at the Faculty of Classics of the University of Cambridge (2005–06), Honorary Research Fellow at the Department of Classics and Ancient History of Durham University (2007–09), and Mairie de Paris Research Fellow at the Centre Léon Robin (Paris, 2009–10), working mainly on Stoicism. He is currently at work on a book in English on the ancient Stoic concept of providence and a new translation with commentary in French of Plotinus' *Treatise 3* (III 1, *On fate*) for the series *Plotin Œuvres complètes*, under the editorship of Jean-Marc Narbonne (Les Belles Lettres). Other research interests include ancient concepts of virtue, fate, and freedom in the Stoa, Alexander of Aphrodisias, and Plotinus. He is currently co-editing a collection of essays on the origin and unity of virtue from Plato to Augustine and Nietzsche.

Sandra Dučić-Collette is an independent scholar and translator who has studied classical philology in the former Yougoslavia (Novi-Sad), Canada (Université de Montréal), Germany (DAAD), and Austria (Universität Wien). As a Culture Communication Fund B.V. Fellow (2004–05), she researched on the ancient Japanese conception of gardens (in the Japanese court of the Heian period) at the International Research Institute for the Humanities in Nichibunken (Kyoto, Japan). She has a wide range of research interests and expertise, from ancient concepts of love to the reception of Plato in Hölderlin. Her current research interests bear on several themes in the history of art and literature, including the poetry of Dante and of the romantic movement, especially Shelley, as well as the aesthetic theories of Raphael and Castiglione. She is currently working on the edition and translation into Serbian of studies by C. L. Frommel on Raphael and Pope Julius II.

Dimitri El Murr is a lecturer in ancient philosophy at the University of Paris 1 Panthéon-Sorbonne and a junior member of the Institut Universitaire de France. His research area is ancient philosophy, especially Socrates and Plato. He has published many articles on different aspects of Plato's thought and was the editor of *Plato, The Journal of the International Plato Society* (from 2007 to 2010). He is the author of a collection of texts on the philosophy of friendship, with introduction and commentaries (*L'Amitié*, Paris, 2001). He co-edited, with A. Brancacci and D. P. Taormina, a collective volume of essays on Plato (*Aglaïa. Autour de Platon. Mélanges offerts à Monique Dixsaut*, Paris, 2010). He has recently edited a volume on the *Theaetetus* (*La Mesure du savoir. Études sur le* Théétète (Paris, Vrin, 2013) and co-edited, with G. Boys-Stones and Ch. Gill, *The Platonic Art of Philosophy* (Cambridge University Press, 2013). He is currently working on a book on Plato's *Politicus*.

Gary M. Gurtler, SJ, is an associate professor of philosophy at Boston College. He was educated at St. John Fisher College, Fordham University, and the Weston School of Theology. His research in ancient philosophy is specifically related to Aristotle and Neoplatonism. His book *Plotinus: The Experience of Unity* (1988) has led to a number of articles on alienation and otherness in Plotinus. He is currently working on a translation and commentary of Plotinus' *Ennead* IV, 4 for the series *The Enneads of Plotinus*, under the editorship of John M. Dillon and Andrew Smith (Parmenides Publishing).

Fergus Kerr, OP graduated at Aberdeen University in 1953; served in the Royal Air Force; entered the Order of Preachers in 1956; studied in Paris, Munich, and Oxford; taught in Oxford from 1966 through 1986; and has been an Honorary Fellow in Divinity at Edinburgh University since 1986. He obtained a DD from Aberdeen University in 1996. A regent at Blackfriars Hall, Oxford, 1998–2004, he has been the editor of *New Blackfriars* since 1995 and was made a fellow of the Royal Society of Edinburgh in 2003. His publications include *Theology after Wittgenstein* (1986; French 1991; Italian 1992; expanded edition 1997); *Immortal Longings: Versions of Transcending Humanity* (1997); *After Aquinas: Versions of Thomism* (2002); *Twentieth*

Century Catholic theologians: From Neoscholasticism to Nuptial Mysticism
(2007; Polish and Japanese 2011).

Harry Lesser is an honorary research fellow and former senior lecturer in
philosophy at the University of Manchester and the author of several articles
on Plato and a chapter on Lucretius, "On the Nature of the Universe," in
vol.1 of *Central Works of Philosophy*, ed. John Shand (Acumen, 2005).

John Panteleimon Manoussakis is the Edward Bennet Williams Fellow
and assistant professor of philosophy at the College of the Holy Cross
and an honorary fellow at the faculty of theology and philosophy of the
Australian Catholic University. He was born in Athens and educated in the
United States (PhD, Boston College). He is also a monastic ordained to the
diaconate in 1995 and to the priesthood in 2011 (Archdiocese of Athens).
His publications focus on philosophy of religion, phenomenology, Plato and
the Neo-Platonic tradition, and Patristics (Dionysius and Maximus). His
publications focus on philosophy of religion, phenomenology (in particular
the postsubjective anthropology of Heidegger and Marion). He is the author
of *God after Metaphysics* (Indiana University Press, 2007) and the editor of
five volumes, most recently of *Phenomenology and Eschatology* (Ashgate, 2009).
He has published over thirty articles in English, Greek, Russian, and Serbian.

Tamer Nawar is a postdoctoral fellow in the faculty of philosophy at the
University of Oxford; he read for a PhD in ancient philosophy at the
University of Cambridge.

John R. Sommerfeldt was educated at the Universities of Michigan and
Notre-Dame and at the Albert-Ludwigs Universität in Freiburg. He is
professor emeritus of History at the University of Dallas, where he also
served as president. He is the author of numerous books and articles on
medieval intellectual history, including *Bernard of Clairvaux on the Life of the
Mind* (2004); *Bernard of Clairvaux: On the Spirituality of Relationship* (2004);
Aelred of Rievaulx: Pursuing Perfect Happiness (2005); *Aelred of Rievaulx: On
Love and Order in the World and the Church* (2006); and *Christianity in
Culture: A Historical Quest* (2009). He established the Medieval Institute at
Western Michigan University and was the moving spirit behind the setting up
of the International Medieval Conference that takes place annually at Kalamazoo
(Western Michigan), editing the proceedings of that conference for close to
thirty years while being also head editor of *Cistercian Studies*. He is currently
writing a book on the cultural history of medieval Germany.

Suzanne Stern-Gillet studied philosophy at the University of Liège (Belgium) and classics at the University of Manchester (U.K.). Having previously taught in universities in continental Europe and the United States, she is now professor of ancient philosophy at the University of Bolton and honorary research fellow in the Department of Classics and Ancient History at the University of Manchester. Having early in her career translated Gilbert Ryle's *The Concept of Mind* into French and published in the tradition of analytical philosophy, she now concentrates her research on ancient Greek philosophy. She is the author of *Aristotle's Philosophy of Friendship* (Ithaca, 1995) and of some fifty articles (in English or in French), mostly on ancient moral psychology and the aesthetics of ancient Greek thinkers. In collaboration with Kevin Corrigan she has edited *Reading Ancient Texts: Essays in Honour of Denis O'Brien* (vol. I: *Presocratics and Plato*, vol. II: *Aristotle and Neoplatonism*). She is currently working on a monograph on Plato's *Ion* for Cambridge University Press and is preparing a translation and commentary on Plotinus' tractate *On the Virtues* (I.2 [19]) for the series *The Enneads of Plotinus*, under the editorship of John M. Dillon and Andrew Smith (Parmenides Publishing).

Andrea Veltman is an associate professor of philosophy at James Madison University in Virginia. In addition to publishing articles on Plato, Aristotle, Simone de Beauvoir, and Hannah Arendt, she has edited *Social and Political Philosophy* (Oxford 2008) and co-edited *Oppression and Moral Agency* (Special Issue of *Hypatia* 24:1) and *Evil, Political Violence and Forgiveness* (Rowman & Littlefield 2009) in collaboration with Kathryn J. Norlock. She is currently working on a book on meaningful work, examining goals of work in the context of theories of human flourishing.

Robin Weiss holds a PhD (2012) in philosophy from DePaul University and was until recently a visiting assistant professor at Mount Allison University. She is now a post-doctoral fellow at the American University in Cairo. Her research interests lie in praxis and the practical intellect in Roman Stoicism, subjects she addressed in her doctoral dissertation, *The Stoics and the Practical: A Roman Reply to Aristotle*. She is currently writing a book on ethics, politics, and their relationship in Stoicism and has written a preliminary article on the subject, "In Cicero's *De Finibus*, An *Ars Vitae* Between *Technê* and *Theôria*," *Epoché* 17:2 (Spring 2013).

NAME INDEX

SUBJECT INDEX

Honor (honors and dishonor), 16, 21,
30, 55, 57, 58, 62–79 passim,
127, 155, 204, 301
Humility, 55, 57, 70, 72, 79, 80, 217,
247, 299

Justice, xi, 4, 36, 43, 47, 52, 61, 62,
64, 89, 90, 96, 113, 135, 166,
167, 197, 199, 202, 216, 217,
229, 233, 256

Kalokagathia (perfect virtue), 56

Legislation, 6, 8, 18–19, 21, 24, 253
Liturgies (leitourgiai), 65
Love
as pedagogy, xii, 87–115
divine love, ix, 238–240, 261
love of god, ix, xiii, xv, 212, 261,
305
love of friends, x, 142, 153, 174,
198, 220, 249
Platonic love, xii, xiv, xv, 3, 29, 30,
95–98 passim, 100, 108, 134–
135, 251–255, 296, 313, Erotic
love, see Erōs
Philosophical love, 14, 98–101,
302
Lust (concupiscentia), 7, 118, 122, 128,
167–168, 201, 205, 218, 219,
248, 250

Megalopsychia (greatness of soul), xi,
52–59, 68–69, 71, 76
Megalopsychos (the great-souled man),
xi, 49, 52–75 passim, 77, 79
Mikropsychia (smallness of soul), xii,
52, 53–55 passim, 68–74, 75, 80
Mikropsychos (the small-souled man),
52, 68–76
Moderation (sōphrosunē), 23, 61, 89,
90, 96, 233
Monarchy, 18–19, 21

Neighbor, neighborly love, x, 44, 191,
198, 199, 200, 212, 218, 223,
248, 249, 261, 262, 263, 274

Objectivity, 274, 275, 278
Oikeiōsis (appropriation,
familiarization), 12, 29, 102, 103,
112, 137, 153, 159, 163

Phantasia (impression, affection of the
soul), 91, 92, 93, 110
Phantasma (mental illusion), 91–93,
99, 110
Philein (to love, to like, see also
agapan), xiv, 41, 165, 174–176,
178–181, 185, 188
Philosophia (monasticism), 181–184,
193
Practical reasoning, 203, 213
Pride, xi, xiii, 53, 57, 70, 75, 76,
203–205, 214, 217, 219, 236,
294

Reciprocity, 9, 12, 16, 29, 98, 101, 102

Sage, xii, 29, 43, 44, 47, 87–115, 133,
151, 166, 167, 273, 280, 313
Selfhood
other selfhood, xii, xv, 41–44, 47,
52, 146, 147, 161, 176, 190,
205–206, 220, 273, 332
self-disclosure, xv, 271–287
self-knowledge and self-ignorance, xv,
38, 42, 47, 72, 271–278, 281,
282, 283, 284, 285
self-love, xii, 35, 38, 40–43, 58,
65–67, 136–151 passim
self-sacrifice, 66, 126
self-sufficiency, xi, 12, 52, 59, 60, 75,
160, 256, 258, 259
Sexuality, 17, 118, 119, 124, 129, 130
Sociability (and sociality), xv, 60, 197,
272, 282